SPANISH
Vocabulary

Second Edition

by

Julianne Dueber

University of Missouri-St. Louis

BARRON'S

BARRON'S EDUCATIONAL SERIES, INC.

To my father, Clarence E. Dueber

© Copyright 2002 by Barron's Educational Series, Inc.
Previous edition, © Copyright 1990 by Barron's Educational Series, Inc.

All inquiries should be addressed to:
Barron's Educational Series, Inc.
250 Wireless Boulevard
Hauppauge, NY 11788
http://www.barronseduc.com

International Standard Book No. 0-7641-1985-0

Library of Congress Cataloging-in-Publication Data

Dueber, Julianne.
    Spanish vocabulary / by Julianne Dueber.—2nd ed.
        p.   cm.
    ISBN 0-7641-1985-0 (alk. paper)
    1. Spanish language—Glossaries, vocabularies, etc.
I. Title.
PC4680 .D8 2002
468.2′421—dc21   2002018507

PRINTED IN CHINA
10 9 8 7 6 5

CONTENTS

PREFACE TO THE SECOND EDITION

Since the world has changed so much since 1990, it was necessary to update *Spanish Vocabulary* in many sections: The Telephone, At the Post Office, Electronic Media, Appliances and Common Household Items, Stationery, Photo/Camera, Jobs and Professions, The Doctor, and Computers. The second edition contains a new section on Internet vocabulary, in addition to updated listings for Controversial Issues. Enjoy learning the new words!

If you have any new vocabulary you would like to see in the next edition of the book, please e-mail me at *jdueber@yahoo.com* with your suggestions.

Julianne Dueber

HOW TO USE THIS BOOK

THIS IS NOT JUST ANOTHER DICTIONARY!

This book will help you to study vocabulary systematically on those topics of special interest to you. It is a programmed study guide to almost 6,000 Spanish words you will need to talk about any subject, and in situations such as buying supplies at the hardware store, discussing environmental problems, and reporting an emergency.

OVERALL DESIGN

Spanish Vocabulary consists of a pronunciation guide, nine chapters, an appendix, and an English-Spanish vocabulary list.

Each chapter is divided into main themes. For example, the chapter entitled People is divided into: (a) family and friends, (b) describing people, and (c) the body. The vocabulary presented in this chapter deals with such diverse topics as family relationships, physical appearance, marital status, religion, personality traits, parts of the body, etc.

USING THIS BOOK FOR DIFFERENT LEARNING GOALS

If you are attempting to learn Spanish by yourself, you will find that *Spanish Vocabulary* provides you with an easy system for acquiring the most important basic vocabulary for dealing with a wide variety of topics. If you already have some knowledge of Spanish, you will easily expand your vocabulary and quickly increase your speaking ability. If you are currently a Spanish student, you will find this guide useful in preparing oral and written reports on specific topics.

FEATURES

Each chapter lists the English word first, followed by its Spanish equivalent or equivalents, and its phonetic pronunciation. Please note that *Spanish Vocabulary* stresses the Latin American pronunciation. If you are visiting or living in Spain, remember to make allowances for the pronunciation of words with *ce, ci,* and *z.*

The English words are arranged in alphabetical order, unless the nature of the theme requires some other logical system of organization (e.g., numbers). Related items, concepts, or specific uses are indented.

GENDER AND PLURALIZATION OF NOUNS

A regular masculine noun in Spanish ends in *-o.* A regular feminine noun in Spanish ends in *-a.* Any noun that does not fall into these categories is marked as masculine (*m*) or feminine (*f*). (See Abbreviations section for all other grammar symbols that are used throughout this book.) Most professions are given in the masculine form only. For the feminine, replace the **o** ending with an **a.** The designation (*m/f*) indicates that the form given is both masculine and feminine.

Nouns ending in a vowel usually add *-s* to form the plural; those ending in a consonant add *-es*. Nouns that do not follow these rules are noted as they occur in the text.

OTHER PARTS OF SPEECH

Other parts of speech are identified as they arise. Spanish has three verb conjugations, each according to the verb endings: *ar, -er,* and *-ir*. Spanish verbs that are irregular in some way are followed by an asterisk (*). (Check the Appendix for the conjugation of irregular verbs.)

Adjectives are given in their masculine singular forms only (*diario, alto*). Some adjectives have the same form for both masculine and feminine (*e.g., verde, importante*).

ABBREVIATIONS

FOR NOUNS

m	masculine noun
f	feminine noun
s	singular form
pl	plural form

FOR VERBS

v	verb
pp	past participle
*	A verb with some irregularity. Look for its conjugation in the verb appendix.

GENERAL ABBREVIATIONS

fam	familiar *you* form	*n*	noun
pol	polite *you* form	*prep*	preposition
adj	adjective	*pron*	pronoun
adv	adverb		
conj	conjunction		

PRONUNCIATION GUIDE

The pronunciation of Spanish is easy when compared to other languages. The following charts will help you pronounce the vowels and consonants. Note the Symbols Used column, which indicates how pronunciation of the Spanish words is given throughout the book.

VOWELS

Spanish vowels	English equivalents	Approximate pronunciation	Symbol used
a _casa_	father	ah	*ah*
e _Pepe_	they	eh	*eh*
i _tipo_	machine	ee	*ee*
o _nota_	cone	oh	*oh*
u _uno_	soon	oo	*oo*

DIPHTHONGS

The combination of strong (*a*, *e*, and *o*) and weak vowels (*u* and *i*) or two weak ones, forms a diphthong, which may not be separated into a syllable unless the weak one carries a written accent: *fiesta*, *familia*, *alegría*, *raúl*.

Spanish	English equivalent	Symbols used
ai (ay) *aire, hay*	I	*ah·ee*
au *causa*	out	*ow*
ei *seis*	pay	*eh·ee*
eu *deuda*	ay-oo	*eh·oo*
ia *diablo*	ee-ah	*ee·ah*
io *serio*	ee-o	*ee·oh*
ie *fiesta*	ee-eh	*ee·eh*
Iu *ciudad*	you	*ee·oo*
oi, oy *hoy, soy*	foil, toy	*oy*
ua *agua*	oo-ah	*wah*
uo *cuota*	whoa	*woh*
ue *bueno*	oo-eh	*weh*
ui *cuidado*	oo-ee	*wee*
uy *muy*	oo-ee	*wee*

CONSONANTS

Most consonants are pronounced like their English equivalents. However, the following consonants and consonant-vowel combinations have special pronunciations.

Spanish	English equivalent	Symbols used
ce	<u>th</u>ink	*th* (Spain)
ce	say	*seh* (Hispanic America)
ci	<u>th</u>ink	*th* (Spain)
ci	see	*see* (Hispanic America)
ge	hay	*heh*
gi	<u>hee</u>p	*hee*
h	is never pronounced	
j	<u>h</u>ope	*h*
ll	<u>y</u>es milli<u>on</u>	*y* (the majority use)
ñ	can<u>y</u>on	*ny*
qui	mos<u>qui</u>to	*kee*
que	Kay	*keh*
r	<u>R</u>oy	*r* (slightly rolled in the middle of a word [*señ orita*]) and trilled at the beginning of a word (*Raúl*)
rr	no English equivalent	*rr* (strongly trilled)
v	<u>b</u>oy	*b* (a soft sound)
x	e<u>x</u>ert	*ks* or *s* (has the sound of *ks* between vowels)
z	<u>s</u>uit	*s* NOTE: In Spain, *z* is pronounced as in <u>th</u>ink

BASIC INFORMATION

1. ARITHMETIC

a. CARDINAL NUMBERS

zero	cero	*'seh-roh*
one	uno	*'oo-noh*
two	dos	*dohs*
three	tres	*trehs*
four	cuatro	*'kwah-troh*
five	cinco	*'seen-koh*
six	seis	*'seh·ees*
seven	siete	*'see·eh-teh*
eight	ocho	*'oh-choh*
nine	nueve	*'nweh-beh*
ten	diez	*dee·'ehs*
eleven	once	*'ohn-seh*
twelve	doce	*'doh-seh*
thirteen	trece	*'treh-seh*
fourteen	catorce	*kah-'tohr-seh*
fifteen	quince	*'keen-seh*
sixteen	dieciséis	*dee·eh-see-'seh·ees*
seventeen	diecisiete	*dee·eh-see-see-'eh-teh*
eighteen	dieciocho	*dee·eh-see-'oh-choh*
nineteen	diecinueve	*dee·eh-see-'nweh-beh*
twenty	veinte	*'beh·een-teh*
twenty-one	veintiuno	*'beh·een-tee-'oo-noh*
twenty-two	veintidós	*'beh·een-tee-'dohs*
twenty-three	veintitrés	*'beh·een-tee-'trehs*
twenty-four	veinticuatro	*'beh·een-tee-'kwah-troh*
twenty-five	veinticinco	*'beh·een-tee-'seen-koh*
twenty-six	veintiséis	*'beh·een-tee-'seh·ees*
twenty-seven	veintisiete	*'beh·een-tee-see-'eh-teh*
twenty-eight	veintiocho	*'beh·een-tee-'oh-choh*
twenty-nine	veintinueve	*'beh·een-tee-'nweh-beh*
thirty	treinta	*'treh·een-tah*
thirty-one	treinta y uno	*'treh·een-tah ee 'oo-noh*
thirty-two	treinta y dos	*'treh·een-tah ee dohs*
forty	cuarenta	*kwah-'rehn-tah*
forty-one	cuarenta y uno	*kwah-'rehn-tah ee 'oo-noh*
forty-two	cuarenta y dos	*kwah-'rehn-tah ee dohs*
fifty	cincuenta	*seen-'kwehn-tah*
fifty-one	cincuenta y uno	*seen-'kwehn-tah ee 'oo-noh*

sixty	sesenta	*seh-'sehn-tah*
sixty-one	sesenta y uno	*seh-'sehn-tah ee 'oo-noh*
seventy	setenta	*seh-'tehn-tah*
eighty	ochenta	*oh-'chehn-tah*
ninety	noventa	*noh-'behn-tah*
one hundred	cien	*see-ehn*
one hundred and one	ciento uno	*see-'ehn-toh 'oo-noh*
one hundred and two	ciento dos	*see-'ehn-toh dohs*
one hundred and twenty	ciento veinte	*see-'ehn-toh 'beh·een-teh*
two hundred	doscientos	*dohs-see-'ehn-tohs*
two hundred and one	doscientos uno	*dohs-see-'ehn-tohs 'oo-noh*
three hundred	trescientos	*trehs-see-'ehn-tohs*
four hundred	cuatrocientos	*kwah-troh-see-'ehn-tohs*
five hundred	quinientos	*kee-nee-'ehn-tohs*
six hundred	seiscientos	*seh-ees-see-'ehn-tohs*
seven hundred	setecientos	*seh-teh-see-'ehn-tohs*
eight hundred	ochocientos	*oh-choh-see-'ehn-tohs*
nine hundred	novecientos	*noh-beh-see-'ehn-tohs*
one thousand	mil	*meel*
one thousand and one	mil y uno	*meel ee 'oo-noh*
one thousand forty	mil cuarenta	*meel kwah-'rehn-tah*
one thousand three hundred	mil trescientos	*meel trehs-see-'ehn-tohs*
1990	mil novecientos noventa	*mil noh-beh-see-'ehn-tohs noh-'behn-tah*
two thousand	dos mil	*dohs meel*
two thousand and one	dos mil y uno	*dohs meel ee 'oo-noh*
two thousand four hundred	dos mil cuatrocientos	*dohs meel kwah-troh-see-'ehn-tohs*
one hundred thousand	cien mil	*see-'ehn meel*
two hundred thousand	doscientos mil	*dohs-see-'ehn-tohs meel*
one million	un millón	*oon mee-'yohn*
two million	dos millones	*dohs mee-'yoh-nehs*
one hundred million	cien millones	*see-'ehn mee-'yoh-nehs*
one billion	mil millones	*meel mee-'yoh-nehs*
two billion	dos mil millones	*dohs meel mee-'yoh-nehs*

b. ORDINAL NUMBERS

first	primero	*pree-'meh-roh*
second	segundo	*seh-'goon-doh*
third	tercero	*tehr-'seh-roh*

fourth	cuarto	*'kwahr-toh*
fifth	quinto	*'keen-toh*
sixth	sexto	*'sehks-toh*
seventh	séptimo	*'sehp-tee-moh*
eighth	octavo	*ohk-'tah-boh*
ninth	noveno	*noh-'behn-oh*
tenth	décimo	*'deh-see-moh*
eleventh	undécimo	*oon-'deh-see-moh*
twelfth	duodécimo	*doo-oh-'deh-see-moh*
thirteenth	decimotercero	*deh-see-moh-tehr-'seh-roh*
fourteenth	decimocuarto	*deh-see-moh-'kwahr-toh*
fifteenth	decimoquinto	*deh-see-moh-'keen-toh*
sixteenth	decimosexto	*deh-see-moh-'sehks-toh*
seventeenth	decimoséptimo	*deh-see-moh-'sehp-tee-moh*
eighteenth	decimoctavo	*deh-see-moh-ohk-'tah-boh*
nineteenth	decimonoveno	*deh-see-moh-noh-'beh-noh*
twentieth	vigésimo	*bee-'heh-see-moh*
twenty-first	vigésimo primero	*bee-'heh-see-moh pree-'meh-roh*
twenty-second	vigésimo segundo	*bee-'heh-see-moh seh-'goon-doh*
thirtieth	trigésimo	*tree-'heh-see-moh*
fortieth	cuadragésimo	*kwah-drah-'heh-see-moh*
fiftieth	quincuagésimo	*keen-kwah-'heh-see-moh*
sixtieth	sexagésimo	*sehks-ah-'heh-see-moh*
seventieth	septuagésimo	*sehp-twah-'heh-see-moh*
eightieth	octogésimo	*ohk-toh-'heh-see-moh*
ninetieth	nonagésimo	*noh-nah-'heh-see-moh*
hundredth	centésimo	*sehn-'teh-see-moh*
thousandth	milésimo	*mee-'leh-see-moh*
millionth	millonésimo	*mee-yoh-'neh-see moh*
billionth	billonésimo	*bee-yoh-'neh-see-moh*

c. FRACTIONS

one-half	un medio	*oon 'meh-dee·oh*
one-third	un tercio	*oon 'tehr-see-oh*
one-fourth	un cuarto	*oon 'kwahr-toh*
two-thirds	dos tercios	*dohs 'tehr-see·ohs*
three-fourths	tres cuartos	*trehs 'kwahr-tohs*

| four-sevenths | cuatro séptimos | *'kwah-troh 'sehp-tee mohs* |
| eight-tenths | ocho décimos | *'oh-choh 'deh-see-mohs* |

d. TYPES OF NUMBERS

number	número	*'noo-meh-roh*
• number	numerar (*v*)	*noo-meh-'rahr*
• numeral	número	*'noo-meh-roh*
• numerical	numérico (*adj*)	*noo-'meh-ree-koh*
Arabic numerals	numeración (*f*) arábica	*noo-meh-rah-see·'ohn ah-'rah-bee-kah*
cardinal number	número cardinal	*'noo-meh-roh kar-dee-'nahl*
complex number	número complejo	*'noo-meh-roh kohm-'pleh-hoh*
digit	dígito	*'dee-hee-toh*
even	par (*adj*)	*pahr*
fractional	fraccionario (*adj*)	*frahk-see·oh·'nah-ree-oh*
• fraction	fracción (*f*)	*frahk-see·'ohn*
imaginary	imaginario (*adj*)	*ee-mah-hee-'nah-ree-oh*
integer	entero	*ehn-'teh-roh*
irrational number	número irracional	*'noo-meh-roh ee-rrah-see·oh-'nahl*
natural	natural (*adj*)	*nah-too-'rahl*
negative	negativo (*adj*)	*neh-gah-'tee-boh*
odd	impar (*adj*)	*eem-'pahr*
ordinal	ordinal (*adj*)	*ohr-dee-'nahl*
positive	positivo (*adj*)	*poh-see-'tee-boh*
prime	primo (*adj*)	*'pree-moh*
rational	racional (*adj*)	*rah-see-oh-'nahl*
real	real (*adj*)	*reh-'ahl*
reciprocal	recíproco (*adj*)	*reh-'see-proh-koh*
Roman numeral	número romano	*'noo-meh-roh roh-'mah-noh*

e. BASIC OPERATIONS

arithmetical operations	operaciones aritméticas (*f, pl*)	*oh-peh-rah-see·'oh-nehs ah-reet-'meh-tee-kahs*
add up	sumar (*v*)	*soo-'mahr*
• addition	suma (*f*)	*'soo-mah*
• plus	más	*mahs*
• Two plus two equals four.	Dos más dos son cuatro.	*Dohs mahs dohs sohn 'kwah-troh*
subtract	restar (*v*)	*rehs-'tahr*
• subtraction	resta (*f*)	*'rehs-tah*
• minus	menos	*'meh-nohs*

• **Three minus two are one.**	Tres menos dos son uno.	*Trehs 'meh-nohs dohs sohn 'oo-noh*
multiply	multiplicar (*v*)	*mool-tee-plee-'kahr*
• **multiplication**	multiplicación (*f*)	*mool-tee-plee-kah-see·'ohn*
• **multiplication table**	tabla de multiplicación	*'tah-blah deh mool-tee-plee-kah-see·'ohn*
• **multiplied by**	multiplicado por	*mool-tee-plee-'kah-doh pohr*
• **Three times two equals six.**	Tres por dos son seis.	*Trehs pohr dohs sohn 'seh·ees*
divide	dividir (*v*)	*dee-bee-'deer*
• **divided by**	dividido por	*dee-bee-'dee-doh pohr*
• **division**	división (*f*)	*dee-bee-see·'ohn*
• **Six divided by two equals three.**	Seis dividido por dos son tres.	*'Seh·ees dee-bee-'dee-doh pohr dohs sohn trehs*
raise to the . . . power	elevar a la . . . potencia	*eh-leh-'bahr ah lah poh-'tehn-see·ah*
• **to the fourth power**	a la cuarta potencia	*ah lah 'kwar-tah poh-'tehn-see·ah*
• **to the nth power**	a la enésima potencia	*ah lah eh-'neh-see-mah poh-'tehn-see·ah*
• **squared**	al cuadrado	*ahl kwah-'drah-doh*
• **cubed**	al cubo	*ahl 'koo-boh*
• **Two squared equals four.**	Dos al cuadrado son cuatro.	*Dohs ahl kwah-'drah-doh sohn 'kwah-troh*
extract a root	extraer (*v**) una raíz	*ehks-trah-'ehr 'oo-nah rah·'ees*
• **square root**	raíz cuadrada	*rah·'ees kwah-'drah-dah*
• **cube root**	raíz cúbica	*rah·'ees 'koo-bee-kah*
• **nth root**	enésima raíz	*eh-'neh-see-mah rah·'ees*
• **The square root of nine is three.**	La raíz cuadrada de nueve es tres.	*lah rah·'ees kwah-'drah-dah deh 'nweh-beh ehs trehs*
ratio	proporción (*f*)	*proh-pohr-see·'ohn*

FOCUS: Arithmetical Operations

Addition—Adición
$2 + 3 = 5$ two plus three equals five   dos más tres son cinco

Subtraction—Substracción
$9 - 3 = 6$ nine minus three   nueve menos tres son seis
     equals six

Multiplication—Multiplicación
$4 \times 2 = 8$ four times two equals eight   cuatro por dos son ocho
$4 \cdot 2 = 8$

Division—División
$10 : 2 = 5$ ten divided by two   diez dividido por dos son
     equals five   cinco

Raising to a power—Elevación a una potencia
$3^2 = 9$ three squared equals nine   tres al cuadrado son
     nueve
$2^3 = 8$ two cubed equals eight   dos al cubo son ocho
$2^4 = 16$ two to the fourth   dos a la cuarta potencia
     power equals sixteen   son dieciséis
x^n x to the nth power x a la enésima potencia

Extraction of root—Extracción de raíz
$\sqrt[2]{4} = 2$ the square root of four   la raíz cuadrada de cuatro
     is two   es dos
$\sqrt[3]{27} = 3$ the cube root of   la raíz cúbica de
     twenty-seven is three   veintisiete es tres
$\sqrt[n]{x}$ the nth root of x   la enésima raíz de x

f. ADDITIONAL MATHEMATICAL CONCEPTS

algebra	álgebra (*m*)	*'ahl-hek-brah*
• **algebraic**	algebraico (*adj*)	*ahl-heh-'brah·ee-koh*
arithmetic	aritmética	*ah-reet-'meh-tee-kah*
• **arithmetic**	aritmético (*adj*)	*ah-reet-'meh-tee-koh*
average	promedio	*proh-'meh-dee·oh*
calculate	calcular (*v*)	*kahl-koo-'lahr*
• **calculation**	cálculo	*'kahl-koo-loh*
decimal	decimal (*adj*)	*deh-see-'mahl*
difference	diferencia	*dee-feh-'rehn-see·ah*

equality	igualdad (f)	ee-gwal-'dahd
• equals	es igual a	ehs ee-'gwal ah
• is not equal to	no es igual a	noh ehs ee-'gwal ah
• is equivalent to	equivale a	eh-kee-'bah-leh ah
• is greater than	es mayor que	ehs mah-'yohr keh
• is less than	es menor que	ehs meh-'nohr keh
• is similar to	es semejante a	ehs seh-meh-'hahn-teh ah
equation	ecuación (f)	eh-kwah-see-'ohn
• quadratic equation	ecuación de segundo grado	eh-kwah-see-'ohn deh seh-'goon-doh 'grah-doh
factor	factor (m)	fahk-'tohr
logarithm	logaritmo	loh-gah-'reet-moh
• logarithmic	logarítmico	loh-gah-'reet-mee-koh
multiple	múltiple (adj)	'mool-tee-pleh
percent	por ciento	pohr see-'ehn-toh
• percentage	porcentaje (m)	pohr-sehn-'tah-heh
problem	problema (m)	proh-'bleh-mah
• problem to solve	problema que resolver	proh-'bleh-mah keh reh-sohl-'behr
product	producto	proh-'dook-toh
quotient	cociente (m)	koh-see-'ehn-teh
set	conjunto	kohn-'hoon-toh
solution	solución (f)	soh-loo-see-'ohn
• solve	resolver (v)	reh-sohl-'behr
statistical	estadístico (adj)	ehs-tah-'dees-tee-koh
• statistics	estadística (f)	ehs-tah-'dees-tee-kah
sum	suma	'soo-mah
• sum up	sumar (v)	soo-'mahr
symbol	símbolo	'seem-boh-loh
variable	variable	bah-ree-'ah-bleh

2. GEOMETRY

a. FIGURES

plane figures	figuras planas	fee-goo-rahs 'plah-nahs
triangle	triángulo	tree-'ahn-goo-loh
• acute-angled	ángulo agudo	'ahn-goo-loh ah-'goo-doh
• equilateral	equilátero (adj)	eh-kee-'lah-teh-roh
• isosceles	isósceles	ee-'soh-seh-lehs
• obtuse-angled	obtuso (adj)	ohb-'too-soh
• right-angled	recto (adj)	'rehk-toh
• scalene	escaleno (adj)	ehs-kah-'leh-noh

four-sided figures	figuras cuadriláteras	*fee-'goo-rahs kwah-dree-'lah-teh-rahs*
• parallelogram	paralelogramo	*pah-rah-leh-loh-'grah-moh*
• rectangle	rectángulo	*rehk-'tahn-goo-loh*
• rhombus	rombo	*'rohm-boh*
• square	cuadrado	*kwah-'drah-doh*
• trapezium (trapezoid)	trapecio	*trah-'peh-see·oh*
n-sided figures	polígonos	*poh-'lee-goh-nohs*
• decagon	decágono	*deh-'kah-goh-noh*
• heptagon	heptágono	*ehp-'tah-goh-noh*
• hexagon	hexágono	*ekhs-'ah-goh-noh*
• octagon	octógono (octágono)	*ohk-'toh-goh-noh (ohk-'tah-goh-noh)*
• pentagon	pentágono	*pehn-'tah-goh-noh*
circle	círculo	*'seer-koo-loh*
• center	centro	*'sehn-troh*
• circumference	circunferencia	*seer-koon-feh-'rehn-see·ah*
• diameter	diámetro	*dee-'ah-meh-troh*
• radius	radio	*'rah-dee·oh*
• tangent	tangente (*f*)	*tahn-'hehn-teh*
solid figures	figuras sólidas	*fee-'goo-rahs 'soh-lee-dahs*
cone	cono	*'koh-noh*
cube	cubo	*'koo-boh*
cylinder	cilindro	*see-'leen-droh*
parallelepiped	paralelopípedo	*pah-rah-leh-loh-'pee-peh-doh*
polyhedron	poliedro	*poh-lee-'eh-droh*
• dodecahedron	dodecaedro	*doh-deh-kah-'eh-droh*
• icosahedron	isocaedro	*ee-koh-sah-'eh-droh*
• octahedron	octaedro	*ohk-tah-'eh-droh*
• tetrahedron	tetraedro	*teh-trah-'eh-droh*
prism	prisma (*m*)	*'prees-mah*
pyramid	pirámide (*f*)	*pee-'rah-mee-deh*
sphere	esfera	*ehs-'feh-rah*

b. CONCEPTS

angle	ángulo (*adj*)	*'ahn-goo-loh*
• acute	agudo (*adj*)	*ah-'goo-doh*

FOCUS: Geometrical Figures

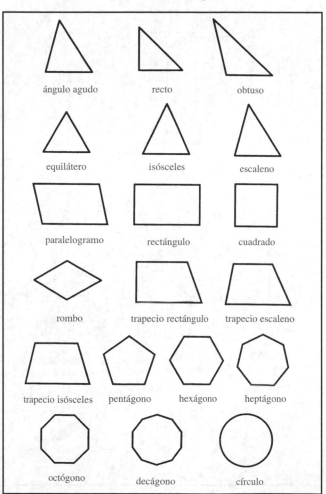

FOCUS: Geometrical Solids

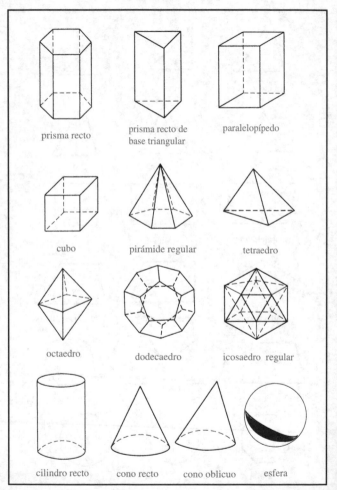

prisma recto

prisma recto de
base triangular

paralelopípedo

cubo

pirámide regular

tetraedro

octaedro

dodecaedro

icosaedro regular

cilindro recto

cono recto

cono oblicuo

esfera

FOCUS: Angles

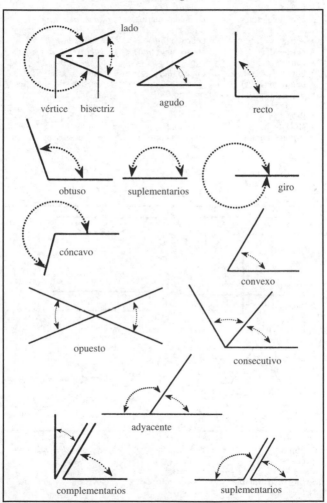

• **adjacent**	adyacente (*adj*)	*ahd-yah-'sehn-teh*
• **bisector**	bisectriz (*f*)	*bee·sehk-'trees*
• **complementary**	complementario (*adj*)	*kohm-pleh-mehn-'tah-ree·oh*
• **concave**	cóncavo (*adj*)	*'kohn-kah-boh*
• **consecutive**	consecutivo (*adj*)	*kohn-seh-koo-'tee-boh*
• **convex**	convexo (*adj*)	*kohn-'behk-soh*
• **obtuse**	obtuso (*adj*)	*ohb-'too-soh*
• **one turn (360°)**	giro (*m*)	*'hee-roh*
• **opposite**	opuesto (*adj*)	*oh-'pwehs-toh*
• **right**	recto (*adj*)	*'rehk-toh*
• **side**	lado	*'lah-doh*
• **straight**	plano (*adj*)	*'plah-noh*
• **supplementary**	suplementario	*soo-pleh-mehn-'tah-ree·oh*
• **vertex**	vértice (*m*)	*'behr-tee-seh*
• **axis**	eje (*m*)	*'eh-heh*

FOCUS: Lines

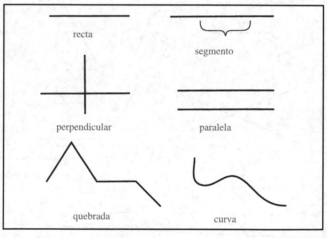

coordinate	coordenada	*koh-ohr-deh-'nah-dah*
degree	grado	*'grah-doh*
draw	trazar (*v*)	*trah-'sahr*
drawing instruments	instrumentos de dibujo	*eens-troo-'mehn-tohs deh dee·'boo-hoh*
• **compass**	compás (*m*)	*kohm-'pahs*

• **eraser**	goma de borrar	*'goh-mah deh boh-'rrahr*
• **pen**	pluma	*'ploo-mah*
• **pencil**	lápiz (*m*)	*'lah-pees*
• **protractor**	transportador (*m*)	*trahns-pohr-tah-'dohr*
• **ruler**	regla	*reh-glah*
geometrical	geométrico	*heh-oh-'meh-tree-koh*
• **geometry**	geometría	*heh-oh-meh-'tree-ah*
line	línea	*'lee-neh-ah*
• **broken**	quebrada (*adj*)	*keh-'brah-dah*
• **curved**	curva (*adj*)	*'koor-bah*
• **parallel**	paralela (*adj*)	*pah-rah-'leh-lah*
• **perpendicular**	perpendicular (*adj*)	*pehr-pehn-dee-koo-'lahr*
• **segment**	segmento	*sehg-'mehn-toh*
• **straight**	recta (*adj*)	*'rehk-tah*
point	punto	*'poon-toh*
space	espacio	*ehs-'pah-see-oh*
trigonometry	trigonometría	*tree-goh-noh-meh-'tree-ah*
• **trigonometric**	trigonométrico	*tree-goh-noh-'meh-tree-koh*
• **cosecant**	cosecante (*f*)	*koh-seh-'kahn-teh*
• **cosine**	coseno	*koh-'seh-noh*
• **cotangent**	cotangente (*f*)	*koh-tahn-'hehn-teh*
• **secant**	secante (*f*)	*seh-'kahn-teh*
• **sine**	seno	*'seh-noh*
• **tangent**	tangente (*f*)	*tahn-'hehn-teh*
vector	vector (*m*)	*behk-'tohr*

3. *QUANTITY AND SPACE*

a. WEIGHTS AND MEASURES

area	área (*f*)	*'ah-reh·ah*
• **hectare**	hectárea	*ehk-'tah-reh·ah*
• **square centimeter**	centímetro cuadrado	*sehn-'tee-meh-troh kwah-'drah-doh*
• **square kilometer**	kilómetro cuadrado	*kee-'loh-meh-troh kwah-'drah-doh*
• **square meter**	metro cuadrado	*'meh-troh kwah-'drah-doh*
• **square millimeter**	milímetro cuadrado	*mee-'lee-meh-troh kwah-'drah-doh*
length	longitud (*f*)	*lohn-hee-'tood*
• **centimeter**	centímetro	*sehn-'tee-meh-troh*
• **kilometer**	kilómetro	*kee-'loh-meh-troh*
• **meter**	metro	*'meh-troh*
• **millimeter**	milímetro	*mee-'lee-meh-troh*

volume	volumen (*m*)	*boh-'loo-mehn*
• cubic centimeter	centímetro cúbico	*sehn-'tee-meh-troh 'koo-bee-koh*
• cubic kilometer	kilómetro cúbico	*kee-'loh-meh-troh 'koo-bee-koh*
• cubic meter	metro cúbico	*'meh-troh 'koo-bee-koh*
• cubic millimeter	milímetro cúbico	*mee-'lee-meh-troh 'koo-bee-koh*
• liter	litro	*'lee-troh*
• quart	cuarto	*'kwahr-toh*
weight	peso	*'peh-soh*
• gram	gramo	*'grah-moh*
• hectogram	hectogramo	*ehk-toh-'grah-moh*
• kilogram	kilogramo	*kee-loh-'grah-moh*
	kilo	*'kee-loh*

b. WEIGHING AND MEASURING

dense	denso (*adj*)	*'dehn-soh*
• density	densidad (*f*)	*dehn-see-'dahd*
dimension	dimensión (*f*)	*dee-mehn-see-'ohn*
extension	extensión (*f*)	*ehks-tehn-see-'ohn*
heavy	pesado (*adj*)	*peh-'sah-doh*
heavy (*liquid*)	espeso (*adj*)	*ehs-'peh-soh*
light	ligero (*adj*)	*lee-'heh-roh*
long	largo (*adj*)	*'lahr-goh*
mass	masa	*'mah-sah*
maximum	máximo (*adj*)	*'mah-ksee-moh*
measure	medir (*v**)	*meh-'deer*
• measuring tape	cinta métrica	*'seen-tah 'meh-tree-kah*
• medium	mediano (*adj*)	*meh-dee-'ah-noh*
• minimum	mínimo (*adj*)	*'mee-nee-moh*
• narrow	estrecho (*adj*)	*ehs-'treh-choh*
• short (*thing*)	corto (*adj*)	*'kohr-toh*
• size	tamaño	*tah-'mah-nyoh*
speed	velocidad (*f*)	*beh-loh-see-'dahd*
• per hour	por hora	*pohr 'oh-rah*
• per minute	por minuto	*pohr mee-'noo-toh*
• per second	por segundo	*pohr seh-'goon-doh*
tall	alto (*adj*)	*'ahl-toh*
thick	espeso (*adj*)	*ehs-'peh-soh*
thin	delgado (*adj*)	*dehl-'gah-doh*
	fino (*adj*)	*'fee-noh*
weigh	pesar (*v*)	*peh-'sahr*
wide	ancho (*adj*)	*'ahn-choh*
• width	anchura	*ahn-'choo-rah*

c. CONCEPTS OF QUANTITY

a lot, much	mucho (*adj, adv*)	'moo-choh
all, everything	todo (*adj, pron*)	'toh-doh
• **everyone**	todos (*pron*)	'toh-dohs
	todo el mundo (*pron*)	'toh-doh ehl 'moon-doh
almost, nearly	casi (*adv*)	'kah-see
approximately	aproximadamente (*adv*)	ah-prohk-see-mah-dah-'mehn-teh
as much as	tanto . . . como	'tahn-toh 'koh-moh
big, large	grande (*adj*)	'grahn-deh
both	ambos (*adj, pron*)	'ahm-bohs
capacity	capacidad (*f*)	kah-pah-see-'dahd
decrease	disminuir (*v**)	dees-mee-'nweer
• **decrease**	disminución (*f*)	dees-mee-noo-see-'ohn
double	doble (*adj*)	'doh-bleh
empty	vacío (*adj*)	bah-'see-oh
• **empty**	vaciar (*v*)	bah-see-'ahr
enough	bastante (*adj, adv*)	bahs-'tahn-teh
• **be enough**	bastar (*v*)	bahs-'tahr
	ser (*v**) bastante	sehr bahs-'tahn-teh
entire	entero (*adj*)	ehn-'teh-roh
every, each	cada (*adv*)	'kah-dah
fill	llenar (*v*)	yeh-'nahr
• **full**	lleno (*adj*)	'yeh-noh
grow	crecer (*v*)	kreh-'sehr
• **growth**	crecimiento	kreh-see-mee-'ehn-toh
half	mitad (*f*)	mee-'tahd
	medio (*adj*)	'meh-dee·oh
how much	¿cuánto? (*adj, pron*)	'kwahn-toh
increase	aumentar (*v*)	ow-mehn-'tahr
• **increase**	aumento	ow-'mehn-toh
less	menos	'meh-nohs
little	pequeño (*adj*)	peh-'keh-nyoh
• **a little**	un poco	oon 'poh-koh
more	más	mahs
no one	nadie (*pron*)	'nah-dee·eh
nothing	nada	'nah-dah
pair	par (*m*)	pahr
part	parte (*f*)	'pahr-teh
piece	pedazo	peh-'dah-soh
portion	porción (*f*)	pohr-see-'ohn
quantity	cantidad (*f*)	kahn-tee-'dahd
several	varios	'bah-ree·ohs
small	pequeño	peh-'keh-nyoh
some	algunos (-as) (*adj*)	ahl-'goo-nohs (-nahs)

suffice	bastar (*v*)	*bahs-'tahr*
	ser (*v**) suficiente	*sehr soo-fee-see·'ehn-teh*
• **sufficient**	suficiente (*adj*)	*soo-fee-see·'ehn-teh*
too much	demasiado (*adj, adv*)	*deh-mah-see·'ah-doh*
triple	triple (*adj*)	*'tree-pleh*

d. CONCEPTS OF LOCATION

above	arriba (*adv*)	*ah-'rree-bah*
	sobre (*prep*)	*'soh-breh*
across	a través de (*prep*)	*ah trah-'behs deh*
ahead	delante (*adj, adv*)	*deh-'lahn-teh*
	al frente (*adj, adv*)	*ahl 'frehn-teh*
among, between	entre (*prep*)	*'ehn-treh*
away (gone)	fuera (*adv*)	*'fweh-rah*
behind	detrás (*adv*)	*deh-'trahs*
beside, next to	junto a (*prep*)	*'hoon-toh ah*
	al lado de (*prep*)	*ahl 'lah-doh deh*
beyond	más allá	*mahs ah-'yah*
bottom	fondo	*'fohn-doh*
• **at the bottom**	en el fondo	*ehn ehl 'fohn-doh*
compass	brújula	*'broo-hoo-lah*
direction	dirección	*dee-rehk-see-'ohn*
distance	distancia	*dees-'tahn-see·ah*
down below	abajo	*ah-'bah-hoh*
east	este (*m*)	*'ehs-teh*
• **eastern**	oriental (*adj*)	*oh-ree·ehn-'tahl*
	este (*adj*)	*'ehs-teh*
• **to the east**	al este	*ahl 'ehs-teh*
edge	borde	*'bohr-deh*
far	lejos (*adv*)	*'leh-hohs*
from	de (*prep*)	*deh*
here	aquí (*adv*)	*ah-'kee*
	acá (*adv*)	*ah-'kah*
horizontal	horizontal (*adj*)	*oh-ree-sohn-'tahl*
in	en (*prep*)	*ehn*
• **inside of**	dentro de (*prep*)	*'dehn-troh deh*
in front of	delante de (*prep*)	*deh-'lahn-teh deh*
in front of (*facing*)	en frente de (*prep*)	*ehn 'frehn-teh deh*
in the middle	en medio de (*prep*)	*ehn 'meh-dee·oh deh*
left	izquierdo (*adj*)	*ees-kee·'ehr-doh*
• **to the left**	a la izquierda	*ah lah ees-kee·'ehr-dah*
level	llano (*adj*)	*'yah-noh*
near	cerca (de) (*adv, prep*)	*'sehr-kah (deh)*

north	norte (*m*)	*'nohr-teh*
• **northern**	septentrional (*adj*)	*sehp-tehn-tree·oh-'nahl*
• **to the north**	al norte	*ahl 'nohr-teh*
nowhere	en ninguna parte (*adv*)	*ehn neen-'goo-nah 'pahr-teh*
on	encima (de) (*adv, prep*)	*ehn-'see-mah (deh)*
outside	fuera (de) (*adv, prep*)	*'fweh-rah (deh)*
place	lugar (*m*)	*loo-'gahr*
position	posición (*f*)	*poh-see-see-'ohn*
right	derecho (*adj*)	*deh-'reh-choh*
• **to the right**	a la derecha	*ah lah deh-'reh-chah*
somewhere	en alguna parte (*adv*)	*ehn ahl-'goo-nah 'pahr-teh*
south	sur (*m*)	*soor*
• **southern**	meridional (*adj*)	*meh-ree-dee·oh-'nahl*
• **to the south**	al sur	*ahl soor*
there	allí	*ah-'yee*
	allá	*ah-'yah*
through	a través de	*ah trah-'behs deh*
to, at	a (*prep*)	*ah*
• **at** (*someone's place*)	en (*prep*)	*ehn*
toward	hacia (*prep*)	*'ah-see·ah*
under	debajo (de) (*adv, prep*)	*deh-'bah-hoh deh*
up	arriba (*adv*)	*ah-'rree-bah*
vertical	vertical (*adj*)	*behr-tee-'kahl*
west	oeste (*m*)	*oh-'ehs-teh*

FOCUS: Compass Points

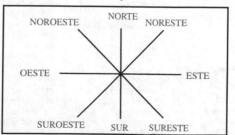

• **western**	occidental (*adj*)	*ohk-see-dehn-'tahl*
• **to the west**	al oeste	*ahl oh-'ehs-teh*
where	donde	*'dohn-deh*

e. MOVEMENT

arrive	llegar (*v*)	*yeh-'gahr*
come	venir (*v**)	*beh-'neer*
drive	manejar (*v*)	*mah-neh-'hahr*
	conducir (*v**)	*kohn-doo-'seer*
enter	entrar (*v*)	*ehn-'trahr*
fall	caer (*v**)	*kah-'ehr*
fast	rápido (*adj*)	*'rah-pee-doh*
follow	seguir (*v**)	*seh-'geer*
get up	levantarse (*v*)	*leh-bahn-'tahr-seh*
go	ir (*v**)	*eer*
• **go away**	irse (*v**)	*'eer-seh*
• **go down**	bajar (*v*)	*bah-'hahr*
• **go on foot**	ir (*v**) a pie	*eer ah pee·'eh*
• **go out, exit**	salir (*v**)	*sah-'leer*
• **go up**	subir (*v*)	*soo-'beer*
leave, depart	partir (*v*)	*pahr-'teer*
	irse (*v**)	*'eer-seh*
lie down	acostarse (*v**)	*ah-koh-'stahr-seh*
	tenderse (*v**)	*tehn-'dehr-seh*
lift	levantar (*v*)	*leh-bahn-'tahr*
	elevar (*v*)	*eh-leh-'bahr*
motion	movimiento	*moh-bee-mee·'ehn-toh*
• **move**	mover (*v**)	*moh-'behr*
• **move oneself**	moverse (*v**)	*moh-'behr-seh*
movement	movimiento	*moh-bee-mee·'ehn-toh*
pass by	pasar (*v*)	*pah-'sahr*
pull	tirar (*v*)	*tee-'rahr*
push	empujar (*v*)	*ehm-poo-'hahr*
put	poner (*v**)	*poh-'nehr*
	meter (*v*)	*meh-'tehr*
quick	rápido (*adj*)	*'rah-pee-doh*
• **quickly**	rápidamente (*adv*)	*'rah-pee-dah-mehn-teh*
return	volver (*v**)	*bohl-'behr*
	regresar (*v*)	*reh-greh-'sahr*
• **return something**	devolver (*v**)	*deh-bohl-'behr*
run	correr (*v*)	*koh-'rrehr*
send	mandar (*v*)	*mahn-'dahr*
sit down	sentarse (*v**)	*sehn-'tahr-seh*
slow	lento (*adj*)	*'lehn-toh*
• **slowly**	lentamente (*adv*)	*lehn-tah-'mehn-teh*
	despacio (*adv*)	*dehs-'pah-see·oh*

stop	parar (*v*)	pah-'rahr
	detener (*v**)	deh-teh-'nehr
• stop oneself	detenerse (*v**)	deh-teh-'nehr-seh
turn	volver (*v**)	bohl-'behr
	girar (*v*)	hee-'rahr
walk	andar (*v*)	ahn-'dahr
	caminar (*v*)	kah-mee-'nahr
• walk	caminata	kah-mee-'nah-tah

4. TIME

a. GENERAL EXPRESSIONS OF TIME

afternoon	tarde (*f*)	'tahr-deh
• in the afternoon	por la tarde	pohr lah 'tahr-deh
• this afternoon	esta tarde	'ehs-tah 'tahr-deh
• tomorrow afternoon	mañana por la tarde	mah-'nyah-nah pohr lah 'tahr-deh
dawn	amanecer (*m*)	ah-mah-neh-'sehr
day	día (*m*)	'dee-ah
• all day	todo el día	'toh-doh ehl 'dee-ah
evening	tarde (*f*)	'tahr-deh
	noche (*f*)	'noh-cheh
• in the evening	por la tarde	pohr lah 'tahr-deh-
• this evening	esta tarde	'ehs-tah 'tahr-deh
• tomorrow evening	mañana por la tarde	mah-'nyah-nah pohr lah 'tahr-deh
midnight	medianoche (*f*)	meh-dee-ah-'noh-cheh
• at midnight	a la medianoche	ah lah meh-dee-ah-'noh-cheh
morning	mañana	mah-'nyah-nah
• in the morning	por la mañana	pohr lah mah-'nyah-nah
• this morning	esta mañana	'ehs-tah mah-'nyah-nah
• tomorrow morning	mañana por la mañana	mah-'nyah-nah pohr lah mah-'nyah-nah
night	noche (*f*)	'noh-cheh
• at night	de noche	deh 'noh-cheh
• last night	anoche	ah-'noh-cheh
• tomorrow night	mañana por la noche	mah-'nyah-nah pohr lah 'noh-cheh
• tonight	esta noche	'ehs-tah 'noh-cheh
noon	mediodía (*m*)	meh-dee-oh-'dee-ah
• at noon	al mediodía	ahl meh-dee-oh-'dee-ah
sunrise	salida del sol	sah-'lee-dah dehl sohl
sunset	puesta del sol	'poo·ehs-tah dehl sohl
time	tiempo	tee·'ehm-poh
• time (*hour*)	hora	'oh-rah

• **time** (*once, twice*)	vez (*f*)	*behs*
today	hoy (*adv*)	*oy*
tomorrow	mañana	*mah-'nyah-nah*
• **day after tomorrow**	pasado mañana	*pah-'sah-doh mah-'nyah-nah*
tonight	esta noche	*'ehs-tah 'noh-cheh*
yesterday	ayer	*ah-'yehr*
• **day before yesterday**	anteayer	*ahn-teh-ah-'yehr*
• **yesterday morning**	ayer por la mañana	*ah-'yehr pohr lah mah-'nyah-nah*

b. TELLING TIME

What time is it?	¿Qué hora es?	*keh 'oh-rah ehs*
• **It's 1:00.**	Es la una.	*ehs lah 'oo-nah*
• **It's 2:00.**	Son las dos.	*sohn lahs dohs*
• **It's 3:00 sharp.**	Son las tres en punto.	*sohn lahs trehs ehn 'poon-toh*
• **It's 1:10.**	Es la una y diez.	*ehs lah 'oo-nah ee dee-'ehs*
• **It's 3:15.**	Son las tres y cuarto.	*sohn lahs trehs ee 'kwahr-toh*
• **It's 3:30.**	Son las tres y media.	*sohn lahs trehs ee 'meh-dee·ah*
• **It's 2:45.**	Son las tres menos cuarto.	*sohn lahs trehs 'meh-nohs 'kwahr-toh*
• **It's 5:50.**	Son las seis menos diez.	*sohn lahs 'seh·ees 'meh-nohs dee·'ehs*
• **It's 5:00 A.M.**	Son las cinco de la mañana.	*sohn lahs 'seen-koh deh lah mah-'nyah-nah*
• **It's 5:00 P.M.**	Son las cinco de la tarde.	*sohn lahs 'seen-koh deh lah 'tahr-deh*
• **It's 10:00 P.M.**	Son las diez de la noche.	*sohn lahs dee·'ehs deh lah 'noh-cheh*
At what time?	¿A qué hora?	*ah keh 'oh-rah*
• **at 1:00**	a la una	*ah lah 'oo-nah*
• **at 2:00**	a las dos	*ah lahs dohs*
• **at 3:00**	a las tres	*ah lahs trehs*

c. UNITS OF TIME

century	siglo	*'see·gloh*
day	día (*m*)	*'dee·ah*
• **daily**	diario (*n, adj*)	*dee·ah-ree·oh*
	cotidiano (*adj*)	*koh-tee-dee·'ah-noh*

decade	década	*'deh-kah-dah*
hour	hora	*'oh-rah*
• hourly (*per hour*)	por hora	*pohr 'oh-rah*
• hourly (*each hour*)	cada hora	*'kah-dah 'oh-rah*
instant	instante	*eens-'tahn-teh*
minute	minuto	*mee-'noo-toh*
moment	momento	*moh-'mehn-toh*
month	mes (*m*)	*mehs*
• monthly	mensual (*adj*)	*mehn-'swahl*
	mensualmente (*adv*)	*mehn-swahl-'mehn-teh*
second	segundo	*seh-'goon-doh*
week	semana	*seh-'mah·nah*
• weekly	semanal (*adj*)	*seh-mah-'nahl*
	por semana (*adv*)	*pohr seh-'mah-nah*
year	año	*'ah-nyoh*
• yearly	anual (*adj*)	*ah-'nwahl*
	anualmente (*adv*)	*ah-nwahl-'mehn-teh*

d. TIMEPIECES

alarm clock	despertador (*m*)	*dehs-pehr-tah-'dohr*
clock	reloj (*m*)	*reh-'loh*
dial	esfera	*ehs-'feh-rah*
grandfather clock	reloj de caja	*reh-'loh deh 'kah-hah*
hand (*of a clock*)	mano (*f*)	*'mah-noh*
watch	reloj (*m*)	*reh-'loh*
• The watch is fast.	El reloj anda adelantado.	*Ehl reh-'loh 'ahn-dah ah-deh-lahn-'tah-doh*
• The watch is slow.	El reloj anda atrasado.	*Ehl reh-'loh 'ahn-dah ah-trah-'sah-doh*
watchband	correa de reloj	*koh-'rreh-ah deh reh-'loh*
watch battery	pila	*'pee-lah*
wind	dar (*v**) cuerda a	*dahr 'kwehr-dah ah*
wristwatch	reloj de pulsera	*reh-'loh deh pool-'seh-rah*

e. CONCEPTS OF TIME

after	después (de) (*adv, prep*)	*dehs-'pwehs (deh)*
again	otra vez	*'oh-trah behs*
ago	hace	*'ah-seh*
almost never	casi nunca	*'kah-see 'noon-kah*
already	ya	*yah*

always	siempre	*see-'ehm-preh*
as soon as	así que	*as-'see keh*
	luego que	*'lweh-goh keh*
	tan pronto como	*tahn 'prohn-toh 'koh-moh*
at the same time	al mismo tiempo	*ahl 'mees-moh tee-'ehm-poh*
be about to	estar para	*ehs-'tahr 'pah-rah*
be on time (*people*)	llegar a tiempo	*yeh-'gahr ah tee-'ehm-poh*
	ser puntual	*sehr poon-'twahl*
• on time (*e.g., trains*)	a tiempo	*ah tee-'ehm-poh*
	a la hora	*ah lah 'oh-rah*

Time is money.	= El tiempo es oro.	
There is time for all things.	= Cada cosa a su tiempo.	
Time is up.	= Es la hora.	

before	antes (de) (*adv, prep*)	*'ahn-tehs (deh)*
	antes (de) que (*conj*)	*'ahn-tehs (deh) keh*
begin	empezar (*v**)	*ehm-peh-'sahr*
	comenzar (*v**)	*koh-mehn-'sahr*
• beginning	principio	*preen-'see-pee·oh*
brief	breve (*adj*)	*'breh-beh*
• briefly	brevemente (*adv*)	*breh-beh-'mehn-teh*
by now	ya	*yah*
change	cambiar (*v*)	*kahm-bee-'ahr*
continue	continuar (*v**)	*kohn-tee-'nwahr*
• continually	continuamente	*kohn-tee-nwah-'mehn-teh*
during	durante	*doo-'rahn-teh*
early	temprano (*adv*)	*tehm-'prah-noh*
• to be early	llegar (*v*) temprano	*yeh-'gahr tehm-'prah-noh*
end, finish	terminar (*v*)	*tehr-mee-'nahr*
• end	fin (*m*)	*feen*
frequent	frecuente (*adj*)	*freh-'kwehn-teh*
• frequently	frecuentemente (*adv*)	*freh-kwehn-teh-'mehn-teh*
	con frecuencia (*adv*)	*kohn freh-'kwehn-see·ah*
happen, occur	pasar (*v*)	*pah-'sahr*
	ocurrir (*v*)	*oh-koo-'reer*
	suceder (*v*)	*soo-seh-'dehr*

in an hour's time	dentro de una hora	*'dehn-troh deh 'oo-nah 'oh-rah*
• **in two minutes' time**	en dos minutos	*ehn dohs mee-'noo-tohs*
in the meantime	mientras tanto	*mee-'ehn-trahs 'tahn-toh*
in time	a tiempo	*ah tee-'ehm-poh*
just	justo *(adj, adv)*	*'hoos-toh*
last	durar *(v)*	*doo-'rahr*
• **last a long time**	durar *(v)* mucho tiempo	*doo-'rahr 'moo-choh tee-'ehm-poh*
• **last a short time**	durar *(v)* poco tiempo	*doo-'rahr 'poh-koh tee-'ehm-poh*
last	pasado *(adj)*	*pah-'sah-doh*
• **last month**	el mes pasado	*ehl mehs pah-'sah-doh*
• **last year**	el año pasado	*ehl 'ah-nyoh pah-'sah-doh*
late	tarde *(adj)*	*'tahr-deh*
• **to be late**	llegar *(v)* tarde	*yeh-'gahr 'tahr-deh*
long-term	a largo plazo	*ah 'lahr-goh 'plah-soh*
look forward to	esperar *(v)* con placer anticipado	*ehs-peh-'rahr kohn plah-'sehr ahn-tee-see-'pah-doh*
never	nunca	*'noon-kah*
• **almost never**	casi nunca	*'kah-see 'noon-kah*
now	ahora	*ah-'oh-rah*
• **for now**	por ahora	*pohr ah-'oh-rah*
• **from now on**	de ahora en adelante	*deh ah-'oh-rah ehn ah-deh-'lahn-teh*
nowadays	hoy día	*oy 'dee-ah*
occasionally	de vez en cuando	*deh behs ehn 'kwahn-doh*
often	con frecuencia	*kohn freh-'kwehn-see-ah*
once	una vez	*'oo-nah behs*
• **twice**	dos veces	*dohs 'beh-sehs*
• **once in a while**	de vez en cuando	*deh behs ehn 'kwan-doh*
• **once upon a time**	hace siglos	*'ah-seh 'see-glohs*
only	solo *(adj)*	*'soh-loh*
	sólo *(adv)*	*'soh-loh*
	solamente *(adv)*	*soh-lah-'mehn-teh*
past	pasado	*pah-'sah-doh*
present	presente *(m)*	*preh-'sehn-teh*
• **present**	actual *(adj)*	*ahk-'twahl*
• **presently**	actualmente *(adv)*	*ahk-twahl-'mehn-teh*
previous	anterior	*ahn-teh-ree-'ohr*
• **previously**	anteriormente *(adv)*	*ahn-teh-ree·ohr-'mehn-teh*
	antes *(adv)*	*'ahn-tehs*

rare	raro *(adj)*	*'rah-roh*
• **rarely**	raramente *(adv)*	*rah-rah-'mehn-teh*
	raras veces *(adv)*	*'rah-rahs 'beh-sehs*
recent	reciente *(adj)*	*reh-see-'ehn-teh*
• **recently**	recientemente *(adv)*	*reh-see·ehn-teh-'mehn-teh*
regular	regular *(adj)*	*reh-goo-'lahr*
	normal *(adj)*	*nohr-'mahl*
• **regularly**	regularmente *(adv)*	*reh-goo-lahr-'mehn-teh*
right away	ahora mismo	*ah-'oh-rah 'mees-moh*
short-term	a corto plazo	*ah 'kohr-toh 'plah-soh*
simultaneous	simultáneo *(adj)*	*see-mool-'tah-neh-oh*
• **simultaneously**	simultáneamente *(adv)*	*see-mool-tah-neh-ah-'mehn-teh*
since, for	desde *(prep)*	*'dehs-deh*
• **since Monday**	desde el lunes	*'dehs-deh ehl 'loo-nehs*
• **since yesterday**	desde ayer	*'dehs-deh ah-'yehr*
• **for three days**	desde hace tres días	*'dehs-deh 'ah-seh trehs 'dee-ahs*
slow	lento *(adj)*	*'lehn-toh*
• **slowly**	lentamente *(adv)*	*lehn-tah-'mehn-teh*
	despacio *(adv)*	*dehs-'pah-see-oh*
soon	pronto	*'prohn-toh*
• **as soon as**	así que	*ah-'see keh*
	tan pronto como	*tahn 'prohn-toh 'koh-moh*
• **sooner or later**	tarde o temprano	*'tahr-deh oh tehm-'prah-noh*
spend time	pasar *(v)*	*pah-'sahr*
sporadic	esporádico *(adj)*	*ehs-poh-'rah-dee-koh*
• **sporadically**	esporádicamente *(adv)*	*ehs-poh-'rah-dee-kah-'mehn-teh*
still	aún *(adv)*	*ah-'oon*
	todavía *(adv)*	*toh-dah-'bee-ah*
take place	tener *(v*)* lugar	*teh-'nehr 'loo-gahr*
temporary	temporáneo *(adj)*	*tehm-poh-'rah-neh·oh*
• **temporarily**	temporáneamente *(adv)*	*tehn-poh'rah-neh-ah-mehn-teh*
then	entonces *(adv)*	*ehn-'tohn-sehs*

Better late than never. = Más vale tarde que nunca.

---

timetable, schedule	horario	*oh-'rah-ree-oh*
to this day	hasta la fecha	*'ahs-tah lah 'feh-chah*
until	hasta *(prep)*	*'ahs-tah*
	hasta que *(conj)*	*'ahs-tah keh*

usually	normalmente	*nohr-mahl-'mehn-teh*
wait for	esperar (*v*)	*ehs-peh-'rahr*
when	cuando (*conj*)	*'kwahn-doh*
while	mientras	*mee'·ehn-trahs*
within	dentro de (*prep*)	*'dehn-troh deh*
yet	todavía (*adv*)	*toh-dah-'bee-ah*

5. DAYS, MONTHS, AND SEASONS

a. DAYS OF THE WEEK

day of the week	día de la semana	*'dee-ah deh lah seh-'mah-nah*
• **Monday**	el lunes	*ehl 'loo-nehs*
• **Tuesday**	el martes	*ehl 'mahr-tehs*
• **Wednesday**	el miércoles	*ehl mee·'ehr-koh-lehs*
• **Thursday**	el jueves	*ehl 'hweh-behs*
• **Friday**	el viernes	*ehl bee·'ehr-nehs*
• **Saturday**	el sábado	*ehl 'sah-bah-doh*
• **Sunday**	el domingo	*ehl doh-'meen-goh*
• **on Mondays**	los lunes	*lohs 'loo-nehs*
• **on Saturdays**	los sábados	*lohs 'sah-bah-dohs*
holiday	día de fiesta	*'dee-ah deh fee·'ehs-tah*
• **Today is a holiday.**	Hoy es fiesta.	*oy ehs fee·'ehs-tah*
weekend	fin de semana (*m*)	*feen deh seh-'mah-nah*
What day is it?	¿Qué día es hoy?	*keh 'dee-ah ehs oy*
workday	día laborable	*'dee-ah lah-boh-'rah-bleh*
	día de trabajo	*'dee-ah deh trah-'bah-hoh*

b. MONTHS OF THE YEAR

month of the year	mes (*m*) del año	*mehs dehl 'ah-nyoh*
• **January**	enero	*eh-'neh-roh*
• **February**	febrero	*feh-'breh-roh*
• **March**	marzo	*'mahr-soh*
• **April**	abril	*ah-'breel*
• **May**	mayo	*'mah-yoh*
• **June**	junio	*'hoo-nee·oh*
• **July**	julio	*'hoo-lee·oh*
• **August**	agosto	*ah-'gohs-toh*
• **September**	septiembre (*m*)	*sehp-tee·'ehm-breh*
• **October**	octubre (*m*)	*ohk-'too-breh*
• **November**	noviembre (*m*)	*noh-bee·'ehm-breh*
• **December**	diciembre (*m*)	*dee-see·'ehm-breh*

calendar	calendario	*kah-lehn-'dah-ree·oh*
leap year	año bisiesto	*'ah-nyoh bee-see-'ehs-toh*
monthly	mensual (*adj*)	*mehn-'swahl*
	mensualmente (*adv*)	*mehn-swahl-'mehn-teh*
school year	año escolar	*ah-'nyoh ehs-koh-'lahr*
What month is it?	¿En qué mes estamos?	*ehn keh mehs ehs-'tah-mohs*

c. SEASONS

season	estación (*f*)	*eh-stah-see·'ohn*
• spring	primavera	*pree-mah-'beh-rah*
• summer	verano	*beh-'rah-noh*
• fall	otoño	*oh-'toh-nyoh*
• winter	invierno	*een-vee-'ehr-noh*
equinox	equinoccio	*eh-kee-'nohk-see·oh*
moon	luna	*'loo-nah*
solstice	solsticio	*sohl-'stee-see·oh*
sun	sol (*m*)	*sohl*

FOCUS: The Seasons

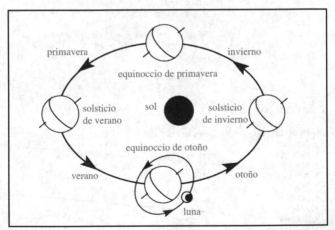

d. THE ZODIAC

> For the planets see Section 13.

horoscope	horóscopo	*oh-'rohs-koh-poh*
zodiac	zodíaco	*soh-'dee-ah-koh*
signs of the zodiac	signos del zodíaco	*'seeg-nohs dehl soh-'dee-ah-koh*
• **Aries**	Aries	*'ah-ree·ehs*
• **Taurus**	Tauro	*'tow-roh*
• **Gemini**	Géminis	*'heh-mee-nees*
• **Cancer**	Cáncer	*'kahn-sehr*
• **Leo**	Leo	*'leh-oh*
• **Virgo**	Virgo	*'veer-goh*
• **Libra**	Libra	*'lee-brah*
• **Scorpio**	Escorpión	*ehs-kohr-pee-'ohn*
• **Sagittarius**	Sagitario	*sah-hee-'tah-ree-oh*
• **Capricorn**	Capricornio	*kah-pree-'kohr-nee·oh*
• **Aquarius**	Acuario	*ah-'kwah-ree·oh*
• **Pisces**	Piscis	*'pees-sees*

e. EXPRESSING THE DATE

What's today's date?	¿Cuál es la fecha de hoy?	*'kwahl ehs lah 'feh-chah deh oy*
• **October first**	el primero de octubre	*ehl pree-'meh-roh deh ohk-'too-breh*
• **February second**	el dos de febrero	*ehl dohs deh feh-'breh-roh*
• **June 3**	el tres de junio	*ehl trehs deh 'hoo-nee·oh*
When were you born?	¿Cuándo nació usted? (*pol*)	*'kwahn-doh nah-see·'oh oos-'tehd*
	¿Cuándo naciste? (*fam*)	*kwahn-doh nah-'sees-teh*
I was born in 1972.	Nací en 1972.	*nah-'see ehn meel noh-beh-see-'ehn-tohs seh-'tehn-tah ee dohs*

f. IMPORTANT DATES

the New Year	el Año Nuevo	*ehl 'ah-nyoh 'nweh-boh*
New Year's Day	el Día de Año Nuevo	*ehl 'dee-ah deh 'ah-nyoh 'nweh-boh*

New Year's Eve	la Nochevieja	*lah noh-cheh-bee·'eh-hah*
	Víspera del Año Nuevo	*'bees-peh-rah dehl 'ah-nyoh 'nweh-boh*
Easter	Pascua Florida	*'pahs-kwah floh-'ree-dah*
Christmas	Navidad (*f*)	*nah-bee-'dahd*
Christmas Eve	la Nochebuena	*lah 'noh-cheh 'bweh-nah*

6. TALKING ABOUT THE WEATHER

a. GENERAL WEATHER VOCABULARY

air	aire (*m*)	*'ah·ee-reh*
atmosphere	atmósfera	*aht-'mohs-feh-rah*
• atmospheric conditions	condiciones atmosféricas	*kohn-dee-see·'oh-nehs aht-mohs-'feh-ree-kahs*
clear	despejado	*deh-speh-'hah-doh*
climate	clima (*m*)	*'klee-mah*
• continental	continental (*adj*)	*kohn-tee-nehn-'tahl*
• dry	seco (*adj*)	*'seh-koh*
• humid	húmedo (*adj*)	*'oo-meh-doh*
• Mediterranean	mediterráneo (*adj*)	*meh-dee-teh-'rrah-neh-oh*
• tropical	tropical (*adj*)	*troh-pee-'kahl*
cloud	nube (*f*)	*'noo-beh*
• cloudy	nublado (*adj*)	*noo-'blah-doh*

> **to be daydreaming** = estar en las nubes

cold	frío (*adj, n*)	*'free·oh*
cool	fresco (*adj*)	*'frehs-koh*
dark	oscuro (*adj*)	*ohs-'koo-roh*
• It's getting dark.	Anochece.	*ah-noh-'cheh-seh*
drop (*e.g., of rain*)	gota	*'goh-tah*
dry	seco (*adj*)	*'seh-koh*
fog	neblina	*neh-'blee-nah*
• foggy	brumoso (*adj*)	*broo-'moh-soh*
freeze	helarse (*v**)	*eh-'lahr-seh*
	congelarse (*v*)	*kohn-heh-'lahr-seh*
• frozen	helado (*pp*)	*eh-'lah-doh*
hail	granizo	*grah-'nee-soh*
• hail	granizar (*v*)	*grah-nee-'sahr*
humid, damp	húmedo	*'oo-meh-doh*

• to be humid	ser (*v**) (estar (*v**)) húmedo	*sehr (ehs-'tahr) 'oo-meh-doh*
• humidity	humedad (*f*)	*oo-meh-'dahd*
hurricane	huracán (*m*)	*ooh-rah-'kahn*
ice	hielo	*ee-'eh-loh*
light	luz (*f*)	*loos*
lightning	relámpago	*reh-'lahm-pah-goh*
• lightning	relampaguear (*v*)	*reh-lahm-pah-geh-'ahr*
mild	templado (*adj*)	*tehm-'plah-doh*
• be mild	ser (*v**) (estar (*v**)) templado	*sehr (ehs-'tahr) tehm-'plah-doh*
moon	luna	*'loo-nah*
• full moon	luna llena	*'loo-nah 'yeh-nah*
• half moon	luna media	*'loo-nah 'meh-dee·ah*
• new moon	luna nueva	*'loo-nah 'nweh-bah*
mugginess	bochorno (*m*)	*boh-'chohr-noh*
• muggy	bochornoso (*adj*)	*boh-chohr-'noh-soh*
• be muggy	ser (*v**) (estar (*v**)) bochornoso	*sehr (ehs-'tahr) boh-chohr-'noh-soh*
rain	lluvia	*'yoo-bee·ah*
• rain	llover (*v*)	*yoh-'behr*
• It's rainy.	Está lluvioso.	*ehs-'tah yoo-bee-'oh-soh*
rainbow	arco iris (*m*)	*'ahr-koh 'ee-rees*
sea	mar (*m/f*)	*mahr*
shadow, shade	sombra	*'sohm-brah*
sky	cielo	*see-'eh-loh*
snow	nieve (*f*)	*nee-'eh-beh*
• snow	nevar (*v**)	*neh-'bahr*
storm	tormenta	*tohr-'mehn-tah*
	tempestad (*f*)	*tehm-pehs-'tahd*
sun	sol (*m*)	*sohl*
thunder	trueno	*'trweh-noh*
• thunder	tronar (*v**)	*troh-'nahr*

---

to quarrel with = tronar con

---

tornado	tornado	*tohr-'nah-doh*
weather	tiempo	*tee·'ehm-poh*
wind	viento	*bee·ehn-toh*

b. REACTING TO THE WEATHER

How's the weather?	¿Qué tiempo hace?	*keh tee·'ehm-poh 'ah-seh*

• It's a bit cold.	Hace un poco de frío.	'ah-seh oon 'poh-koh deh 'free-oh
• It's terrible.	Hace mal tiempo.	'ah-seh mahl tee·'ehm-poh
• It's beautiful.	Hace muy buen tiempo.	'ah-seh mwee bwehn tee·'ehm-poh
• It's cloudy.	Está nublado.	eh-'stah noo-'blah-doh
• It's cold.	Hace frío.	'ah-seh 'free·oh
• It's cool.	Hace fresco.	'ah-seh 'frehs-koh
• It's hot.	Hace calor.	'ah-seh kah-'lohr
• It's humid.	Es (Está) húmedo.	ehs (ehs-'tah) 'oo-meh-doh
• It's mild.	Es (Está) templado.	ehs (ehs-'tah) tehm-'plah-doh
• It's muggy.	Es (Está) bochornoso.	ehs (ehs-'tah) boh-chohr-'noh-soh
• It's pleasant.	Es (Está) agradable.	ehs (ehs-'tah) ah-grah-'dah-bleh
• It's raining.	Está lloviendo.	ehs-'tah yoh-bee·'ehn-doh
• It's snowing.	Está nevando.	ehs-'tah neh-'bahn-doh
• It's sunny.	Hace sol.	'ah-seh sohl
• It's thundering.	Truena.	'trweh-nah
• It's very cold.	Hace mucho frío.	'ah-seh 'moo-choh 'free-oh
• It's very hot.	Hace mucho calor.	'ah-seh 'moo-choh kah-'lohr
• It's windy.	Hace viento.	'ah-seh bee·'ehn-toh
• It's lightning.	Relampaguea.	reh-lahm-pah-'geh-ah
be cold	tener (v*) frío	teh-'nehr 'free·oh
• I can't stand the cold.	No puedo soportar el frío.	noh 'pweh-doh soh-pohr-'tahr ehl 'free·oh
• I love the cold.	Me encanta el frío.	meh ehn-'tahn-tah ehl 'free·oh
be hot	tener (v*) calor	teh-'nehr kah-'lohr
• I can't stand the heat.	No puedo soportar el calor.	noh 'pweh-doh soh-pohr-'tahr ehl kah-'lohr
• I love the heat.	Me encanta el calor.	meh ehn-'kahn-tah ehl kah-'lohr
catch a chill	enfriarse (v*)	ehn-free·'ahr-seh
perspire	sudar (v)	soo-'dahr
warm up	calentarse (v*)	kah-lehn-'tahr-seh

c. WEATHER-MEASURING INSTRUMENTS AND ACTIVITIES

barometer	barómetro	bah-'roh-meh-troh
• barometric pressure	presión barométrica (f)	preh-see·'ohn bah-roh-'meh-tree-kah

Celsius	Celsio	*'sehl-see-oh*
Fahrenheit	Fahrenheit	*fah-rehn-'heh·eet'*
mercury	mercurio	*mehr-'koo-ree-oh*
temperature	temperatura	*tehm-peh-rah-'too-rah*
• high (*temp*)	alta	*'ahl-tah*
• low	baja	*'bah-hah*
• maximum	máxima	*'mahk-see-mah*
• minimum	mínima	*'mee-nee-mah*
thermometer	termómetro	*tehr-'moh-meh-troh*
• boiling point	punto de ebullición	*'poon-toh deh eh-boo-yee-see-'ohn*
• melting point	punto de fusión	*'poon-toh deh foo-see-'ohn*
thermostat	termostato	*tehr-mohs-'tah-toh*
weather forecast	pronóstico del tiempo	*proh-'nohs-tee-koh dehl tee-'ehm-poh*
weather report	boletín meteorológico	*boh-leh-'teen meh-teh-oh-roh-'loh-hee-koh*
zero	cero	*'seh-roh*
• below zero	bajo cero	*'bah-hoh 'seh-roh*

7. COLORS

a. BASIC COLORS

What color is it?	¿De qué color es?	*deh keh koh-'lohr ehs*
• black	negro	*'neh-groh*
• blue	azul	*ah-'sool*
• dark blue	azul oscuro	*ah-'sool ohs-'koo-roh*
• navy blue	azul marino	*ah-'sool mah-'ree-noh*
• light blue	azul claro	*ah-'sool 'klah-roh*
• brown	marrón	*mah-'rrohn*
• gold	dorado	*doh-'rah-doh*
• gray	gris	*grees*
• green	verde	*'behr-deh*
• orange	anaranjado	*ah-nah-rahn-'hah-doh*
• pink	rosado	*roh-'sah-doh*
• purple	morado	*moh-'rah-doh*
• red	rojo	*'roh-hoh*
• silver	plateado	*plah-teh-'ah-doh*
• white	blanco	*'blahn-koh*
• yellow	amarillo	*ah-mah-'ree-yoh*

---

to blush	= ponerse (*v**) rojo
to get as red as a beet	= ponerse (*v**) de mil colores
to be very pessimistic	= verlo todo negro

b. DESCRIBING COLORS

bright	vivo (*adj*)	*'bee-boh*
dark	oscuro (*adj*)	*ohs-'koo-roh*
dull	apagado (*adj*)	*ah-pah-'gah-doh*
light	claro (*adj*)	*'klah-roh*
lively	vivo (*adj*)	*'bee-boh*
opaque	opaco (*adj*)	*oh-'pah-koh*
pure	puro (*adj*)	*'poo-roh*
transparent	transparente (*adj*)	*trahns-pah-'rehn-teh*
vibrant	vibrante (*adj*)	*bee-'brahn-teh*

c. ADDITIONAL VOCABULARY: COLORS

color	color (*m*)	*koh-'lohr*
• color	colorear (*v*)	*koh-loh-reh-'ahr*
• colored	coloreado (*pp*)	*koh-loh-reh-'ah-doh*
• coloring	coloración (*f*)	*koh-loh-rah-see·'ohn*
• food coloring	colorante alimentario (*m*)	*koh-loh-'rahn-teh ah-lee-mehn-'tah-ree·oh*
crayon	creyón (*m*)	*kreh-'yohn*
• coloring book	libro para colorear	*'lee-broh 'pah-rah koh-loh-reh-'ahr*
painter	pintor(a)	*peen-'tohr (rah)*
• paint	pintar (*v*)	*peen-'tahr*
• paint	pintura (*f*)	*peen-'too-rah*
• canvas	lienzo	*lee-'ehn-soh*
pen	pluma	*'ploo-mah*
• felt pen	rotulador (*m*)	*roh-too-lah-'dohr*
tint (*hair dye*)	tinte (*m*)	*'teen-teh*
• tint	teñir (*v**)	*teh-'nyeer*

8. BASIC GRAMMAR

a. GRAMMATICAL TERMS

adjective	adjetivo	*ahd-heh-'tee-boh*
• demonstrative	demostrativo	*deh-mohs-trah-'tee-boh*
• descriptive	descriptivo	*dehs-kreep-'tee-boh*
• indefinite	indefinido	*een-deh-feh-'nee-doh*
• interrogative	interrogativo	*een-teh-rroh-gah-'tee-boh*
• possessive	posesivo	*poh-seh-'see-boh*
adverb	adverbio	*ahd-'behr-bee·oh*
alphabet	alfabeto	*ahl-fah-'beh-toh*
• accent	acento	*ah-'sehn-toh*
• consonant	consonante	*kohn-soh-'nahn-teh*

• letter	letra	*'leh-trah*
• phonetics	fonética	*foh-'neh-tee-kah*
• pronunciation	pronunciación (*f*)	*proh-noon-see-ah-see-'ohn*
• vowel	vocal (*f*)	*boh-'kahl*
article	artículo	*ahr-'tee-koo-loh*
• definite	definido	*deh-fee-'nee-doh*
• indefinite	indefinido (*adj*)	*een-deh-fee-'nee-doh*
clause	cláusula	*'clow-soo-lah*
• main	principal (*adj*)	*preen-see-'pahl*
• relative	relativo (*adj*)	*reh-lah-'tee-boh*
• subordinate	subordinado (*adj*)	*soo-bohr-dee-'nah-doh*
comparison	comparación (*f*)	*kohm-pah-rah-see-'ohn*
conjugation	conjugación (*f*)	*kohn-hoo-gah-see-'ohn*
conjunction	conjunción (*f*)	*kohn-hoon-see-'ohn*
discourse	discurso	*dees-'koor-soh*
• direct	directo (*adj*)	*dee-'rehk-toh*
• indirect	indirecto (*adj*)	*een-dee-'rehk-toh*
gender	género	*'heh-neh-roh*
• feminine	femenino	*feh-meh-'nee-noh*
• masculine	masculino	*mahs-koo-'lee-noh*
grammar	gramática	*grah-'mah-tee-kah*
interrogative	interrogativo (*adj*)	*een-teh-rroh-gah-'tee-boh*
mood	modo	*'moh-doh*
• imperative	imperativo	*eem-peh-rah-'tee-boh*
• indicative	indicativo	*een-dee-kah-'tee-boh*
• subjunctive	subjuntivo	*soob-hoon-'tee-boh*
noun	sustantivo	*soos-tahn-'tee-boh*
number	número	*'noo-meh-roh*
• plural	plural (*adj*)	*ploo-'rahl*
• singular	singular (*adj*)	*seen-goo-'lahr*
object	complemento	*kohm-pleh-'mehn-toh*
• direct	directo (*adj*)	*dee-'rehk-toh*
• indirect	indirecto (*adj*)	*een-dee-'rehk-toh*
participle	participio	*pahr-tee-'see-pee·oh*
• past	pasado (*adj*)	*pah-'sah-doh*
• present	presente (*adj*)	*preh-'sehn-teh*
person	persona	*pehr-'soh-nah*
• first	primera (*adj*)	*pree-'meh-rah*
• second	segunda (*adj*)	*seh-'goon-dah*
• third	tercera (*adj*)	*tehr-'seh-rah*
predicate	predicado	*preh-dee-'kah-doh*
pronoun	pronombre (*m*)	*proh-'nohm-breh*
• demonstrative	demostrativo (*adj*)	*deh-mohs-trah-'tee-boh*
• interrogative	interrogativo (*adj*)	*een-teh-rroh-gah-'tee-boh*

• **object**	complemento	*kohm-pleh-'mehn-toh*
• **personal**	personal (*adj*)	*pehr-soh-'nahl*
• **possessive**	posesivo (*adj*)	*poh-seh-'see-boh*
• **reflexive**	reflexivo (*adj*)	*reh-fleh-'ksee-boh*
• **relative**	relativo (*adj*)	*reh-lah-'tee-boh*
• **subject**	sujeto (*adj*)	*soo-'heh-toh*
sentence	frase (*f*)	*'frah-seh*
	oración (*f*)	*oh-rah-see-'ohn*
• **active voice**	voz activa (*f*)	*bohs ahk-'tee-bah*
• **declarative**	enunciativo (*adj*)	*eh-noon-see-ah-'tee-boh*
• **interrogative**	interrogativo (*adj*)	*een-teh-rroh-gah-'tee-boh*
• **passive voice**	voz pasiva (*f*)	*bohs pah-'see-bah*
spelling	deletreo	*deh-leh-'treh·oh*
subject	sujeto	*soo-'heh-toh*
tense	tiempo	*tee·'ehm-poh*
• **conditional**	condicional	*kohn-dee-see-oh-'nahl*
• **future**	futuro	*foo-'too-roh*
• **imperfect**	imperfecto	*eem-pehr-'fehk-toh*
• **pluperfect**	pluscuamperfecto	*ploos-kwahm-pehr-'fehk-toh*
• **present**	presente	*preh-'sehn-teh*
• **present perfect**	presente perfecto	*preh-'sehn-teh pehr-'fehk-toh*
• **preterite**	pretérito	*preh-'teh-ree-toh*
verb	verbo	*'behr-boh*
• **conjugation**	conjugación (*f*)	*kohn-hoo-gah-see-'ohn*
• **ending**	terminación (*f*)	*tehr-mee-nah-see-'ohn*
• **gerund**	gerundio	*heh-'roon-dee-oh*
• **infinitive**	infinitivo	*een-fee-nee-'tee-boh*
• **intransitive**	intransitivo	*een-trahn-see-'tee-boh*
• **irregular**	irregular	*ee-rreh-goo-'lahr*
• **reflexive**	reflexivo	*reh-fleh-'ksee-boh*
• **regular**	regular	*reh-goo-'lahr*
• **transitive**	transitivo	*trahn-see-'tee-boh*

b. DEFINITE ARTICLES

the	el (*m, s*)	*ehl*
	la (*f, s*)	*lah*
	los (*m, pl*)	*lohs*
	las (*f, pl*)	*lahs*

	SINGULAR	PLURAL
Masculine	el	los
Feminine	la	las

c. INDEFINITE ARTICLES

a, an	un (*m, s*)	*oon*
	una (*f, s*)	*'oo-nah*

	SINGULAR	PLURAL
Masculine	un	unos
Feminine	una	unas

d. DEMONSTRATIVE ADJECTIVES

this	este (*m, s*)	*'ehs-teh*
	esta (*f, s*)	*'ehs-tah*
that (*nearby*)	ese (*m, s*)	*'eh-seh*
	esa (*f, s*)	*'eh-sah*
that (*farther away*)	aquel (*m, s*)	*ah-'kehl*
	aquella (*f, s*)	*ah-'keh-yah*
these	estos (*m, pl*)	*'ehs-tohs*
	estas (*f, pl*)	*'ehs-tahs*
those (*nearby*)	esos (*m, pl*)	*'eh-sohs*
	esas (*f, pl*)	*'eh-sahs*
those (*farther away*)	aquellos (*m, pl*)	*ah-'keh-yohs*
	aquellas (*f, pl*)	*ah-'keh-yahs*

e. POSSESSIVE ADJECTIVES

my	mi (*m/f, s*)	*mee*
	mis (*m/f, pl*)	*mees*
your	tu (*m/f, s, fam*)	*too*
	tus (*m/f, pl*)	*toos*
your	su (*m/f, s pol*)	*soo*
	sus (*m/f, pl*)	*soos*
his, her, their	su (*m/f, s*)	*soo*
	sus (*m/f, pl*)	*soos*

our	nuestro (*m, s*)	'nwehs-troh
	nuestra (*f, s*)	'nwehs-trah
	nuestros (*m, pl*)	'nwehs-trohs
	nuestras (*f, pl*)	'nwehs-trahs

Adjective	Pronoun	
mi	el mío/la mía	
tu	el tuyo/la tuya	
su	el suyo/la suya	singular
nuestro/nuestra	el nuestro/la nuestra	
vuestro/vuestra	el vuestro/la vuestra	
mis	los míos/las mías	
tus	los tuyos/las tuyas	
sus	los suyos/las suyas	
nuestros/nuestras	los nuestros/las nuestras	plural
vuestros/vuestras	los vuestros/las vuestras	

Este es **mi** dibujo. ¿Cuál es el **tuyo**? = This is **my** drawing.
Which one is **yours**?

f. POSSESSIVE PRONOUNS

mine	mío (*m, s*), mía (*f, s*)	'mee-oh, 'mee-ah
	míos (*m, pl*), mías (*f, pl*)	'mee-ohs, 'mee-ahs
yours	tuyo (*m, s, fam*), tuya (*f, s, fam*)	'too-yoh, 'too-yah
	tuyos (*m, pl, fam*), tuyas (*f, pl, fam*)	'too-yohs, 'too-yahs
yours	suyo (*m, s, pol*), suya (*f, s, pol*)	'soo-yoh, 'soo-yah
	suyos (*m, s, pol*), suyas (*f, s, pol*)	'soo-yohs, 'soo-yahs
yours	vuestro (*m, s, fam*), vuestra (*f, s, fam*)	'vwehs-troh, 'vwehs-trah
	vuestros (*m, pl, fam*), vuestras (*f, pl, fam*)	'vwehs-trohs, 'vwehs-trahs
ours	nuestro (*m, s*), nuestra (*f, s*)	noo·'ehs-troh, noo·'ehs-trah
	nuestros (*m, pl*), nuestras (*f, pl*)	noo·'ehs-trohs, noo·'ehs-trahs

g. PREPOSITIONS

among	entre	*'ehn-treh*
at	en, a	*ehn, ah*
besides	además de	*ah-deh-'mahs deh*
between	entre	*'ehn-treh*
for	por, para	*pohr, 'pah-rah*
from	de	*deh*
in	en	*ehn*
of	de	*deh*
on	en, sobre	*ehn, 'soh-breh*
	encima de	*ehn-'see-mah deh*
to	a	*ah*
with	con	*kohn*

h. SUBJECT PRONOUNS

I	yo	*yoh*
you	tú (*s, fam*)	*too*
you	usted (*s, pol*)	*oos-'tehd*
he	él	*ehl*
she	ella	*'eh-yah*
we	nosotros (*m*)	*noh-'soh-trohs*
	nosotras (*f*)	*noh-'soh-trahs*
you	vosotros (*m, pl, fam*)	*boh-'soh-trohs*
	vosotras (*f, pl, fam*)	*boh-'soh-trahs*
you	ustedes (*pl, pol*)	*oos-'teh-dehs*
they	ellos (*m*)	*'eh-yohs*
	ellas (*f*)	*'eh-yahs*

i. DIRECT OBJECT PRONOUNS

me	me	*meh*
you	te (*s, fam*)	*teh*
you	lo (*m, pol*)	*loh*
	la (*f, pol*)	*lah*
him	lo, le	*loh, leh*
her	la	*lah*
it	lo (*m, s*)	*loh*
	la (*f, s*)	*lah*
us	nos	*nohs*
you	os (*pl, fam*)	*ohs*
you	los (*m, pol*)	*lohs*
	las (*f, pol*)	*lahs*
them	los (*m, pl*)	*lohs*
	las (*f, pl*)	*lahs*

j. INDIRECT OBJECT PRONOUNS

to me	me	*meh*
to you	te (*s, fam*)	*teh*
to you	le (*s, pol*)	*leh*
to him	le	*leh*
to her	le	*leh*
to us	nos	*nohs*
to you	os (*pl, fam*)	*ohs*
to you	les (*pl, pol*)	*lehs*
to them	les	*lehs*

k. REFLEXIVE PRONOUNS

myself	me	*meh*
yourself	te (*s, fam*)	*teh*
yourself	se (*s, pol*)	*seh*
himself	se	*seh*
herself	se	*seh*
ourselves	nos	*nohs*
yourselves	os (*pl, fam*)	*ohs*
yourselves	se (*pl, pol*)	*seh*
themselves	se	*seh*

Adjective		Pronoun
cuyo (s), cuya (s)	= WHOSE =	de quién (es)

*Ése es el cantante **cuya** música es muy popular hoy día.* = This is the singer whose music is very popular nowadays.

*Van Gogh es el artista **cuyas** pinturas tienen colores vibrantes.* = Van Gogh is the artist whose paintings have vibrant colors.

*Esta pluma azul, ¿**de quién** es?* = This blue pen, whose is it?
*¿**De quiénes** son todos esos libros?* = Whose are all those books?

---

l. RELATIVE ADJECTIVE

whose	cuyo (*m, s*), cuya (*f, s*)	*'koo-yoh, 'koo-yah*
	cuyos (*m, pl*), cuyas (*f, pl*)	*'koo-yohs, 'koo-yahs*

m. RELATIVE PRONOUNS

that, which, who	que	*keh*
he, she, who	quien	*kee·'ehn*
whose	de quién	*deh kee·'ehn*
	de quiénes	*deh kee·'ehn-ehs*

n. OTHER PRONOUNS

everyone	todos	*'toh-dohs*
	todo el mundo	*'toh-doh ehl 'moon-doh*
everything	todo	*'toh-doh*
many	muchos (*m*)	*'moo-chohs*
	muchas (*f*)	*'moo-chahs*
no one	nadie	*'nah-dee·eh*
others	otros	*'oh-trohs*
some (*people*)	algunos (*m*)	*ahl-'goo-nohs*
	algunas (*f*)	*ahl-'goo-nahs*
someone	alguien	*'ahl-gee·ehn*
something	algo	*'ahl-goh*

> **some is better than none** = algo es algo

o. CONJUNCTIONS

after	después (de) que	*dehs-poo·'ehs (deh) keh*
although	aunque	*ah·'oon-keh*
and	y (e)	*ee, (eh)*
as	como	*'koh-moh*
as if	como si	*'koh-moh see*
because	porque	*'pohr-keh*
before	antes (de) que	*'ahn-tehs (deh) keh*
but	pero (sino que)	*'peh-roh ('see-noh keh)*
even though	aunque	*'ah·oon-keh*
if, whether	si	*see*
in case	en caso (de) que	*ehn 'ka-soh (deh) keh*
in order that, so that	para que	*'pah-rah keh*
	de modo que	*deh 'moh-doh keh*
provided that	con tal (de) que	*kohn tahl (deh) keh*
since	desde que	*'dehs-deh keh*
	puesto que	*poo·'ehs-toh keh*
unless	a menos que	*ah 'meh-nohs keh*
until	hasta que	*'ahs-tah keh*
while	mientras	*mee·'ehn-trahs*
without	sin	*seen*

9. REQUESTING INFORMATION

answer	respuesta	*rehs-'pwehs-tah*
• **answer**	responder (*v*)	*rehs-pohn-'dehr*
	contestar (*v*)	*kohn-tehs-'tahr*
ask	preguntar (*v*)	*preh-goon-'tahr*
• **ask a question**	hacer (*v**) una pregunta	*ah-'sehr 'oo-nah preh-'goon-tah*
Can you tell me . . . ?	¿Puede usted decirme . . . ?	*poo-'eh-deh oos-'tehd deh-'seer-meh*
How?	¿Cómo?	*'koh-moh*
How do you say . . . in Spanish?	¿Cómo se dice . . . en español?	*'koh-moh seh 'dee-seh ehn ehs-pah-'nyohl*
How come . . . ?	¿Cómo es que . . . ?	*'koh-moh ehs keh*
How much?	¿Cuánto?	*'kwahn-toh*
I don't understand.	No comprendo.	*noh kohm-'prehn-doh*
	No entiendo.	*noh ehn-tee-'ehn-doh*
What?	¿Cómo?	*'koh-moh*
What does . . . mean?	¿Qué quiere decir . . . ?	*keh kee-'eh-reh deh-'seer*
When?	¿Cuándo?	*'kwahn-doh*
Where?	¿Dónde?	*'dohn-deh*
Which (one)?	¿Cuál?	*kwahl*
Who?	¿Quién? (*s*)	*kee-'ehn*
	¿Quiénes? (*pl*)	*kee-'ehn-ehs*
Why?	¿Por qué?	*pohr keh*

PEOPLE

10. FAMILY AND FRIENDS

a. FAMILY MEMBERS

aunt	tía	*'tee-ah*
brother	hermano	*ehr-'mah-noh*
• **brother-in-law**	cuñado	*koo-'nyah-doh*
cousin	primo(a)	*'pree-moh (-mah)*
dad	papá	*pah-'pah*
daughter	hija	*'ee-hah*
• **daughter-in-law**	nuera	*'nweh-rah*
	hija política	*'ee-hah poh-'lee-tee-kah*
family	familia	*fah-'mee-lee-ah*
father	padre	*'pah-dreh*
• **father-in-law**	suegro	*'sweh-groh*
grandchild	nieto(a)	*nee·'eh-toh (-tah)*
grandfather	abuelo	*ah-'bweh-loh*
grandmother	abuela	*ah-'bweh-lah*
great-aunt	tía abuela	*'tee-ah ah-'bweh-lah*
great grandchild	bisnieto(a)	*bees-nee·'eh-toh (-tah)*
great grandfather	bisabuelo	*bees-ah-'bweh-loh*
great grandmother	bisabuela	*bees-ah-'bweh-lah*
great-uncle	tío abuelo	*'tee-oh ah-'bweh-loh*
husband	marido	*mah-'ree-doh*
	esposo	*ehs-'poh-soh*
mom	mamá	*mah-'mah*
mother	madre	*'mah-dreh*
• **mother-in-law**	suegra	*'sweh-grah*
nephew	sobrino	*soh-'bree-noh*
niece	sobrina	*soh-'bree-nah*
parents	padres (*m, pl*)	*'pah-drehs*
quadruplets	cuatrillizos	*kwah-tree-'yee-sohs*
relatives	parientes (*m, pl*)	*pah-ree·'ehn-tehs*
sister	hermana	*ehr-'mah-nah*
• **sister-in-law**	cuñada	*koo-'nyah-dah*
	hermana política	*ehr-'mah-nah poh-'lee-tee-kah*
son	hijo	*'ee-hoh*
• **son-in-law**	yerno	*'yehr-noh*
	hijo político	*'ee-hoh poh-'lee-tee-koh*
stepbrother	hermanastro	*ehr-mah-'nahs-troh*
stepdaughter	hijastra	*ee-'hahs-trah*
stepfather	padrastro	*pah-'drahs-troh*
stepmother	madrastra	*mah-'drahs-trah*

stepsister	hermanastra	*ehr-mah-'nahs-trah*
stepson	hijastro	*ee-'hahs-troh*
triplets	trillizos	*tree-'yee-sohs*
twin	gemelo(a)	*heh-'meh-loh (-lah)*
	mellizo(a)	*meh-'yee-soh (-sah)*
• twin brother	hermano gemelo	*ehr-'mah-noh heh-'meh-loh*
• twin sister	hermana gemela	*ehr-'mah-nah heh-'meh-lah*
uncle	tío	*'tee-oh*
wife	esposa	*ehs-'poh-sah*
	mujer (*f*)	*moo-'hehr*

b. FRIENDS

acquaintance	conocido(a)	*koh-noh-'see-doh (-dah)*
boyfriend	novio	*'noh-bee·oh*
	amigo	*ah-'mee-goh*
colleague	colega (*m/f*)	*koh-'leh-gah*
enemy	enemigo(a)	*eh-neh-'mee-goh (-gah)*
fiancé	novio	*'noh-bee·oh*
fiancée	novia	*'noh-bee·ah*
friend	amigo(a)	*ah-'mee-goh (-gah)*
• become friends	hacerse (*v**) amigos	*ah-'sehr-seh ah-'mee-gohs*
• between friends	entre amigos	*'ehn-treh ah-'mee-gohs*
• break off a friendship	romper (*v*) una amistad	*rohm-'pehr 'oo-nah ah-mees-'tahd*
• close friends	amigos íntimos	*ah-'mee-gohs 'een-tee-mohs*
• family friend	amigo de familia	*ah-'mee-goh deh fah-'mee-lee·ah*
• friendship	amistad (*f*)	*ah-mees-'tahd*
girlfriend	novia	*'noh-bee·ah*
	amiga	*ah-'mee-gah*
lover	amante (*m/f*)	*ah-'mahn-teh*
• love affair	amorío	*ah-moh-'ree-oh*

11. DESCRIBING PEOPLE

a. GENDER AND APPEARANCE

attractive	atractivo (*adj*)	*ah-trahk-'tee-boh*
beautiful	hermoso (*adj*)	*ehr-'moh-soh*
• beauty	belleza	*beh-'yeh-sah*
big	grande (*adj*)	*'grahn-deh*
• bigness	grandeza	*grahn-'deh-sah*
• make big	engrandecer (*v**)	*ehn-grahn-deh-'sehr*

blond	rubio (*adj*)	'*roo-bee·oh*
body	cuerpo	'*kwehr-poh*
• bodily physique	físico	'*fee-see-koh*
boy	chico	'*chee-koh*
	muchacho	*moo-'chah-choh*
brunette	moreno (*adj*)	*moh-'reh-noh*
• dark-haired	de pelo oscuro	*deh 'peh-loh ohs-* '*koo-roh*
clean	limpio (*adj*)	'*leem-pee·oh*
curly	rizado (*adj*)	*ree-'sah-doh*
• curly-haired	de pelo rizado	*deh 'peh-loh ree-* '*sah-doh*
dirty	sucio (*adj*)	'*soo-see·oh*
elegant	elegante (*adj*)	*eh-leh-'gahn-teh*
• elegance	elegancia	*eh-leh-'gahn-see·ah*
• elegantly	elegantemente (*adv*)	*eh-leh-gahn-teh-* '*mehn-teh*
• inelegant	poco elegante (*adj*)	'*poh-koh eh-leh-* '*gahn-teh*
fat	gordo (*adj*)	'*gohr-doh*
• become fat	engordar (*v*)	*ehn-gohr-'dahr*
• obesity	obesidad (*f*)	*oh-beh-see-'dahd*
female (*sex*)	(sexo) femenino (*adj*)	'*seh-ksoh feh-meh-* '*nee-noh*
• female (*animals*)	hembra (*adj*)	'*ehm-brah*
• a female voice	una voz de mujer	'*oo-nah bohs deh* *moo-'hehr*
• feminine	femenino (*adj*)	*feh-meh-'nee-noh*
gentleman	caballero	*kah-bah-'yeh-roh*
	señor	*seh-'nyohr*
girl	chica	'*chee-kah*
	muchacha	*moo-'chah-chah*
handicapped	minusválido	*meen-oos-'vah-* *lee-doh*
	incapacitado (*adj*)	*een-kah-pah-see-* '*tah-doh*
health	salud (*f*)	*sah-'lood*
• be in good health	estar (*v**) bien de salud	*ehs-'tahr bee·'ehn deh* *sah-'lood*
• healthy	sano, saludable (*adj*)	'*sah-noh, sah-loo-* '*dah-bleh*
height	estatura	*ehs-tah-'too-rah*
• How tall are you?	¿Cuánto mide usted?	'*kwahn-toh 'mee-deh* *oos-'tehd*
• I am . . . tall.	Tengo . . . de alto.	'*tehn-goh deh* '*ahl-toh*
• of medium height	de estatura mediana	*deh ehs-tah-'too-rah* *meh-dee·'ah-nah*

• short	bajo (*adj*)	*'bah-hoh*
• tall	alto (*adj*)	*'ahl-toh*
lady	señora	*seh-'nyoh-rah*
• young lady	señorita	*seh-nyoh-'ree-tah*
large	grande (*adj*)	*'grahn-deh*
male (*sex*)	(sexo) masculino	*'seh-ksoh mahs-koo-'lee-noh*
• male (*animals*)	macho (*n, adj*)	*'mah-choh*
• male (*person*)	varón (*n, adj*)	*bah-'rohn*
• virile	viril (*adj*)	*bee-'reel*
man	hombre (*m*)	*'ohm-breh*
• young man	joven	*'hoh-behn*
physical appearance	aspecto físico	*ah-'spehk-toh 'fee-see-koh*
red-haired	pelirrojo (*adj*)	*peh-lee-'roh-hoh*
sexy	atractivo (*adj*)	*ah-trahk-'tee-boh*
sick	enfermo (*adj*)	*ehn-'fehr-moh*
• sickness	enfermedad (*f*)	*ehn-fehr-meh-'dahd*
• become sick	enfermarse (*v*)	*ehn-fehr-'mahr-seh*
small, little	pequeño (*adj*)	*peh-'keh-nyoh*
strength	fuerza	*'fwehr-sah*
• strong	fuerte (*adj*)	*'fwehr-teh*
ugly	feo (*adj*)	*'feh-oh*
• ugliness	fealdad (*f*)	*feh-ahl-'adhd*
weak	débil (*adj*)	*'deh-beel*
• weakness	debilidad (*f*)	*deh-bee-lee-'dahd*
• become weak	debilitarse (*v*)	*deh-bee-lee-'tahr-seh*
weight	peso	*'peh-soh*
• heavy	pesado (*adj*)	*peh-'sah-doh*
• How much do you weigh?	¿Cuánto pesa usted?	*'kwahn-toh 'peh-sah oos-'tehd*
• I weigh . . .	Peso . . .	*'peh-soh*
• light	ligero (*adj*)	*lee-'heh-roh*
• skinny, thin	delgado (*adj*)	*dehl-'gah-doh*
	flaco (*adj*)	*'flah-koh*
• weigh oneself	pesarse (*v*)	*peh-'sahr-seh*
• pound	libra	*'lee-brah*
• kilo	kilo	*'kee-loh*
• become thin	adelgazar (*v*)	*ah-dehl-gah-'sahr*
• lose weight	perder (*v**) peso	*pehr-'dehr 'peh-soh*
• slim, slender	esbelto (*adj*)	*ehs-'behl-toh*
woman	mujer (*f*)	*moo-'hehr*

b. CONCEPTS OF AGE

adolescence	juventud (*f*)	*hoo-behn-'tood*
• adolescent, teenager	joven (*m/f*)	*'hoh-behn*

adult	adulto	*ah-'dool-toh*
age	edad (*f*)	*eh-'dahd*
baby	bebé (*m/f*)	*beh-'beh*
boy	chico	*'chee-koh*
	muchacho	*moo-'chah-choh*
child	niño(a)	*'nee-nyoh (-nyah)*
• **children**	niños(as)	*'nee-nyohs (-nyahs)*
elderly person	viejo(a)	*bee·'eh-hoh (-hah)*
• **elderly people**	personas de mayor edad	*pehr-'soh-nahs deh mah-'yohr eh-'dahd*
• **have white hair**	tener (*v**) canas	*teh-'nehr 'kah-nahs*
girl	chica	*'chee-kah*
	muchacha	*moo-'chah-chah*
old	viejo (*adj*)	*bee·'eh-hoh*
• **become old**	envejecerse (*v**)	*ehn-beh-heh-'sehr-seh*
• **older**	mayor	*mah-'yohr*
• **older brother**	hermano mayor	*ehr-'mah-noh mah-'yohr*
• **older sister**	hermana mayor	*ehr-'mah-nah mah-'yohr*
• **How old are you?**	¿Cuántos años tiene usted?	*'kwahn-tohs 'ah-nyohs tee·'eh-neh oos-'tehd*
• **I am . . . old.**	Tengo . . . años.	*'tehn-goh . . . 'ah-nyohs*
• **two-year old**	de dos años	*deh dohs 'ah-nyohs*
• **twenty-year old**	de veinte años	*deh 'beh·een·teh 'ah-nyohs*
young	joven (*m/f*)	*'hoh-behn*
• **younger**	menor	*meh-'nohr*
• **younger brother**	hermano menor	*ehr-'mah-noh meh-'nohr*
• **younger sister**	hermana menor	*ehr-'mah-nah meh-'nohr*
• **youthful**	juvenil (*adj*)	*hoo-beh-'neel*

c. MARRIAGE AND THE HUMAN LIFE CYCLE

anniversary	aniversario	*ah-nee-behr-'sah-ree·oh*
• **golden anniversary**	aniversario de oro	*ah-nee-behr-'sah-ree·oh deh 'oh-roh*
• **silver anniversary**	aniversario de plata	*ah-nee-behr-'sah-ree·oh deh 'plah-tah*
bachelor	soltero(a)	*sohl-'teh-roh (-rah)*
birth	nacimiento	*nah-see-mee·'ehn-toh*
• **be born**	nacer (*v**)	*nah-'sehr*
• **I was born on the (*day*) of (*month*).**	Nací el . . . de . . .	*nah-'see ehl . . . deh . . .*
birthday	cumpleaños (*m*)	*koom-pleh-'ah-nyohs*
• **celebrate one's birthday**	celebrar (*v*) el cumpleaños	*seh-leh-'brahr ehl koom-pleh-'ah-nyohs*

• **Happy Birthday!**	¡Feliz cumpleaños!	*feh-'lees koom-pleh-* *'ah-nyohs*
bride	novia	*'noh-bee·ah*
death	muerte (*f*)	*'mwehr-teh*
• **die**	morir (*v**)	*moh-'reer*
divorce	divorciarse (*v*)	*dee-bohr-see·'ahr-seh*
• **divorce**	divorcio (*m*)	*dee-'bohr-see·oh*
• **divorced (be)**	estar (*v**) divorciado (*adj*)	*ehs-'tahr* *dee-bohr-see·'ah-doh*
engaged	prometido	*proh-meh-'tee-doh*
	comprometido	*kohm-proh-meh-* *'tee-doh*
• **become engaged**	prometerse (*v*)	*proh-meh-'tehr-seh*
	comprometerse (*v*)	*kohm-proh-meh-* *'tehr-seh*
• **engagement**	noviazgo	*noh-bee·'ahs-goh*
• **engagement ring**	anillo de compromiso	*ah-'nee-yoh deh kohm-* *proh-'mee-soh*
fiancé	novio	*'noh-bee·oh*
fiancée	novia	*'noh-bee·ah*
get used to	acostumbrarse (*v*)	*ah-kohs-toom-* *'brahr-seh*
gift	regalo	*reh-'gah-loh*
• **give a gift**	regalar (*v*)	*reh-gah-'lahr*
go to school	asistir (*v*) a la escuela	*ah-sees-'teer ah lah ehs-* *'kweh-lah*
groom	novio	*'noh-bee·oh*
heredity	herencia	*eh-'rehn-see·ah*
• **inherit**	heredar (*v*)	*eh-reh-'dahr*
honeymoon	luna de miel	*'loo-nah deh mee·'ehl*
	viaje de novios	*bee·'ah-heh deh 'noh-* *bee·ohs*
husband	marido	*mah-'ree-doh*
kiss	besar (*v*)	*beh-'sahr*
• **kiss**	beso	*'beh-soh*
life	vida	*'bee-dah*
• **live**	vivir (*v*)	*bee-'beer*
love	querer (*v**)	*keh-'rehr*
	amar (*v*)	*ah-'mahr*
• **love**	amor (*m*)	*ah-'mohr*
• **fall in love**	enamorarse (*v*)	*eh-nah-moh-'rahr-seh*
• **in love**	enamorado (*adj*)	*eh-nah-moh-'rah-doh*
marriage, matrimony	matrimonio	*mah-tree-'moh-nee·oh*
• **get married**	casarse (*v*)	*kah-'sahr-seh*
• **marriage ceremony**	boda	*'boh-dah*
• **married**	casado (*adj*)	*kah-'sah-doh*
• **married couple**	matrimonio	*mah-tree-'moh-nee·oh*
• **unmarried**	soltero(a)	*sohl-'teh-roh (-rah)*

marital status	estado civil	*ehs-'tah-doh see-'beel*
pregnancy	embarazo	*ehm-bah-'rah-soh*
• **be pregnant**	estar (*v**) embarazada	*ehs-'tahr ehm-bah-rah-* *'sah-dah*
• **give birth**	dar (*v**) a luz	*dahr ah loos*
• **have a baby**	tener (*v**) un niño	*teh-'nehr oon 'nee-nyoh*
raise (*someone*)	criar (*v*)	*kree-'ahr*
reception	recepción (*f*)	*reh-sehp-see-'ohn*
separation	separación (*f*) matrimonial	*seh-pah-rah-see-'ohn* *mah-tree-moh-nee-'ahl*
• **separate**	separarse (*v*)	*seh-pah-'rahr-seh*
• **separated**	separado (*adj*)	*seh-pah-'rah-doh*
spouse	esposo	*ehs-'poh-soh*
	esposa	*ehs-'poh-sah*
wedding	boda	*'boh-dah*
• **wedding dress**	traje de novia (*m*)	*'trah-heh deh 'noh-* *bee-ah*
• **wedding** **invitation**	invitación (*f*) de boda	*een-bee-tah-see-'ohn* *deh 'boh-dah*
• **wedding ring**	anillo de boda	*ah-'nee·yoh deh* *'boh-dah*
widow	viuda	*bee-'oo-dah*
widower	viudo	*bee-'oo-doh*
wife	esposa	*ehs-'poh-sah*
	mujer	*moo-'hehr*

d. RELIGION AND RACE

For nationalities, see Section 30.

agnostic	agnóstico	*ahg-'nohs-tee-koh*
atheism	ateísmo	*ah-teh-'ees-moh*
• **atheist**	ateo	*ah-'teh·oh*
baptism	bautismo	*bow-'tees-moh*
• **baptized**	bautizado	*bow-tee-'sah-doh*
Baptist	bautista (*m/f*)	*bow-'tees-tah*
belief	creencia	*kreh-'ehn-see·ah*
• **believe**	creer (*v*)	*kreh-'ehr*
• **believer**	creyente (*m/f*)	*kreh-'yehn-teh*
Buddhism	budismo	*boo-'dees-moh*
• **Buddhist**	budista (*m/f*)	*boo-'dees-tah*
catechism	catecismo	*kah-teh-'sees-moh*
Catholic	católico	*kah-'toh-lee-koh*
• **Catholicism**	catolicismo	*kah-toh-lee-'sees-moh*

Christian	cristiano	*krees-tee·'ah-noh*
• **Christianity**	cristianismo	*krees-tee·ah-'nees-moh*
church	iglesia	*ee-'gleh-see·ah*
confirmation	confirmación (*f*)	*kohn-feer-mah-see-'ohn*
faith	fe (*f*)	*feh*
• **faithful**	fiel (*adj*)	*fee-'ehl*
God	Dios	*dee-'ohs*
Hindu	hindú (*m/f*)	*een-'dooh*
human	humano	*oo-'mah-noh*
• **human being**	ser humano	*sehr oo-'mah-noh*
• **humanity**	humanidad (*f*)	*oo-mah-nee-'dahd*
Islamic	islámico	*ees-'lah-mee-koh*
Jewish	judío	*hoo-'dee·oh*
• **Judaism**	judaísmo	*hoo-dah·'ees-moh*
lay person	laico	*'lah·ee-koh*
• **laity**	laicado	*lah·ee-'kah-doh*
Lutheran	luterano	*loo-teh-'rah-noh*
Mass	misa	*'mee-sah*
Methodist	metodista (*m/f*)	*meh-toh-'dees-tah*
minister	ministro	*mee-'nees-troh*
monk	monje (*m*)	*'mohn-heh*
mosque	mezquita	*mehs-'kee-tah*
Muslim	musulmán(a) (*adj*)	*moo-sool-'mahn (ah)*
myth	mito	*'mee-toh*
nun	monja	*'mohn-hah*
oriental	oriental (*n, adj*)	*oh-ree·ehn-'tahl*
pagan	pagano	*pah-'gah-noh*
people	gente (*f*)	*'hehn-teh*
person	persona	*pehr-'soh-nah*
pray	rezar (*v*)	*reh-'sahr*
	orar (*v*)	*oh-'rahr*
• **prayer**	oración (*f*)	*oh-rah-see·'ohn*
Presbyterian	presbiteriano	*prehs-bee-teh-ree· 'ah-noh*
priest	cura (*m*)	*'koo-rah*
	sacerdote (*m*)	*sah-sehr-'doh-teh*
Protestantism	protestantismo	*proh-tehs-tahn- 'tees-moh*
• **Protestant**	protestante	*proh-tehs-'tahn-teh*
rabbi	rabino	*rah-'bee-noh*
• **Rabbi**	rabí	*rah-'bee*
race	raza	*'rah-sah*
religion	religión (*f*)	*reh-lee-hee·'ohn*
• **religious**	religioso (*adj*)	*reh-lee-hee·'oh-soh*
rite	rito	*'ree-toh*
sermon	sermón (*m*)	*sehr-'mohn*
soul	alma (*f*)	*'ahl-mah*

spirit	espíritu (*m*)	*ehs-'pee-ree-too*
• spiritual	espiritual (*adj*)	*ehs-pee-ree-too·'ahl*
synagogue	sinagoga	*see-nah-'goh-gah*
temple	templo	*'tehm-ploh*
western	occidental (*adj*)	*ok-see-dehn-'tahl*

e. CHARACTERISTICS AND SOCIAL TRAITS

active	activo (*adj*)	*ahk-'tee-boh*
• activity	actividad (*f*)	*ahk-tee-bee-'dahd*
adapt	adaptar (*v*)	*ah-dahp-'tahr*
• adaptable	adaptable (*adj*)	*ah-dahp-'tah-bleh*
addict	adicto (*n*)	*ah-'deek-toh*
• addict (*oneself*)	enviciar(se) (*v*)	*ehn-bee-see-'ahr (-seh)*
affection	afecto	*ah-'fehk-toh*
	cariño (*adj*)	*kah-'ree-nyoh*
• affectionate	afectuoso (*adj*)	*ah-fehk-'twoh-soh*
	cariñoso (*adj*)	*kah-ree-'nyoh-soh*
aggressive	agresivo (*adj*)	*ah-greh-'see-boh*
• aggressiveness	agresividad (*f*)	*ah-greh-see-bee-'dahd*
altruism	altruismo	*ahl-'trwees-moh*
• altruistic, altruist	altruista (*m/f*)	*ahl-'trwees-tah*
ambition	ambición (*f*)	*ahm-bee-see·'ohn*
• ambitious	ambicioso (*adj*)	*ahm-bee-see·'oh-soh*
anger	ira	*'ee-rah*
	enojo	*eh-'noh-hoh*
• angry	enojado (*adj*)	*eh-noh-'hah-doh*
	enfadado (*adj*)	*ehn-fah-'dah-doh*
• become angry	enojarse (*v*)	*eh-noh-'hahr-seh*
	enfadarse (*v*)	*ehn-fah-'dahr-seh*
anxious	inquieto (*adj*)	*een-kee·'eh-toh*
• anxiousness	inquietud (*f*)	*een-kee·eh-'tood*
arrogant	arrogante (*adj*)	*ah-rroh-'gahn-teh*
artistic	artístico (*adj*)	*ahr-'tees-tee-koh*
astute	astuto (*adj*)	*ahs-'too-toh*
• astuteness	astucia	*ahs-'too-see·ah*
attractive	atractivo (*adj*)	*ah-trahk-'tee-boh*
avarice, greed	avaricia	*ah-bah-'ree-see·ah*
• avaricious	avaro (*adj*)	*ah-'bah-roh*
• greedy	avaricioso (*adj*)	*ah-bah-ree-see·'oh-soh*
bad, mean	malo (*adj*)	*'mah-loh*
• meanness	maldad (*f*)	*mahl-'dahd*
bold	audaz (*adj*)	*ow-'dahs*
brash	atrevido (*adj*)	*ah-treh-'bee-doh*
brilliant	brillante (*adj*)	*bree-'yahn-teh*
calm	tranquilo (*adj*)	*trahn-'kee-loh*

• **calmness**	tranquilidad (*f*)	*trahn-kee-lee-'dahd*
character	carácter (*m*)	*kah-'rahk-tehr*
• **characteristic**	característica	*kah-rahk-teh-'rees-tee-kah*
• **characterize**	caracterizar (*v*)	*kah-rahk-teh-ree-'sahr*
conformist	conformista (*m/f*)	*kohn-fohr-'mees-tah*
• **nonconformist**	disidente (*m/f*)	*dee-see-'dehn-teh*
conscience	conciencia	*kohn-see-'ehn-see·ah*
• **conscientious**	concienzudo (*adj*)	*kohn-see·ehn-'soo-doh*
conservative	conservador (-dora) (*n, adj*)	*kohn-sehr-bah-'dohr (-doh-rah)*
courage	valor (*m*)	*bah-'lohr*
• **courageous**	valiente (*adj*)	*bah-lee-'ehn-teh*
courteous	cortés (*adj*)	*kohr-'tehs*
• **courtesy**	cortesía	*kohr-teh-'see·ah*
• **discourteous**	descortés (*adj*)	*dehs-kohr-'tehs*
crazy, mad	loco (*adj*)	*'loh-koh*
• **madness**	locura	*loh-'koo-rah*
creativity	creatividad (*f*)	*kreh·ah-tee-bee-'dahd*
• **create**	crear (*v*)	*kreh-'ahr*
• **creative**	creativo (*adj*)	*kreh-ah-'tee-boh*
critical	crítico (*adj*)	*'kree-tee-koh*
cry	llorar (*v*)	*yoh-'rahr*
• **crying**	llanto	*'yahn-toh*
cultured	culto (*adj*)	*'kool-toh*
curiosity	curiosidad (*f*)	*koo-ree·oh-see-'dahd*
delicate	delicado (*adj*)	*deh-lee-'kah-doh*
diligence	diligencia	*dee-lee-'hehn-see·ah*
• **diligent**	diligente (*adj*)	*dee-lee-'hehn-teh*
diplomatic	diplomático (*adj*)	*dee-ploh-'mah-tee-koh*
dishonest	deshonesto (*adj*)	*dehs-oh-'nehs-toh*
• **dishonesty**	deshonestidad (*f*)	*dehs-oh-nehs-tee-'dahd*
disorganized	desorganizado (*adj*)	*dehs-ohr-gah-nee-'sah-doh*
dynamic	dinámico (*adj*)	*dee-'nah-mee-koh*
eccentric	excéntrico (*adj*)	*ehks-'sehn-tree-koh*
egoism	egoísmo	*eh-goh·'ees-moh*
• **egoist, egoistic**	egoísta (*adj*)	*eh-goh·'ees-tah*
eloquence	elocuencia	*eh-loh-'kwehn-see·ah*
• **eloquent**	elocuente (*adj*)	*eh-loh 'kwehn-teh*
energetic	enérgico (*adj*)	*eh-'nehr-hee-koh*
	vigoroso (*adj*)	*bee-goh-'roh-soh*
• **energy**	energía	*eh-nehr-'hee·ah*
envious	envidioso (*adj*)	*ehn-bee-dee-'oh-soh*
• **envy**	envidia	*ehn-'bee-dee·ah*
faithful	fiel (*adj*)	*fee-'ehl*
fascinate	fascinar (*v*)	*fah-see-'nahr*
• **fascinating**	fascinante (*adj*)	*fah-see-'nahn-teh*

• **fascination**	fascinación (*f*)	*fah-see-nah-see-'ohn*
	encanto	*ehn-kahn-toh*
fear	miedo	*'myeh-doh*
fool, clown	tonto	*'tohn-toh*
	bufón (*m*)	*boo-'fohn*
• **foolish, silly**	tonto (*adj*)	*'tohn-toh*
friendly	amistoso (*adj*)	*ah-mees-'toh-soh*
funny	cómico (*adj*)	*'koh-mee-koh*
fussy	exigente (*adj*)	*eks-ee-'hehn-teh*
generosity	generosidad (*f*)	*heh-neh-roh-see-'dahd*
• **generous**	generoso (*adj*)	*heh-neh-'roh-soh*
gentle (*mild*)	suave (*adj*)	*'swah-beh*
gentle (*tame*)	manso (*adj*)	*'mahn-soh*
good, kind	bueno (*adj*)	*'bweh-noh*
	bondadoso (*adj*)	*bohn-dah-'doh-soh*
• **goodness, kindness**	bondad (*f*)	*bohn-'dahd*
graceful	gracioso (*adj*)	*grah-see-'oh-soh*
habit	hábito	*'ah-bee-toh*
happiness	felicidad (*f*)	*feh-lee-see-'dahd*
• **happy**	alegre (*adj*)	*ah-'leh-greh*
	contento (*adj*)	*kohn-'tehn-toh*
hate	odio	*'oh-dee·oh*
• **hate**	odiar (*v*)	*oh-dee-'ahr*
• **hateful**	odioso (*adj*)	*oh-dee-'oh-soh*
honest	honesto (*adj*)	*oh-'nehs-toh*
	recto (*adj*)	*'rehk-toh*
• **honesty**	honradez (*f*)	*ohn-rah-'dehs*
humanitarian	humanitario (*adj*)	*oo-mah-nee-'tah-ree·oh*
• **humanitarianism**	humanitarismo	*oo-mah-nee-tah-'rees-moh*
humble	humilde (*adj*)	*oo-'meel-deh*
• **humility**	humildad (*f*)	*oo-meel-'dahd*
humor	humor (*m*)	*oo-'mohr*
• **sense of humor**	sentido del humor	*sehn-'tee-doh dehl oo-'mohr*
idealism	idealismo	*ee-deh·ah-'lees-moh*
• **idealist**	idealista (*m/f*)	*ee-deh·ah-'lees-tah*
• **idealistic**	idealista (*adj*)	*ee-deh·ah-'lees-tah*
imagination	imaginación (*f*)	*ee-mah-hee-nah-see·'ohn*
• **imaginative**	imaginativo (*adj*)	*ee-mah-hee-nah-'tee-boh*
impudence	insolencia	*een-soh-'lehn-see·ah*
• **impudent**	insolente (*adj*)	*een-soh-'lehn-teh*
impulse	impulso	*eem-'pool-soh*
• **impulsive**	impulsivo (*adj*)	*eem-pool-'see-boh*

indecision	indecisión (*f*)	*een-deh-see-see-'ohn*
• indecisive	indecisivo (*adj*)	*een-deh-see-'see-boh*
independent	independiente (*adj*)	*een-deh-pehn-dee-'ehn-teh*
ingenious	ingenioso (*adj*)	*een-heh-nee-'oh-soh*
• ingeniousness	ingenio	*een-'heh-nee-oh*
innocence	inocencia	*ee-noh-'sehn-see-ah*
• innocent	inocente (*adj*)	*ee-noh-'sehn-teh*
insolent	insolente	*een-soh-'lehn-teh*
intelligence	inteligencia	*een-teh-lee-'hehn-see-ah*
• intelligent	inteligente (*adj*)	*een-teh-lee-'hehn-teh*
irascible	colérico (*adj*)	*koh-'leh-ree-koh*
irony	ironía	*ee-roh-'nee-ah*
• ironic	irónico (*adj*)	*ee-'roh-nee-koh*
irritable	irritable (*adj*)	*ee-rree-'tah-bleh*
jealousy	celos (*m*)	*'seh-lohs*
• jealous	celoso (*adj*)	*seh-'loh-soh*
laugh	reírse (*v**)	*rreh-'eer-seh*
• laughter	risa	*'rree-sah*
laziness	pereza	*peh-'reh-sah*
• lazy	perezoso (*adj*)	*peh-reh-'soh-soh*
liberal	liberal (*adj*)	*lee-beh-'rahl*
lively	vivo (*adj*)	*'bee-boh*
love	amor (*m*)	*ah-'mohr*
• love	amar (*v*)	*ah-'mahr*
	querer (*v**)	*keh-'rehr*
• lovable	amable (*adj*)	*ah-'mah-bleh*
• loving	cariñoso (*adj*)	*kah-ree-'nyoh-soh*
malicious	malévolo (*adj*)	*mah-'leh-boh-loh*
mischievous	travieso (*adj*)	*trah-bee-'eh-soh*
mood	humor (*m*)	*oo-'mohr*
• bad mood	mal humor	*mahl oo-'mohr*
• good mood	buen humor	*bwehn oo'-mohr*
naïve	ingenuo	*een-'heh-noo-oh*
neat	limpio (*adj*)	*'leem-pee-oh*
	ordenado (*adj*)	*ohr-deh-'nah-doh*
nice	simpático (*adj*)	*seem-'pah-tee-koh*
not nice, odious	antipático (*adj*)	*ahn-tee-'pah-tee-koh*
obstinate	obstinado (*adj*)	*ohbs-tee-'nah-doh*
optimism	optimismo	*ohp-tee-'mees-moh*
• optimist	optimista (*m/f*)	*ohp-tee-'mees-tah*
• optimistic	optimista (*adj*)	*ohp-tee-'mees-tah*
original	original (*adj*)	*oh-ree-hee-'nahl*
outgoing	extravertido	*ehks-trah-vehr-'tee-doh*
patience	paciencia	*pah-see-'ehn-see-ah*
• impatient	impaciente (*adj*)	*eem-pah-see-'ehn-teh*
• patient	paciente (*adj*)	*pah-see-'ehn-teh*

perfection	perfección (*f*)	*pehr-feks-see-'ohn*
• **perfect**	perfecto (*adj*)	*pehr-'fek-toh*
• **perfectionist**	perfeccionista (*adj*)	*pehr-'fek-see-oh-'nees-tah*
personality	personalidad (*f*)	*pehr-soh-nah-lee-'dahd*
pessimism	pesimismo	*peh-see-'mees-moh*
• **pessimist**	pesimista (*m/f*)	*peh-see-'mees-tah*
• **pessimistic**	pesimista (*adj*)	*peh-see-'mees-tah*
picky	difícil (*adj*)	*dee-'fee-seel*
pleasant, likable	agradable (*adj*)	*ah-grah-'dah-bleh*
• **unpleasant**	desagradable (*adj*)	*dehs-ah-grah-'dah-bleh*
poor	pobre (*adj*)	*'poh-breh*
possessive	posesivo (*adj*)	*poh-seh-'see-boh*
presumptuous	presuntuoso (*adj*)	*preh-soon-'twoh-soh*
pretentious	pretencioso (*adj*)	*preh-tehn-see-'oh-soh*
proud	orgulloso (*adj*)	*ohr-goo-'yoh-soh*
prudent	prudente (*adj*)	*proo-'dehn-teh*
• **imprudent**	imprudente (*adj*)	*eem-proo-'dehn-teh*
rebellious	rebelde (*adj*)	*reh-'behl-deh*
refined	refinado (*adj*)	*reh-fee-'nah-doh*
reserved	reservado (*adj*)	*reh-sehr-'bah-doh*
restless	incansable	*een-kahn-'sah-bleh*
rich	rico (*adj*)	*'ree-koh*
romantic	romántico (*adj*)	*roh-'mahn-tee-koh*
rough	áspero (*adj*)	*'ash-peh-roh*
rude	descortés (*adj*)	*dehs-kohr-'tehs*
	mal educado (*adj*)	*mahl eh-doo-'kah-doh*
sad	triste (*adj*)	*'trees-teh*
• **sadness**	tristeza	*trees-'teh-sah*
sarcasm	sarcasmo	*sahr-'kahs-moh*
• **sarcastic**	sarcástico (*adj*)	*sahr-'kahs-tee-koh*
seduction	seducción (*f*)	*seh-dook-see-'ohn*
• **seductive**	seductivo (*adj*)	*seh-dook-'tee-boh*
selfish	egoísta (*adj*)	*eh-goh-'ees-tah*
self-sufficient	independiente (*adj*)	*een-deh-pehn-dee-'ehn-teh*
sensitive	sensible (*adj*)	*sehn-'see-bleh*
	sensitivo (*adj*)	*sehn-see-'tee-boh*
sentimental	sentimental (*adj*)	*sehn-tee-mehn-'tahl*
serious	serio (*adj*)	*'seh-ree-oh*
shrewd	sagaz (*adj*)	*sah-'gahs*
	listo (*adj*)	*'lees-toh*
• **shrewdness**	sagacidad (*f*)	*sah-gah-see-'dahd*
shy	tímido (*adj*)	*'tee-mee-doh*
simple	sencillo (*adj*)	*sehn-'see-yoh*
sincere	sincero (*adj*)	*seen-'seh-roh*
• **sincerity**	sinceridad (*f*)	*seen-seh-ree-'dahd*

sloppy	desorganizado (*adj*)	*dehs-ohr-gah-nee-'sah-doh*
smart	listo (*adj*)	*'lees-toh*
snobbish	presuntuoso (*adj*)	*preh-soon-'twoh-soh*
stingy	mezquino (*adj*)	*mehs-'kee-noh*
	tacaño (*adj*)	*tah-'kah-nyoh*
• **stinginess**	mezquindad (*f*)	*mehs-keen-'dahd*
strong	fuerte (*adj*)	*'fwehr-teh*
stubborn	terco (*adj*)	*'tehr-koh*
stupid	estúpido (*adj*)	*ehs-'too-pee-doh*
superstitious	supersticioso (*adj*)	*soo-pehr-stee-see-'oh-soh*
sweet	dulce (*adj*)	*'dool-seh*
traditional	tradicional (*adj*)	*trah-dee-see-oh-'nahl*
troublemaker	perturbador (*m*)	*pehr-toor-bah-'dohr*
vain	vanidoso (*adj*)	*bah-nee-'doh-soh*
versatile	versátil (*adj*)	*behr-'sah-teel*
weak	débil (*adj*)	*'deh-beel*
well-mannered	cortés (*adj*)	*kohr-'tehs*
	bien educado (*adj*)	*bee-'ehn eh-doo-'kah-doh*
willing	dispuesto (*adj*)	*dees-'pwehs-toh*
wisdom	sabiduría	*sah-bee-doo-'ree-ah*
• **wise**	sabio (*adj*)	*'sah-bee-oh*

f. BASIC PERSONAL INFORMATION

> For jobs and professions see Section 38.

address	dirección, señas	*dee-rehk-see-'ohn, 'seh-nyahs*
• **avenue**	avenida	*ah-beh-'nee-dah*
• **square**	plaza	*'plah-sah*
• **street**	calle (*f*)	*'kah-yeh*
• **Where do you live?**	¿Dónde vive usted?	*'dohn-deh 'bee-beh oos-'tehd*
• **I live on ... street.**	Vivo en la calle ...	*'bee-boh ehn lah 'kah-yeh*
• **house number**	número de casa	*'noo-meh-roh deh 'kah-sah*
be from	ser (*v**) de	*sehr deh*
• **city**	ciudad (*f*)	*see-oo-'dahd*
• **country**	país (*m*)	*peh-'ees*

• **state**	estado	*ehs-'tah-doh*
• **town**	pueblo	*'pweh-bloh*
career	carrera	*kah-'rreh-rah*
date of birth	fecha de nacimiento	*'feh-chah deh nah-see-mee·'ehn-toh*
education	enseñanza	*ehn-seh-'nyahn-sah*
• **go to school**	asistir (*v*) a la escuela	*ah-sees-'teer ah lah ehs-'kweh-lah*
• **finish school**	terminar la escuela	*tehr-mee-'nahr lah ehs-'kweh-lah*
• **university degree**	título universitario	*'tee-too-loh oo-nee-behr-see-'tah-ree-oh*
• **diploma**	diploma (*m*)	*dee-'ploh-mah*
• **register, enroll**	matricularse (*v*)	*mah-tree-koo-'lahr-seh*
identification	identificación (*f*)	*ee-dehn-tee-fee-kah-see·'ohn*
job	trabajo	*trah-'bah-hoh*
name	nombre (*m*)	*'nohm-breh*
• **first name**	nombre (de pila)	*'nohm-breh (deh 'pee-lah)*
• **family name, surname**	apellido	*ah-peh-'yee-doh*
• **be called**	llamarse (*v*)	*yah-'mahr-seh*
• **How do you spell your name?**	¿Cómo se escribe (deletrea) su nombre?	*'koh-moh seh ehs-'kree-beh (deh-leh-'treh-ah) soo 'nohm-breh*
• **Print your name.**	Escriba su nombre con letras de molde (imprenta).	*ehs-'kree-bah soo 'nohm-breh kohn 'leh-trahs deh 'mohl-deh (eem-'prehn-tah)*
• **What's your name?**	¿Cómo se llama usted?	*'koh-moh seh 'yah-mah oos-'tehd*
• **My name is . . .**	Me llamo . . .	*meh 'yah-moh*
• **sign**	firmar (*v*)	*feer-'mahr*
• **signature**	firma	*'feer-mah*
nationality	nacionalidad (*f*)	*nah-see·oh-nah-lee-'dahd*
place of birth	lugar de nacimiento	*loo-'gahr deh nah-see-mee·'ehn-toh*
place of employment	lugar de trabajo	*loo-'gahr deh trah-'bah-hoh*
profession	profesión (*f*)	*proh-feh-see·'ohn*
• **professional**	profesional (*adj*)	*proh-feh-see·oh-'nahl*
residence	residencia	*reh-see-'dehn-see·ah*
telephone number	número de teléfono	*'noo-meh-roh deh teh-'leh-foh-noh*
title	título	*'tee-too-loh*
• **Dr.**	Doctor(a) (Dr.)	*dohk-'tohr (-rah)*
• **Miss**	Señorita (Srta.)	*seh-nyoh-'ree-tah*

• **Mr.**	Señor (Sr.)	*seh-'nyohr*
• **Mrs.**	Señora (Sra.)	*seh-'nyoh-rah*
• **Prof.**	Profesor(a) (Prof.)	*proh-feh-'sohr (-rah)*
work	trabajo	*trah-'bah-hoh*
• **work**	trabajar (*v*)	*trah-bah-'hahr*
• **line of work**	tipo de trabajo	*'tee-poh deh tra-'bah-hoh*

12. THE BODY

a. PARTS OF THE BODY

See also Section 40.

ankle	tobillo	*toh-'bee-yoh*
arm	brazo	*'brah-soh*
back	espalda	*eh-'spahl-dah*
beard	barba	*'bahr-bah*
blood	sangre (*f*)	*'sahn-greh*
body	cuerpo	*'kwehr-poh*
bone	hueso	*'weh-soh*
brain	cerebro	*seh-'reh-broh*
breast	seno	*'seh-noh*
buttocks	trasero	*trah-'seh-roh*
calf	pantorrilla	*pahn-toh-'rree-yah*
cheek	mejilla	*meh-'hee-yah*
chest	pecho	*'peh-choh*
chin	barbilla	*bahr-'bee-yah*
ear	oreja	*oh-'reh-hah*
elbow	codo	*'koh-doh*
eye	ojo	*'oh-hoh*
eyebrow	ceja	*'seh-hah*
eyelash	pestaña	*pehs-'tah-nyah*
eyelid	párpado	*'pahr-pah-doh*
face	cara	*'kah-rah*
finger	dedo	*'deh-doh*
fingernail	uña	*'oo-nyah*
foot	pie (*m*)	*'pee·eh*
forehead	frente (*f*)	*'frehn-teh*
hair	pelo	*'peh-loh*
	cabello	*kah-'beh-yoh*
hand	mano (*f*)	*'mah-noh*
head	cabeza	*kah-'beh-sah*

> **Two heads are better than one.** = Más ven cuatro ojos que dos.
> **word for word** = al pie de la letra
> **to get on one's feet** = levantar cabeza

heart	corazón (*m*)	*koh-rah-'sohn*
hip	cadera	*kah-'deh-rah*
index finger	dedo índice	*'deh-doh 'een-dee-seh*
jaw	mandíbula	*mahn-'dee-boo-lah*
knee	rodilla	*roh-'dee-yah*
knuckle	nudillo	*noo-'dee-yoh*
leg	pierna	*pee·'ehr-nah*
lip	labio	*'lah-bee·oh*
little finger	dedo meñique	*'deh-doh meh-'nyee-keh*
lung	pulmón (*m*)	*pool-'mohn*
middle finger	dedo medio	*'deh-doh 'meh-dee·oh*
mouth	boca	*'boh-kah*
muscle	músculo	*'moos-koo-loh*
mustache	bigote (*m*)	*bee-'goh-teh*
neck	cuello	*'kweh-yoh*
nose	nariz (*f*)	*nah-'rees*
nostril	nariz, narices (*f*)	*nah-'rees (ehs)*
penis	pene	*'peh-neh*
pubis	pubis	*'poo-bees*
ring finger	dedo anular	*'deh-doh ah-noo-'lahr*
shoulder	hombro	*'ohm-broh*
skin	piel (*f*)	*pee·'ehl*
stomach	estómago	*ehs-'toh-mah-goh*
thigh	muslo	*'moos loh*
throat	garganta	*gahr-'gahn-tah*
thumb	pulgar (*m*)	*pool-'gahr*
toe	dedo del pie	*'deh-doh dehl pee·'eh*
tongue	lengua	*'lehn-gwah*
tooth	diente (*m*)	*dee·'ehn-teh*
	muela	*moo·'eh-lah*
vagina	vagina	*vah-'hee-nah*
waist	cintura	*seen-'too-rah*
wrist	muñeca	*moo-'nyeh-kah*

FOCUS: Parts of the Body

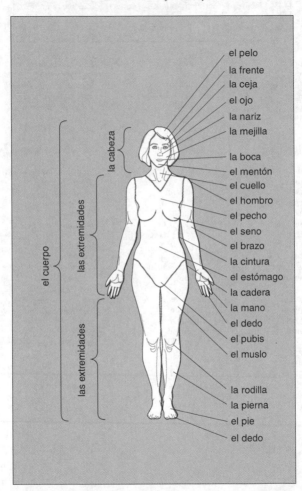

el pelo
la frente
la ceja
el ojo
la nariz
la mejilla
la boca
el mentón
el cuello
el hombro
el pecho
el seno
el brazo
la cintura
el estómago
la cadera
la mano
el dedo
el pubis
el muslo
la rodilla
la pierna
el pie
el dedo

la cabeza
las extremidades
el cuerpo
las extremidades

b. PHYSICAL STATES AND ACTIVITIES

be cold	tener (*v**) frío	*teh-'nehr 'free·oh*
be hot	tener (*v**) calor	*teh-'nehr kah-'lohr*
be hungry	tener (*v**) hambre	*teh-'nehr 'ahm-breh*
• **hunger**	hambre (*f*)	*'ahm-breh*
be sleepy	tener (*v**) sueño	*teh-'nehr 'sweh-nyoh*
be thirsty	tener (*v**) sed	*teh-'nehr sehd*
• **thirst**	sed (*f*)	*sehd*
be tired	estar cansado	*ehs-'tahr kahn-'sah-doh*
breathe	respirar (*v*)	*rehs-pee-'rahr*
drink	beber (*v*)	*beh-'behr*
eat	comer (*v*)	*koh-'mehr*
fall asleep	dormirse (*v**)	*dohr-'meer-seh*
feel badly	sentirse (*v**) mal	*sehn-'teer-seh mahl*
feel well	sentirse (*v**) bien	*sehn-'teer-seh bee-'ehn*
get up	levantarse (*v*)	*leh-bahn-'tahr-seh*
go to bed	acostarse (*v**)	*ah-kohs-'tahr-seh*
relax	relajarse (*v*)	*reh-lah-'hahr-seh*
rest	descansar (*v*)	*dehs-kahn-'sahr*
run	correr (*v*)	*koh-'rrehr*
sleep	dormir (*v**)	*dohr-'meer*
urinate	orinar (*v*)	*oh-ree-'nahr*
wake up	despertarse (*v**)	*dehs-pehr-'tahr-seh*
walk	andar (*v*)	*ahn-'dahr*

c. SENSORY PERCEPTION

blind (person)	ciego	*see·'eh-goh*
• **blindness**	ceguera	*seh-'geh-rah*
deaf (person)	sordo	*'sohr-doh*
• **deafness**	sordera	*sohr-'deh-rah*
flavor	sabor	*sah-'bohr*
• **taste**	probar (*v**)	*proh-'bahr*
hear	oír (*v**)	*oh-'eer*
• **hearing**	oído	*oh-'ee-doh*
listen (to)	escuchar (*v*)	*ehs-koo-'chahr*
look at	mirar (*v*)	*mee-'rahr*
mute (person)	mudo	*'moo-doh*
noise	ruido	*'rwee-doh*
• **noisy**	ruidoso	*rwee-'doh-soh*
perceive	percibir (*v*)	*pehr-see-'beer*
• **perception**	percepción (*f*)	*pehr-sehp-see-'ohn*
see	ver (*v**)	*behr*
• **sight**	vista	*'bees-tah*
sense, feel	sentirse (*v**)	*sehn-'teer-seh*
• **sense**	sentido	*sehn-'tee-doh*

smell	oler (*v**)	*oh-'lehr*
• **sense of smell**	olfato	*ohl-'fah-toh*
sound	sonido	*soh-'nee-doh*
touch	tocar (*v*)	*toh-'kahr*
• **sense of touch**	el sentido del tacto	*ehl sehn-'tee-doh dehl 'tahk-toh*

d. PERSONAL CARE

bald	calvo (*adj*)	*'kahl-boh*
bangs	flequillo	*fleh-'kee-yoh*
barber	barbero	*bahr-'beh-roh*
• **barber shop**	barbería	*bahr-beh-'ree-ah*
	peluquería	*peh-loo-keh-'ree-ah*
beautician	peluquero(a)	*peh-loo-'keh-roh (-rah)*
brush	cepillarse (*v*)	*seh-pee-'yahr-seh*
• **brush**	cepillo	*seh-'pee-yoh*
clean oneself	limpiarse (*v*)	*leem-pee-'ahr-seh*
clippers	maquinilla	*mah-kee-'nee-yah*
comb	peinar (*v*)	*peh·ee-'nahr*
comb one's hair	peinarse (*v*)	*peh-ee-'nahr-seh*
• **comb**	peine (*m*)	*'peh·ee-neh*
curls	bucles (*m*)	*'boo-klehs*
• **loose curls**	bucles flojos	*'boo-klehs 'floh-hohs*
curlers	rulos	*'roo-lohs*
	rizadores (*m*)	*ree-sah-'doh-rehs*
curling iron	tenacillas	*teh-nah-'see-yahs*
cut	cortar (*v*)	*kohr-'tahr*
cut one's hair	cortarse (*v*) el pelo	*kohr-'tahr-seh ehl 'peh-loh*
dirty	sucio	*'soo-see·oh*
dry	secar (*v*)	*seh-kahr*
dry oneself	secarse (*v*)	*seh-'kahr-seh*
frosted hair	pelo escarchado	*'peh-loh ehs-kahr-'chah-doh*
hair	pelo	*'peh-loh*
• **permanent**	permanente (*f*)	*pehr-mah-'nehn-teh*
haircut	corte (*m*) de pelo	*'kohr-teh deh 'peh-loh*
• **in the back**	por detrás	*pohr deh-'trahs*
• **in the front**	por delante	*pohr deh-'lahn-teh*
• **on the sides**	a los lados	*ah lohs 'lah-dohs*
• **on top**	de arriba	*deh ah-'rree-bah*
hairdresser	peluquero(a)	*peh-loo-'keh-roh (-rah)*
hairdryer	secador (*m*)	*seh-kah-'dohr*
hair spray	laca	*'lah-kah*
hygiene	higiene (*f*)	*ee-hee·'eh-neh*
• **hygienic**	higiénico (*adj*)	*ee-hee·'eh-nee-koh*
long	largo (*adj*)	*'lahr-goh*

makeup	maquillaje (*m*)	*mah-kee-'yah-heh*
• **put on makeup**	ponerse (*v**) el maquillaje	*poh-'nehr-seh ehl mah-kee-'yah-heh*
manicure	manicura	*mah-nee-'koo-rah*
mascara	rimmel (*m*)	*ree-'mehl*
massage	masaje (*m*)	*mah-'sah-heh*
nail polish	esmalte para las uñas	*ehs-'mahl-teh 'pah-rah lahs 'oo-nyahs*
perfume	perfume (*m*)	*pehr-'foo-meh*
• **put on perfume**	ponerse (*v**) perfume	*poh-'nehr-seh pehr-'foo-meh*
permanent	permanente (*f*)	*pehr-mah-'nehn-teh*
razor	afeitadora	*ah-feh·ee-tah-'doh-rah*
• **electric razor**	afeitadora eléctrica	*ah-feh·ee-tah-'doh-rah eh-'lehk-tree-kah*
rinse	enjuague	*ehn-'hwah-geh*
scissors	tijeras	*tee-'heh-rahs*
set	arreglar (*v*)	*ah-rreh-'glahr*
shampoo	champú (*m*)	*chahm-'poo*
shave	afeitarse (*v*)	*ah-feh·ee-'tahr-seh*
short	corto (*adj*)	*'kohr-toh*
sideburn	patilla	*pah-'tee-yah*
soap	jabón (*m*)	*hah-'bohn*
toothbrush	cepillo de dientes	*seh-'pee-yoh deh dee-'ehn-tehs*
toothpaste	crema dental	*'kreh-mah dehn-'tahl*
	pasta dentífrica	*'pahs-tah dehn-'tee-free-kah*
touch up	retoque (*m*)	*reh-'toh-keh*
towel, handcloth	toalla	*toh·ah-yah*
	paño	*'pah-nyoh*
trim	recortar (*v*)	*reh-kohr-'tahr*
wash	lavado	*lah-'bah-doh*
wash oneself	lavarse (*v*)	*lah-'bahr-seh*
• **wash one's hair**	lavarse (*v*) el pelo	*lah-'bahr-seh ehl 'peh-loh*

THE PHYSICAL, PLANT, AND ANIMAL WORLDS

13. THE PHYSICAL WORLD

a. THE UNIVERSE

> For signs of the zodiac see Section 5.

astronomy	astronomía	*ahs-troh-noh-'mee-ah*
comet	cometa (*m*)	*koh-'meh-tah*
cosmos	cosmos (*m*)	*'kohs-mohs*
eclipse	eclipse (*m*)	*eh-'kleep-seh*
• **lunar eclipse**	eclipse lunar	*eh-'kleep-seh loo-'nahr*
• **solar eclipse**	eclipse solar	*eh-'kleep-seh soh-'lahr*
galaxy	galaxia	*gah-'lahk-see·ah*
gravitation	gravitación	*grah-bee-tah-see·'ohn*
• **gravity**	gravedad (*f*)	*grah-beh-'dahd*
light	luz (*f*)	*loos*
• **infrared light**	luz infrarroja	*loos een-frah-'rroh-hah*
• **light year**	año luz	*'ah-nyoh loos*
• **ultraviolet light**	luz ultravioleta	*loos ool-trah-bee·oh-'leh-tah*
meteor	meteoro	*meh-teh-'oh-roh*
moon	luna	*'loo-nah*
• **full moon**	luna llena	*loo-nah 'yeh-nah*
• **moonbeam (ray)**	rayo de luna	*'rah-yoh deh 'loo-nah*
• **new moon**	luna nueva	*'loo-nah 'nweh-bah*
orbit	estar (*v*) en órbita	*ehs-'tahr ehn 'ohr-bee-tah*
• **orbit**	órbita	*'ohr-bee-tah*
planet	planeta (*m*)	*plah-'neh-tah*
• **Earth**	Tierra	*tee·'eh-rrah*
• **Jupiter**	Júpiter (*m*)	*'hoo-pee-tehr*
• **Mars**	Marte (*m*)	*'mahr-teh*
• **Mercury**	Mercurio	*mehr-koo-'ree·oh*
• **Neptune**	Neptuno	*nehp-'too-noh*
• **Pluto**	Plutón (*m*)	*ploo-'tohn*
• **Saturn**	Saturno	*sah-'toor-noh*
• **Uranus**	Urano	*oo-'rah-noh*
• **Venus**	Venus (*m*)	*'beh-noos*

satellite	satélite (*m*)	*sah-'teh-lee-teh*
space	espacio	*ehs-'pah-see·oh*
• three-dimensional space	espacio tridimensional	*ehs-'pah-see·oh tree-dee-mehn-see·oh-'nahl*
star	estrella	*ehs-'treh-yah*
	astro	*ahs-troh*
sun	sol (*m*)	*sohl*
solar system	sistema solar (*m*)	*sees-'teh-mah soh-'lahr*
• sunbeam (ray)	rayo de sol	*'ra-yoh de sohl*
• sunlight	luz del sol	*loos dehl sohl*
universe	universo	*oo-nee-'behr-soh*
world	mundo	*'moon-doh*

to publish	= sacar (*v*) a luz
to give birth to	= dar (*v*) a luz
in the twilight	= entre dos luces
my sweet	= luz de mis ojos

b. THE ENVIRONMENT

See also Sections 13 and 44.

archipelago	archipiélago	*ahr-chee-pee-'eh-lah-goh*
atmosphere	atmósfera	*aht-'mohs-feh-rah*
• **atmospheric**	atmosférico (*adj*)	*aht-mohs-'feh-ree-koh*
basin	cuenca	*'kwehn-kah*
bay	bahía	*bah-'ee·ah*
beach	playa	*'plah-yah*
canal	canal (*m*)	*kah-'nahl*
cape	cabo	*'kah-boh*
cave	cueva	*'kweh-bah*
channel	cauce (*m*)	*'kow-seh*
cloud	nube (*f*)	*'noo-beh*
coast	costa	*'kohs-tah*

countryside	campo	'kahm-poh
	campiña	kahm-'pee-nyah
dam	dique	'dee-keh
	presa	'preh-sah
desert	desierto	deh-see·'ehr-toh
earthquake	terremoto	teh-rreh-'moh-toh
environment	ambiente (m)	ahm-bee·'ehn-teh
farmland	tierras de labrantío	tee·'eh-rrahs deh lah-brahn-'tee·oh
field	campo	'kahm-poh
forest	selva	'sehl-bah
	bosque	'bohs-keh
• tropical forest	selva tropical	'sehl-bah troh-pee-'kahl
grass	hierba	ee·'ehr-bah
gulf	golfo	'gohl-foh
hill	colina	koh-'lee-nah
	cerro	'seh-rroh
hurricane	huracán	oo-rah-'kahn
ice	hielo	ee·'eh-loh
island	isla	'ees-lah
jungle	selva	'sehl-bah
	jungla	'hoon-glah
lake	lago	'lah-goh
land	tierra	tee·'eh-rrah
	terreno	teh-'rreh-noh
landscape	paisaje (m)	pah·'eeh-sah-heh
layer	estrato	ehs-trah-toh
marsh	pantano	pahn-'tah-noh
• wetland	tierra pantanosa	tee·'eh-rrah pahn-tah-'noh-sah
meadow	prado	'prah-doh
mountain	montaña	mohn-'tah-nyah
• mountain range	cordillera	kohr-dee-'yeh-rah
• mountainous	montañoso (adj)	mohn-tah-'nyoh-soh
• peak	pico	'pee-koh
nature	naturaleza	nah-too-rah-'leh-sah
• natural	natural	nah-too-'rahl
ocean	océano	oh-'seh-ah-noh
• Antarctic	Antártico	ahnt-'ahr-tee-koh
• Arctic	Ártico	'ahr-tee-koh
• Atlantic	Atlántico	aht-'lahn-tee-koh
• Indian	Indico	'een-dee·koh
• Pacific	Pacífico	pah-'see-fee-koh
peninsula	península	peh-'neen-soo-lah
plain	llano	'yah-noh
pond	estanque (m)	ehs-'tahn-keh
	laguna	lah-'goo-nah

river	río	'ree·oh
• flow	fluir (v)	floo·'eer
• navigable	navegable (adj)	nah-beh-'gah-bleh
rock	roca	'roh-kah
	peña	'peh-nyah
sand	arena	ah-'reh-nah
sea	mar (m)	mahr
sky	cielo	see·'eh-loh
stone	piedra	pee·'eh-drah
strait	estrecho	ehs-'treh-choh
tide	marea	mah-'reh-ah
valley	valle (m)	'bah-yeh
vegetation	vegetación	beh-heh-tah-see·'ohn
volcano	volcán (m)	bohl-'kahn
• eruption	erupción (f)	eh-roop-see·'ohn
• lava	lava	'lah-bah
wave	ola	'oh-lah
woods	bosque (m)	'bohs-keh

c. MATTER AND THE ENVIRONMENT

> See also Section 44.

acid	ácido	'ah-see-doh
air	aire (m)	'ah·ee-reh
ammonia	amoniaco	ah-moh-nee·'ah-koh
atom	átomo	'ah-toh-moh
• charge	carga	'kahr-gah
• electron	electrón (m)	eh-lehk-'trohn
• neutron	neutrón (m)	neh·oo-'trohn
• nucleus	núcleo	'noo-kleh-oh
• proton	protón (m)	proh-'tohn
brass	latón (m)	lah-'tohn
bronze	bronce (m)	'brohn-ceh
carbon	carbono	kahr-'boh-noh
chemical	producto químico	proh-'dook-toh 'kee-mee-koh
• chemistry	química	'kee-mee-kah
chlorine	cloro	'kloh-roh
clay	arcilla	ahr-'see-yah
coal	carbón (m)	kahr-'bohn
• coal mine	mina de carbón	'mee-nah deh kahr-'bohn
• coal mining	extracción del carbón (f)	ehks-trahk-see·'ohn dehl kahr-'bohn

compound	compuesto	*kohm-'pwehs-toh*
copper	cobre (*m*)	*'koh-breh*
cotton	algodón (*m*)	*ahl-goh-'dohn*
electricity	electricidad (*f*)	*eh-lehk-tree-see-'dahd*
• electrical	eléctrico (*adj*)	*eh-'lehk-tree-koh*
element	elemento	*eh-leh-'mehn-toh*
energy	energía	*eh-nehr-'hee·ah*
• fossil	fósil (*adj*)	*'foh-seel*
• nuclear	nuclear (*adj*)	*noo-kleh-'ahr*
• radioactive	radioactivo (*adj*)	*rah-dee-oh-ahk-'tee-boh*
• solar	solar (*adj*)	*soh-'lahr*
fiber	fibra	*'fee-brah*
fire	fuego	*foo·'eh-goh*
fuel	combustible (*m*)	*kohm-boos-'tee-bleh*
• fossil fuel	combustibles (*m*) de fósil	*kohm-boos-'tee-blehs deh 'foh-seel*
gas	gas (*m*)	*gahs*
• gasoline	gasolina	*gah-soh-'lee-nah*
• natural gas	gas natural	*gahs nah-too-'rahl*
gold	oro	*'oh-roh*
heat	calor (*m*)	*kah-'lohr*
heat (for home)	calefacción (*f*)	*kah-leh-fahk-see·'ohn*
hydrogen	hidrógeno	*ee-'droh-heh-noh*
industrial	industrial (*adj*)	*een-doos-tree-'ahl*
• industry	industria	*een-'doos-tree·ah*
iodine	yodo	*'yoh-doh*
iron	hierro	*ee·'eh-rroh*
laboratory	laboratorio	*lah-boh-rah-'toh-ree·oh*
lead	plomo	*'ploh-moh*
leather	de cuero (*adj*)	*deh koo-'eh-roh*
	de piel (*adj*)	*deh pee·ehl*
liquid	líquido	*'lee-kee-doh*
material	materia	*mah-'teh-ree·ah*
	material	*mah-teh-ree-'ahl*
matter	materia	*mah-'teh-ree·ah*
mercury	mercurio	*mehr-'koo-ree·oh*
metal	metal (*m*)	*meh-'tahl*
methane	metano	*meh-'tah-noh*
microscope	microscopio	*mee-kroh-'skoh-pee·oh*
mineral	mineral (*m*)	*mee-neh-'rahl*
molecule	molécula	*moh-'leh-koo-lah*
• model	modelo	*moh-'deh-loh*
• molecular	molecular (*adj*)	*moh-leh-koo-'lahr*
• molecular formula	fórmula molecular	*'fohr-moo-lah moh-leh-koo-'lahr*
• structure	estructura	*ehs-trook-'too-rah*

natural resources	recursos naturales	*rreh-'koor-sohs nah-too-rah-lehs*
organic	orgánico (*adj*)	*ohr-'gah-nee-koh*
• **inorganic**	inorgánico (*adj*)	*een-ohr-'gah-nee-koh*
oxygen	oxígeno	*ohks-'ee-heh-noh*
particle	partícula	*pahr-'tee-koo-lah*
petroleum	petróleo	*peh-'troh-leh-oh*
physical	físico (*adj*)	*'fee-see-koh*
• **physics**	física	*'fee-see-kah*
plastic	plástico (*n, adj*)	*'plahs-tee-koh*
platinum	platino	*plah-'tee-noh*
pollution	contaminación (*f*)	*kohn-tah-mee-nah-see·'ohn*
salt	sal (*f*)	*sahl*
silk	seda	*'seh-dah*
silver	plata	*'plah-tah*
smoke	humo	*'oo-moh*
sodium	sodio	*'soh-dee·oh*
steel	acero	*ah-'seh-roh*
• **stainless steel**	acero inoxidable	*ah-'seh-roh een-ohks-ee-'dah-bleh*
substance	substancia	*soob-'stahn-see·ah*
sulphur	azufre (*m*)	*ah-'soo-freh*
• **sulphuric acid**	ácido sulfúrico	*'ah-see-doh sool-'foo-ree-koh*
textile	textil	*tehks-'teel*
	tejido	*teh-'hee-doh*
tin	estaño	*ehs-'tah-nyoh*
vapor	vapor (*m*)	*bah-'pohr*
water	agua (*f*)	*'ah-gwah*
wool	lana	*'lah-nah*

d. CHARACTERISTICS OF MATTER

artificial	artificial (*adj*)	*ahr-tee-fee-see·'ahl*
authentic	auténtico (*adj*)	*ow-'tehn-tee-koh*
elastic	elástico (*adj*)	*eh-'lahs-tee-koh*
fake	falso (*adj*)	*'fahl-soh*
hard	duro (*adj*)	*'doo-roh*
heavy	pesado (*adj*)	*peh-'sah-doh*
light	ligero (*adj*)	*lee-'heh-roh*
malleable	maleable (*adj*)	*mah-leh-'ah-bleh*
opaque	opaco (*adj*)	*oh-'pah-koh*
pure	puro (*adj*)	*'poo-roh*
resistant	resistente (*adj*)	*reh-sees-'tehn-teh*
robust	robusto (*adj*)	*roh-'boos-toh*

rough	áspero (*adj*)	'*ahs-peh-roh*
smooth	liso (*adj*)	'*lee-soh*
soft	blando (*adj*)	'*blahn-doh*
soluble	soluble (*adj*)	*soh-*'*loo-bleh*
stable	estable (*adj*)	*ehs-*'*tah-bleh*
strong	fuerte (*adj*)	'*fwehr-teh*
synthetic	sintético (*adj*)	*seen-*'*teh-tee-koh*
transparent	transparente (*adj*)	*trahns-pah-*'*rehn-teh*
weak	débil (*adj*)	'*deh-beel*

e. GEOGRAPHY

For names of countries, cities, etc., see Section 30.

Antarctic Circle	Círculo Antártico	'*seer-koo-loh ahnt-*'*ahr-tee-koh*
Arctic Circle	Círculo Ártico	'*seer-koo-loh* '*ahr-tee-koh*
area	área (*f*)	'*ah-reh-ah*
border	frontera	*frohn-*'*teh-rah*
city	ciudad (*f*)	*see·oo-*'*dahd*
• **capital**	capital (*f*)	*kah-pee-*'*tahl*
continent	continente (*m*)	*kohn-tee-*'*nehn-teh*
• **continental**	continental (*adj*)	*kohn-tee-nehn-*'*tahl*
country	país (*m*)	*pah·*'*ees*
equator	ecuador (*m*)	*eh-kwah-*'*dohr*
geography	geografía	*heh-oh-grah-*'*fee-ah*
• **geographical**	geográfico (*adj*)	*heh-oh-*'*grah-fee-koh*
globe	globo	'*gloh-boh*
hemisphere	hemisferio	*eh-mees-*'*feh-ree-oh*
• **hemispheric**	hemisférico (*adj*)	*eh-mees-*'*feh-ree-koh*
latitude	latitud (*f*)	*lah-tee-*'*tood*
longitude	longitud (*f*)	*lohn-hee-*'*tood*
locate	localizar (*v*)	*loh-kah-lee-*'*zahr*
• **location**	localización (*f*)	*loh-kah-lee-sah-see·*'*ohn*
• **be located**	estar (*v**) ubicado (situado)	*ehs-*'*tahr oo-bee-*'*kah-doh (see-*'*twah-doh)*
map	mapa (*m*)	'*mah-pah*
meridian	meridiano (*adj*)	*meh-ree-dee·*'*ah-noh*
• **prime meridian**	primer meridiano	*pree-*'*mehr meh-ree-dee·*'*ah-noh*

nation	nación (*f*)	*nah-see-'ohn*
• **national**	nacional (*adj*)	*nah-see·oh-'nahl*
pole	polo	*'poh-loh*
• **North Pole**	Polo Norte	*'poh-loh 'nohr-teh*
• **South Pole**	Polo Sur	*'poh-loh soor*
province	provincia	*proh-'been-see·ah*
region	región (*f*)	*reh-hee-'ohn*
state	estado	*ehs-'tah-doh*
territory	territorio	*teh-rree-'toh-ree·oh*
tropic	trópico	*'troh-pee·koh*
• **Tropic of Cancer**	trópico de Cáncer	*'troh-pee-koh deh 'kahn-sehr*
• **Tropic of Capricorn**	trópico de Capricornio	*'troh-pee-koh deh kah-pree-'kohr-nee·oh*
• **tropical**	tropical	*troh-pee-'kahl*
zone	zona	*'soh-nah*

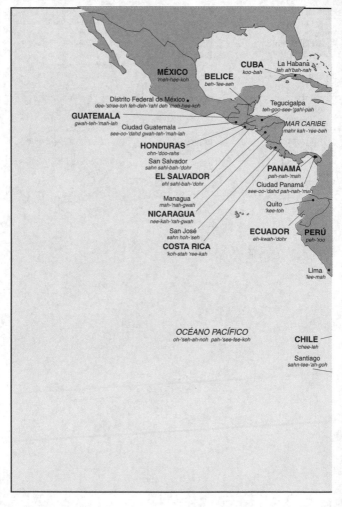

MÉXICO
meh-hee-koh

BELICE
beh-'lee-seh

CUBA
koo-bah

La Habana
lah ah'bah-nah

Distrito Federal de México
dee-'stree-toh feh-deh-'rahl deh 'meh-hee-koh

Tegucigalpa
teh-goo-see-'gahl-pah

GUATEMALA
gwah-teh-'mah-lah

Ciudad Guatemala
see-oo-'dahd gwah-teh-'mah-lah

MAR CARIBE
mahr kah-'ree-beh

HONDURAS
ohn-'doo-rahs

San Salvador
sahn sahl-bah-'dohr

EL SALVADOR
ehl sahl-bah-'dohr

PANAMÁ
pah-nah-'mah

Ciudad Panamá
see-oo-'dahd pah-nah-'mah

Managua
mah-'nah-gwah

NICARAGUA
nee-kah-'rah-gwah

Quito
'kee-toh

San José
sahn hoh-'seh

COSTA RICA
'koh-stah 'ree-kah

ECUADOR
eh-kwah-'dohr

PERÚ
peh-'roo

Lima
'lee-mah

OCÉANO PACÍFICO
oh-'seh-ah-noh pah-'see-fee-koh

CHILE
'chee-leh

Santiago
sahn-tee-'ah-goh

Puerto Príncipe
'pwehr-toh 'preen-see-peh

HAITÍ
ah-ee'tee

Santo Domingo
'sahn-toh doh-'meen-goh

REPÚBLICA DOMINICANA
reh-'poo-blee-kah doh-mee-nee-'kah-nah

San Juan
sahn wahn

PUERTO RICO
'pwehr-toh 'ree-koh

JAMAICA
jah-'mah•ee-kah

Caracas
kah-'rah-kahs

VENEZUELA
beh-neh-soo-'eh-lan

Bogotá
boh-goh-'tah

GUYANA
goo-'yah-nah

SURINAM
soo-ree-'nahm

GUAYANA
gwah-'yah-nah

AMÉRICA LATINA
ah-'meh-ree-kah lah-'tee-nah

OCÉANO ATLÁNTICO
oh-'seh-ah-noh aht-'lahn-tee-koh

COLOMBIA
koh-'lohm-bee•ah

BRASIL
brah-'seel

BOLIVIA
boh-'lee-bee•ah

Brasilia
brah-'see-lee•ah

La Paz
lah pahs

PARAGUAY
pah-rah-'gwah•ee

Asunción
ah-soon-see-'ohn

Río de Janeiro
'ree-oh deh hah-'neh•ee-roh

URUGUAY
oo-roo-'gwah•ee

ARGENTINA
ahr-hehn-'tee-nah

Montevideo
mohn-teh-bee-'deh-oh

Buenos Aires
'bweh-nohs 'ah•ee-rehs

Islas Malvinas
'ees-lahs mahl-'bee-nahs

14. PLANTS

a. GENERAL VOCABULARY

agriculture	agricultura	*ah-gree-kool-'too-rah*
bloom	florecer (*v*)	*floh-reh-'sehr*
botanical	botánico (*adj*)	*boh-'tah-nee-koh*
• **botany**	botánica	*boh-'tah-nee-kah*
branch	rama	*'rah-mah*
bud	brote (*m*)	*'broh-teh*
• **in bud**	en capullo	*ehn kah-'poo-yoh*
bulb	bulbo	*'bool-boh*
bush	arbusto	*ahr-'boos-toh*
cell	célula	*'seh-loo-lah*
• **nucleus**	núcleo	*'noo-kleh-oh*
chlorophyll	clorofila	*kloh-roh-'fee-lah*
cultivate	cultivar (*v*)	*kool-tee-'bahr*
• **cultivation**	cultivo	*kool-'tee-boh*
dig	cavar (*v*)	*kah-'bahr*
flower	florecer (*v*)	*floh-reh-'sehr*
foliage	follaje (*m*)	*foh-'yah-heh*
gather	recoger (*v*)	*reh-koh-'hehr*
grain	grano	*'grah-noh*
greenhouse	invernadero	*een-behr-nah-'deh-roh*
hedge	seto vivo	*'seh-toh 'bee-boh*
horticulture	horticultura	*ohr-tee-kool-'too-rah*
leaf	hoja	*'oh-hah*
look after	cuidar (*v*)	*kwee-'dahr*
membrane	membrana	*mehm-'brah-nah*
organism	organismo	*ohr-gah-'nees-moh*
photosynthesis	fotosíntesis (*f*)	*foh-toh-'seen-teh-sees*
plant	planta	*'plahn-tah*
• **plant**	plantar (*v*)	*plahn-'tahr*
	sembrar (*v**)	*sehm-'brahr*
pollen	polen (*m*)	*'poh-lehn*
reproduce	reproducir (*v**)	*reh-proh-doo-'seer*
• **reproduction**	reproducción (*f*)	*reh-proh-dook-see-'ohn*
ripe	maduro (*adj*)	*mah-'doo-roh*
root	raíz (*f*)	*rah-'ees*
rotten	podrido (*adj*)	*poh-'dree-doh*
seed	semilla	*seh-'-mee-yah*
• **seed**	sembrar (*v**)	*sehm-'brahr*
species	especie (*f*)	*ehs-'peh·see·eh*
stem	tallo	*'tah-yoh*
	pedúnculo	*peh-'doon-koo-loh*
transplant	trasplantar (*v*)	*trahs-plahn-'tahr*
• **transplant**	trasplante (*m*)	*trahs-'plahn-teh*
trunk	tronco	*'trohn-koh*

| water | regar (*v**) | *reh-'gahr* |
| wheat | trigo | *'tree-goh* |

b. FLOWERS

carnation	clavel (*m*)	*klah-'behl*
cyclamen	ciclamen (*m*)	*see-'klah-mehn*
dahlia	dalia	*'dah-lee·ah*
daisy	margarita	*mahr-gah-'ree-tah*
flower	flor (*f*)	*flohr*
• bouquet of flowers	ramo de flores	*'rah-moh deh 'floh-rehs*
• flowerbed	macizo	*mah-'see-soh*
	arriate (*m*)	*ah-rree·'ah-teh*
• pick flowers	recoger (*v**) flores	*reh-koh-'gehr 'floh-rehs*
• wilted flower	flor marchita	*flohr mahr-'chee-tah*
geranium	geranio	*heh-'rah-nee·oh*
gladiolus	gladiolo	*glah-dee·'oh-loh*
lily	azucena	*ah-soo-'seh-nah*
orchid	orquídea	*ohr-'kee-deh·ah*
petal	pétalo	*'peh-tah-loh*
petunia	petunia	*peh-'too-nee·ah*
poppy	amapola	*ah-mah-'poh-lah*
rose	rosa	*'roh-sah*
thorn	espina	*ehs-'pee-nah*
tulip	tulipán (*m*)	*too-lee-'pahn*
violet	violeta	*bee·oh-'leh-tah*

c. TREES

beech tree	haya	*'ah-yah*
cypress tree	ciprés (*m*)	*see-'prehs*
fir tree	abeto	*ah-'beh-toh*
fruit tree	frutero	*froo-'teh-roh*
• apple tree	manzano	*mahn-'zah-noh*
• cherry tree	cerezo	*seh-'reh-soh*
• fig tree	higuera	*ee-'geh-rah*
• lemon tree	limonero	*lee-moh-'neh-roh*
• olive tree	olivo	*oh-'lee-boh*
• orange tree	naranjo	*nah-'rahn-hoh*
• peach tree	duraznero	*doo-rahs-'neh-roh*
	melocotonero	*meh-loh-koh-toh-'neh-roh*
• pear tree	peral (*m*)	*peh-'rahl*
• walnut tree	nogal (*m*)	*noh-'gahl*
maple tree	arce (*m*)	*'ahr-seh*
oak tree	roble (*m*)	*'roh-bleh*
palm tree	palma	*'pahl-mah*

pine tree	pino	*'pee-noh*
poplar tree	álamo	*'ah-lah-moh*
tree	árbol (*m*)	*'ahr-bohl*

d. FRUITS

apple	manzana	*mahn-'zah-nah*
apricot	albaricoque (*m*)	*ahl-bah-ree-'koh-keh*
banana	banana	*bah-'nah-nah*
	plátano	*'plah-tah-noh*
blackberry	zarzamora	*sahr-sah-'moh-rah*
cherry	cereza	*seh-'reh-sah*
chestnut	castaña	*kah-'stah-nyah*
citrus	fruta agria	*'froo-tah 'ah-gree·ah*
• **citric**	cítrico (*adj*)	*'see-tree-koh*
date	dátil (*m*)	*'dah-teel*
dried fruit	frutas secas	*'froo-tahs 'seh-kahs*
fig	higo	*'ee-goh*
fruit	fruta	*'froo-tah*
grapefruit	toronja	*toh-'rohn-hah*
	pomelo	*poh-'meh-loh*
grapes	uvas	*'oo-bahs*
lemon	limón	*lee-'mohn*
mandarin orange	mandarina	*mahn-dah-'ree-nah*
melon	melón	*meh-'lohn*
olive	oliva	*oh-'lee-bah*
orange	naranja	*nah-'rahn-hah*
peach	durazno	*doo-'rahs-noh*
	melocotón	*meh-loh-koh-'tohn*
peanut	cacahuete (*m*)	*kah-kah-'weh-teh*
	maní (*m*)	*mah-'nee*
pear	pera	*'peh-rah*
pineapple	piña	*'pee-nyah*
plum	ciruela	*see-'rweh-lah*
prune	ciruela pasa	*see-'rweh-lah 'pah-sah*
raspberry	frambuesa	*frahm-'bweh-sah*
strawberry	fresa	*'freh-sah*
walnut	nuez (*f*)	*'nwehs*
watermelon	sandía	*sahn-'dee-ah*

e. VEGETABLES AND HERBS

artichoke	alcachofa	*ahl-kah-'choh-fah*
asparagus	espárrago	*ehs-'pah-rrah-goh*
basil	albahaca	*al-bah-'ah-kah*
beans	frijoles (*m*, *pl*)	*free-'hoh-lehs*
	habas (*f*, *pl*)	*'ah-bahs*
beet	remolacha	*reh-moh-'lah-chah*

broccoli	brécol (*m*)	*'breh-kohl*
	bróculi (*m*)	*'broh-koo-lee*
cabbage	col (*f*)	*kohl*
	repollo	*reh-'poh-yoh*
carrot	zanahoria	*sah-nah-'oh-ree-ah*
cauliflower	coliflor (*f*)	*koh-lee-'flohr*
celery	apio	*'ah-pee-oh*
corn	maíz (*m*)	*mah-'ees*
cucumber	pepino	*peh-'pee-noh*
eggplant	berenjena	*beh-rehn-'heh-nah*
fennel	hinojo	*ee-'noh-hoh*
garden	jardín (*m*)	*hahr-'deen*
• **vegetable garden**	huerta	*'wehr-tah*
garlic	ajo	*'ah-hoh*
grass	césped (*m*)	*'sehs-pehd*
	hierba	*ee-'ehr-bah*
green pepper	pimiento verde	*pee-mee-'ehn-toh*
		'vehr-deh
lentil	lenteja	*lehn-'teh-hah*
lettuce	lechuga	*leh-'choo-gah*
lima bean	frijol de media luna	*free-'hohl deh 'meh-*
	(*m*)	*dee-ah 'loo-nah*
mint	menta	*'mehn-tah*
mushroom	seta	*'seh-tah*
	hongo	*'ohn-goh*
onion	cebolla	*seh-'boh-yah*
parsley	perejil (*m*)	*peh-reh-'heel*
pea	guisante (*m*)	*gee-'sahn-teh*
potato	papa	*'pah-pah*
	patata	*pah-'tah-tah*
pumpkin	calabaza	*kah-lah-'bah-sah*
radish	rábano	*'rah-bah-noh*
rhubarb	ruibarbo	*rwee-'bahr-boh*
rosemary	romero	*roh-'meh-roh*
spinach	espinaca	*ehs-pee-'nah-kah*
string bean	judía verde	*hoo-'dee-ah 'behr-deh*
tomato	tomate (*m*)	*toh-'mah-teh*
turnip	nabo	*'nah-boh*
vegetable	legumbre (*f*)	*leh-'goom-breh*
	vegetal (*m, adj*)	*beh-heh-'tahl*
zucchini	calabacín (*m*)	*kah-lah-bah-'seen*

15. THE ANIMAL WORLD

a. ANIMALS

animal	animal (*m*)	*ah-nee-'mahl*
bat	murciélago	*moor-see-'eh-lah-goh*

bear	oso	'oh-soh
beast	bestia	'behs-tee·ah
buffalo	búfalo	'boo-fah-loh
bull	toro	'toh-roh
camel	camello	kah-'meh-yoh
cat	gato	'gah-toh
• meow	maullar (v*)	mow-'yahr
cow	vaca	'bah-kah
deer	venado	beh-'nah-doh
dog	perro	'peh-rroh
• bark	ladrar (v)	lah-'drahr
donkey	burro	'boo-rroh
elephant	elefante (m)	eh-leh-'fahn-teh
farm	granja	'grahn-hah
	hacienda	ah-see-'ehn-dah
• barn	establo	ehs-'tah-bloh
• farmer	campesino	kahm-peh-'see-noh
	labrador (m)	lah-brah-'dohr
• fence	cerca	'sehr-kah
fox	zorro	'soh-rroh
giraffe	jirafa	hee-'rah-fah
goat	cabra	'kah-brah
hare	liebre (f)	lee-'eh-breh
hippopotamus	hipopótamo	ee-poh-'poh-tah-moh
horse	caballo	kah-'bah-yoh
• neigh	relinchar (v)	reh-leen-'chahr
hunter	cazador (m)	kah-sah-'dohr
• hunt	cazar (v)	kah-'sahr
• hunting	caza	kah-sah
hyena	hiena	ee·'eh-nah
lamb	cordero	kohr-'deh-roh
leopard	leopardo	leh-oh-'pahr-doh
lion	león	leh-'ohn
• roar	rugir (v*)	roo-'heer
mammal	mamífero	mah-'mee-feh-roh
mole	topo	'toh-poh
monkey	mono	'moh-noh
mountain lion, cougar	puma (m)	'poo-mah
mouse	ratón (m)	rah-'tohn
mule	mulo	'moo-loh
ox	buey (m)	'bweh-ee
paw	pata	'pah-tah
pet	animal doméstico	ah-nee-'mahl doh-'mehs-tee-koh
pig	cerdo	'sehr-doh
primate	primate (m)	pree-'mah-teh
rabbit	conejo	koh-'neh-hoh

rat	rata	'rah-tah
rhinoceros	rinoceronte (m)	ree-noh-seh-'rohn-teh
sheep	carnero	kahr-'neh-roh
	oveja	oh-'beh-hah
• bleat	balar (v)	bah-'lahr
tail	cola	'koh-lah

> **to line up** = hacer cola

tiger	tigre	'tee-greh
vertebrate	vertebrado	behr-teh-'brah-doh
• invertebrate	invertebrado	een-behr-teh-'brah-doh
wild animal	animal salvaje	ah-nee-'mahl sahl-'bah-heh
wolf	lobo	'loh-boh
• howl	aullar (v*)	ow-'yahr
zebra	cebra	'seh-brah
zoo	parque (m) zoológico	'pahr-keh soh-oh-'loh-hee-koh
• zoological	zoológico (adj)	soh-oh-'loh-hee-koh
• zoology	zoología	soh-oh-loh-'hee-ah

b. BIRDS AND FOWL

albatross	albatros (m)	ahl-'bah-trohs
beak	pico	'pee-koh
bird	pájaro	'pah-hah-roh
blackbird	mirlo	'meer-loh
dove	paloma	pah-'loh-mah
duck	pato	'pah-toh
eagle	águila (f)	'ah-gee-lah
feather	pluma	'ploo-mah
• plumage	plumaje (m)	ploo-'mah-heh
goose	ánsar	'ahn-sahr
	ganso (m)	'gahn-soh
hen	gallina	gah-'yee-nah
nightingale	ruiseñor (m)	rwee-seh-'nyohr
ostrich	avestruz (f)	ah-beh-'stroos
owl	buho	'boo-oh
parakeet	perico	peh-'ree-koh
parrot	loro	'loh-roh
pelican	pelícano	peh-'lee-kah-noh
pigeon	pichón	pee-'chohn

> **to kill two birds with one stone** = matar dos pájaros en un tiro

rooster	gallo	*'gah-yoh*
seagull	gaviota	*gah-bee·'oh-tah*
sparrow	gorrión (*m*)	*goh-rree·'ohn*
swan	cisne (*m*)	*'sees-neh*
turkey	pavo	*'pah-boh*
vulture	buitre (*m*)	*'bwee-treh*
wing	ala	*'ah-lah*

c. FISH, REPTILES, AMPHIBIANS, AND MARINE MAMMALS

amphibian	anfibio (*n, adj*)	*ahn-'fee-bee·oh*
codfish	bacalao	*bah-kah-'lah-oh*
crocodile	cocodrilo	*koh-koh-'dree-loh*
dolphin	delfín (*m*)	*dehl-'feen*
eel	anguila	*ahn-'gee-lah*
fish	pez (in water)	*pehs*
	pescado (food)	*pehs-'kah-doh*
• **fin**	aleta	*ah-'leh-tah*
• **fishbone**	espina	*ehs-'pee-nah*
• **fish**	pescar (*v*)	*pehs-'kahr*
• **fisherman**	pescador (*m*)	*pehs-kah-'dohr*
• **fishing**	pesca	*'pehs-kah*
• **fishing rod**	caña de pescar	*'kah-nyah deh pehs-'kahr*
• **hook**	anzuelo	*ahn-soo·'eh-loh*
frog	rana	*rah-nah*
goldfish	carpa dorada	*'kahr-pah doh-'rah-dah*
hake	merluza	*mehr-'loo-sah*
octopus	pulpo	*'pool-poh*
red snapper	huachinango	*wah-chee-'nahn-goh*
reptile	reptil (*m*)	*rehp-'teel*
salamander	salamandra	*sah-lah-'mahn-drah*
sardine	sardina	*sahr-'dee-nah*
sea lion, seal	foca	*'foh-kah*
shark	tiburón (*m*)	*tee-boo-'rohn*
snake	serpiente (*f*)	*sehr-pee·'ehn-teh*
sole fish	lenguado	*lehn-'gwah-doh*
swordfish	pez espada (*m*)	*pehs ehs-'pah-dah*
toad	sapo	*'sah-poh*
trout	trucha	*'troo-chah*
tuna	atún (*m*)	*ah-'toon*
turtle	tortuga	*tohr-'too-gah*
whale	ballena	*bah-'yeh-nah*

d. INSECTS AND OTHER INVERTEBRATES

ant	hormiga	*ohr-'mee-gah*
bedbug	chinche (*f*)	*'cheen-cheh*
bee	abeja	*ah-'beh-hah*
bug	insecto	*een-'sehk-toh*
butterfly	mariposa	*mah-ree-'poh-sah*
caterpillar	oruga	*oh-'roo-gah*
cockroach	cucaracha	*koo-kah-'rah-chah*
cricket	grillo	*'gree-yoh*
firefly	luciérnaga	*loo-see-'ehr-nah-gah*
flea	pulga	*'pool-gah*
fly	mosca	*'mohs-kah*
grasshopper	saltamontes (*m*)	*sahl-tah-'mohn-tehs*
	chapulín (*m*)	*chah-poo-'leen*
insect	insecto	*een-'sehk-toh*
louse	piojo	*pee-'oh-hoh*
metamorphosis	metamorfosis (*f*)	*meh-tah-mohr-'foh-sees*
mosquito	mosquito	*mohs-'kee-toh*
moth	polilla	*poh-'lee-yah*
scorpion	alacrán (*m*)	*ah-lah-'krahn*
spider	araña	*ah-'rah-nyah*
termite	comején (*m*)	*koh-meh-'hehn*
tick	garrapata	*gah-rrah-'pah-tah*
wasp	avispa	*ah-'bees-pah*
worm	gusano	*goo-'sah-noh*

COMMUNICATING, FEELING, AND THINKING

16. BASIC SOCIAL EXPRESSIONS

a. GREETINGS AND FAREWELLS

Good afternoon.	Buenas tardes.	*'bweh-nahs 'tahr-dehs*
Good evening.	Buenas tardes.	*'bweh-nahs 'tahr-dehs*
Good morning.	Buenos días.	*'bweh-nohs 'dee·ahs*
Good night.	Buenas noches.	*'bweh-nahs 'noh-chehs*
Good bye.	Adiós.	*ah-dee·'ohs*
Hello.	Hola.	*'oh-lah*
How are you?	¿Cómo está usted? (*pol*)	*'koh-moh ehs-'tah oos-'tehd*
	¿Cómo estás? (*fam*)	*'koh-moh ehs-'tahs*
	¿Qué tal?	*keh tahl*
How's it going?	¿Cómo le va?	*'koh-moh leh bah*
Badly.	Mal.	*mahl*
Fine.	Bien.	*bee·'ehn*
Quite well.	Bastante bien.	*bahs-'tahn-teh bee·'ehn*
So, so.	Regular.	*reh-goo-'lahr*
Very well.	Muy bien.	*mwee bee·'ehn*
Pleased to meet you.	Mucho gusto en conocerlo(la).	*'moo-choh 'goos-toh ehn koh-noh-'sehr-loh (-lah)*
See you.	Hasta luego.	*'ahs-tah 'lweh-goh*
• **See you soon.**	Hasta pronto.	*'ahs-tah 'prohn-toh*
• **See you Sunday.**	Hasta el domingo.	*'ahs-tah ehl doh-'meen-goh*
• **See you tomorrow.**	Hasta mañana.	*'ahs-tah mah-'nyah-nah*
Shake hands with . . .	Dar la mano a . . .	*dahr lah 'mah-noh ah*
• **handshake**	apretón de manos (*m*)	*ah-preh-'tohn deh 'mah-nohs*

b. FORMS OF ADDRESS AND INTRODUCTIONS

A pleasure.	Mucho gusto.	*'moo-choh 'goos-toh*
• **The pleasure is mine.**	El gusto es mío.	*ehl 'goos-toh ehs 'mee·oh*
• **Likewise.**	Igualmente.	*ee-gwahl-'mehn-teh*
Allow me to introduce myself.	Permítame presentarme.	*pehr-'mee-tah-meh preh-sehn-'tahr-meh*

Allow me to introduce you to . . .	Permítame presentarlo(la) a . . .	*pehr-'mee-tah-meh preh-sehn-'tahr-loh (-lah) ah*
be on a first-name basis	tutear (v)	*too-teh-'ahr*
calling card	tarjeta de visita	*tahr-'heh-tah deh bee-'see-tah*
Come in. (Enter)	Pase usted.	*'pah-seh oos-'tehd*
	Pasen ustedes. (pl)	*'pah-sehn oos-'teh-dehs*
Delighted.	Encantado(a).	*ehn-kahn-'tah-doh (-dah)*
introduce oneself	presentarse (v)	*preh-sehn-'tahr-seh*
• **introduction**	presentación	*preh-sehn-tah-see-'ohn*
know someone	conocer (v*)	*koh-noh-'sehr*
title	título	*'tee-too-loh*
• **Dr.**	Doctor(a) (Dr.)	*dohk-'tohr(ah)*
• **Miss**	Señorita (Srta.)	*seh-nyoh-'ree-tah*
• **Mr.**	Señor (Sr.)	*seh-'nyohr*
• **Mrs.**	Señora (Sra.)	*seh-'nyoh-rah*
What's your name?	¿Cómo se llama usted?	*'koh-moh seh 'yah-mah oos-'tehd*
• **My name is . . .**	Me llamo . . .	*meh 'yah-moh*
• **I'm . . .**	Soy . . .	*soy*

c. COURTESY

Bless you. (*after a sneeze*)	Salud.	*sah-'lood*
Cheers.	Salud.	*sah-'lood*
Congratulations.	Enhorabuena.	*ehn-oh-rah-'bweh-nah*
	Felicitaciones.	*feh-lee-see-tah-see-'oh-nehs*
Don't mention it.	No hay de qué.	*noh 'ah·ee deh keh*
Eat up.	Buen apetito.	*bwehn ah-peh-'tee-toh*
	Buen provecho.	*bwehn proh-'beh-choh*
Excuse me.	Perdón.	*pehr-'dohn*
	Discúlpeme.	*dees-'kool-peh-meh*
Good luck.	Buena suerte.	*'bweh-nah 'swehr-teh*
Happy Birthday.	Feliz cumpleaños.	*feh-'lees koom-pleh-'ah-nyohs*
Happy New Year.	Feliz Año Nuevo.	*feh-'lees 'ah-nyoh 'nweh-boh*
Have a good holiday.	¡Qué pase(n) buenas vacaciones!	*keh 'pah-sehn 'bweh-nahs bah-kah-see-'oh-nehs*
Have a good time.	¡Diviértase!	*dee-bee-'ehr-tah-seh*
	¡Diviértanse! (pl)	*dee-bee-'ehr-tahn-seh*

Have a good trip.	Buen viaje.	*bwehn bee-'ah-heh*
Many thanks.	Muchas gracias.	*'moo-chahs 'grah-see·ahs*
May I come in?	¿Puedo pasar?	*'pweh-doh pah-'sahr*
May I help you?	¿En qué puedo servirlo(la)?	*ehn keh 'pweh-doh sehr-'beer-loh (-lah)*
Merry Christmas.	Feliz Navidad.	*feh-'lees nah-bee-'dahd*
Please.	Por favor.	*pohr fah-'bohr*
You're welcome.	De nada.	*deh 'nah-dah*
Thank you.	Gracias.	*'grah-see·ahs*

17. SPEAKING AND TALKING

a. SPEECH ACTIVITIES AND TYPES

advice	consejo	*kohn-'seh-hoh*
• advise	aconsejar (*v*)	*ah-kohn-seh-'hahr*
allude	aludir (*v*)	*ah-loo-'deer*
analogy	analogía	*ah-nah-loh-'gee-ah*
announce	anunciar (*v*)	*ah-noon-see-'ahr*
• announcement	anuncio	*ah-'noon-see-oh*
answer	responder (*v*)	*rehs-pohn-'dehr*
	contestar (*v*)	*kohn-tehs-'tahr*
• answer	respuesta	*rehs-'pwehs-tah*
argue	reñir (*v**)	*reh-'nyeer*
• argument	disputa	*dees-'poo-tah*
articulate	articular (*v*)	*ahr-tee-koo-'lahr*
ask	preguntar (*v*)	*preh-goon-'tahr*
beg to do something	rogarle (*v**) hacer una cosa	*roh-'gahr-leh ah-'sehr 'oo-nah 'koh-sah*
call	llamar (*v*)	*yah-'mahr*
change the subject	cambiar (*v*) de tema	*kahm-bee-'ahr deh 'teh-mah*
chat	charlar (*v*)	*chahr-'lahr*
communicate	comunicar (*v*)	*koh-moo-nee-'kahr*
• communication	comunicación (*f*)	*koh-moo-nee-kah-see-'ohn*
compare	comparar (*v*)	*kohm-pah-'rahr*
• comparison	comparación (*f*)	*kohm-pah-rah-see-'ohn*
conclude	concluir (*v**)	*konh-kloo-'eer*
• conclusion	conclusión (*f*)	*kohn-kloo-see-'ohn*
congratulate	felicitar (*v*)	*feh-lee-see-'tahr*
conversation	conversación (*f*)	*kohn-behr-sah-see-'ohn*
debate	debatir (*v*)	*deh-bah-'teer*
• debate	debate (*m*)	*deh-'bah-teh*
declare	declarar (*v*)	*deh-klah-'rahr*
deny	negar (*v**)	*neh-'gahr*

describe	describir (*v*)	*dehs-kree-'beer*
• description	descripción (*f*)	*dehs-kreep-see·'ohn*
develop	desarrollar (*v*)	*dehs-ah-rroh-'yahr*
dictate	dictar (*v*)	*deek-'tahr*
digress	divagar (*v*)	*dee-bah-'gahr*
discuss	discutir (*v*)	*dees-koo-'teer*
• discussion	discusión (*f*)	*dees-koo-see·'ohn*
emphasize	enfatizar (*v*)	*ehn-fah-tee-'sahr*
• emphasis	énfasis (*m*)	*'ehn-fah-sees*
excuse oneself	disculparse (*v*)	*dees-kool-'pahr-seh*
• excuse	excusa	*ehks-'koo-sah*
explain	explicar (*v*)	*ehks-plee-'kahr*
• explanation	explicación (*f*)	*ehks-plee-kah-see·'ohn*
express oneself	expresarse (*v*)	*ehks-preh-'sahr-seh*
• express	expresar (*v*)	*ehks-preh-'sahr*
• expression	expresión (*f*)	*ehks-preh-see·'ohn*
figure of speech	figura retórica	*fee-'goo-rah reh-'toh-ree-kah*
• allegory	alegoría	*ah-leh-goh-'ree·ah*
• literal	literal (*adj*)	*lee-teh-'rahl*
• metaphor	metáfora	*meh-'tah-foh-rah*
• symbol	símbolo	*'seem-boh-loh*
gossip	chismear (*v*)	*chees-meh-'ahr*
• gossip	chisme (*m*)	*'chees-meh*
hesitate	vacilar (*v*)	*bah-see-'lahr*
• hesitation	vacilación (*f*)	*bah-see-lah-see·'ohn*
identify	identificar (*v*)	*ee-dehn-tee-fee-'kahr*
indicate, point out	señalar (*v*)	*seh-nyah-'lahr*
• indication	indicación (*f*)	*een-dee-kah-see·'ohn*
inform	avisar (*v*)	*ah-bee-'sahr*
interrupt	interrumpir (*v*)	*een-teh-rroom-'peer*
• interruption	interrupción (*f*)	*een-teh-rroop-see·'ohn*
invite	invitar (*v*)	*een-bee-'tahr*
• invitation	invitación (*f*)	*een-bee-tah-see·'ohn*
jest	bromear (*v*)	*broh-meh-'ahr*
joke	chiste (*m*)	*'chees-teh*
• tell a joke	contar (*v**) un chiste	*kohn-'tahr oon 'chees-teh*
keep quiet	callarse (*v*)	*kah-'yahr-seh*
lecture	conferencia	*kohn-feh-'rehn-see·ah*
• lecture	dar (*v**) una conferencia	*dahr 'oo-nah kohn-feh-'rehn-see·ah*
lie	mentir (*v**)	*mehn-'teer*
• lie	mentira	*mehn-'tee-rah*
listen to	escuchar (*v*)	*ehs-koo-'chahr*
malign, speak badly	hablar (*v*) mal de	*ah-'blahr mahl deh*

mean	querer (*v**) decir (*v*)	*keh-'rehr deh-'seer*
	significar (*v*)	*seeg-nee-fee-'kahr*
• meaning	significado	*seeg-nee-fee-'kah-doh*
mention	mencionar (*v*)	*mehn-see-oh-'nahr*
mumble	mascullar (*v*)	*mahs-koo-'yahr*
murmur	murmurar (*v*)	*moor-moor-'ahr*
nag	regañar (*v*)	*reh-gah-'nyahr*
offend	ofender (*v*)	*oh-fehn-'dehr*
oral	oral (*adj*)	*oh-'rahl*
• orally	oralmente (*adv*)	*oh-rahl-'mehn-teh*
order	mandar (*v*)	*mahn-'dahr*
• order	mandato	*mahn-'dah-toh*
outspoken	franco (*adj*)	*'frahn-koh*
praise	alabar (*v*)	*ah-lah-'bahr*
pray	rezar (*v*)	*reh-'sahr*
	orar (*v*)	*oh-'rahr*
• prayer	oración (*f*)	*oh-rah-see-'ohn*
preach	predicar (*v*)	*preh-dee-'kahr*
• sermon	sermón (*m*)	*sehr-'mohn*
predict	predecir (*v**)	*preh-deh-'seer*
promise	prometer (*v*)	*proh-meh-'tehr*
• promise	promesa	*proh-'meh-sah*
pronounce	pronunciar (*v*)	*proh-noon-see-'ahr*
• pronunciation	pronunciación (*f*)	*proh-noon-see-ah-see-'ohn*
propose	proponer (*v**)	*proh-poh-'nehr*
recommend	recomendar (*v**)	*reh-koh-mehn-'dahr*
relate	relatar (*v*)	*reh-lah-'tahr*
repeat	repetir (*v**)	*reh-peh-'teer*
• repetition	repetición (*f*)	*reh-peh-tee-see-'ohn*
report	relatar (*v*)	*reh-lah-'tahr*
• report	informe (*m*)	*een-'fohr-meh*
reproach	reprochar (*v*)	*reh-proh-'chahr*
request	pedir (*v**)	*peh-'deer*
• request	petición (*f*)	*peh-tee-see-'ohn*
rhetoric	retórica	*reh-'toh-ree-kah*
• rhetorical	retórico (*adj*)	*reh-'toh-ree-koh*
• rhetorical question	pregunta retórica	*preh-'goon-tah reh-'toh-ree-kah*
rumor	rumor (*m*)	*roo-'mohr*
• Rumor has it that . . .	Se dice que . . .	*seh 'dee-seh keh*
say, tell	decir (*v**)	*deh-'seer*
share	compartir (*v*)	*kohm-pahr-'teer*
shout, yell	gritar (*v*)	*gree-'tahr*
• shout, yell	grito	*'gree-toh*
shut up	callarse (*v*)	*kah-'yahr-seh*

silence	silencio	see-'lehn-see·oh
• silent	silencioso (adj)	see-lehn-see·'oh-soh
speak, talk	decir (v*)	deh-'seer
• speech, talk	discurso	dees-'koor-soh
state	declarar (v)	deh-klah-'rahr
• statement	declaración (f)	deh-klah-rah-see·'ohn
story	cuento	'kwehn-toh
• tell a story	contar (v*)	kohn-'tahr
suggest	sugerir (v*)	soo-heh-'reer
summarize	resumir (v)	reh-soo-'meer
• summary	resumen	reh-'soo-mehn
swear (in court)	jurar (v)	hoo-'rahr
swear (profanity)	maldecir (v*)	mahl-deh-'seer
thank	agradecer (v*)	ah-grah-deh-'sehr
threaten	amenazar (v)	ah-meh-nah-'sahr
• threat	amenaza	ah-meh-'nah-sah
toast	brindar (v)	breen-'dahr
• toast	brindis (m)	'breen-dees
translate	traducir (v*)	trah-doo-'seer
• translation	traducción (f)	trah-dook-see·'ohn
utter	pronunciar (v)	proh-noon-see·'ahr
vocabulary	vocabulario	boh-kah-boo-'lah-ree·oh
warn	advertir (v*)	ahd-behr-'teer
• warning	aviso	ah-'bee-soh
	advertencia	ahd-behr-'tehn-see·ah
whisper	cuchichear (v)	koo-chee-cheh-'ahr
	susurrar (v)	soo-soo-'rrahr
word	palabra	pah-'lah-brah
	vocablo	boh-'kah-bloh
yawn	bostezar (v)	bohs-teh-'sahr
• yawn	bostezo	bohs-'teh-soh
yell	gritar (v)	gree-'tahr

b. USEFUL EXPRESSIONS

actually	en realidad	ehn reh-ah-lee-'dahd
as a matter of fact	en realidad	ehn reh-ah-lee-'dahd
	de hecho	deh 'eh-choh
briefly	brevemente (adv)	breh-beh-'mehn-teh
by the way	a propósito	ah proh-'poh-see-toh
Go ahead.	¡Adelante!	ah-deh-'lahn-teh
I didn't understand.	No entendí.	noh ehn-tehn-'dee
How do you say . . .	¿Cómo se dice . . .	'koh-moh seh 'dee-seh
in Spanish?	en español?	ehn ehs-pah-'nyohl
I'm sure that . . .	Estoy seguro(a) de	ehs-'toy seh-'goo-roh
	que . . .	(-rah) deh keh
Isn't it so?	¿Verdad?	behr-'dahd

It seems that . . .	Parece que . . .	*pah-'reh-seh keh*
It's not true.	No es verdad.	*noh ehs behr-'dahd*
It's obvious that . . .	Es obvio que . . .	*ehs 'ohb-bee-oh keh*
It's true!	¡Es verdad!	*ehs behr-'dahd*
Listen!	¡Escuche!	*ehs-'koo-cheh*
now	ahora	*ah-'oh-rah*
to sum up	en resumen	*ehn reh-'soo-mehn*
You don't say!	¡No me digas!	*non me 'dee-gahs*
Who knows?	¿Quién sabe?	*kee·'ehn 'sah-beh*

18. THE TELEPHONE

a. TELEPHONES AND ACCESSORIES

answering machine	contestador automático	*kohn-tehs-tah-'dohr ow-toh-'mah-tee-koh*
cable	cable (*m*)	*'kah-bleh*
fax machine	fax (*m*)	*fahks*
intercom	interfono	*een-tehr-'foh-noh*
plug	clavija	*klah-'bee-hah*
receiver, earphone	auricular (*m*)	*ow-ree-koo-'lahr*
	receptor (*m*)	*reh-seph-'tohr*
telecommunication	telecomunicación (*f*)	*teh-leh-koh-moo-nee-kah-see·'ohn*
• **telecommunications satellite**	satélite de telecomunicación	*sah-'teh-lee-teh deh teh-leh-koh-moo-nee-kah-see·'ohn*
telephone	teléfono	*teh-'leh-foh-noh*
• **outlet**	toma	*'toh-mah*
• **pay telephone**	teléfono público	*teh-'leh-foh-noh 'poo-blee-koh*
• **portable telephone**	teléfono remoto	*teh-'leh-foh-noh reh-'moh-toh*
• **telephone book**	guía de teléfonos	*'gee·ah deh teh-'leh-foh-nohs*
token	ficha	*'fee-chah*
• **slot** (*for tokens*)	ranura	*rah-'noo-rah*
yellow pages	páginas amarillas	*'pah-hee-nahs ah-mah-'ree-yahs*

b. USING THE TELEPHONE

answer	responder a (*v*)	*rehs-pohn-'dehr ah*
	contestar a (*v*)	*kohn-tehs-'tahr ah*
area code	zona teléfonica	*'soh-nah teh-leh-'foh-nee-kah*
calling card	tarjeta telefónica	*tahr-'heh-tah teh-leh-'foh-nee-kah*

collect call	llamada de cobro revertido	*yah-'mah-dah deh 'koh-broh reh-behr-'tee-doh*
dial	marcar (*v*)	*mahr-'kahr*
• **direct dialing**	marcación directa (*f*)	*mahr-kah-see-'ohn dee-'rehk-tah*
• **dial direct**	marcar directo (*v*)	*mahr-'kahr dee-'rehk-toh*
fax	fax (*m*)	*fahks*
hang up	colgar (*v**)	*kohl-'gahr*
information	información (*f*)	*een-fohr-mah-see-'ohn*
long-distance call	llamada de larga distancia	*yah-'mah-dah deh 'lahr-gah dees-'tahn-see·ah*
make a call	hacer (*v**) una llamada	*ah-'sehr 'oo-nah yah-'mah-dah*
• **Hello**	Aló (*Latin America*)	*ah-'loh*
	Bueno (*Mexico*)	*'bweh-noh*
	Diga (*Spain*)	*'dee-gah*
• **Is . . . in?**	¿Está . . . ?	*ehs-'tah*
• **This is . . .**	Habla . . .	*'ah-blah*
• **Who's speaking?**	¿De parte de quién?	*deh 'pahr-teh deh kee-'ehn*
• **Wrong number.**	Número equivocado.	*'noo-meh-roh eh-kee-boh-'kah-doh*
message	mensaje (*m*)	*mehn-'sah-heh*
operator	telefonista (*m, f*), operador(a)	*teh-leh-foh-'nees-tah, oh-peh-rah-'dohr (-rah)*
phone	llamar (*v*) por teléfono	*yah-'mahr pohr teh-'leh-foh-noh*
pound sign	signo de libra	*'seeg-noh deh 'lee-brah*
ring	sonar (*v**)	*soh-'nahr*
star	asterisco	*ah-steh-'rees-koh*
telephone bill	cuenta telefónica	*'kwehn-tah teh-leh-'foh-nee-kah*
telephone line	línea telefónica	*'lee-neh-ah teh-leh-'foh-nee-kah*
• **busy** (*line*)	ocupada	*oh-koo-'pah-dah*
• **free** (*line*)	libre	*'lee-breh*
telephone number	número de teléfono	*'noo-meh-roh deh teh-'leh-foh-noh*
toll-free	sin cargo, gratis	*seen 'kahr-goh, 'grah-tees*

19. LETTER WRITING

a. FORMAL SALUTATIONS/CLOSINGS

Dear Sir(s):	Estimado(s) señor(es):	*ehs-tee-'mah-doh(s) seh-'nyohr (-'nyoh-rehs)*

Dear Madam:	Estimada señora:	ehs-tee-'mah-dah seh-'nyoh-rah
To Whom It May Concern:	A quien corresponda:	ah kee-'ehn koh-rrehs-'pohn-dah
Attentively,	Atentamente,	ah-tehn-tah-'mehn-teh
Attentively yours,	De usted atentamente,	deh oos-'tehd ah-tehn-tah-'-mehn-teh
Sincerely,	Sinceramente,	seen-seh-rah-'mehn-teh

b. FAMILIAR SALUTATIONS/CLOSINGS

Dear . . . ,	Querido(a) . . . ,	keh-'ree-doh (-dah)
With love,	Con cariño,	kohn kah-'ree-nyoh
Affectionately,	Cariñosamente,	kah-ree-nyoh-sah-'mehn-teh
With much love,	Con mucho cariño,	kohn 'moo-choh kah-'ree-nyoh
A kiss,	Un beso,	oon 'beh-soh
A hug,	Un abrazo,	oon ah-'brah-soh

c. PARTS OF A LETTER/PUNCTUATION

body	cuerpo	'kwehr-poh
closing	despedida	dehs-peh-'dee-dah
date	fecha	'feh-chah
heading	membrete(m)	mehm-'breh-teh
parenthesis	paréntesis (m)	pah-'rehn-teh-sees
place	lugar (m)	loo-'gahr
punctuation	puntuación (f)	poon-twah-see-'ohn
• accent	acento	ah-'sehn-toh
• apostrophe	apóstrofe (m)	ah-'pohs-troh-feh
• asterisk	asterisco	ahs-teh-'rees-koh
• bracket	paréntesis (m)	pah-'rehn-teh-sees
• capital letter	mayúscula	mah-'yohs-koo-lah
• colon	dos puntos	dohs 'poon-tohs
• comma	coma	'koh-mah
• exclamation mark	signo de admiración	'seeg-noh deh ahd-mee-rah-see-'ohn
• hyphen	guión (m)	gee-'ohn
• italics	bastardilla	bahs-tahr-'dee-yah
• period	punto	'poon-toh
• question mark	signo de interrogación	'seeg-noh deh een-teh-rroh-gah-see-'ohn
• quotation mark	comillas	koh-'mee-yahs
• semicolon	punto y coma	'poon-toh ee 'koh-mah
• small letter	minúscula	mee-'noos-koo-lah
• square bracket	corchete (m)	kohr-'cheh-teh
• underlining	subrayado	soob-rrah-'yah-doh

salutation	salutación (*f*)	*sah-loo-tah-see-'ohn*
	saludo	*sah-'loo-doh*
signature	firma	*'feer-mah*
• **sign**	firmar (*v*)	*feer-'mahr*
text	texto	*'tehks-toh*
• **abbreviation**	abreviatura	*ah-breh-bee-ah-'too-rah*
• **letter** (*of the alphabet*)	letra	*'leh-trah*
• **line**	línea	*'lee-neh-ah*
• **margin**	margen (*m*)	*'mahr-hehn*
• **P. S.**	P. D. (postdata)	*pohs-'dah-tah*
• **paragraph**	párrafo	*'pah-rrah-foh*
• **phrase**	frase (*f*)	*'frah-seh*
• **sentence**	oración (*f*)	*oh-rah-see-'ohn*
• **spelling**	ortografía	*ohr-toh-grah-'fee·ah*
• **word**	palabra	*pah-'lah-brah*
	vocablo	*boh-'kah-bloh*

FOCUS: Letters

Madrid, 24 junio 2002	**Place and date** Lugar y fecha
Estimados señores:	**Salutation** Saludo
En respuesta a su carta con fecha de. . . .	**Body of the letter** Texto de la carta
De usted atentamente.	**Complimentary close** Despedida
José González	**Signature** Firma

d. WRITING MATERIALS AND ACCESSORIES

adhesive tape	cinta adhesiva	*'seen-tah ahd-eh-'see-bah*
computer	computadora (*Latin America*)	*kohm-poo-tah-'doh-rah*
	ordenador (*m*) (*Spain*)	*ohr-deh-nah-'dohr*
envelope	sobre (*m*)	*'soh-breh*
eraser	goma de borrar	*'goh-mah deh boh-'rrahr*

glue	pegamento	*peh-gah-'mehn-toh*
ink	tinta	*'teen-tah*
letter	carta	*'kahr-tah*
letterhead	papel con membrete *(m)*	*pah-'pehl kohn mehm-'breh-teh*
marker	marcador *(m)*	*mahr-kah-'dohr*
pad	bloc *(m)*	*blohk*
page	página	*'pah-hee-nah*
paper	papel *(m)*	*pah-'pehl*
paper clip	sujetapapeles *(m)*	*soo-heh-tah-pah-'peh-lehs*
pen	pluma	*'ploo-mah*
• ballpoint pen	bolígrafo	*boh-'lee-grah-foh*
• felt pen	rotulador *(m)*	*roh-too-lah-'dohr*
pencil	lápiz *(m)*	*'lah-pees*
ruler	regla	*'reh-glah*
scissors	tijeras *(f)*	*tee-'heh-rahs*
staple	grapa	*'grah-pah*
• stapler	engrapador *(m)*	*ehn-grah-pah-'dohr*
string	cordel *(m)*	*kohr-'dehl*
typewriter	máquina de escribir	*'mah-kee-nah deh ehs-kree-'beer*
• carriage	carro	*'kah-rroh*
• keyboard	teclado	*teh-'klah-doh*
• margin	margen *(m)*	*'mahr-hehn*
• ribbon	cinta de máquina de escribir	*'seen-tah deh 'mah-kee-nah deh ehs-kree-'beer*
• space bar	espaciador *(m)*	*ehs-pah-see·ah-'dohr*
• tab	tabulador *(m)*	*tah-boo-lah-'dohr*
word processor	procesador de texto *(m)*	*proh-seh-sah-'dohr deh 'tehks-toh*

For additional computer terms, see Section 42.

e. AT THE POST OFFICE

abroad	al extranjero	*ahl ehks-trahn-'heh-roh*
address	dirección *(f)*	*dee-rehk-see·'ohn*
	señas	*'seh-nyahs*
• return address	dirección del remitente *(m)*	*dee-rehk-see·'ohn dehl reh-mee-'tehn-teh*
addressee	destinatario	*dehs-tee-nah-'tah-ree·oh*
airmail	por avión	*pohr ah-bee-'ohn*
business letter	carta comercial	*'kahr-tah koh-mehr-see·'ahl*

clerk	dependiente	*deh-pehn-dee-'ehn-teh*
clerk's window	ventanilla	*behn-tah-'nee-yah*
COD	contra reembolso	*'kohn-trah reh-ehm-'bohl-soh*
correspondence	correspondencia	*koh-rrehs-pohn-'dehn-see·ah*
courier	mensajero	*mehn-sah-'heh-roh*
envelope	sobre (*m*)	*'soh-breh*
insured	asegurado	*ah-seh-goo-'rah-doh*
letter carrier	cartero	*kahr-'teh-roh*
mail	correo	*koh-'rreh-oh*
• **mail**	echar (*v*) al correo	*eh-'chahr ahl koh-'rreh-oh*
mail delivery	distribución (*f*) de correo	*dees-tree-boo-see-'ohn deh koh-'rreh-oh*
mailbox	buzón (*m*)	*boo-'sohn*
money order	giro postal	*'hee-roh pohs-'tahl*
note	nota	*'noh-tah*
package	paquete (*m*)	*pah-'keh-teh*
postage	franqueo	*frahn-'keh-oh*
postcard	tarjeta postal	*tahr-'heh-tah pohs-'tahl*
postal code	código postal	*'koh-dee-goh pohs-'tahl*
postal rate	tarifa postal	*tah-'ree-fah pohs-'tahl*
printed matter	impresos	*eem-'preh-sohs*
registered letter	carta certificada	*'kahr-tah sehr-tee-fee-'kah-dah*
receive	recibir (*v*)	*reh-see-'beer*
reply	responder	*rehs-pohn-'dehr*
	contestar (*v*)	*kohn-tehs-'tahr*
send	mandar (*v*)	*mahn-'dahr*
sender	remitente (*m*)	*reh-mee-'tehn-teh*
special delivery	correo urgente	*koh-'rreh-oh oor-'hehn-teh*
	entrega inmediata	*ehn-'treh-gah een-meh-dee-'ah-tah*
stamp	estampilla	*ehs-tahm-'pee-yah*
	sello	*'seh-yoh*
	timbre (*m*)	*'teem-breh*
wait for	esperar (*v*)	*ehs-peh-'rahr*
write	escribir (*v*)	*ehs-kree-'beer*

20. THE MEDIA

a. PRINT MEDIA

advertising	publicidad (*f*)	*poo-blee-see-'dahd*
	propaganda	*proh-pah-'gahn-dah*
appendix	apéndice (*m*)	*ah-'pehn-dee-seh*

atlas	atlas (*m*)	*'aht-lahs*
author	autor(a)	*ow-'tohr (-ah)*
book	libro	*'lee-broh*
comics	tiras cómicas	*'tee-rahs 'koh-mee-kahs*
cover	portada	*pohr-'tah-dah*
essay	ensayo	*ehn-'sah·yoh*
fiction	ficción	*feehk-'see·ohn*
• **non-fiction**	literatura no novelesca	*lee-teh-rah-'too-rah noh noh-beh-'lehs-kah*
index	índice (*m*)	*'een-dee-seh*
magazine	revista	*reh-'beehs-tah*
• **article**	artículo	*ahr-'tee-koo-loh*
• **criticism**	crítica	*'kree-tee-kah*
• **daily newspaper**	diario	*dee-'ah-ree·oh*
• **editor**	redactor (*m*)	*reh-dahk-'tohr*
• **editorial**	editorial (*m*)	*eh-dee-toh-ree-'ahl*
• **front page**	primera plana	*pree-'meh-rah 'plah-nah*
• **headline**	titular (*m*)	*tee-too-'lahr*
• **illustration**	ilustración (*f*)	*ee-loos-trah-see·'ohn*
• **interview**	entrevista	*ehn-treh-'bees-tah*
• **journalist**	periodista (*m/f*)	*peh-ree·oh-'dees-tah*
• **news**	noticias	*noh-'tee-see·ahs*
• **obituary**	obituario	*oh-bee-'twah-ree·oh*
• **obituaries**	necrología (*f, pl*)	*neh-kroh-loh-'hee·ah*
• **photo(graph)**	foto(grafía)	*'foh-toh (foh-toh-grah-'fee·ah)*
• **reader**	lector(a)	*lehk-'tohr (-rah)*
• **reporter**	reportero	*reh-pohr-'teh-roh*
• **review**	reseña	*reh-'seh-nyah*
note	nota	*'noh-tah*
• **footnote**	nota	*'noh-tah*
novel	novela	*noh-'beh-lah*
• **adventure**	aventura	*ah-behn-'too-rah*
• **best seller**	éxito de librería	*'ehks-ee-toh deh lee-breh-'ree-ah*
• **mystery**	misterio	*mees-'teh-ree·oh*
• **plot**	trama	*'trah-mah*
• **romance**	romántica	*roh-'mahn-tee-kah*
page	página	*'pah-hee-nah*
pamphlet, brochure	folleto	*foh-'yeh-toh*
play	drama (*m*)	*'drah-mah*
	obra de teatro	*'oh-brah deh teh-'ah-troh*
• **comedy**	comedia	*koh-'meh-dee·ah*
• **drama**	drama (*m*)	*'drah-mah*
• **tragedy**	tragedia	*trah-'heh-dee·ah*

poem	poema (*m*)	*poh-'eh-mah*
• poetry	poesía	*poh-eh-'see·ah*
print	impresión (*f*)	*eem-preh-see·'ohn*
• in print	publicado	*poo-blee-'kah-doh*
	impreso	*eem-'preh-soh*
• out of print	agotado	*ah-goh-'tah-doh*
• printing	imprenta	*eem-'prehn-tah*
• typography	tipografía	*tee-poh-grah-'fee·ah*
publish	publicar (*v*)	*poo-blee-'kahr*
• publisher	editor (*m*)	*eh-dee-'tohr*
read	leer (*v*)	*leh-'ehr*
reference book	libro de consulta	*'lee-broh deh kohn-'sool-tah*
• definition	definición (*f*)	*deh-fee-nee-see·'ohn*
• dictionary	diccionario	*deek-see·oh-'nah-ree·oh*
• encyclopedia	enciclopedia	*ehn-see-kloh-'peh-dee·ah*
science fiction	ciencia ficción	*see·'ehn-see·ah feek-see·'ohn*
short story	cuento	*'kwehn-toh*
text	texto	*'tehks-toh*
title	título	*'tee-too-loh*
turn (pages), leaf through	hojear (*v*)	*oh-heh-'ahr*
write	escribir (*v*)	*ehs-kree-'beer*

b. ELECTRONIC MEDIA

adapter	adaptador (*m*)	*ah-dahp-tah-'dohr*
antenna	antena	*ahn-'teh-nah*
audio equipment	equipo auditivo	*eh-'kee-poh ow-dee-'tee-boh*
• amplifier	amplificador (*m*)	*ahm-plee-fee-kah-'dohr*
• cassette	casete (*m*)	*kah-'seh-teh*
• cassette player	tocacintas (*m*)	*toh-kah-'seen-tahs*
• compact disc	disco compacto	*'dees-koh kohm-'pahk-toh*
• headphones	auriculares (*m*)	*ow-ree-koo-'lah-rehs*
• microphone	micrófono	*mee-'kroh-foh-noh*
• play (a recording)	tocar (*v*)	*toh-'kahr*
• receiver	receptor (*m*)	*reh-sehp-'tohr*
• record	grabar (*v*)	*grah-'bahr*
• speaker	altavoz (*m*)	*ahl-tah-'bohs*
• tape recorder	grabadora	*grah-bah-'doh-rah*
• tuner	sintonizador (*m*)	*seen-toh-nee-sah-'dohr*
battery charger	cargador (*m*) de pilas	*kahr-gah-'dohr deh 'pee-lahs*

cellphone	teléfono celular, móvil	*teh-'leh-foh-noh ceh-loo-'lahr, 'moh-beel*
copier	copiadora	*koh-pee·ah-'doh-rah*
cordless phone	teléfono remoto	*teh-'leh-foh-noh reh-'moh-toh*
digital image stabilization	estabilización (*f*) de imagen	*eh-stah-bee-lee-sah-see-'ohn deh ee-'mah-hehn*
digital video camera	videocámara digital	*bee-deh-oh-'kah-mah-rah dee-hee-'tahl*
DVD player	grabadora de DVD	*grah-bah-'doh-rah deh deh beh deh*
earphones with microphone (for cellphones)	auriculares con micrófono	*ow-ree-koo-'lah-rehs kohn mee-'kroh-foh-noh*
GPS (global position satellite)	sistema de posicionamiento global	*see-'steh-mah deh poh-see-see·oh-nah-mee-'ehn-toh gloh-'bahl*
lithium battery	batería de litio, pila de litio	*bah-teh-'ree-ah deh 'lee-tee·oh, 'pee-lah deh 'lee-tee·oh*
mobile phone	teléfono móvil	*teh-'leh-foh-noh 'moh-beel*
mp3 player	reproductor (*m*) de mp3	*reh-proh-dook-'tohr deh 'eh-meh peh trehs*
organizer	organizador (*m*)	*ohr-gah-nee-sah-'dohr*
pager	localizador (*m*) alfanumérico	*loh-kah-lee-sah-'dohr ahl fah-noo-'meh-ree-koh*
portable CD player	reproductor (*m*) portátil de CD	*reh-proh-dook-'toh pohr-'tah-teel deh seh-deh*
program	programa (*m*)	*proh-'grah-mah*
projector	proyector (*m*)	*proh-yehk-'tohr*
• slide projector	proyector de diapositivas	*proh-yehk-'tohr deh dee·ah-poh-see-'tee-bahs*
radio	radio	*'rah-dee·oh*
• car radio	radio	*'rah-dee·oh*
• listen to	escuchar (*v*)	*ehs-koo-'chahr*
• news report	noticias	*noh-'tee·see·ahs*
• newscast	noticiario	*noh-tee-see-'ah-ree·oh*
• pocket radio	radio de bolsillo	*'rah-dee·oh deh bohl-see·yoh*
• station	estación (*f*)	*ehs-tah-see-'ohn*
remote control	control (*m*) remoto	*kohn-'trohl reh-'moh-toh*
show	función (*f*)	*foon-see-'ohn*
stereo system	equipo estéreo (*m*)	*eh-'kee-poh ehs-'teh-reh·oh*

television	televisión (*f*)	*teh-leh-bee-see·'ohn*
• **be on the air**	estar (*v**) transmitiendo	*ehs-'tahr trahns-mee-tee·'ehn-doh*
• **channel**	canal (*m*)	*kah-'nahl*
• **closed circuit**	circuito cerrado	*seer-'kwee-toh seh-'rrah-doh*
• **commercial**	anuncio	*ah-'noon-see·oh*
• **documentary**	documental	*doh-koo-mehn-'tahl*
• **interview**	entrevista	*ehn-tre-'bees-tah*
• **look at, watch**	mirar (*v*)	*mee-'rahr*
• **network**	cadena	*kah-'deh-nah*
• **remote control**	control remoto	*kohn-'trohl reh-'moh-toh*
• **series**	serie (*f*)	*'seh-ree·eh*
• **soap opera**	telenovela	*teh-leh-noh-'beh-lah*
• **television set**	televisor (*m*)	*teh-leh-bee-'sohr*
• **transmission**	transmisión (*f*)	*trahns-mee-see·'ohn*
• **video game**	juego electrónico	*hoo'eh-goh eh-lehk-'troh-nee-koh*
• **videocassette**	videocasete (*m*)	*bee·deh-oh-kah-'seh-teh*
• **videotape**	cinta (magnética) de video	*'seen-tah (mahg-'neh-tee-kah) deh 'bee-deh·oh*
turn off	apagar (*v*)	*ah-pah-'gahr*
turn on	poner (*v**)	*poh-'nehr*
VCR	videograbadora	*bee-deh-oh-grah-bah-'doh-rah*
	videocasetera	*bee·deh-oh-kah-seh-'teh-rah*
wireless phone	teléfono móvil	*teh-'leh-foh-noh 'moh-beel*
wireless	inalámbrico	*een-ah-'lahmb-ree-koh*

21. FEELINGS

a. MOODS/ATTITUDES/EMOTIONS

affection	cariño	*kah-'ree-nyoh*
agree	estar (*v*) de acuerdo	*ehs-'tahr deh ah-'kwehr-doh*
anger	enojo	*eh-'noh-hoh*
	ira	*'ee-rah*
anxiety, anxiousness	ansia	*'ahn-see·ah*
• **anxious**	ansioso (*adj*)	*ahn-see·'oh-soh*
	inquieto (*adj*)	*een-kee·'eh-toh*
assure	asegurar (*v*)	*ah-seh-goo-'rahr*

attitude	actitud (*f*)	*ahk-tee-'tood*
be able to	poder (*v**)	*poh-'dehr*

Where there's a will, there's a way = Querer es poder

---

bore	aburrir (*v*)	*ah-boo-'rreer*
• become bored	aburrirse (*v*)	*ah-boo'rreer-seh*
• bored	aburrido (*adj*)	*ah-boo-'rree-doh*
• boredom	aburrimiento	*ah-boo-rree-mee·'ehn-toh*
complain	quejarse (*v*)	*keh-'hahr-seh*
• complaint	queja	*'keh-hah*
cry	llorar (*v*)	*yoh-'rahr*
• crying	llanto	*'yahn-toh*
depressed	deprimido (*adj*)	*deh-pree-'mee-doh*
• depression	depresión (*f*)	*deh-preh-see·'ohn*
desperate	desesperado (*adj*)	*dehs-ehs-peh-'rah-doh*
• desperation	desesperación (*f*)	*dehs-ehs-peh-rah-see·'ohn*
disagree	no estar (*v**) de acuerdo	*noh ehs-'tahr deh ah-'kwehr-doh*
• disagreement	desacuerdo	*deh-sah-'kwehr-doh*
• be against	estar (*v**) en contra de	*ehs-'tahr ehn 'kohn-trah deh*
disappoint	decepcionar (*v*)	*deh-sehp-see·oh-'nahr*
• disappointed	decepcionado (*adj*)	*deh-sehp-see·oh-'nah-doh*
dissatisfaction	descontento	*dehs-kohn-'tehn-toh*
• dissatisfied	descontento	*dehs-kohn-'tehn-toh*
encourage	animar (*v*)	*ah-nee-'mahr*
	estimular (*v*)	*ehs-tee-moo-'lahr*
faith, trust	fe (*f*)	*feh*
	confianza	*kohn-fee·'ahn-sah*
• trust	tener (*v**) confianza	*teh-'nehr kohn-fee·'ahn-sah*
feel	sentirse (*v**)	*sehn-'teer-seh*
• feel like	tener (*v**) ganas de	*teh-'nehr 'gah-nahs deh*
flatter	adular (*v*)	*ah-doo-'lahr*
• flattery	adulación (*f*)	*ah-doo-lah-see·'ohn*
fun, enjoyment	alegría	*ah-leh-'gree·ah*
	diversión (*f*)	*dee-behr-see·'ohn*
• have fun	divertirse (*v**)	*dee-behr-'teer-seh*
happiness	felicidad (*f*)	*feh-lee-see-'dahd*
• happy	feliz (*adj*)	*feh-'lees*
	contento (*adj*)	*kohn-'tehn-toh*

have to	tener (*v**) que	*teh-'nehr keh*
hope	esperar (*v*)	*ehs-peh-'rahr*
• **hope**	esperanza	*ehs-peh-'rahn-sah*
indifference	indiferencia	*een-dee-feh-'rehn-see·ah*
• **indifferent**	indiferente (*adj*)	*een-dee-feh-'rehn-teh*
joy	alegría	*ah-leh-'gree·ah*
laugh	reír (*v**)	*reh-'eer*
• **laughter**	risa	*'ree-sah*

> **He who laughs last laughs best** = El que ríe al último ríe mejor

---

matter	importar (*v*)	*eem-pohr-'tahr*
mood	humor (*m*)	*oo-'mohr*
• **bad mood**	mal humor	*mahl oo-'mohr*
• **good mood**	buen humor	*bwehn oo-'mohr*
need	necesitar (*v*)	*neh-seh-see-'tahr*
• **need**	necesidad (*f*)	*neh-seh-see-dahd*
patience	paciencia	*pah-see·'ehn-see·ah*
• **have patience**	tener (*v**) paciencia	*teh-'nehr pah-see·'ehn-see·ah*
relief	alivio	*ah-'lee-bee·oh*
• **relieve**	aliviar (*v*)	*ah-lee-bee-'ahr*
	liberar (*v*)	*lee-beh-'rahr*
sad	triste (*adj*)	*'trees-teh*
• **sadness**	tristeza	*trees-'teh-sah*
• **become sad**	entristecerse (*v**)	*ehn-trees-teh-'sehr-seh*
satisfaction	satisfacción (*f*)	*sah-tees-fahks-see·'ohn*
• **satisfied**	satisfecho (*adj*)	*sah-tees-'feh-choh*
shame	vergüenza	*behr-'gwehn-sah*
• **be ashamed**	tener (*v**) vergüenza	*teh-'nehr behr-'gwehn-sah*
smile	sonreír (*v**)	*sohn-reh·'eer*
• **smile**	sonrisa	*sohn-'ree-sah*
sorrow	dolor (*m*)	*doh-'lohr*
	pena	*'peh-nah*
surprise	sorpresa	*sohr-'preh-sah*
• **surprise**	sorprender (*v*)	*sohr-prehn-'dehr*
• **surprised**	sorprendido (*adj*)	*sohr-prehn-'dee-doh*
sympathy (*over a death*)	pésame (*m*)	*'peh-sah-meh*
	condolencia	*kohn-doh-'lehn-see·ah*
• **sympathetic**	compasivo (*adj*)	*kohm-pah-'see-boh*
thankfulness	agradecimiento	*ah-grah-deh-see-mee·'ehn-toh*
• **thankful**	agradecido (*adj*)	*ah-grah-deh-'see-doh*
• **thank**	agradecer (*v**)	*ah-grah-deh-'sehr*

tolerance	tolerancia	*toh-leh-'rahn-see·ah*
• **tolerate**	tolerar (*v*)	*toh-leh-'rahr*
want to	querer (*v**)	*keh-'rehr*

b. LIKES AND DISLIKES

accept	aceptar (*v*)	*ah-sehp-'tahr*
• **acceptable**	aceptable (*adj*)	*ah-sehp-'tah-bleh*
• **unacceptable**	inaceptable (*adj*)	*een-ah-sehp-'tah-bleh*
approval	aprobación (*f*)	*ah-proh-bah-see-'ohn*
• **approve**	aprobar (*v**)	*ah-proh-'bahr*
be fond of	estar (*v**) encariñado con	*ehs-'tahr ehn-kah-ree-'nyah-doh kohn*
	ser (*v**) aficionado a	*sehr ah-fee-see-oh-'nah-doh ah*
detest	detestar (*v*)	*deh-tehs-'tahr*
	odiar (*v*)	*oh-dee-'ahr*
disgust	disgusto	*dees-'goos-toh*
• **disgusted**	disgustado (*adj*)	*dees-goos-'tah-doh*
hate	odiar (*v*)	*oh-dee-'ahr*
• **hatred**	odio	*'oh-dee·oh*
kiss	besar (*v*)	*beh-'sahr*
• **kiss**	beso	*'beh-soh*
like	gustarle a uno	*goos-'tahr-leh ah 'oo-noh*
• **dislike**	tener (*v**) aversión a	*teh-'nehr ah-behr-see-'ohn ah*
• **liking**	cariño	*kah-'ree-nyo*
love	amar (*v*)	*ah-'mahr*
	querer (*v**)	*keh-'rehr*
• **love**	amor (*m*)	*ah-'mohr*
mediocre	mediocre (*adj*)	*meh-dee-'oh-kreh*
pleasant	agradable (*adj*)	*ah-grah-'dah-bleh*
• **unpleasant**	desagradable (*adj*)	*dehs-ah-grah-'dah-bleh*
prefer	preferir (*v**)	*preh-feh-'reer*

c. EXPRESSING EMOTIONS

Are you joking?	¿Habla en serio?	*'ah-blah ehn 'seh-ree-oh*
Be careful.	Tenga cuidado.	*'tehn-gah 'kwee-'dah-doh*
Enough.	¡Basta!	*'bahs-tah*
Good heavens!	¡Dios mío!	*dee-'ohs 'mee-oh*
How fortunate!	¡Qué suerte!	*keh 'swehr-teh*
I can't stand him!	¡No puedo soportarlo!	*noh 'pweh-doh soh-pohr-'tahr-loh*
I don't believe it!	¡No lo puedo creer!	*noh loh 'pweh-doh kre-'ehr*

I don't feel like . . .	No tengo ganas de . . .	*noh 'tehn-goh 'gah-nahs deh*
I wish . . .	Ojalá . . .	*oh-hah-'lah*
I'm serious.	Hablo en serio.	*'ah-bloh ehn 'seh-ree·oh*
I'm sorry.	Lo siento.	*loh see-'ehn-toh*
Impossible.	Imposible.	*eem-poh-'see-bleh*
It doesn't matter	No importa.	*noh eem-'pohr-tah*
My God!	¡Dios mío!	*dee-'ohs 'mee-oh*
Poor man!	¡Pobrecito!	*poh-breh-'see-toh*
Poor woman!	¡Pobrecita!	*poh-breh-'see-tah*
Quiet!	¡Silencio!	*see-'lehn-see·oh*
Really?	¿De veras?	*deh 'beh-rahs*
Shut up!	¡Cállense!	*'kah-yehn-seh*
Thank goodness!	¡Gracias a Dios!	*'grah-see·ahs ah dee-'ohs*
Too bad!	¡Qué lástima!	*keh 'lahs-tee-mah*
Ugh!	¡Uf!	*oof*
Unbelievable!	¡Increíble!	*een-kreh-'ee-bleh*
Unfortunately!	Desafortunadamente.	*dehs-ah-fohr-too-nah-dah-'mehn-teh*
What a bore!	¡Qué bárbaro(a)!	*keh 'bahr-bah-roh (-rah)*
	¡Qué lata!	*keh 'lah-tah*

22. THINKING

a. DESCRIBING THOUGHT

complicated	complicado (*adj*)	*kohm-plee-'kah-doh*
concept	concepto	*kohn-'sehp-toh*
conscience	conciencia	*kohn-see-'ehn-see·ah*
conscientious	concienzudo (*adj*)	*kohn-see·ehn-'soo-doh*
difficult	difícil (*adj*)	*dee-'fee-seel*
doubt	duda	*'doo-dah*
easy	fácil (*adj*)	*'fah-seel*
existence	existencia	*ehks-ees-'tehn-see·ah*
hypothesis	hipótesis (*f*)	*ee-'poh-teh-sees*
idea	idea	*ee-'deh-ah*
ignorant	ignorante (*adj*)	*eeg-noh-'rahn-teh*
imagination	imaginación (*f*)	*ee-mah-hee-nah-see-'ohn*
interesting	interesante (*adj*)	*een-teh-reh-'sahn-teh*
judgment	juicio	*'hwee-see·oh*
knowledge	conocimiento	*koh-noh-see-mee-'ehn-toh*
knowledgeable	informado (*adj*)	*een-fohr-'mah-doh*
mind	mente (*f*)	*'mehn-teh*
opinion	opinión (*f*)	*oh-pee-nee-'ohn*
• in my opinion	a mi parecer	*ah mee pah-reh-'sehr*

English	Spanish	Pronunciation
problem	problema (m)	proh-'bleh-mah
• No problem.	Sin (ningún) problema	seen (neen-'goon) proh-'bleh-mah
reason	razón (f)	rah-'sohn
simple	sencillo (adj)	sehn-'see-yoh
thought	pensamiento	pehn-sah-mee-'ehn-toh
wisdom	sabiduría	sah-bee-doo-'ree-ah

b. BASIC THOUGHT PROCESSES

English	Spanish	Pronunciation
agree	estar (v*) de acuerdo	ehs-'tahr deh ah-'kwehr-doh
be interested in	tener (v*) interés en	teh-'nehr een-teh-'rehs ehn
be right	tener (v*) razón	teh-'nehr rah-'sohn
be wrong	no tener (v*) razón	noh teh-'nehr rah-'sohn
believe	creer (v)	kreh-'ehr
convince	convencer (v*)	kohn-behn-'sehr
demonstrate	demostrar (v*)	deh-mohs-'trahr
doubt	dudar (v)	doo-'dahr
forget	olvidarse de (v)	ohl-bee-'dahr-seh deh
imagine	imaginar (v)	ee-mah-hee-'nahr
know	saber (v*)	sah-'behr
	conocer (v*)	koh-noh-'sehr
learn	aprender (v)	ah-prehn-'dehr
persuade	persuadir (v)	pehr-swah-'deer
reason	razonar (v)	rah-soh-'nahr
reflect	reflexionar (v)	reh-fleh-ksee-oh-'nahr
	meditar (v)	meh-dee-'tahr
remember	recordar (v*)	reh-kohr-'dahr
study	estudiar (v*)	ehs-too-dee-'ahr
think	pensar (v)	pehn-'sahr
understand	comprender (v)	kohm-prehn-'dehr
	entender (v*)	ehn-tehn-'dehr
• What do you think?	¿Qué opina usted?	keh oh-'pee-nah oos-'tehd

DAILY LIFE

23. AT HOME

a. PARTS OF THE HOUSE

attic	ático	'ah-tee-koh
balcony	balcón (m)	bahl-'kohn
basement	sótano	'soh-tah-noh
bathtub	bañera	bah-'nyeh-rah
ceiling	techo	'teh-choh
chimney	chimenea	chee-meh-'neh-ah
closet	ropero	roh-'peh-roh
corridor	pasillo	pah-'see-yoh
door	puerta	'pwehr-tah
doorbell	timbre (m)	'teem-breh
entrance	entrada	ehn-'trah-dah
faucet	grifo	'gree-foh
fireplace	chimenea	chee-meh-'neh-ah
floor	suelo	'sweh-loh
floor (*level*)	piso	'pee-soh
garage	garaje (m)	gah-'rah-heh
garden	jardín (m)	har-'deen
ground floor	planta baja	'plahn-tah 'bah-hah
house	casa	'kah-sah
mailbox	buzón (m)	boo-'sohn
pantry	despensa	dehs-'pehn-sah
porch	portal	pohr-'tahl
	terraza cubierta	teh-'rrah-sah koo-bee·'ehr-tah
roof	tejado	teh-'hah-doh
shelf	estante (m)	ehs-'tahn-teh
shower	ducha	'doo-chah
sink	lavabo	lah-'bah-boh
stairs	escalera	ehs-kah-'leh-rah
switch	interruptor (m)	een-teh-rroop-'tohr
terrace	terraza	teh-'rrah-sah
toilet	retrete (m)	reh-'treh-teh
	excusado	ehks-coo-'sah-doh
wall (*inside*)	pared (f)	pah-'rehd
wall (*exterior*)	muro	'moo-roh
window	ventana	behn-'tah-nah
window ledge, sill	antepecho	ahn-teh-'peh-choh
yard	patio	'pah-tee·oh

b. ROOMS

bathroom	cuarto de baño	*kwahr-toh deh 'bah-nyoh*
bedroom	alcoba	*ahl-'koh-bah*
	cuarto	*'kwahr-toh*
	habitación (*f*)	*ah-bee-tah-see·'ohn*
closet, cupboard	armario	*ahr-'mah-ree-oh*
corner (of a room)	rincón (*m*)	*reen-'kohn*
dining room	comedor (*m*)	*koh-meh-'dohr*
hall	vestíbulo	*behs-'tee-boo-loh*
kitchen	cocina	*koh-'see-nah*
living room	sala (de estar)	*'sah-lah (deh ehs-'tahr)*
room	cuarto	*'kwahr-toh*
washroom	servicios	*sehr-'bee-see·ohs*
wine cellar	bodega	*boh-'deh-gah*

c. FURNITURE AND DECORATION

armchair	sillón (*m*)	*see-'yohn*
ashtray	cenicero	*seh-nee-'seh-roh*
bed	cama	*'kah-mah*
bedside table	mesilla de noche	*meh-'see-yah deh 'noh-cheh*
bookcase	estante (*m*)	*ehs-'tahn-teh*
carpet, rug	alfombra	*ahl-'fohm-brah*
chair	silla	*'see-yah*
chest of drawers, dresser	cómoda	*'koh-moh-dah*
curtain	cortina	*kohr-'tee-nah*
cushion	cojín (*m*)	*koh-'heen*
decor	decoración (*f*)	*deh-koh-rah-see·'ohn*
drawer	cajón (*m*)	*kah-'hohn*
dresser	tocador (*m*)	*toh-kah-'dohr*
furniture	muebles (*m*)	*'mweh-blehs*
• **piece of furniture**	mueble (*m*)	*'mweh-bleh*
lamp	lámpara	*'lahm-pah-rah*
mirror	espejo	*ehs-'peh-hoh*
painting	pintura	*peen-'too-rah*
	cuadro	*'kwah-droh*
sofa	sofá (*m*)	*soh-'fah*
stool	banquillo	*bahn-'kee-yoh*
table	mesa	*'meh-sah*
• **coffee table**	mesa de centro	*'meh-sah deh 'sehn-troh*
• **end table**	mesa auxiliar	*'meh-sah ow-ksee-lee·'ahr*
upholstery	tapizado	*tah-pee-'sah-doh*

venetian blinds	persianas	*pehr-see-·'ah-nahs*
wallpaper	empapelado	*ehm-pah-peh-'lah-doh*
writing desk	escritorio	*ehs-kree-'toh-ree-oh*

d. APPLIANCES AND COMMON HOUSEHOLD ITEMS

bag	saco	*'sah-koh*
	bolsa	*'bohl-sah*
barrel	barril (*m*)	*bah-'rreel*
basket	cesta	*'sehs-tah*
	canasta	*kah-'nahs-tah*
blanket	manta	*'mahn-tah*
blender	licuadora	*lee-kwah-'doh-rah*
bottle	botella	*boh-'teh-yah*
bowl	tazón (*m*)	*tah-'sohn*
box	caja	*'kah-hah*
broom	escoba	*ehs-'koh-bah*
can	lata	*'lah-tah*
case	estuche (*m*)	*ehs-'too-cheh*
china	procelana	*pohr-seh-'lah-nah*
clothes hanger	percha	*'pehr-chah*
	gancho	*'gahn-choh*
coffee pot	cafetera	*kah-feh-'teh-rah*
colander	colador (*m*)	*koh-lah-'dohr*
corkscrew	sacacorchos (*m*)	*sah-kah-'kohr-chohs*
cup	taza	*'tah-sah*
dishwasher	lavaplatos (*m*)	*lah-bah-'plah-tohs*
dryer	secadora	*seh-kah-'dohr*
flour sifter	cernidor (*m*) de harina	*sehr-nee-'dohr deh ah-'ree-nah*
fork	tenedor (*m*)	*teh-neh-'dohr*
freezer	congelador (*m*)	*kohn-geh-lah-'dohr*
frying pan	sartén (*f*)	*sahr-'tehn*
funnel	embudo	*ehm-'boo-doh*
glass (*drinking*)	vaso	*'bah-soh*
grater	rallador (*m*)	*rah-yah-'dohr*
iron	plancha	*'plahn-chah*
kettle	hervidor (*m*)	*ehr-bee-'dohr*
	cafetera	*kah-feh-'teh-rah*
key	llave (*f*)	*'ya-beh*
knife	cuchillo	*koo-'chee-yoh*
• **blade**	hoja	*'oh-hah*
• **handle**	mango	*'mahn-goh*
ladle	cucharón (*m*)	*koo-chah-'rohn*
lid	tapa	*'tah-pah*
measuring cups	juego de tazas de medir	*'hweh-goh deh 'tah-sahs deh meh-'deer*

measuring spoons	juego de cucharitas de medir	*'hweh-goh deh koo-chah-'ree-tahs deh meh-'deer*
microwave oven	horno de microondas	*'ohr-noh deh mee-kroh-'ohn-dahs*
mixer	batidora	*bah-tee-'doh-rah*
napkin	servilleta	*sehr-bee-'yeh-tah*
oven	horno	*'ohr-noh*
pail	cubo	*'koo-boh*
pan	cacerola	*kah-seh-'roh-lah*
pillow	almohada	*ahl-moh-'ah-dah*
pillowcase	funda	*'foon-dah*
plate	plato	*'plah-toh*
pot	olla	*'oh-yah*
radio	radio	*'rah-dee·oh*
recipe	receta	*reh-'seh-tah*
refrigerator	nevera	*neh-'beh-rah*
	frigorífico	*free-goh-'ree-fee-koh*
	refrigerador (*m*)	*reh-free-heh-rah-'dohr*
saucer	platillo	*plah-'tee-yoh*
sewing machine	máquina de coser	*'mah-kee-nah deh koh-'sehr*
sheet (*bed*)	sábana	*'sah-bah-nah*
skillet	sartén (*f*)	*sahr-'tehn*
spatula	espátula	*ehs-'pah-too-lah*
spoon	cuchara	*koo-chah-rah*
• **teaspoon**	cucharita	*koo-char-'ree-tah*
• **teaspoonful**	cucharadita	*koo-chah-rah-'dee-tah*
stove	estufa	*ehs-'too-fah*
tablecloth	mantel (*m*)	*mahn-'tehl*
teapot	tetera	*teh-'teh-rah*
television set	televisor (*m*)	*teh-leh-bee-'sohr*
toaster	tostador (*m*)	*tohs-tah-'dohr*
tools	herramientas	*eh-rrah-mee·'ehn-tahs*
toothpick	palillo	*pah-'lee-yoh*
tray	bandeja	*bahn-'deh-hah*
utensils	utensilios (*m, pl*)	*oo-tehn-'see-lee·ohs*
vacuum cleaner	aspirador (a) (*m/f*)	*ahs-pee-rah-'dohr (-rah)*
vase	florero	*floh-'reh-roh*
washing machine	lavadora	*lah-bah-'doh-rah*

e. SERVICES

air conditioning	aire (*m*) acondicionado	*'ah-ee-reh ah-kohn-dee-see·oh-'nah-doh*
electricity	electricidad (*f*)	*eh-lehk-tree-see-'dahd*
furnace	calorífero	*kah-loh-'ree-feh-roh*
gas	gas (*m*)	*gahs*

heating	calefacción (*f*)	*kah-leh-fahk-see·'ohn*
telephone	teléfono	*teh-'leh-foh-noh*
water	agua (*f*)	*'ah-gwah*

f. ADDITIONAL HOUSEHOLD VOCABULARY

at home	en casa	*ehn 'kah-sah*
build	construir (*v**)	*kohns-'trweer*
buy	comprar (*v*)	*kohm-'prahr*
clean	limpiar (*v*)	*leem-pee·'ahr*
clear the table	quitar (*v*) la mesa	*kee-'tahr lah 'meh-sah*
decorate	decorar (*v*)	*deh-koh-'rahr*
live (in)	vivir (*v*) (en)	*bee-'beer (ehn)*
make the bed	hacer (*v**) la cama	*ah-'sehr lah 'kah-mah*
move	mudarse (*v*)	*moo-'dahr-seh*
paint	pintar (*v*)	*peen-'tahr*
put a room in order	arreglar (*v*) un cuarto	*ah-rreh-'glahr oon 'kwahr-toh*
restore	restaurar (*v*)	*rehs-tow-'rahr*
sell	vender (*v*)	*behn-'dehr*
set the table	poner (*v**) la mesa	*poh-'nehr lah 'meh-sah*
wash	lavar (*v*)	*lah-'bahr*
• wash the clothes	lavar (*v*) la ropa	*lah-'bahr lah 'roh-pah*
• wash the dishes	lavar (*v*) los platos	*lah-'bahr lohs 'plah-tohs*

g. LIVING IN AN APARTMENT

apartment	apartamento	*ah-pahr-tah-'mehn-toh*
	piso	*'pee-soh*
apartment house	casa de pisos	*'kah-sah deh 'pee-sohs*
building	edificio	*eh-dee-'fee-see·oh*
condominium	condominio	*kohn-doh-'mee-nee·oh*
elevator	ascensor (*m*)	*ah-sehn-'sohr*
ground floor	planta baja	*'plahn-tah 'bah-hah*
landlord	propietario	*proh-pee·eh-'tah-ree·oh*
	patrón	*pah-'trohn*
rent	alquilar (*v*)	*ahl-kee-'lahr*
• rent	alquiler (*m*)	*ahl-kee-'lehr*
tenant	arrendatario	*ah-rrehn-dah-'tah-ree·oh*
	inquilino	*een-kee-'lee-noh*

24. EATING AND DRINKING

a. MEALS

| breakfast | desayuno | *deh-sah-'yoo-noh* |
| • eat breakfast | desayunar(se) (*v*) | *deh-sah-yoo-'nahr (seh)* |

dinner	cena	'seh-nah
• eat dinner	cenar (v)	seh-'nahr
food	comida	koh-'mee-dah
lunch	almuerzo	ahl-'mwehr-soh
• eat lunch	almorzar (v*)	ahl-mohr-'sahr
meal	comida	koh-'mee-dah
snack	bocadillo	boh-kah-'dee-yoh
• snack	comer(se) (v)	koh-'mehr (-seh) oon
	un bocadillo	boh-kah-'dee-yoh

b. PREPARATION OF FOOD

baked	asado (adj)	ah-'sah-doh
boiled	guisado (adj)	gee-'sah-doh
broiled	a la parrilla	ah lah pah-'rree-yah
fried	frito	'free-toh
medium	a término medio	ah 'tehr-mee-noh 'meh-dee·oh
rare	poco asado (adj)	'poh-koh ah-'sah-doh
well-done	bien asado (adj)	bee·'ehn ah-'sah-doh

c. MEAT AND POULTRY

bacon	tocino	toh-'see-noh
beefsteak	bistec (m)	bees-'tehk
chicken	pollo	'poh-yoh
cold cuts	fiambres (m)	fee-'ahm-brehs
goat	cabrito	kah-'bree-toh
ham	jamón (m)	hah-'mohn
lamb	cordero	kohr-'deh-roh
liver	hígado	'ee-gah-doh
pork	cerdo	'sehr-doh
• pork chops	chuletas de cerdo	choo-'leh-tahs deh 'sehr-doh
sausage	salchicha	sahl-'chee-chah
turkey	pavo	'pah-boh
veal	ternera	tehr-'neh-rah

d. FISH, SEAFOOD, AND SHELLFISH

anchovy	anchoa	ahn-'choh-ah
clam	almeja	ahl-'meh-hah
codfish	bacalao	bah-kah-'lah-oh
eel	anguila	ahn-'gee-lah
fish	pescado	pehs-'kah-doh
herring	arenque (m)	ah-'rehn-keh
lobster	langosta	lahn-'gohs-tah
mussels	mejillones (m)	meh-hee-'yoh-nehs
oyster	ostra	'ohs-trah

salmon	salmón (m)	*sahl-'mohn*
sardine	sardina	*sahr-'dee-nah*
seafood	pescado y marisco	*pehs-'kah-doh ee mah-'rees-koh*
shellfish	marisco(s)	*mah-'rees-koh(s)*
shrimp	gambas	*'gahm-bahs*
sole	lenguado	*lehn-'gwah-doh*
squid	camarones (m)	*kah-mah-'roh-nehs*
	calamares (m)	*kah-lah-'mah-rehs*
trout	trucha	*'troo-chah*
tuna	atún (m)	*ah-'toon*

e. VEGETABLES

artichoke	alcachofa	*ahl-kah-'choh-fah*
asparagus	espárrago	*ehs-'pah-rrah-goh*
avocado	aguacate (m)	*ah-gwah-'kah-teh*
beans	frijoles (m)	*free-'hoh-lehs*
beet	remolacha	*reh-moh-'lah-chah*
broccoli	brécol (m)	*'breh-kohl*
	bróculi (m)	*'broh-koo-lee*
cabbage	col (m)	*kohl*
	repollo	*reh-'poh-yoh*
carrot	zanahoria	*sah-nah-'oh-ree-ah*
cauliflower	coliflor (f)	*koh-lee-'flohr*
celery	apio	*'ah-pee·oh*
cucumber	pepino	*peh-'pee-noh*
eggplant	berenjena	*beh-rehn-'heh-nah*
lettuce	lechuga	*leh-'choo-gah*
mushroom	champiñón (m)	*chahm-pee-'nyohn*
	hongo	*'ohn-goh*
olive	aceituna	*ah-seh·ee-'too-nah*
onion	cebolla	*seh-'boh-yah*
pea	guisante (m)	*gee-'sahn-teh*
potato	papa	*'pah-pah*
	patata	*pah-'tah-tah*
spinach	espinaca	*ehs-pee-'nah-kah*
string bean	judía verde	*hoo-'dee-ah 'behr-deh*
sweet potato	batata	*bah-'tah-tah*
tomato	tomate (m)	*toh-'mah-teh*
vegetables	verduras	*behr-'doo-rahs*
	legumbres (f, pl)	*leh-'goom-brehs*

f. FRUITS

| apple | manzana | *mahn-'sah-nah* |
| apricot | albaricoque (m) | *ahl-bah-ree-'koh-keh* |

banana	banana	*bah-'nah-nah*
	plátano	*'plah-tah-noh*
blueberry	mirtilo	*meer-'tee-loh*
cherry	cereza	*seh-'reh-sah*
date	dátil (*m*)	*'dah-teel*
fig	higo	*'ee-goh*
fruit	fruta	*'froo-tah*
grapefruit	toronja	*toh-'rohn-hah*
	pomelo	*poh-'meh-loh*
grapes	uvas	*'oo-bahs*
lemon	limón (*m*)	*lee-'mohn*
lime	lima	*'lee-mah*
melon	melón (*m*)	*meh-'lohn*
orange	naranja	*nah-'rahn-hah*
peach	melocotón (*m*)	*meh-loh-koh-'tohn*
	durazno	*doo-'rahs-noh*
peanut	cacahuete (*m*)	*kah-kah-'weh-teh*
	maní (*m*)	*mah-'nee*
pineapple	piña	*'pee-nyah*
plum	ciruela	*see-'rweh-lah*
prune	ciruela pasa	*see-'rweh-lah 'pah-sah*
raspberry	frambuesa	*frahm-'bweh-sah*
strawberry	fresa	*'freh-sah*
tangerine	mandarina	*mahn-dah-'ree-nah*
watermelon	sandía	*sahn-'dee·ah*

g. MEAL AND MENU COMPONENTS

aperitif	aperitivo	*ah-peh-ree-'tee-boh*
appetizer	tapa	*'tah-pah*
	bocadillo	*boh-kah-'dee-yoh*
broth	caldo	*'kahl-doh*
cake	torta	*'tohr-tah*
course	plato	*'plah-toh*
cutlet	chuleta	*choo-'leh-tah*
dessert	postre (*m*)	*'pohs-treh*
filet	filete (*m*)	*fee-'leh-teh*
French fries	papas fritas	*'pah-pahs 'free-tahs*
menu	menú (*m*)	*meh-'noo*
	lista de platos	*'lees-tah deh 'plah-tohs*
pie	pastel (*m*)	*pahs-'tehl*
pudding	budín (*m*)	*booh-'deen*
salad	ensalada	*ehn-sah-'lah-dah*
sandwich	torta (*Mexico*)	*'tohr-tah*
	bocadillo (*Spain*)	*boh-kah-'dee-yoh*
	emparedado (*Latin America*)	*ehm-pah-reh-'dah-doh*
soup	sopa	*'soh-pah*

h. DAIRY PRODUCTS, EGGS, AND RELATED FOODS

butter	mantequilla	*mahn-teh-'kee-yah*
cheese	queso	*'keh-soh*
cream	crema	*'kreh-mah*
dairy product	productos lácteos	*proh-'dook-tohs 'lahk-teh-ohs*
egg	huevo	*'weh-boh*
ice cream	helado	*eh-'lah-doh*
margarine	margarina	*marh-gah-'ree-nah*
milk	leche (*f*)	*'leh-cheh*
omelette	tortilla (*Spain*)	*tohr-'tee-yah*
whipped cream	crema batida	*'kreh-mah bah-'tee-dah*
yogurt	yogur (*m*)	*yoh-'goor*

i. GRAINS AND GRAIN PRODUCTS

barley	cebada	*seh-'bah-dah*
biscuit	bizcocho	*bees-'koh-choh*
bread	pan (*m*)	*pahn*
cookie	galleta	*gah-'yeh-tah*
corn	maíz (*m*)	*mah-'ees*
flour	harina	*ah-'ree-nah*
noodles	fideos	*fee-'deh-ohs*
oat	avena	*ah-'beh-nah*
pastry	pastel (*m*)	*pahs-'tehl*
rice	arroz (*m*)	*ah-'rrohs*
wheat	trigo	*'tree-goh*
• **whole wheat bread**	pan integral	*pahn een-teh-'grahl*

j. CONDIMENTS AND SPICES

basil	albahaca	*ahl-bah-'ah-kah*
cinnamon	canela	*kah-'neh-lah*
garlic	ajo	*'ah-hoh*
herb	hierba	*'ee·ehr-bah*
	yerba	*'yehr-bah*
honey	miel (*f*)	*mee·ehl*
horseradish	rábano picante	*'rah-bah-noh pee-'kahn-teh*
jam, marmalade	mermelada	*mehr-meh-'lah-dah*
ketchup	salsa de tomate	*'sahl-sah deh toh-'mah-teh*
mayonnaise	mayonesa	*mah-yoh-'neh-sah*
mint	menta	*'mehn-tah*
mustard	mostaza	*mohs-'tah-sah*

oil	aceite (*m*)	*ah-'seh·ee-teh*
parsley	perejil (*m*)	*peh-reh-'heel*
pepper	pimienta	*pee-mee-'ehn-tah*
rosemary	romero	*roh-'meh-roh*
salt	sal (*f*)	*sahl*
spice	especia	*ehs-'peh-see·ah*
sugar	azúcar (*m*)	*ah-'soo-kahr*
vinegar	vinagre (*m*)	*bee-'nah-greh*

k. DRINKS

alcoholic drink	bebida alcohólica	*beh-'bee-dah ahl-koh-'oh-lee-kah*
beer	cerveza	*sehr-'beh-sah*
coffee	café (*m*)	*kah-'feh*
• instant coffee	café instantáneo	*kah-'feh een-stahn-'tah-neh-oh*
drink	bebida	*beh-'bee-dah*
juice	jugo	*'hoo-goh*
	zumo	*'soo-moh*
liqueur	licor (*m*)	*lee-'kohr*
milk	leche (*f*)	*'leh-cheh*
mineral water	agua mineral (*f*)	*'ah-gwah mee-neh-'rahl*
soft drink	refresco	*reh-'frehs-koh*
tea	té (*m*)	*teh*
water	agua (*f*)	*'ah-gwah*
whiskey	whiski (*m*)	*'wees-kee*
wine	vino	*'bee-noh*

l. AT THE TABLE

bottle	botella	*boh-'teh-yah*
bowl	tazón (*m*)	*tah-'sohn*
cup	taza	*'tah-sah*
fork	tenedor (*m*)	*teh-neh-'dohr*
glass (*drinking*)	vaso	*'bah-soh*
knife	cuchillo	*koo-'chee-yoh*
napkin	servilleta	*sehr-bee-'yeh-tah*
pepper shaker	pimentero	*pee-mehn-'teh-roh*
plate	plato	*'plah-toh*
salt shaker	salero	*sah-'leh-roh*
saucer	platillo	*pla-'tee-yoh*
silverware (place setting)	cubierto	*koo-bee-'ehr-toh*
spoon	cuchara	*koo-'chah-rah*
table	mesa	*'meh-sah*
tablecloth	mantel (*m*)	*mahn-'tehl*
teaspoon	cucharita	*koo-'chah-'ree-tah*

toothpick	palillo	*pahl-'lee-yoh*
tray	bandeja	*bahn-'deh-hah*
water glass	vaso para agua	*'vah-soh 'pah-rah 'ah-gwah*
wineglass	vaso para vino	*'vah-soh 'pah-rah 'bee-noh*
	copa	*'koh-pah*

> **Cheers!** = ¡Salud!
> **Enjoy your meal!** = ¡Buen provecho!

---

m. DINING OUT

bartender	cantinero	*kahn-tee-'neh-roh*
bill, check	cuenta	*'kwehn-tah*
cafeteria	cafetería	*kah-feh-teh-'ree-ah*
cover charge	precio del cubierto	*'preh-see·oh dehl koo-bee·'ehr-toh*
fixed price	precio fijo	*'preh-see·oh 'fee-hoh*
price	precio	*'preh-see·oh*
reservation	reservación (*f*)	*reh-sehr-bah-see·'ohn*
• reserved	reservado (*adj*)	*reh-sehr-'bah-doh*
restaurant	restaurante (*m*)	*rehs-tow-'rahn-teh*
service	servicio	*sehr-'bee-see·oh*
snack bar	bar	*bahr*
	cafetería	*kah-feh-teh-'ree-ah*
tip	propina	*proh-'pee-nah*
• tip	dar (*v**) una propina	*dahr 'oo-nah proh-'pee-nah*
waiter	camarero	*kah-mah-'reh-roh*
	mesero	*meh-'seh-roh*
waitress	camarera	*kah-mah-'reh-rah*
wine list	lista de vinos	*'lees-tah deh 'bee-nohs*

n. BUYING FOOD AND DRINK

bakery	panadería	*pah-nah-deh-'ree-ah*
butcher shop	carnicería	*kahr-nee-seh-'ree-ah*
dairy	lechería	*leh-cheh-'ree-ah*
fish store	pescadería	*pehs-kah-deh-'ree-ah*
fruit store	frutería	*froo-teh-'ree-ah*
grocery store	tienda de comestibles	*'tee·ehn-dah deh koh-mehs-'tee-blehs*

ice cream parlor	heladería	eh-lah-deh-'ree-ah
market	mercado	mehr-'kah-doh
pastry shop	pastelería	pahs-teh-leh-'ree-ah
supermarket	supermercado	soo-pehr-mehr-'kah-doh

o. FOOD AND DRINK: ACTIVITIES

add up the bill	sumar (v) la cuenta	soo-'mahr lah 'kwehn-tah
be hungry	tener (v*) hambre	teh-'nehr 'ahm-breh
be thirsty	tener (v*) sed	teh-'nehr sehd
clear the table	quitar (v) la mesa	kee-'tahr lah 'meh-sah
	limpiar (v) la mesa	leem-pee-'ahr lah 'meh-sah
cook	cocinar (v)	koh-see-'nahr
cost	costar (v*)	kohs-'tahr
cut	cortar (v)	kohr-'tahr
drink	beber (v)	beh-'behr
	tomar (v)	toh-'mahr
eat	comer (v)	koh-'mehr
have a snack	merendar (v*)	meh-rehn-'dahr
have dinner	cenar (v)	seh-'nahr
have lunch	almorzar (v*)	ahl-mohr-'sahr
order	pedir (v*)	peh-'deer
peel	pelar (v)	peh-'lahr
pour	verter (v*)	behr-'tehr
serve	servir (v*)	sehr-'beer
set the table	poner (v*) la mesa	poh-'nehr lah 'meh-sah
shop for food	comprar (v) comestibles	kohm-'prahr koh-mehs-'tee-blehs
slice	rebanar (v)	reh-bah-'nahr
	tajar (v)	tah-'hahr
toast	tostar (v*)	tohs-'tahr
weigh	pesar (v)	peh-'sahr

p. DESCRIBING FOOD AND DRINK

appetizing	apetitoso (adj)	ah-peh-tee-'toh-soh
bad	malo (adj)	'mah-loh
baked	asado al horno (adj)	ah-'sah-doh ahl 'ohr-noh
cheap	barato (adj)	bah-'rah-toh
cold	frío (adj)	'free-oh
expensive	caro (adj)	'kah-roh
fried	frito (adj)	'free-toh
good	bueno (adj)	'bweh-noh
hot	caliente (adj)	kah-lee-'ehn-teh

mild	suave (*adj*)	'swah-beh
salty	salado (*adj*)	sah-'lah-doh
sour	agrio (*adj*)	'ah-gree-oh
spicy	picante (*adj*)	pee-'kahn-teh
sweet	dulce (*adj*)	'dool-seh
tasty	sabroso (*adj*)	sah-'broh-soh
with ice	con hielo	kohn ee·'eh-loh

25. SHOPPING AND ERRANDS

a. GENERAL VOCABULARY

antique	antigüedad (*f*)	ahn-tee-gweh-'dahd
bag	saco	'sah-koh
	bolsa	'bohl-sah
become	hacerse (*v**)	ah-'sehr-seh
bill	cuenta	'kwehn-tah
• bill	facturar (*v*)	fahk-too-'rahr
bring	traer (*v**)	trah-'ehr
buy	comprar (*v*)	kohm-'prahr
cash register	caja registradora	'kah-hah reh-hees-trah-'doh-rah
• cashier	cajero	kah-'heh-roh
change (*money*)	cambiar (*v*)	kahm-bee-'ahr
cost	costar (*v**)	kohs-'tahr
• How much does it cost?	¿Cuánto cuesta?	'kwahn-toh 'kwehs-tah
• How much is it?	¿Cuánto es?	'kwahn-toh ehs

> **It costs an arm and a leg** = Cuesta un ojo de la cara

counter	mostrador (*m*)	mohs-trah-'dohr
customer	cliente (*m/f*)	klee-'ehn-teh
department (*in store*)	departamento	deh-pahr-tah-'mehn-toh
entrance	entrada	ehn-'trah-dah
elevator	ascensor (*m*)	ah-sehn-'sohr
escalator	escalera movediza	ehs-kah-leh-'rah moh-beh-'dee-sah
exchange (*of merchandise*)	canje (*m*)	'kahn-heh
• exchange	canjear (*v*)	kahn-heh-'ahr
exit	salida	sah-'lee-dah
free	gratis	'grah-tees
gift	regalo	reh-'gah-loh
lack	faltar (*v*)	fahl-'tahr
look for something	buscar (*v*) algo	boos-'kahr 'ahl-goh

package	paquete (*m*)	*pah-'keh-teh*
pay	pagar (*v*)	*pah-'gahr*
• **cash**	en efectivo	*ehn eh-fehk-'tee-boh*
• **check**	cheque (*m*)	*'cheh-keh*
• **credit card**	tarjeta de crédito	*tahr-'heh-tah deh 'kreh-dee-toh*
price	precio	*'preh-see·oh*
• **discount**	descuento	*dehs-'kwehn-toh*
• **expensive**	caro (*adj*)	*'kah-roh*
• **fixed price**	precio fijo	*'preh-see·oh 'fee-hoh*
• **inexpensive**	barato (*adj*)	*bah-'rah-toh*
• **reduced price**	precio reducido	*'preh-see·oh reh-doo-'see-doh*
• **tag, label**	etiqueta	*eh-tee-'keh-tah*
purchase	comprar (*v*)	*kohm-'prahr*
• **purchase**	compra	*kohm-prah*
refund	reembolso	*rreh-ehm-'bohl-soh*
• **refund**	reembolsar (*v*)	*rreh-ehm-bohl-'sahr*
return	devolución (*f*)	*deh-boh-loo-see-'ohn*
• **return** (*an object*)	devolver (*v**)	*deh-bohl-'behr*
sale	venta	*'behn-tah*
• **for sale**	de venta	*deh 'behn-tah*
	se vende	*seh 'behn-deh*
• **on sale**	en venta	*ehn 'behn-tah*
shop	ir (*v**) de compras	*eer deh 'kohm-prahs*
• **shop**	tienda	*tee-'ehn-dah*
souvenir	recuerdo	*reh-'kwehr-doh*
spend	gastar (*v*)	*gahs-'tahr*
store	tienda	*tee-'ehn-dah*
• **closed**	cerrado (*adj*)	*seh-'rrah-doh*
• **closing time**	hora de cerrar	*'oh-rah deh seh-'rrahr*
• **department store**	almacén (*m*)	*ahl-mah-'sehn*
• **open**	abierto (*adj*)	*ah-bee·ehr-toh*
• **opening hour**	hora de abrir	*'oh-rah deh ah-'breer*
• **store clerk**	dependiente(a)	*deh-pehn-dee-'ehn-teh (-tah)*
take	tomar (*v*)	*toh-'mahr*
• **take back**	devolver (*v**)	*deh-bohl-'behr*

b. HARDWARE

battery (*radios, etc.*)	pila	*'pee-lah*
• **battery** (*car*)	acumulador	*ah-koo-moo-lah-'dohr*
cable	cable (*m*)	*'kah-bleh*
clamp	abrazadera	*ah-brah-sah-'deh-rah*

drill	taladro	*tah-'lah-droh*
• drill	taladrar (*v*)	*tah-lah-'drahr*
electrical	eléctrico (*adj*)	*eh-'lehk-tree-koh*
file	lima	*'lee-mah*
flashlight	linterna	*leen-'tehr-nah*
fuse	fusible (*m*)	*foo-'see-bleh*
hammer	martillo	*mahr-'tee-yoh*
hardware store	ferretería	*feh-rreh-teh-'ree-ah*
insulation wire	alambre (*m*) aislante	*ah-'lahm-breh ah·ees-'lahn-teh*
light bulb	bombilla	*bohm-'bee-yah*
• fluorescent	fluorescente (*adj*)	*flwoh-reh-'sehn-teh*
• neon light	alumbrado de neón	*ah-loom-'brah-doh deh neh-'ohn*
masking tape	cinta adhesiva	*'seen-tah ahd-eh-'see-bah*
mechanical	mecánico (*adj*)	*meh-'kah-nee-koh*
nail	clavo	*'kla-boh*
• nail	clavar (*v*)	*klah-'bahr*
nut	tuerca	*'twehr-kah*
outlet (*electrical*)	toma	*'toh-mah*
paintbrush	brocha	*'broh-chah*
pick	piqueta	*pee-'keh-tah*
pincers	tenazas	*teh-'nah-sahs*
plane	cepillo	*seh-'pee-yoh*
pliers	alicates (*m*)	*ah-lee-'kah-tehs*
plug	enchufe (*m*)	*ehn-'choo-feh*
plumbing	fontanería	*fohn-tah-neh-'ree-ah*
punch	punzón (*m*)	*poon-'sohn*
saw	sierra	*see-'eh-rrah*
screwdriver	destornillador (*m*)	*dehs-tohr-nee-yah-'dohr*
• screw	tornillo	*tohr-'nee-yoh*
• screw	atornillar (*v*)	*ah-tohr-nee-'yahr*
• unscrew	destornillar (*v*)	*dehs-tohr-nee-'yahr*
shovel	pala	*'pah-lah*
tool	herramienta	*eh-rrah-mee-'ehn-tah*
transformer	transformador (*m*)	*trahns-fohr-mah-'dohr*
wire	alambre (*m*)	*ah-'lahm-breh*
wrench	llave inglesa	*'yah-beh een-'gleh-sah*

c. STATIONERY

adhesive tape	cinta adhesiva	*'seen-tah ahd-eh-'see-bah*
ballpoint pen	bolígrafo	*boh-'lee-grah-foh*
briefcase	cartera, portafolio (*m*)	*kahr-'teh-rah, pohr-tah-'foh-lee·oh*

business card	tarjeta de visita	*tahr-'heh-tah deh vee-'see-tah*
copy paper	papel (*m*) de fotocopiadora	*pah-'pehl deh foh-toh-koh-pee-ah-'doh-rah*
envelope	sobre (*m*)	*'soh-breh*
glue	pegamento	*peh-gah-'mehn-toh*
handheld organizer	organizador (*m*) de mano	*ohr-gah-nee-sah-'dohr deh 'mah-noh*
hanging folder	carpeta colgante	*kahr-'peh-tah kohl-'gahn-teh*
holepuncher	perforadora	*pehr-foh-rah-'doh-rah*
label	rótulo	*'roh-too-loh*
	etiqueta	*eh-tee-'keh-tah*
marker	marcador (*m*)	*mahr-kah-'dohr*
note pad	bloc de papel (*m*)	*blohk deh pah-'pehl*
paper	papel (*m*)	*pah-'pehl*
paper clip	ganchito	*gahn-'chee-toh*
paper cutter	guillotina	*gee-yoh-'tee-nah*
paper feeder	bandeja de alimentación	*bahn-'deh-hah deh ah-lee-mehn-tah-see'-ohn*
pen	pluma	*'ploo-mah*
pencil sharpener	sacapuntas (*m*)	*sah-kah-'poon-tahs*
rubber bands	gomitas	*goh-'mee-tahs*
sheet (*of paper*)	hoja	*'oh-hah*
staple	grapa	*'grah-pah*
• stapler	engrapador (*m*)	*ehn-grah-pah-'dohr*
staple remover	sacagrapas (*m*)	*sah-kah-'grah-pahs*
stationery store	papelería	*pah-peh-leh-'ree-ah*
string	cordel (*m*)	*kohr-'dehl*
writing paper	papel (*m*) de escribir	*pah-'pehl deh ehs-kree-'beer*

d. PHOTO/CAMERA

camera	cámara	*'kah-mah-rah*
• movie camera	cámara cinematográfica	*'kah-mah-rah cee-neh-mah-toh-'grah-fee-kah*
• videocamera	videocámara	*bee-deh-oh-'kah-mah-rah*
darkroom	cámara oscura	*'kah-mah-rah ohs-'koo-rah*
	cuarto oscuro	*'kwahr-toh ohs-'koo-roh*
develop	revelar (*v*)	*reh-beh-'lahr*
digital camera	cámara digital	*'kah-mah-rah dee-hee-'tahl*
• lens (camera)	lente (*m*)	*'lehn-teh*

• **megapixel**	megapíxel (*m*)	*meh-gah-'peek-sehl*
• **memory card reader**	lector (*m*) de tarjeta de memoria	*lehk-'tohr deh tahr-'heh-tah deh meh-'moh-ree-ah*
• **memory card**	tarjeta de memoria	*tahr-'heh-tah deh meh-'moh-ree-ah*
• **rechargeable batteries**	pilas recargables	*'peeh-lahs reh-kahr-'gah-blehs*
enlargement	ampliación (*f*)	*ahm-plee·ah-see·'ohn*
• **enlarge**	ampliar (*v*)	*ahm-plee·'ahr*
film	película	*peh-'lee-koo-lah*
• **roll of film**	rollo de película	*'roh-yoh deh peh-'lee-koo-lah*
flash	flash (*m*)	*flahsh*
glossy finish	con acabado brillante	*kohn ah-kah-'bah-doh bree-'yahn-teh*
matte finish	con acabado mate	*kohn ah-kah-'bah-doh 'mah-teh*
photo (graph)	foto(grafía) (*f*)	*'foh-toh (grah-'fee-ah)*
• **black and white**	en blanco y negro	*ehn 'blahn-koh ee 'neh-groh*
• **clear**	clara (*adj*)	*'klah-rah*
• **focus**	enfocar (*v*)	*ehn-foh-'kahr*
• **in color**	en colores	*ehn koh-'loh-rehs*
• **in focus**	enfocada (*adj*)	*ehn-foh-'kah-dah*
• **out of focus**	fuera de foco	*'fweh-rah deh 'foh-koh*
• **take a picture**	sacar (*v*) una foto	*sah-'kahr 'oo-nah 'foh-toh*
• **It (the picture) turned out badly.**	Salió mal.	*sah-lee-'oh mahl*
• **It (the picture) turned out well.**	Salió bien.	*sah-lee-'oh bee-'ehn*
print	prueba positiva	*'prweh-bah poh-see-'tee-bah*
screen	pantalla	*pahn-'tah-yah*
slide	diapositiva	*dee·ah-poh-see-'tee-bah*
zoom	zoom (*m*)	*soom*

e. TOBACCO

cigar	puro	*'poo-roh*
	cigarro	*see-'gah-rroh*
cigarette	cigarrillo	*see-gah-'rree-yoh*
lighter	mechero	*meh-'cheh-roh*
	encendedor (*m*)	*ehn-sehn-deh-'dohr*

matches	fósforos	*'fohs-foh-rohs*
	cerillas	*seh-'ree-yahs*
pipe	pipa	*'pee-pah*
tobacco	tabaco	*tah-'bah-koh*
tobacco shop	tabaquería	*tah-bah-keh-'ree-ah*

f. COSMETICS/TOILETRIES

bath oil	aceite (*m*) de baño	*ah-'seh-ee-teh deh 'bah-nyoh*
blush, rouge	colorete (*m*)	*koh-loh-'reh-teh*
bobbypins	horquillas	*ohr-'kee-yahs*
brush	cepillo	*seh-'pee-yoh*
cologne	colonia	*koh-'loh-nee-ah*
comb	peine (*m*)	*'peh·ee-neh*
cosmetics/perfume store	perfumería	*pehr-foo-meh-'ree-ah*
cream	crema	*'kreh-mah*
curler	rizador (*m*)	*ree-sah-'dohr*
deodorant	desodorante (*m*)	*dehs-oh-doh-'rahn-teh*
electric razor	afeitadora eléctrica	*ah-feh·ee-tah-'doh-rah eh-'lehk-tree-kah*
face powder	polvos para la cara	*'pohl-bohs 'pah-rah lah 'kah-rah*
hair dryer	secador (*m*)	*seh-kah-'dohr*
lipstick	lápiz (*m*) de labios	*'lah-pees deh 'lah-bee·ohs*
lotion	loción (*f*)	*loh-see-'ohn*
makeup	maquillaje (*m*)	*mah-kee-'yah-heh*
mascara	rimmel (*m*)	*ree-'mehl*
nail clippers	cortauñas (*m*)	*kohr-tah-'oo-nyahs*
nail polish	esmalte (*m*) para las uñas	*ehs-'mahl-teh 'pah-rah lahs 'oo-nyahs*
perfume	perfume (*m*)	*pehr-'foo-meh*
razor	navaja de afeitar	*nah-'bah-hah deh ah-feh·ee-'tahr*
• razor blade	hoja de afeitar	*'oh-hah deh ah-feh-ee-'tahr*
shampoo	champú (*m*)	*chahm-'poo*
shaving cream	crema de afeitar	*'kreh-mah deh ah-feh·ee-'tahr*
soap	jabón (*m*)	*hah-'bohn*
talcum powder	talco	*'tahl-koh*
tweezers	pinzas	*'peen-sahs*

g. LAUNDRY

| button | botón (*m*) | *boh-'tohn* |
| • buttonhole | ojal (*m*) | *oh-'hahl* |

clean	limpiar (v)	*leem-pee-'ahr*
clothes	ropa	*'roh-pah*
• clothes basket	cesta para la ropa sucia	*'sehs-tah 'pah-rah lah 'roh-pah 'soo-see·ah*
• clothespin	pinza	*'peen-sah*
dirty	sucio (adj)	*'soo-see·oh*
dry cleaner	tintorería	*teen-toh-reh-'ree-ah*
hole	agujero	*ah-goo-'heh-roh*
iron	planchar (v)	*plahn'-chahr*
• iron	plancha	*'plahn-chah*
• ironing board	tabla de planchar	*'tah-blah deh plahn-'chahr*
• scorch	chamuscar (v)	*chah-moos'kahr*
laundry	lavandería	*lah-vahn-deh-'ree-ah*
lining (of a coat)	forro	*'foh-rroh*
mend	remendar (v*)	*reh-mehn'dahr*
pocket	bolsillo	*bohl-'see-yoh*
sew	coser (v)	*koh-'sehr*
sleeve	manga	*'mahn-gah*
soap powder	jabón de polvo	*hah-'bohn deh 'pohl-boh*
spot, stain	mancha	*'mahn-chah*
starch	almidón (m)	*ahl-mee-'dohn*
• starched	almidonado (adj)	*ahl-mee-doh-'nah-doh*
stitch	coser (v)	*koh-'sehr*
wash	lavar (v)	*lah-'bahr*
• washable	lavable (adj)	*lah-'bah-bleh*
wear	llevar (v)	*yeh-'bahr*
zipper	cremallera	*kreh-mah-'yeh-rah*

h. PHARMACY/DRUGSTORE

antibiotic	antibiótico	*ahn-tee-bee-'oh-tee-koh*
aspirin	aspirina	*ahs-pee-'ree-nah*
bandage	venda	*'behn-dah*
condom	condón (m)	*kohn-'dohn*
	hule (m)	*'oo-leh*
cortisone	cortisona	*kohr-tee-'soh-nah*
dental floss	hilo dental	*'ee-loh dehn-'tahl*
drugstore/pharmacy	farmacia	*fahr-'mah-see·ah*
injection	inyección (m)	*een-yehk-see-'ohn*
insulin	insulina	*een-soo-'lee-nah*
laxative	laxante (m)	*lahk-'sahn-teh*
medicine	medicina	*meh-dee-'see-nah*
ointment	ungüento	*oon-'gwehn-toh*
penicillin	penicilina	*peh-nee-see-'lee-nah*
pharmacist	farmacéutico(a)	*fahr-mah-'seh·oo-tee-koh (-kah)*

pill	píldora	*'peel-doh-rah*
powder	polvo	*'pohl-boh*
prescription	receta	*reh-'seh-tah*
sanitary napkins	toallitas higiénicas	*toh-ah-'yee-tahs ee-hee-'eh-nee-kahs*
sodium bicarbonate	bicarbonato de sodio	*bee-kahr-boh-'nah-toh deh 'soh-dee·oh*
suppository	supositorio	*soo-poh-see-'toh-ree·oh*
syrup	jarabe *(m)*	*hah-'rah-beh*
tablet	pastilla	*pahs-'tee-yah*
tampons	tampones *(m)*	*tahm-'poh-nehs*
thermometer	termómetro	*tehr-'moh-meh-troh*
tincture of iodine	tintura de yodo	*teen-'too-rah deh 'yoh-doh*
tissue	pañuelo de papel	*pah-nee·oh-'eh-loh deh pah-'pehl*
toothbrush	cepillo de dientes	*seh-'pee-yoh deh dee-'ehn-tehs*
toothpaste	pasta dentífrica	*'pahs-tah dehn-'tee-free-kah*
vitamin	vitamina	*bee-tah-'mee-nah*

i. JEWELRY

amethyst	amatista	*ah-mah-'teehs-tah*
artificial	artificial *(adj)*	*ahr-tee-fee-see-'ahl*
bracelet	pulsera	*pool-'seh-rah*
brooch	broche *(m)*	*'broh-cheh*
carat	quilate *(m)*	*kee-'lah-teh*
chain	cadena	*kah-'deh-nah*
charm	dije *(m)*	*'dee-heh*
diamond	diamante *(m)*	*dee-ah-'mahn-teh*
earring	arete *(m)*	*ah-'reh-teh*
	pendiente *(m)*	*pehn-dee·'ehn-teh*
emerald	esmeralda	*ehs-meh-'rahl-dah*
false	falso *(adj)*	*'fahl-soh*
fix	reparar *(v)*	*reh-pah-'rahr*
gold	oro	*'oh-roh*
ivory	marfil *(m)*	*mahr-'feel*
jewel	joya	*'hoh-yah*
jewelry store	joyería	*ho-yeh-'ree-ah*
necklace	collar *(m)*	*koh-'yahr*
opal	ópalo	*'oh-pah-loh*
pearl	perla	*'pehr-lah*
precious	precioso *(adj)*	*preh-see·'oh-soh*
ring (*with stone*)	sortija	*sohr-'lee-hah*
ring (*without stone*)	anillo	*ah-'nee-yoh*

ruby	rubí (*m*)	*roo-'bee*
sapphire	zafiro	*sah-'fee-roh*
silver	plata	*'plah-tah*
topaz	topacio	*toh-'pah-see·oh*
true	verdadero (*adj*)	*behr-dah-'deh-roh*
watch, clock	reloj (*m*)	*reh-'loh*
• alarm clock	despertador (*m*)	*desh-pehr-tah-'dohr*
• dial	esfera	*ehs-'feh-rah*
• hand	mano (*f*)	*'mah-noh*
	manecilla	*mah-neh-'see-yah*
• spring	muelle (*m*)	*'mweh-yeh*
• wind	dar (*v**) cuerda a	*dahr 'kwehr-dah ah*
• wristband	muñequera	*moo-nyeh-'keh-rah*
	correa	*koh-'rreh-ah*

j. MUSIC

cassette	casete (*m*)	*kah-'seh-teh*
classical music	música clásica	*'moo-see-kah 'klah-see-kah*
compact disk	disco compacto	*'dees-koh kohm-'pahk-toh*
composer	compositor(a)	*kohm-poh-see-'tohr (-rah)*
dance music	música de baile	*'moo-see-kah deh 'bah·ee-leh*
jazz	jazz (*m*)	*yahs*
music	música	*'moo-see-kah*
record	disco	*'dees-koh*
rock music	música rock	*'moo-see-kah rohk*
singer	cantante (*m/f*)	*kahn-'tahn-teh*
song	canción (*f*)	*kahn-see·'ohn*
tape	cinta	*'seen-tah*

k. CLOTHING

articles of clothing	prendas de vestir	*'prehn-dahs deh behs-'teer*
bathing suit	traje (*m*) de baño	*'trah-heh deh 'bah-nyoh*
belt	cinturón (*m*)	*seen-too-'rohn*
blouse	blusa	*'bloo-sah*
bra	sostén (*m*)	*sohs-'tehn*
briefs	calzoncillos	*kahl-sohn-'see-yohs*
changing room	vestuario	*behs-'twah-ree·oh*
clothing store	tienda de ropa	*tee-'ehn-dah deh 'roh-pah*
coat	abrigo	*ah-'bree-goh*

dress	vestido	*behs-'tee-doh*
fashion	moda	*'moh-dah*
fur coat	abrigo de piel	*ah-'bree-goh deh pee-'ehl*
glove	guante (*m*)	*'gwahn-teh*
handkerchief	pañuelo	*pah-'nyweh-loh*
hat	sombrero	*sohm-'breh-roh*
jacket	chaqueta	*chah-'keh-tah*
pajamas	pijamas	*pee-'hah-mahs*
panties	bragas	*'brah-gahs*
pants	pantalones (*m*)	*pahn-tah-'loh-nehs*
raincoat	impermeable (*m*)	*eem-pehr-meh-'ah-bleh*
scarf	bufanda	*boo-'fahn-dah*
shirt	camisa	*kah-'mee-sah*
shorts (*underwear*)	calzoncillos	*kahl-sohn-'see-yohs*
size	talla	*'tah-yah*
skirt	falda	*'fahl-dah*
slip	combinación (*f*)	*kohm-bee-nah-see-'ohn*
suit	traje (*m*)	*'trah-heh*
sweater	suéter (*m*)	*'sweh-tehr*
sweatshirt	sudadera	*soo-dah-'deh-rah*
T-shirt	camiseta	*kah-mee-'seh-tah*
tie	corbata	*kohr-'bah-tah*
underwear	ropa interior	*'roh-pah een-teh-ree-'ohr*

1. DESCRIBING CLOTHING

> For colors, see Section 7.

beautiful	precioso (*adj*)	*preh-see-'oh-soh*
	hermoso (*adj*)	*ehr-'moh-soh*
big	grande (*adj*)	*'grahn-deh*
brocade	brocado	*broh-'kah-doh*
corduroy	pana	*'pah-nah*
cotton	algodón (*m*)	*ahl-goh-'dohn*
elegant	elegante (*adj*)	*eh-leh-'gahn-teh*
fabric	tela	*'teh-lah*
	paño	*'pah-nyoh*
felt	fieltro	*fee-'ehl-troh*
flannel	franela	*frah-'neh-lah*
in the latest style	de la última moda	*deh lah 'ool-tee-mah 'moh-dah*
lace	encaje (*m*)	*ehn-'kah-heh*
leather	cuero	*'kweh-roh*

loose	suelto (*adj*)	*'swehl-toh*
nylon	nailon, nilón (*m*)	*'nah·ee-lohn, nee-'lohn*
permanent press	inarrugable (*adj*)	*een-ah-rroo-'gah-bleh*
plaid	a cuadros	*ah 'kwah-drohs*
polka dots	a lunares (*m*)	*ah loo-'nah-rehs*
polyester	poliéster (*m*)	*poh-lee·'ehs-tehr*
silk	seda	*'seh-dah*
small	pequeño (*adj*)	*peh-'keh-nyoh*
striped	rayado (*adj*)	*rrah·'yah-doh*
suede	gamuza	*gah-'moo-sah*
This looks bad on you.	Esto te queda mal.	*'ehs-toh teh 'keh-dah mahl*
This looks good on you.	Esto te queda bien.	*'ehs-toh teh 'keh-dah bee·'ehn*
tight	ceñido (*adj*)	*seh-'nyee-doh*
ugly	feo (*adj*)	*'feh-oh*
velvet	terciopelo	*tehr-see·oh-'peh-loh*
wool	lana	*'lah-nah*

m. CLOTHING: ACTIVITIES

enlarge	agrandar (*v*)	*ah-grahn-'dahr*
	ampliar (*v*)	*ahm-plee·'ahr*
get dressed	vestirse (*v**)	*behs-'teer-seh*
lengthen	alargar (*v*)	*ah-lahr-'gahr*
put on	ponerse (*v**)	*poh-'nehr-seh*
shorten	acortar (*v*)	*ah-kohr-'tahr*
take off	quitarse (*v*)	*kee-'tahr-seh*
tighten	apretar (*v**)	*ah-preh-'tahr*
try on	probar (*v**)	*proh-'bahr*
undress	desnudarse (*v*)	*dehs-noo-'dahr-seh*
wear	llevar (*v*)	*yeh-'bahr*

n. SHOES

boot	bota	*'boh-tah*
pair	par (*m*)	*pahr*
purse	bolsa	*'bohl-sah*
shoe	zapato	*sah-'pah-toh*
shoe polish	betún (*m*), crema para zapato	*beh-'toon, 'kreh-mah 'pah-rah sah-'pah-toh*
shoe store	zapatería	*sah-pah-tah-'ree-ah*
shoelace	cordón (*m*) de zapato	*kohr-'dohn deh sah-'pah-toh*
size (*of shoe*)	número	*'noo-meh-roh*
slipper	zapatilla	*sah-pah-'tee-yah*
sock	calcetín (*m*)	*kahl-seh-'teen*
stockings	medias	*'meh-dee·ahs*

o. BOOKS

adventure book	libro de aventura	*'lee-broh deh ah-behn-'too-rah*
book	libro	*'lee-broh*
• **best-seller**	éxito de librería	*'ehks-ee-toh deh lee-breh-'ree-ah*
bookstore	librería	*lee-breh-'ree-ah*
comics	historieta	*ees-toh-ree-'eh-tah*
dictionary	diccionario	*deek-see-oh-'nah-ree-oh*
encyclopedia	enciclopedia	*ehn-see-kloh-'peh-dee-ah*
guidebook	guía del viajero (*f*)	*'gee-ah dehl bee-ah-'heh-roh*
magazine	revista	*reh-'bees-tah*
mystery novel	novela policíaca	*noh-'beh-lah poh-lee-'see-ah-kah*
newspaper	periódico	*peh-ree-'oh-dee-koh*
novel	novela	*noh-'beh-lah*
paperback book	libro en rústica	*'lee-broh ehn 'roos-tee-kah*
poetry	poesía	*poh-eh-'see-ah*
reference book	libro de consulta	*'lee-broh deh kohn-'sool-tah*
romance book	novela romántica	*noh-'beh-lah roh-'mahn-tee-kah*
science fiction book	libro de ciencia ficción	*'lee-broh deh 'see-ehn-see-ah feek-see-'ohn*
technical book	libro técnico	*'lee-broh 'tehk-nee-koh*
textbook	libro de texto	*'lee-broh deh 'tehks-toh*
theater	teatro	*teh-'ah-troh*

26. *BANKING AND COMMERCE*

> For numerical concepts, see Section 1.

account	cuenta	*'kwehn-tah*
• **close an account**	liquidar una cuenta	*lee-kee-'dahr 'oo-nah 'kwehn-tah*
• **open an account**	abrir una cuenta	*ah-'breer 'oo-nah 'kwehn-tah*
bank	banco	*'bahn-koh*
• **head office**	oficina central	*oh-fee-'see-nah sehn-'trahl*
bank book	libreta de depósitos	*lee-'breh-tah deh de-'poh-see-tohs*

bank rate	tipo de descuento bancario	*'tee-poh deh des-'kwehn-toh bahn-'kah-ree·oh*
• **fixed**	fijo	*'fee-hoh*
• **variable**	variable (*adj*)	*bah-ree-'ah-bleh*
bill, banknote	billete (*m*)	*bee-'yeh-teh*
• **dollar**	dólar (*m*)	*'doh-lahr*
• **large bill**	billete grande	*bee-'yeh-teh 'grahn-deh*
• **small bill**	billete pequeño	*bee-'yeh-teh peh-'keh-nyoh*
bond	bono	*'boh-noh*
budget	presupuesto	*preh-soo-'pwehs-toh*
cash	dinero en efectivo	*dee-'neh-roh ehn eh-fehk-'tee-boh*
• **cash**	cobrar (*v*)	*koh-'brahr*
	cambiar (*v*)	*kahm-bee-'ahr*
• **cash account**	cuenta de caja	*'kwehn-tah deh 'kah-hah*
• **cash payment**	pago al contado	*'pah-goh ahl kohn-'tah-doh*
cashier, teller	cajero(a)	*kah-'heh-roh (-rah)*
check	cheque (*m*)	*'cheh-keh*
• **checkbook**	libreta de cheques	*lee-'breh-tah deh 'cheh-kehs*
• **checking account**	cuenta corriente	*'kwehn-tah koh-rree-'ehn-teh*
coin	moneda	*moh-'neh-dah*
compound interest	interés compuesto	*een-teh-'rehs kohm-'pwehs-toh*
cost of living	coste (*m*) de vida	*'kohs-teh deh 'bee-dah*
credit	crédito	*'kreh-dee-toh*
• **credit card**	tarjeta de crédito	*tahr-'heh-tah deh 'kreh-dee-toh*
current account	cuenta corriente	*kwehn-tah koh-rree-'ehn-teh*
currency	dinero en circulación	*dee-'neh-roh ehn seer-koo-lah-see-'ohn*
customer	cliente (*m/f*)	*klee-'ehn-teh*
debt	deuda	*'deh·oo-dah*
deposit	depósito	*deh-'poh-see-toh*
• **deposit**	depositar (*v*)	*deh-poh-see-'tahr*
• **deposit slip**	hoja de depósito	*'oh-hah deh deh-'poh-see-toh*
discount	descuento	*dehs-'kwehn-toh*
draft	letra de cambio	*'leh-trah deh 'kahm-bee·oh*
employee	empleado(a)	*ehm-pleh-'ah-doh (-dah)*
endorse	endosar (*v*)	*ehn-doh-'sahr*
• **endorsement**	endoso	*ehn-'doh-soh*

exchange	cambiar (v)	*kahm-bee·'ahr*
• exchange	cambio	*'kahm-bee·oh*
• rate of exchange	tipo de cambio	*'tee-poh deh 'kahm-bee·oh*
expiration date	fecha de vencimiento	*'feh-chah deh behn-see-mee·'ehn-toh*
foreign exchange	divisas	*dee-'bee-sahs*
income	ingresos	*een-'greh-sohs*
insurance	seguro	*seh-goo-roh*
• insurance policy	póliza de seguros	*'poh-lee-sah deh seh-'goo-rohs*
• insurance premium	prima de seguros	*'pree-mah deh seh-'goo-rohs*
interest	interés (m)	*een-teh-'rehs*
• interest rate	tasa de interés	*'tah-sah deh een-teh-'rehs*
invest	invertir (v*)	*een-behr-'teer*
• investment	inversión (f)	*een-behr-see·'ohn*
line up	hacer (v*) cola	*ah-'sehr 'koh-lah*
• line	cola	*'koh-lah*
loan	préstamo	*'prehs-tah-moh*
• get a loan	obtener (v*) un préstamo	*ohb-teh-'nehr oon 'prehs-tah-moh*
• loan officer	oficial de préstamos (m/f)	*oh-fee-see·'ahl deh 'prehs-tah-mohs*
loss	pérdida	*'pehr-dee-dah*
manager	gerente (m/f)	*heh-'rehn-teh*
money	dinero	*dee-'neh-roh*
money order	giro postal	*'hee-roh pohs-'tahl*
mortgage	hipoteca	*ee-poh-'teh-kah*
pay	pagar (v)	*pah-'gahr*
• pay off debts	saldar (v) las deudas	*sahl-'dahr lahs dee·'oo-dahs*
• payment	pago	*'pah-goh*
postdate	posfechar (v)	*pohs-feh-'chahr*
• postdate	posfecha	*pohs-'feh-chah*
profit	ganancia	*gah-'nahn-see·ah*
real estate	bienes raíces (m)	*bee·'eh-nehs rah-'ee-sehs*
receipt	recibo	*reh-'see-boh*
retail	venta al por menor	*'behn-tah ahl pohr meh-'nohr*
safe	caja fuerte	*'kah-hah 'fwehr-teh*
• safe deposit box	caja de seguridad	*'kah-hah deh seh-goo-ree-'dahd*
salary	salario	*sah-'lah-ree·oh*
	sueldo	*'soo·ehl-doh*

save	ahorrar (v)	ah-oh-'rrahr
• savings	ahorros	ah-'oh-rrohs
• savings account	cuenta de ahorros	'kwehn-tah deh ah-'oh-rrohs
• savings bank	caja de ahorros	'kah-hah deh ah-'oh-rrohs
securities (*stocks and bonds*)	valores (m)	bah-'loh-rehs
sign	firmar (v)	feer-'mahr
• signature	firma	'feer-mah
stock market	bolsa de valores	'bohl-sah deh bah-'loh-rehs
stock, share	acción (f)	ahk-see-'ohn
tax	impuesto	eem-'pwehs-toh
• tax exemption	exención (f) del impuesto	ehks-ehn-see-'ohn dehl eem-'pwehs-toh
teller's window	ventanilla	behn-tah-'nee-yah
traveler's check	cheque de viajero	'cheh-keh deh bee-ah-'heh-roh
wholesale	venta al por mayor	behn-tah ahl pohr mah-'yohr
withdraw	retirar (v)	reh-tee-'rahr
• withdrawal	retiro	reh-'tee-roh
• withdrawal slip	hoja de retiro	'oh-hah deh reh-'tee-roh

27. GAMES AND SPORTS

a. GAMES, HOBBIES, AND PHYSICAL FITNESS

billiards	billar (m)	bee-'yahr
• billiard ball	bola de billar	'boh-lah deh bee-'yahr
• billiard table	mesa de billar	'meh-sah deh bee-'yahr
• billiard cloth	paño	'pah-nyoh
• cue	taco	'tah-koh
• pocket	bolsillo	bohl-'see-yoh
bingo	bingo	'been-goh
• bingo card	tarjeta de bingo	tahr-'heh-tah deh 'been-goh
body build	desarrollar (v) la musculatura	dehs-ah-rroh-'yahr lah moos-koo-lah-'too-rah
• weightlift	levantar (v) pesas	leh-bahn-'tahr 'peh-sahs
bowling	bolo	'boh-loh
	boliche	boh-'lee-cheh
• bowl	jugar (v*) a los bolos (al boliche)	hoo-'gahr ah lohs 'boh-lohs (ahl boh-'lee-cheh)
• bowling alley	bolera	boh-'leh-rah
• bowling ball	bola	'boh-lah

checkers	damas	*'dah-mahs*
• **checkerboard**	tablero de damas	*tah-'bleh-roh deh 'dah-mahs*
chess	ajedrez (*m*)	*ah-heh-'drehs*
• **bishop**	alfil (*m*)	*ahl-'feel*
• **checkmate**	jaque mate (*m*)	*'hah-keh 'mah-teh*
• **chessboard**	tablero de ajedrez	*tah-'bleh-roh deh ah-heh-'drehs*
• **king**	rey (*m*)	*'reh-ee*
• **knight**	caballo	*kah-'bah-yoh*
• **pawn**	peón (*m*)	*peh-'ohn*
• **queen**	reina	*'reh-ee-nah*
• **rook**	torre (*f*)	*'toh-rreh*
coin	moneda	*moh-'neh-dah*
• **coin collecting**	numismática	*noo-mess-'mah-tee-kah*
darts	dardos	*'dahr-dohs*
dice	dados	*'dah-dohs*
game	juego	*'hweh-goh*
gymnasium	gimnasio	*heem-'nah-see·oh*
• **work out**	hacer (*v**) gimnasia	*ah-'sehr geem-'nah-see·ah*
hobby	pasatiempo	*pah-sah-tee-'ehm-poh*
instrument	instrumento	*eens-troo-'mehn-toh*
• **play an instrument**	tocar (*v*) un instrumento	*toh-'kahr oon eens-troo-'mehn-toh*
jog	correr (*v*) a trote corto	*koh-'rrehr ah 'troh-teh 'kohr-toh*
mountain climbing	alpinismo	*ahl-pee-'nees-moh*
• **backpack**	mochila	*moh-'chee-lah*
• **rope**	cuerda	*'kwehr-dah*
play (*a game*)	jugar (*v**)	*hoo-'gahr*
playing cards	cartas	*'kahr-tahs*
	naipes (*m*)	*'nah-ee-pehs*
• **clubs**	bastos	*'bahs-tohs*
• **diamonds**	diamantes (*m*)	*dee-ah-'mahn-tehs*
• **hearts**	corazones (*m*)	*koh-rah-'soh-nehs*
• **spades**	picos	*'pee-kohs*
	espadas	*ehs-'pah-dahs*
• **shuffle**	barajar (*v*)	*bah-rah-'hahr*
run	correr (*v*)	*koh-'rrehr*
skate	patinar (*v*)	*pah-tee-'nahr*
• **skating**	patinaje (*m*)	*pah-tee-'nah-heh*
• **roller skating**	patinaje sobre ruedas	*pah-tee-'nah-heh 'soh-breh 'rweh-dahs*
stamp	estampilla	*ehs-tahm-'pee-yah*
	sello	*'seh-yoh*
• **stamp collecting**	filatelia	*fee-lah-'teh-lee-ah*

| swim | nadar (*v*) | *nah-'dahr* |
| • swimming | natación (*f*) | *nah-tah-see·'ohn* |

b. SPORTS

amateur	aficionado (*adj*)	*ah-fee-see·oh-'nah-doh*
athlete	atleta (*m/f*)	*aht-'leh-tah*
ball	pelota	*peh-'loh-tah*
• **catch** (*ball*)	agarrar (coger (*v**)) (*v*)	*ah-gah-'rrahr (koh-'hehr)*
• **hit** (*ball*)	pegar (le) (*v*) a	*peh-'gahr (-leh) ah*
• **kick** (*ball*)	patear (*v*)	*pah-teh-'ahr*
• **pass** (*ball*)	pasar (*v*)	*pah-'sahr*
• **throw** (*ball*)	lanzar (*v*)	*lahn-'sahr*
baseball	béisbol (*m*)	*'beh·ees-bohl*
• **ball**	pelota de béisbol	*peh-'loh-tah deh 'beh·ees-bohl*
• **base**	base	*'bah-seh*
• **bat**	bate (*m*)	*'bah-teh*
• **batter**	bateador (*m*)	*bah-teh-ah-'dohr*
• **glove**	guante (*m*)	*'gwahn-teh*
• **home base**	base meta	*'bah-seh 'meh-tah*
• **home run**	jonrón (*m*)	*hohn-'rohn*
basketball	básquetbol (*m*)	*'bahs-keht-bohl*
	baloncesto	*bah-lohn-'sehs-toh*
• **basket**	canasta	*kah-'nahs-tah*
• **basketball**	balón de básquetbol	*bah-'lohn deh 'bahs-keht-bohl*
• **basketball court**	cancha	*'kahn-chah*
bicycle racing	ciclismo	*see-'klees-moh*
binoculars	prismáticos	*prees-'mah-tee-kohs*
boxing	boxeo	*boh-'kseh-oh*
• **boxing gloves**	guantes de boxeo	*'gwahn-tehs deh boh-'kseh-oh*
• **boxing ring**	ring (*m*)	*reengh*
car racing	carreras de coches	*kah-'rreh-rahs deh 'koh-chehs*
coach	entrenador(a)	*ehn-treh-nah-'dohr (-rah)*
competition	competencia	*kohm-peh-'tehn-see·ah*
fencing	esgrima	*ehs-'gree-mah*
• **fencing bout**	encuentro de esgrima	*ehn-'kwehn-troh deh ehs-'gree-mah*
field	campo	*'kahm-poh*
football	fútbol americano	*'foot-bohl ah-meh-ree-'kah-noh*
game, match	partido	*pahr-'tee-doh*

goal	gol (*m*)	*gohl*
golf	golf (*m*)	*gohlf*
helmet	casco	*'kahs-koh*
hockey	hockey (*m*)	*'hoh-kee*
• **field hockey**	hockey sobre hierba	*'hoh-kee 'soh-breh ee·'ehr-boh*
• **ice hockey**	hockey sobre hielo	*'hoh-kee soh-breh ee·'eh-loh*
• **puck**	disco	*'dees-koh*
• **skate**	patinar (*v*)	*pah-tee-'nahr*
martial arts	artes marciales (*f*)	*'ahr-tehs mahr-see-'ah-lehs*
net	red (*f*)	*rehd*
pass	pase (*m*)	*'pah-seh*
penalty	tiro penal	*'tee-roh peh-'nahl*
play	jugada	*hoo-'gah-dah*
• **player**	jugador(a)	*hoo-gah-'dohr (-rah)*
• **playoffs**	partido de desempate	*pahr-'tee-doh deh dehs-ehm-'pah-teh*
point	punto	*'poon-toh*
	tanto	*'tahn-toh*
professional	profesional (*adj*)	*proh-feh-see·oh-'nahl*
race	carrera	*kah-'rreh-rah*
• **horse racing**	carreras de caballo	*kah-'rreh-rahs deh kah-'bah-yoh*
• **racetrack**	hipódromo	*ee-'poh-droh-moh*
referee	árbitro	*'ahr-bec-troh*
score	marcar (*v*)	*mahr-'kahr*
• **draw, tie**	empate (*m*)	*ehm-'pah-teh*
• **tie**	empatar (*v*)	*ehm-pah-'tahr*
• **lose**	perder (*v**)	*pehr-'dehr*
• **loss**	pérdida	*'pehr-dee-dah*
• **win**	victoria	*beek-'toh-ree·ah*
• **win**	ganar (*v*)	*gah-'nahr*
scuba diving	submarinismo	*soob-mahr-ee-'nees-moh*
ski	esquiar (*v**)	*ehs-kee-'ahr*
• **ski**	esquí (*m*)	*ehs-'kee*
• **water ski**	esquiar (*v*) en el agua	*ehs-kee-'ahr ehn ehl 'ah-gwah*
• **water skiing**	esquí acuático	*ehs-'kee ah-'kwah-tee-koh*
soccer	fútbol (*m*)	*'foot-bohl*
• **soccer ball**	balón de fútbol (*m*)	*bah-'lohn deh 'foot-bohl*
• **soccer player**	futbolista (*m/f*)	*foot-boh-'lees-tah*
• **goalie**	portero	*pohr-'teh-roh*
sport	deporte (*m*)	*deh-'pohr-teh*
• **practice a sport**	practicar (*v*) un deporte	*prahk-tee-'kahr oon deh-'pohr-teh*

• **sports event**	encuentro deportivo	*ehn-'kwehn-troh deh-pohr-'tee-boh*
• **sports fan**	aficionado deportivo	*ah-fee-see·oh-'nah-doh deh-pohr-'tee-boh*
stadium	estadio	*ehs-'tah-dee·oh*
team	equipo	*eh-'kee-poh*
tennis	tenis (*m*)	*'teh-nees*
• **racket**	raqueta	*rah-'keh-tah*
ticket	boleto	*boh-'leh-toh*
track	pista	*'pees-tah*
track and field	atletismo en pista	*aht-leh-'tees-moh ehn 'pees-tah*
volleyball	voleibol (*m*)	*boh-leh·ee-'bohl*
water polo	polo acuático	*'poh-loh ah-'kwah-tee-koh*
wrestling	lucha libre	*'loo-chah 'lee-breh*

28. THE ARTS

a. CINEMA

actor	actor	*ahk-'tohr*
actress	actriz	*ahk-'trees*
aisle	pasillo	*pah-'see-yoh*
box office	taquilla	*tah-'kee-yah*
lobby	vestíbulo	*beh-'stee-boo-loh*
movie, film	película	*peh-'lee-koo-lah*
• **make a movie**	filmar (*v*) una película	*feel-'mahr 'oo-nah peh-'lee-koo-lah*
• **premiere showing**	estreno	*ehs-'treh-noh*
movie director	director cinematográfico	*dee-rehk-'tohr see-neh-mah-toh-'grah-fee-koh*
movie star	estrella de cine	*ehs-'treh-yah deh 'see-neh*
movies	películas	*peh-'lee-koo-lahs*
row	fila	*'fee-lah*
screen	pantalla	*pahn-'tah-yah*
seat	asiento	*ah-'see-ehn-toh*
soundtrack	banda sonora	*'bahn-dah soh-'noh-rah*

b. ART/SCULPTURE/ARCHITECTURE

| **architecture** | arquitectura | *ahr-kee-tehk-'too-rah* |
| • **blueprint** | cianotipo | *see-ah-noh-'tee-poh* |

art	arte (*m/f*)	'*ahr-teh*
artist	artista (*m/f*)	*ahr-*'*tees-tah*
brush	pincel (*m*)	*peen-*'*sehl*
canvas	lienzo	*lee-*'*ehn-soh*
drawing	dibujo	*dee-*'*boo-hoh*
easel	caballete (*m*)	*kah-bah-*'*yeh-teh*
etching	aguafuerte (*m*)	*ah-gwah-*'*fwehr-teh*
exhibition	exhibición (*f*)	*enk-see-bee-see-*'*ohn*
fresco painting	fresco	'*frehs-koh*
masterpiece	obra maestra	'*oh-brah mah-*'*ehs-trah*
oil painting	óleo	'*oh-leh-oh*
paint	pintar (*v*)	*peen-*'*tahr*
• paint	pintura	*peen-*'*too-rah*
• painter	pintor(a)	*peehn-*'*tohr* ('*toh-rah*)
• painting	pintura	*peen-*'*too-rah*
	cuadro	*kwah-droh*
palette	paleta	*pah-*'*leh-tah*
pastel	pastel (*m*)	*pahs-*'*tehl*
portrait	retrato	*reh-*'*trah-toh*
sculpt	esculpir (*v*)	*ehs-kool-*'*peer*
• sculptor	escultor	*ehs-*'*kool-*'*tohr*
• sculptress	escultora	*ehs-kool-*'*toh-rah*
• sculpture	escultura	*ehs-kool-*'*too-rah*
tapestry	tapicería	*tah-pee-seh-*'*ree-ah*
watercolor	acuarela	*ah-kwah-*'*reh-lah*

c. MUSIC/DANCE

accordion	acordeón (*m*)	*ah-kohr-deh-*'*ohn*
ballet	ballet (*m*)	*bah-*'*leht*
brass instruments	cobres (*m*)	'*koh-brehs*
• horn	corneta	*kohr-*'*neh-tah*
• trombone	trombón (*m*)	*trohm-*'*bohn*
• trumpet	trompeta	*trohm-*'*peh-tah*
• tuba	tuba	'*too-bah*
classical music	música clásica	'*moo-see-kah* '*klah-see-kah*
composer	compositor(a)	*kom-poh-see-*'*tohr (-rah)*
• composition	composición	*kohm-poh-see-see-*'*ohn*
concert	concierto	*kohn-see-*'*ehr-toh*
dance	baile (*m*)	'*bah·ee-leh*
• dance	bailar (*v*)	*bah·ee-*'*lahr*
• dancer	bailarín, bailarina	*bah·ee-lah-*'*reen, bah·ee-la-*'*ree-nah*
folk music	música folklórica	'*moo-see-kah fohl-*'*kloh-ree-kah*

guitar	guitarra	*gee-'tah-rrah*
• **guitarist**	guitarrista (*m/f*)	*gee-tah-'rrees-tah*
harmony	armonía	*ahr-moh-'nee·ah*
harp	arpa (*f*)	*'ahr-pah*
instrument	instrumento	*eens-troo-'mehn-toh*
• **play an instrument**	tocar (*v*) un instrumento	*toh-'kahr oon eens-troo-'mehn-toh*
jazz	jazz (*m*)	*yahs*
keyboard instruments	instrumentos de teclado	*eens-troo-'mehn-tohs de teh-'klah-doh*
• **grand piano**	piano de cola	*pee·'ah-noh deh 'koh-lah*
• **harpsichord**	clavicordio	*klah-bee-'kohr-dee·oh*
• **organ**	órgano	*'ohr-gah-noh*
• **piano**	piano	*pee·'ah-noh*
• **synthesizer**	sintetizador (*m*)	*seen-teh-tee-sah-'dohr*
• **upright piano**	piano vertical	*pee·'ah-noh behr-tee-'kahl*
light music	música ligera	*'moo-see-kah lee-'heh-rah*
mandolin	mandolina	*mahn-doh-'lee-nah*
music	música	*'moo-see-kah*
• **musician**	músico(a)	*'moo-see-koh (-kah)*
note	nota	*'noh-tah*
opera	ópera	*'oh-peh-rah*
orchestra	orquesta	*ohr-'kehs-tah*
orchestra conductor	director de orquesta	*dee-rehk-'tohr deh ohr-'kehs-tah*
percussion instruments	instrumentos de percusión	*eens-troo-'mehn-tohs deh pehr-koo-see-'ohn*
• **bass drum**	bombo	*'bohm-boh*
• **cymbals**	címbalos	*'seem-bah-lohs*
• **drum**	tambor (*m*)	*tahm-'bohr*
• **set of drums**	tambores (*m*)	*tahm-'boh-rehs*
• **timpani**	timbales (*m*)	*teem-'bah-lehs*
pianist	pianista (*m, f*)	*pee·ah-'nees-tah*
player	músico(a)	*'moo-see-koh (-kah)*
prelude	preludio	*preh-'loo-dee·oh*
rhythm	ritmo	*'reet-moh*
rock music	música rock	*'moo-see-kah rohk*
• **rock group**	grupo de rock	*'groo-poh deh rohk*
show	espectáculo	*ehs-pehk-'tah-koo-loh*
song	canción (*f*)	*kahn-see·'ohn*
• **sing**	cantar (*v*)	*kahn-'tahr*
• **singer**	cantante (*m/f*)	*kahn-'tahn-teh*
string instruments	instrumentos de cuerda	*eens-troo-'mehn-tohs deh 'kwehr-dah*

• bow	arco	*'ahr-koh*
• cello	violoncelo	*bee·oh-lohn-'seh-loh*
• double bass	contrabajo	*kohn-trah-'bah-hoh*
• string	cuerda	*'kwehr-dah*
• viola	viola	*bee·'oh-lah*
• violin	violín	*bee·oh-'leen*
• violinist	violinista (*m/f*)	*bee·oh-lee-'nees-tah*
symphony	sinfonía	*seen-foh-'nee·ah*
wind instruments	instrumentos de viento	*eens-troo-'mehn-tohs deh vee·'ehn-toh*
• bagpipes	gaita	*'ga·ee-tah*
• bassoon	bajón (*m*)	*bah-'hohn*
• clarinet	clarinete (*m*)	*klah-ree-'neh-teh*
• flute	flauta	*'flow-tah*
• oboe	oboe (*m*)	*oh-'boh-eh*
• saxophone	saxofón	*sah-ksoh-'fohn*

d. LITERATURE

analogy	analogía	*ah-nah-loh-'hee·ah*
antithesis	antítesis (*f*)	*ahn-'tee-teh-sees*
appendix	apéndice (*m*)	*ah-'pehn-dee-seh*
autobiography	autobiografía	*ow-toh-bee·oh-grah-'fee·ah*
ballad	romance (*m*)	*roh-'mahn-seh*
baroque	barroco (*n, adj*)	*bah-'rroh-koh*
Bible	Biblia	*'bee-blee·ah*
biography	biografía	*bee·oh-grah-'fee·ah*
chapter	capítulo	*kah-'pee-too-loh*
character (*in a book, play, etc.*)	personaje (*m*)	*pehr-soh-'nah-heh*
conflict	conflicto	*kohn-'fleek-toh*
criticism	crítica	*'kree-tee-kah*
dialogue	diálogo	*dee·'ah-loh-goh*
essay	ensayo	*ehn-'sah-yoh*
euphemism	eufemismo	*eh·oo-feh-'mees-moh*
fable	fábula	*'fah-boo-lah*
fairy tale	cuento de hadas	*'kwehn-toh deh 'ah-dahs*
fiction	ficción (*f*)	*feek-see·'ohn*
folklore	folklore (*m*)	*fohl-'klohr-eh*
genre	género	*'heh-neh-roh*
hyperbole	hipérbole (*f*)	*ee-'pehr-boh-leh*
idiom	modismo	*moh-'dees-moh*
irony	ironía	*ee-roh-'nee·ah*
legend	leyenda	*leh-'yehn-dah*
literature	literatura	*lee-teh-rah-'too-rah*
main character	protagonista (*m/f*)	*proh-tah-goh-'nees-tah*
metaphor	metáfora	*meh-'tah-foh-rah*

monologue	monólogo	*moh-'noh-loh-goh*
myth	mito	*'mee-toh*
mythology	mitología	*mee-toh-loh-'hee-ah*
novel	novela	*noh-'beh-lah*
onomatopoeia	onomatopeya	*oh-noh-mah-toh-'peh-yah*
parable	parábola	*pah-'rah-boh-lah*
paradox	paradoja	*pah-rah-'doh-hah*
pen name	seudónimo	*seh·oo-'doh-nee-moh*
personification	personificación (*f*)	*pehr-soh-nee-fee-kah-see·'ohn*
• personify	personificar (*v*)	*pehr-soh-nee-fee-'kahr*
plagiarism	plagio	*'plah-gee·oh*
plot	trama (*f*)	*'trah-mah*
poet	poeta	*poh·'eh-tah*
	poetisa	*poh·eh-'tee-sah*
point of view	punto de vista	*'poon-toh deh 'bees-tah*
preface	prefacio	*preh-'fah-see·oh*
prologue	prólogo	*'proh-loh-goh*
proverb	proverbio	*proh-'behr-bee·oh*
pun	retruécano	*reh-'trweh-kah-noh*
rhetoric	retórica	*reh-'toh-ree-kah*
rhyme	rima	*'ree-mah*
satire	sátira	*'sah-tee-rah*
short story	cuento	*'kwehn-toh*
simile	símil (*m*)	*'see-meel*
soliloquy	soliloquio	*soh-lee-'loh-kee·oh*
sonnet	soneto	*soh-'neh-toh*
symbol	símbolo	*'seem-boh-loh*
style	estilo	*eh-'stee-loh*
theme	tema (*m*)	*'teh-mah*
verse	verso	*'behr-soh*
work	obra	*'oh-brah*
writer	escritor(a)	*ehs-kree-'tohr (-'toh-rah)*

e. THEATER

act	acto	*'ahk-toh*
• act	actuar (*v*)	*ahk-'twahr*
applause	aplauso	*ah-'plow-soh*
• applaud	aplaudir (*v*)	*ah-plow-'deer*
audience	público	*'poo-blee-koh*
cast	reparto	*reh-'pahr-toh*
character	personaje (*m*)	*pehr-soh-'nah-heh*
comedian	comediante (*m/f*)	*koh-meh-dee·'ahn-teh*
comedy	comedia	*koh-'meh-dee·ah*

curtain	telón (*m*)	*teh-'lohn*
drama	drama (*m*)	*'drah-mah*
hero	héroe (*m*)	*'eh-roh-eh*
heroine	heroína (*f*)	*eh-roh-'ee-nah*
intermission	entreacto	*ehn-treh-'ahk-toh*
open (*play*)	estrenar (*v*)	*ehs-treh-'nahr*
opening night	estreno	*ehs-'treh-noh*
perform	representar (*v*)	*reh-preh-sehn-'tahr*
• performance	representación (*f*)	*reh-preh-sehn-tah-see·'ohn*
play the role of	hacer (*v**) el papel de	*ah-'sehr ehl pah-'pehl deh*
playwright	dramaturgo	*drah-mah-'toor-goh*
plot	argumento	*ahr-goo-'mehn-toh*
	trama	*'trah-mah*
program	programa (*m*)	*proh-'grah-mah*
rehearse	ensayar (*v*)	*ehn-sah-'yahr*
role	papel (*m*)	*pah-'pehl*
scene	escena	*ehs-'seh-nah*
scenery	decorado	*deh-koh-'rah-doh*
stage	escenario	*ehs-seh-'nah-ree·oh*
theater	teatro	*teh-'ah-troh*
tragedy	tragedia	*trah-'heh-dee·ah*
usher	acomodador (*m*)	*ah-koh-moh-dah-'dohr*
wings (*of stage*)	bastidores (*m*)	*bahs-tee-'doh-rehs*

29. HOLIDAYS AND GOING OUT

a. HOLIDAYS/SPECIAL OCCASIONS

anniversary	aniversario	*ah-nee-behr-'sah-ree·oh*
birthday	cumpleaños (*m*)	*koom-pleh-'ah-nyohs*
Christmas	Navidad (*f*)	*nah-bee-'dahd*
engagement	noviazgo	*noh-bee-'ahs-goh*
holiday (*official*)	día de fiesta	*'dee-ah deh fee-'ehs-tah*
holidays	días de fiesta	*'dee-ahs deh fee-'ehs-tah*
New Year's Day	día del Año Nuevo	*'dee-ah dehl 'ah-nyoh 'nweh-boh*
New Year's Eve	Nochevieja	*noh-cheh-vee-'eh-hah*
picnic	picnic (*m*)	*'peek-neek*
vacation	vacaciones (*f*)	*bah-kah-see·'oh-nehs*
• go on vacation	ir (*v**) de vacaciones	*eer deh bah-kah-see·'oh-nes*
wedding	boda	*'boh-dah*

b. GOING OUT

dance	bailar (v)	*bah·ee-'lahr*
• dance	baile (m)	*'bah·ee-leh*
disco	discoteca	*dees-koh-'teh-kah*
go out	salir (v*)	*sah-'leer*
have fun	divertirse (v*)	*dee-behr-'teer-seh*
party	fiesta	*fee-'ehs-tah*
• invitation	invitación (f)	*een-bee-tah-see-'ohn*
remain, stay	quedarse (v)	*keh-'dahr-seh*
return	volver (v*)	*bohl-'behr*
	regresar (v)	*reh-greh-'sahr*
visit	visitar (v)	*bee-see-'tahr*

c. SPECIAL GREETINGS

Best wishes.	Vaya con Dios.	*'bah-yah kohn dee-'ohs*
Congratulations!	¡Felicitaciones!	*feh-lee-see-tah-see-'oh-nehs,*
	¡Enhorabuena!	*ehn-oh-rah-'bweh-nah*
Happy Birthday.	Feliz cumpleaños.	*feh-'lees koom-pleh-'ah-nyohs*
Happy New Year.	Feliz Año Nuevo.	*feh-'lees 'ah-nyoh 'nweh-boh*
Have a good holiday!	¡Qué pasen buenas vacaciones!	*keh 'pah-sehn 'bweh-nahs bah-kah-see-'oh-nehs*
Have fun.	Diviértase.	*dee-bee-'ehr-tah-seh*
Merry Christmas.	Feliz Navidad.	*feh-'lees nah-bee-'dahd*

TRAVEL

30. CHOOSING A DESTINATION

a. AT THE TRAVEL AGENCY

abroad	al extranjero	*ahl ehks-trahn-'heh-roh*
brochure	folleto	*foh-'yeh-toh*
charter flight	vuelo fletado	*'bweh-loh fleh-'tah-doh*
city	ciudad (*f*)	*see·oo-'dahd*
• **capital city**	ciudad capital	*see·oo-'dahd kah-pee-'tahl*
class	clase (*f*)	*'klah-seh*
• **economy class**	clase turista (*f*)	*'klah-seh too-'rees-tah*
• **first class**	primera clase	*pree-'meh-rah 'klah-seh*
continent	continente (*m*)	*kohn-'tee-'nehn-teh*
country	país (*m*)	*pah-'ees*
downtown	centro	*'sehn-troh*
insurance	seguros	*seh-'goo-rohs*
nation	nación (*f*)	*nah-see-'ohn*
outskirts, suburbs	afueras	*ah-'fweh-rahs*
see	ver (*v*)	*behr*
ticket	boleto	*boh-'leh-toh*
	billete	*bee-'yeh-teh*
• **buy a ticket**	comprar un boleto (billete)	*kohm-'prahr oon boh'leh-toh (bee-'yeh-teh)*
• **return** (*ticket*)	de regreso	*deh reh-'greh-soh*
• **round-trip** (*ticket*)	de ida y vuelta	*deh 'ee-dah ee 'bwehl-tah*
tour, excursion	gira	*'hee-rah*
	excursión (*f*)	*ehks-koor-see-'ohn*
• **tour guide**	guía (*m/f*) de turismo	*'gee-ah deh too-'rees-moh*
• **touring bus**	autobús de turismo	*ow-toh-'boos deh too-'rees-moh*
tourist	turista (*m/f*)	*too-'rees-tah*
travel	viajar (*v*)	*bee·ah-'hahr*
• **by boat**	en barco	*ehn 'bahr-koh*
• **by plane**	en avión	*ehn ah-bee·'ohn*
• **by train**	en tren	*ehn trehn*
• **travel agency**	agencia de viajes	*ah-'hehn-see·ah deh bee·'ah-hehs*
trip	viaje (*m*)	*bee·'ah-heh*
• **Have a nice trip.**	Buen viaje.	*bwehn bee·'ah-heh*

| • take a trip | hacer (v*) un viaje | ah-'sehr oon bee·'ah-heh |
| world | mundo | 'moon-doh |

b. COUNTRIES AND CONTINENTS

Africa	Africa	'ah-free-kah
America	América	ah-'meh-ree-kah
• Latin America	Latinoamérica	lah-tee-noh-ah-'meh-ree-kah
• North America	Norteamérica	nohr-teh-ah-'meh-ree-kah
• South America	Sudamérica	sood-ah-'meh-ree-kah
Asia	Asia	'ah-see-ah
Australia	Australia	ows-'trah-lee-ah
Austria	Austria	'ows-tree-ah
Belgium	Bélgica	'behl-hee-kah
Brazil	Brasil (m)	brah-'seel
Canada	Canadá (m)	kah-nah-'dah
China	China	'chee-nah
Denmark	Dinamarca	dee-nah-'mahr-kah
Egypt	Egipto	eh-'heep-toh
England	Inglaterra	een-glah-'teh-rrah
Europe	Europa	ee·oo-'roh-pah
Finland	Finlandia	feen-'lahn-dee·ah
France	Francia	'frahn-see·ah
Germany	Alemania	ah-leh-'mah-nee·ah
Greece	Grecia	'greh-see·ah
Greenland	Groenlandia	groh-ehn-'lahn-dee·ah
Holland	Holanda	oh-'lahn-dah
Ireland	Irlanda	'eer-'lahn-dah
Israel	Israel	ees-rrah-'ehl
Italy	Italia	ee-'tah-lee·ah
Japan	Japón (m)	hah-'pohn
Luxembourg	Luxemburgo	loo-ksehm-'boor-goh
Mexico	México	'meh-hee-koh
Norway	Noruega	noh-roo-'eh-gah
Poland	Polonia	poh-'loh-nee·ah
Portugal	Portugal	pohr-too-'gahl
Russia	Rusia	'roo-see·ah
Scotland	Escocia	ehs-'koh-see·ah
Spain	España	ehs-'pah-nyah
Sweden	Suecia	'sweh-see·ah
Switzerland	Suiza	'swee-sah
United States	los Estados Unidos	lohs ehs-'tah-dohs oo-'nee-dohs

c. A FEW CITIES

Berlin	Berlín	*behr-'leen*
Lisbon	Lisboa	*lees-'boh-ah*
London	Londres	*'lohn-drehs*
Mexico City	Ciudad de México	*see·oo-dahd deh*
		'meh-hee-koh
Moscow	Moscú	*mohs-'koo*
New York	Nueva York	*'nweh-bah yohrk*
Paris	París	*pah-'rees*
Rome	Roma	*'roh-mah*
Stockholm	Estocolmo	*ehs-toh-'kohl-moh*
Tokyo	Tokio	*'toh-kee·oh*

d. NATIONALITIES AND LANGUAGES

> All nationalities are given in their masculine form. The principal language spoken in the country is written in parentheses.

American	americano (inglés)	*ah-meh-ree-'kah-noh*
		(een-'glehs)
Arabic	árabe (árabe)	*'ah-rah-beh*
Argentinian	argentino (español)	*ahr-hehn-'tee-noh*
Australian	australiano (inglés)	*ows-trah-lee-'ah-noh*
Belgian	belga (flamenco, francés)	*'behl-gah*
Bolivian	boliviano (español)	*boh-lee-bee-'ah-noh*
Brazilian	brasileño (portugués)	*brah-see-'leh-'nyoh*
Canadian	canadiense (inglés, francés)	*kah-nah-dee-'ehn-seh*
Chilean	chileno (español)	*chee-'leh-noh*
Chinese	chino (chino)	*'chee-noh*
Colombian	colombiano (español)	*koh-lohm-bee-'ah-noh*
Costa Rican	costarricense (español)	*kohs-tah-ree-'sehn-seh*
Cuban	cubano (español)	*koo-'bah-noh*
Danish	danés (danés)	*dah-'nehs*
Dominican (*Dominican Republic*)	dominicano (español)	*doh-mee-nee-'kah-noh*
Dutch	holandés (holandés)	*oh-lahn-'dehs*
Ecuadorian	ecuatoriano (español)	*eh-kwah-toh-ree-'ah-noh*
English	inglés (inglés)	*een-'glehs*
French	francés (francés)	*frahn-'sehs*
German	alemán (alemán)	*ah-leh-'mahn*
Greek	griego (griego)	*gree-'eh-goh*

Guatemalan	guatemalteco (español)	*gwah-teh-mahl-'teh-koh*
Honduran	hondureño (español)	*ohn-doo-'reh-nyoh*
Irish	irlandés (inglés)	*eer-lahn-'dehs*
Israeli	israelí (israelí)	*ees-rah-eh-'lee*
Italian	italiano (italiano)	*ee-tah-lee-'ah-noh*
Japanese	japonés (japonés)	*hah-poh-'nehs*
Nicaraguan	nicaragüense (español)	*nee-kah-rah-'gwehn-seh*
Norwegian	noruego (noruego)	*noh-'rweh-goh*
Panamanian	panameño (español)	*pah-nah-'meh-nyoh*
Paraguayan	paraguayo (español)	*pah-rah-'gwah-yoh*
Peruvian	peruano (español)	*peh-'rwah-noh*
Polish	polaco (polaco)	*poh-'lah-koh*
Portuguese	portugués (portugués)	*pohr-too-'gehs*
Puerto Rican	puertorriqueño (español)	*pwehr-toh-rree-'keh-nyoh*
Russian	ruso (ruso)	*'rroo-soh*
Salvadoran	salvadoreño (español)	*sahl-bah-doh-'reh-nyoh*
Spanish	español (español)	*ehs-pah-'nyohl*
Swedish	sueco (sueco)	*'sweh-koh*
Swiss	suizo (alemán, italiano, francés)	*'swee-soh*
Uruguayan	uruguayo (español)	*oo-roo-'gwah-yoh*
Venezuelan	venezolano (español)	*beh-neh-soh-'lah-noh*

31. PACKING AND GOING THROUGH CUSTOMS

backpack	mochila	*moh-'chee-lah*
baggage, luggage	equipaje (*m*)	*eh-kee-'pah-heh*
• hand luggage	equipaje de mano	*eh-kee-'pah-heh deh 'mah-noh*
border	frontera	*frohn-'teh-rah*
carry	llevar (*v*)	*yeh-'bahr*
customs	aduana	*ah-'dwah-nah*
• customs officer	aduanero	*ah-dwah-'neh-roh*
declare	declarar (*v*)	*deh-klah-'rahr*
• nothing to declare	nada que declarar	*'nah-dah keh deh-klah-'rahr*
• something to declare	algo que declarar	*'ahl-goh keh deh-klah-'rahr*
documents	documentos	*doh-koo-'mehn-tohs*
duty tax	derechos de aduana	*deh-'reh-chohs deh ah-'dwah-nah*
• pay duty	pagar (*v*) los derechos de aduana	*pah-'gahr lohs deh-'reh-chohs de ah-'dwah-nah*
foreign currency	moneda extranjera	*moh-'neh-dah ehks-trahn-'heh-rah*

foreigner	extranjero(a)	*ehks-trahn-'heh-roh (rah)*
form (*to fill out*)	formulario	*fohr-moo-'lah-ree·oh*
• **fill out**	llenar (*v*)	*yeh-'nahr*
identification card	tarjeta de identificación	*tahr-'heh-tah deh ee-dehn-tee-fee-kah-see-'ohn*
import	importar (*v*)	*eem-pohr-'tahr*
original invoice	factura original	*fahk-'too-rah oh-ree-hee-'nahl*
passport	pasaporte (*m*)	*pah-sah-'pohr-teh*
receipt	recibo	*reh-'see-boh*
suitcase	maleta	*mah-'leh-tah*
tariff	tarifa	*tah-'ree-fah*
visa	visado	*bee-'sah-doh*
	visa	*'bee-sah*
weight	peso	*'peh-soh*
• **heavy**	pesado (*adj*)	*peh-'sah-doh*
• **light**	ligero (*adj*)	*lee-'heh-roh*
• **maximum**	máximo (*adj*)	*'mah-ksee-moh*

32. TRAVELING BY AIR

a. IN THE TERMINAL

airline	línea aérea	*'lee-neh-ah ah-'eh-reh-ah*
air marshal	alguacil aéreo	*ahl-gwah-'seel ah-'eh-reh-oh*
airport	aeropuerto	*ah-eh-roh-'pwehr-toh*
arrival	llegada	*yeh-'gah-dah*
board	subir (*v*) a	*soo-'beer ah*
• **boarding**	embarque (*m*)	*ehm-'bahr-keh*
• **boarding pass**	tarjeta de embarque	*tahr-'heh-tah deh ehm-'bahr-keh*
check (*luggage*)	facturar (*v*)	*fahk-too-'rahr*
	depositar (*v*)	*deh-poh-see-'tahr*
connection	conexión (*f*)	*koh-neh-ksee-'ohn*
• **make a connection**	hacer (*v**) conexión	*ah-'sehr koh-neh-ksee-'ohn*
departure	salida	*sah-'lee-dah*
economy class	clase turista	*'klah-seh too-'rees-tah*
first class	primera clase	*pree-'meh-rah 'klah-seh*
flight	vuelo	*'bweh-loh*
gate	puerta	*'pwehr-tah*
lost and found	oficina de objetos perdidos	*oh-fee-'see-nah deh ohb-'heh-tohs pehr-'dee-dohs*

luggage inspection	inspección del equipaje	*een-spehk-see-'ohn dehl eh-kee-'pah-heh*
no smoking	no fumar	*noh foo-'mahr*
• **no smoking section**	sección de no fumar	*sehk-see-'ohn deh noh foo-'mahr*
• **smoking section**	sección de fumar	*sehk-see-'ohn deh foo-'mahr*
porter	maletero, mozo	*mah-leh-'teh-roh, 'moh-soh*
reservation	reservación (*f*)	*reh-sehr-bah-see-'ohn*
	reserva	*reh-'sehr-bah*
security check	inspección de seguridad	*een-spehk-see-'ohn deh seg-goo-ree-'dahd*
terminal	terminal (*f*)	*tehr-mee-'nahl*
ticket	boleto	*boh-'leh-toh*
	billete (*m*)	*bee-'yeh-teh*
ticket agent	vendedor de boletos (billetes)	*behn-deh-'dohr deh boh-'leh-tohs (bee-'yeh-tehs)*
waiting room	sala de espera	*'sah-lah deh ehs-'peh-rah*

b. FLIGHT INFORMATION

canceled	cancelado (*adj*)	*kahn-seh-'lah-doh*
direct flight	vuelo directo	*'bweh-loh dee-'rehk-toh*
early	temprano	*tehm-'prah-noh*
late	tarde	*'tahr-deh*
non-stop flight	vuelo sin escala	*'bweh-loh seen eh-'skah-lah*
on time	a tiempo	*ah tee-'ehm-poh*

c. ON THE PLANE

airplane	avión (*m*)	*ah-bee-'ohn*
aisle	pasillo	*pah-'see-yoh*
altitude	altitud (*f*)	*ahl-tee-'tood*
cabin	cabina	*kah-'bee-nah*
copilot	copiloto	*koh-pee-'loh-toh*
crew	tripulación (*f*)	*tree-poo-lah-see-'ohn*
emergency procedures	procedimientos de emergencia	*proh-seh-dee-mee-'ehn-tohs deh eh-mehr-'hehn-see-ah*
flight attendant	aeromozo(a)	*ah-ee-roh-'moh-soh (-sah)*
	azafata	*ah-sah-'fah-tah*
fly	volar (*v**)	*boh-'lahr*
headphones	audífonos (*m*)	*ow-'dee-foh-nohs*
	auriculares (*m*)	*ow-ree-koo-'lah-rehs*
helicopter	helicóptero	*eh-lee-'kohp-teh-roh*

land	aterrizar (v)	*ah-teh-rree-'sahr*
• **landing**	aterrizaje (m)	*ah-teh-rree-'sah-heh*
life jacket	chaleco salvavidas	*chah-'leh-koh sahl-bah-'bee-dahs*
liftoff	despegue (m)	*dehs-'peh-geh*
make a stop	hacer (v*) una escala	*ah-'sehr 'oo-nah ehs-'kah-lah*
oxygen	oxígeno	*ohks-'ee-heh-noh*
passenger	pasajero	*pah-sah-'heh-roh*
runway	pista	*'pees-tah*
seat	asiento	*ah-see-'ehn-toh*
• **aisle seat**	asiento de pasillo	*ah-see-'ehn-toh deh pah-'see-yoh*
• **window seat**	asiento de ventanilla	*ah-see-'ehn-toh deh behn-tah-'nee-yah*
seat belt	cinturón (m) de seguridad	*seen-too-'rohn deh seh-goo-ree-'dahd*
• **buckle up**	abrocharse (v)	*ah-broh-'chahr-seh*
• **fasten**	asegurar (v)	*ah-seh-goo-'rahr*
• **unbuckle**	desabrocharse (v)	*dehs-ah-broh-'chahr-seh*
sit down	sentarse (v*)	*sehn-'tahr-seh*
take off	despegar (v)	*dehs-peh-'gahr*
• **take off**	despegue (m)	*dehs-'peh-geh*
toilet	retrete (m)	*reh-'treh-teh*
tray	bandeja	*bahn-'deh-hah*
turbulence	turbulencia	*toor-boo-'lehn-see·ah*
wheel	rueda	*'rweh-dah*
wing	ala (f)	*'ah-lah*

33. ON THE ROAD

a. VEHICLES

ambulance	ambulancia	*ahm-boo-'lahn-see·ah*
automobile	automóvil	*ow-toh-'moh-beel*
bicycle	bicicleta	*bee-see-'kleh-tah*
• **brake**	freno	*'freh-noh*
• **chain**	cadena	*kah-'deh-nah*
• **chain guard**	cárter (m)	*'kahr-tehr*
• **handlebar**	manillar (m)	*mah-nee-'yahr*
• **pedal**	pedal (m)	*peh-'dahl*
• **seat**	sillín (m)	*see-'yeen*
• **spoke**	radio	*'rah-dee-oh*
• **tire**	neumático	*neh-oo-'mah-tee-koh*
• **tube**	llanta	*'yahn-tah*
bus	autobús (m)	*ow-toh-'boos*
	camión (Mexico)	*kah-mee-'ohn*
• **streetcar**	tranvía (m)	*trahn-'bee·ah*

car	carro	'kah-rroh
	coche (m)	'koh-cheh
• rented car	coche alquilado	'koh-cheh ahl-kee-'lah-doh
• sports car	coche deportivo	'koh-cheh deh-pohr-'tee-boh
compact car	coche pequeño	'koh-cheh peh-'keh-nyoh
motorcycle	moto	'moh-toh
	motocicleta	moh-toh-see-'kleh-tah
taxi	taxi (m)	'tah-ksee
• taxi driver	taxista (m/f)	tah-'ksees-tah
tow truck	grúa de remolque	'groo-ah deh reh-'mohl-keh
trailer	remolque (m)	reh-'mohl-keh
truck	camión (m)	kah-mee-'ohn
• truck driver	camionero	kah-mee-oh-'neh-roh
van	furgón (m)	foor-'gohn
vehicle	vehículo	beh-'ee-koo-loh

b. DRIVING: PEOPLE AND DOCUMENTS

driver	conductor(a)	kohn-dook-'tohr (-'toh-rah)
driver's license	licencia para conducir	lee-'sehn-see-ah 'pah-rah kohn-doo-'seer
insurance card	tarjeta de seguro	tahr-'heh-tah deh seh-'goo-roh
passenger	pasajero	pah-sah-'heh-roh
pedestrian	peatón (m)	peh-ah-'tohn
police	policía (f)	poh-lee-'see-ah
• policeman	policía (m)	poh-lee-'see-ah
• policewoman	policía (f)	poh-lee-'see-ah
• traffic policeman	guardia de tráfico (m)	'gwahr-dee-ah deh 'trah-fee-koh
• traffic policewoman	guardia de tráfico (f)	'gwahr-dee-ah deh 'trah-fee-koh
road map	mapa (m) de carreteras	'mah-pah deh kah-rreh-'teh-rahs
title of ownership	título	'tee-too-loh

c. DRIVING: ADDITIONAL VOCABULARY

accident	accidente (m)	ahk-see-'dehn-teh
back up	retroceder (v)	reh-troh-seh-'dehr
block (city)	cuadra	'kwah-drah
	manzana	mahn-'sah-nah
brake	frenar (v)	freh-'nahr

bridge	puente (*m*)	'pwehn-teh
change gears	cambiar (*v*) de velocidad	kahm-bee-'ahr deh beh-loh-see-'dahd
corner (*street*)	esquina	ehs-'kee-nah
curve	curva	'koor-bah
distance	distancia	dees-'tahn-see-ah
downhill	calle abajo	'kah-yeh ah-'bah-hoh
drive	conducir (*v**)	kohn-doo-'seer
	manejar (*v*)	mah-neh-'hahr
fine, ticket	multa	'mool-tah
gas station	gasolinera	gah-soh-lee-'neh-rah
• check the oil	mirar (*v*) el nivel del aceite	mee-'rahr ehl nee-'behl dehl ah-'seh·ee-teh
• diesel	diesel (*m*)	dee·eh-'sehl
• fill up	llenar (*v*)	yeh-'nahr
• fix	reparar (*v*)	reh-pah-'rahr
• gasoline	gasolina	gah-soh-'lee-nah
• leaded gas	gasolina con plomo	gah-soh-'lee-nah kohn 'ploh-moh
• mechanic	mecánico	meh-'kah-nee-koh
• self-service	autoservicio	ow-toh-sehr-'bee-see·oh
• tools	herramientas	eh-rrah-mee-'ehn-tahs
• unleaded gas	gasolina sin plomo	gah-soh-'lee-nah seen 'ploh-moh
go forward	adelantar (*v*)	ah-deh-lahn-'tahr
go through a red light	pasar (*v*) por una luz roja	pah-'sahr pohr 'oo-nah loos 'rroh-hah
highway	carretera	kah-rreh-'teh-rah
intersection	bocacalle (*f*)	boh-kah-'kah-yeh
	cruce (*m*)	'kroo-seh
lane (*traffic*)	carril (*m*)	kah-'rreel
park	estacionar (*v*)	ehs-tah-see·oh-'nahr
• parking	estacionamiento	ehs-tah-see·oh-nah-mee-'ehn-toh
• public parking	estacionamiento público	ehs-tah-see·oh-nah-mee-'ehn-toh 'poo-blee-koh
pass	pasar (*v*)	pah-'sahr
	adelantar (*v*)	ad-deh-lahn-'tahr
pedestrian crossing	paso de peatones (*m*)	pah-soh deh peh-ah-'toh-nehs
ramp	rampa	'rahm-pah
road	camino	kah-'mee-noh
rush hour	hora punta	'oh-rah 'poon-tah
signal	señal (*f*)	seh-'nyahl

speed	velocidad (*f*)	*beh-loh-see-'dahd*
• **slow down**	ir (*v**) más despacio	*eer mahs dehs-'pah-see·oh*
• **speed up**	acelerar (*v*)	*ah-seh-leh-'rahr*
start (*the car*)	arrancar (*v*)	*ah-rrahn-'kahr*
toll	peaje (*m*)	*peh-'ah-heh*
• **toll booth**	barrera de peaje	*bah-'rreh-rah deh peh-'ah-heh*
traffic	tráfico	*'trah-fee-koh*
traffic light	semáforo	*seh-'mah foh-roh*
tunnel	túnel (*m*)	*'too-nehl*
turn	dar (*v**) la vuelta	*dahr lah 'bwehl-tah*
• **to the left**	a la izquierda	*ah lah ees-kee-'ehr-dah*
• **to the right**	a la derecha	*ah lah deh-'reh-chah*
uphill	calle arriba	*'kah-yeh ah-'rree-bah*

d. ROAD SIGNS

caution	cuidado	*kwee-'dah-doh*
danger	peligro	*peh-'lee-groh*
dangerous crossing	cruce (*m*) peligroso	*'kroo-seh peh-lee-'groh-soh*
detour	desvío	*dehs-'bee·oh*
emergency lane	carril (*m*) de emergencia	*kah-'rreel deh eh-mehr-'hehn-see·ah*
intersection	intersección (*f*) cruce (*m*)	*een-tehr-sehk-see-'ohn 'kroo-seh*
keep to the right	conserve su derecha	*kohn-'sehr-beh soo deh-'reh-chah*
level crossing	paso a nivel	*'pah-soh ah nee-'behl*
merge	empalme (*m*)	*ehm-'pahl-meh*
narrow bridge	puente angosto	*'pwehn-teh ahn-'gohs-toh*
no entry	dirección prohibida	*dee-rehk-see-'ohn proh-ee'bee-dah*
no left turn	prohibido girar a la izquierda	*proh-ee-'bee-doh hee-'rahr ah lah ees-kee-'ehr-dah*
no parking	prohibido estacionar	*proh-ee-'bee-doh ehs-tah-see·oh-'nahr*
no passing	prohibido adelantar	*proh-ee-'bee-doh ah-deh-lahn-'tahr*
no right turn	prohibido girar a la derecha	*proh-ee-'bee-doh hee-'rahr ah lah deh-'reh-chah*
no U-turn	prohibido dar la vuelta	*proh-ee-'bee-doh dahr lah 'bwehl-tah*
no stopping	prohibido parar	*proh-ee-'bee-doh pah-'rahr*

one way	dirección única	*dee-rehk-see-'ohn 'oo-nee-kah*
pedestrian crosswalk	paso de peatones	*'pah-soh deh peh-ah-'toh-nehs*
slippery when wet	resbaladizo cuando mojado	*rehs-bah-lah-'dee-soh 'kwahn-doh moh-'hah-doh*
slow	despacio	*dehs-'pah-see-oh*
speed limit	velocidad máxima	*beh-loh-see-'dahd 'mah-ksee-mah*
stop	alto	*'ahl-toh*
	parada	*pah-'rah-dah*
toll	peaje (*m*)	*peh-'ah-heh*
tow-away zone	zona de remolque	*'soh-nah deh reh-'mohl-keh*
underpass	paso subterráneo	*'pah-soh soob-teh-'rrah-neh-oh*
wind gusts	vientos fuertes	*bee-'ehn-tohs 'fwehr-tehs*
work in progress	obras	*'oh-brahs*
yield	ceder (*v*) el paso	*seh-'dehr ehl 'pah-soh*

e. THE CAR

air conditioning	aire acondicionado	*'ah·ee-reh ah-kohn-dee-see-oh-'nah-doh*
battery	acumulador	*ah-koo-moo-lah-'dohr*
brake	freno	*'freh-noh*
bumper	parachoques (*m*)	*pah-rah-'choh-kehs*
car body	carrocería	*kah-rroh-seh-'ree·ah*
car window	ventanilla	*behn-tah-'nee-yah*
carburetor	carburador (*m*)	*kahr-boo-rah-'dohr*
clutch	embrague (*m*)	*ehm-'brah-geh*
dashboard	tablero de instrumentos	*tah-'bleh-roh deh eens-troo-'mehn-tohs*
door	puerta	*'pwehr-tah*
electrical system	sistema eléctrico	*sees-'teh-mah eh-'lehk-tree-koh*
fan	ventilador (*m*)	*behn-tee-lah-'dohr*
• fan belt	correa de ventilador	*koh-'rreh-ah deh behn-tee-lah-'dohr*
fender	parachoques (*m*)	*pah-rah-'choh-kehs*
filter	filtro	*'feel-troh*
gas pedal	acelerador (*m*)	*ah-seh-leh-rah-'dohr*
gas tank	tanque (*m*)	*'tahn-keh*
gearshift	cambio de velocidad	*'kahm-bee-oh deh beh-loh-see-'dahd*
generator	generador (*m*)	*heh-neh-rah-'dohr*

No U-turn

No passing

Border crossing

Traffic signal ahead

Speed limit
(Kilometers)

Traffic circle (roundabout)
ahead

Minimum speed limit
(Kilometers)

All traffic turns left

End of no passing zone

DIRECCIÓN ÚNICA

One-way street

DESVÍO

Detour

Danger ahead

Entrance to expressway

Expressway ends

Guarded railroad crossing

Yield

Stop

Right of way

Dangerous intersection ahead

Gasoline ahead

Parking

No vehicles allowed

Dangerous curve

Pedestrian crossing

Oncoming traffic has right of way

No bicycles allowed

No parking allowed

No entry

No left turn

glove compartment	guantera	*gwahn-'teh-rah*
handle	manija	*mah-'nee-hah*
hazard flash	luces de emergencia	*'loo-sehs deh eh-mehr-'gehn-see·ah*
headlight	faro delantero	*'fah-roh deh-lahn-'teh-roh*
heater	calefacción (*f*)	*kah-leh-fahk-see·'ohn*
hood	capó (*m*)	*kak-'poh*
horn	claxon (*m*), bocina	*'klah-ksohn, boh-'see-nah*
horsepower	caballo de fuerza	*kah-'bah-yoh deh 'fwehr-sah*
ignition	encendido	*ehn-sehn-'dee-doh*
jack	gato	*'gah-toh*
license plate	placa	*'plah-kah*
lights	luces (*f*)	*'loo-sehs*
mileage	kilometraje (*m*)	*kee-loh-meh-'trah-heh*
motor, engine	motor (*m*)	*moh-'tohr*
muffler	silenciador	*see-len-see·ah·'dohr*
rearview mirror	espejo retrovisor	*eh-'speh-hoh reh-troh-vee-'sohr*
repair	reparar (*v*)	*reh-pah-'rahr*
spark plug	bujía	*boo-'hee·ah*
speedometer	velocímetro	*beh-loh-'see-meh-troh*
starter	arranque (*m*)	*ah-'rrahn-keh*
steering wheel	volante (*m*)	*boh-'lahn-teh*
tire	neumático	*neh-oo-'mah-tee-koh*
• flat tire	pinchazo	*peen-'chah-soh*
	neumático desinflado	*neh-oo-'mah-tee-koh dehs-een-'flah-doh*
traffic jam	atasco	*ah-'tahs-koh*
transmission	transmisión (*f*)	*trahs-mee-see·'ohn*
trunk	baúl (*m*)	*bah-'ool*
	valija	*bah-'lee-hah*
turn signal	indicador (*m*) de dirección	*een-dee-kuh-'dohr deh dee-rehk-see·'ohn*
wheel	rueda	*'rweh-dah*
windshield	parabrisas (*m*)	*pah-rah-'bree-sahs*
• windshield washer	limpiaparabrisas (*m*)	*leem-pee·ah-pah-rah-'bree-sahs*

34. TRAIN, BUS, AND SUBWAY

bus	autobús (*m*)	*ow-toh-'boos*
bus driver	conductor(a)	*kohn-dok-'tohr (-rah)*
bus station	estación (*f*) de autobuses	*ehs-tah-see·'ohn deh ow-toh-'boo-sehs*

conductor (*train*)	revisor (*m*)	*reh-bee-'sohr*
conductor (*bus*)	conductor (*m*)	*kohn-dook-'tohr*
compartment	compartimiento	*kohm-pahr-tee-mee·'ehn-toh*
• **no smoking**	de no fumar	*deh·noh foo-'mahr*
• **smoking**	de fumar	*de foo-'mahr*
connection	enlace (*m*)	*ehn-'lah-seh*
	conexión (*f*)	*koh-neh-ksee·'ohn*
direct train	tren (*m*) directo	*trehn dee-'rehk-toh*
express (*bus/train*)	expreso	*ehks-'preh-soh*
leave, depart	salir (*v**)	*sah-'leer*
	partir (*v*)	*pahr-'teer*
miss (*the train, etc.*)	perder (*v**) (el tren)	*pehr-'dehr (ehl trehn)*
local train	tren de cercanías	*trehn deh sehr-kah-'nee·ahs*
newsstand	quiosco	*kee-'ohs-koh*
platform	andén (*m*)	*ahn-'dehn*
porter	maletero	*mah-leh-'teh-roh*
railroad	ferrocarril (*m*)	*feh-rroh-kah-'rreel*
• **railroad station**	estación (*f*) de ferrocarril	*ehs-tah-see·'ohn deh feh-rroh-kah-'rreel*
schedule	horario	*oh-'rah-ree·oh*
• **early**	temprano	*tehm-'prah-noh*
• **late**	tarde	*'tahr-deh*
• **on time**	a tiempo	*ah tee·'ehm-poh*
seat	asiento	*ah-see·'ehn-toh*
• **economy**	clase turista	*'klah-seh too-'rees-tah*
• **first class**	primera clase	*pree-'meh-rah 'klah-seh*
stop	parada	*pah-'rah-dah*
subway	metro	*'meh-tro*
	subterráneo	*soob-teh-'rrah-neh-oh*
• **subway station**	estación del metro	*ehs-tah-see·'ohn del 'meh-troh*
take (*the train, etc.*)	tomar (*v*) el tren	*toh-'mahr ehl trehn*
ticket	boleto	*boh-'leh-toh*
	billete (*m*)	*bee-'yeh-teh*
• **buy a ticket**	comprar (*v*) un boleto	*kohm-'prahr oon boh-'leh-toh*
• **ticket agent**	vendedor (*m*) de boletos	*behn-deh-'dohr deh boh-'leh-tohs*
• **ticket counter**	taquilla	*tah-'kee-yah*
	boletería	*boh-leh-teh-'ree·ah*
track	vía	*bee-ah*
train	tren (*m*)	*trehn*
• **All aboard!**	¡Todos a bordo!	*'toh-dohs ah 'bohr-doh*
• **coach**	vagón (*m*)	*bah-'gohn*
• **coach class**	segunda clase	*seh-'goon-dah 'klah-seh*

| train station | estación de trenes | *ehs-tah-see-'ohn deh 'treh-nehs* |
| wait for | esperar (v) | *ehs-peh-'rahr* |

35. HOTELS

a. LODGING

boardinghouse	casa de huéspedes	*'kah-sah deh 'wehs-peh-dehs*
	pensión (f)	*pehn-see-'ohn*
guesthouse	casa de huéspedes	*'kah-sah deh 'weh-speh-dehs*
hotel	hotel (m)	*oh-'tehl*
• luxury hotel	hotel de primera categoría	*oh-'tehl deh pree-'meh-rah kah-teh-goh-'ree·ah*
inn	posada	*poh-'sah-dah*
	hostería	*oh-steh-'ree-ah*
motel	motel (m)	*moh-'tehl*
youth hostel	albergue juvenil (m)	*ahl-'behr-geh hoo-beh-'neel*

b. STAYING IN HOTELS

bellboy	botones (m)	*boh-'toh-nehs*
bill	cuenta	*'kwehn-tah*
• ask for the bill	pedir (v*) la cuenta	*peh-'deer lah 'kwehn-tah*
breakfast	desayuno	*dehs-ah-'yoo-noh*
• breakfast included	desayuno incluido	*dehs-ah-'yoo-noh een-'klwee-doh*
call for a taxi	pedir (v*) un taxi	*peh-'deer oon 'tah-ksee*
complain	quejarse (v)	*keh-'dahr-seh*
• complaint	queja	*'keh-hah*
doorman	portero	*pohr-'teh-roh*
electric adaptor	adaptador eléctrico (m)	*ah-dahp-tah-'dohr eh-'lehk-tree-koh*
elevator	ascensor (m)	*ahs-sehn-'sohr*
entrance	entrada	*ehn-'trah-dah*
exit	salida	*sah-'lee-dah*
floor	piso	*'pee-soh*
garage	garaje (m)	*gah-'rah-heh*
hotel clerk	dependiente(a)	*deh-pehn-dee-'ehn-teh (-tah)*

ice cubes	cubitos de hielo	*koo-'bee-tohs deh ee·'eh-loh*
identification card	tarjeta de identificación	*tahr-'heh-tah deh ee-dehn-tee-fee-kah-see·'ohn*
key	llave (*f*)	*'yah-beh*
• **return the key before leaving**	devolver (*v**) la llave antes de salir	*deh-bohl-'behr lah 'llah-beh 'ahn-tehs deh sah-'leer*
lobby	vestíbulo	*behs-'tee-boo-loh*
• **main door**	puerta principal	*'pwehr-tah preen-see-'pahl*
• **main floor**	planta baja	*'plahn-tah 'bah-hah*
luggage	equipaje (*m*)	*eh-kee-'pah-heh*
• **luggage rack**	portaequipajes (*m*)	*pohr-tah-eh-kee-'pah-hehs*
maid	criada	*kree-'ah-dah*
manager	gerente (*m/f*)	*heh-'rehn-teh*
message	mensaje (*m*)	*mehn-'sah-heh*
passport	pasaporte (*m*)	*pah-sah-'pohr-teh*
pay	pagar (*v*)	*pah-'gahr*
• **by check**	con cheque	*kohn 'cheh-keh*
• **cash**	en efectivo	*ehn eh-fehk-'tee-boh*
• **credit card**	con tarjeta de crédito	*kohn tahr-'heh-tah deh 'kreh-dee-toh*
• **traveler's check**	con cheque de viajeros	*kohn 'cheh-keh deh bee·ah-heh-rohs*
pool	alberca	*ahl-'behr-kah*
	piscina	*pees-'see-nah*
porter	maletero	*mah-leh-'teh-roh*
price	precio	*'preh-see·oh*
• **high season**	temporada alta	*tehm-poh-'rah-dah 'ahl-tah*
• **low season**	temporada baja	*tehm-poh-'rah-dah 'bah-hah*
receipt	recibo	*reh-'see-boh*
reception desk	recepción (*f*)	*reh-seph-see·'ohn*
reservation	reservación (*f*)	*reh-sehr-bah-see·'ohn*
room	cuarto	*'kwahr-toh*
	habitación (*f*)	*ah-bee-tah-see·'ohn*
• **Do you have a vacant room?**	¿Tiene usted un cuarto libre?	*tee·'eh-neh oos-'tehd oon 'kwahr-toh 'lee-breh*
• **double room**	cuarto doble	*'kwahr-toh 'doh-bleh*
• **double bed**	cama matrimonial	*'kah-mah mah-tree-moh-nee·'ahl*
• **single bed**	cama sencilla	*'kah-mah sehn-'see-yah*

• **room with two beds**	cuarto con dos camas	*'kwahr-toh kohn dohs 'kah-mahs*
• **single room**	cuarto sencillo	*'kwahr-toh sehn-'see-yoh*
services	servicios	*sehr-'bee-see-ohs*
stairs	escalera	*ehs-kah-'leh-rah*
view	vista	*'bee-stah*

c. THE HOTEL ROOM

See also Section 23.

armchair	sillón (*m*)	*see-'yohn*
balcony	balcón (*m*)	*bahl-'kohn*
• **sliding door**	puerta corrediza	*poo-'ehr-tah koh-rreh-'dee-sah*
bathroom	baño	*'bah-nyoh*
bathtub	bañera	*bah-'nyeh-rah*
bed	cama	*'kah-mah*
• **double bed**	cama matrimonial	*'kah-mah mah-tree-moh-nee-'ahl*
bedside table	mesilla de noche	*meh-'see-yah deh 'noh-cheh*
bedspread	cubrecama (*m*)	*koo-breh-'kah-mah*
blanket	manta	*'mahn-tah*
chest of drawers	cómoda	*'koh-moh-dah*
closet	armario	*ahr-mah-ree-'oh*
clothes hanger	percha	*'pehr-chah*
	gancho	*'gahn-choh*
curtains	cortinas	*kohr-'tee-nahs*
dresser	tocador (*m*)	*toh-kah-'dohr*
faucet	grifo	*'gree-foh*
lamp	lámpara	*'lahm-pah-rah*
lights	luces (*f*)	*'loo-sehs*
• **current**	corriente (*m*)	*koh-rree-'ehn-teh*
• **light switch**	interruptor (*m*)	*een-teh-rroop-'tohr*
• **turn off**	apagar (*v*)	*ah-pah-'gahr*
• **turn on**	encender (*v**)	*ehn-sehn-'dehr*
mirror	espejo	*ehs-'peh-hoh*
pillow	almohada	*ahl-moh-'ah-dah*
radio	radio	*'rah-dee-oh*
reading lamp	lámpara para leer	*'lahm-pah-rah 'pah-rah leh-'ehr*

soap bar	pastilla de jabón	*pahs-'tee-yah deh hah-'bohn*
shampoo	champú (*m*)	*chahm-'poo*
sheets	sábanas	*'sah-bah-nahs*
shower	ducha	*'doo-chah*
sink, wash basin	lavabo	*lah-'bah-boh*
• cold water	agua fría	*'ah-gwah 'free·ah*
• hot water	agua caliente	*'ah-gwah cah-lee·'ehn-teh*
table	mesa	*'meh-sah*
telephone	teléfono	*teh-'leh-foh-noh*
television set	televisor (*m*)	*teh-leh-bee-'sohr*
thermostat	termostato	*tehr-mohs-'tah-toh*
toilet	inodoro	*een-oh-'doh-roh*
• toilet paper	papel higiénico	*pah-'pehl ee-hee·'ehn-nee-koh*
towel	toalla	*toh-'ah-yah*

36. ON VACATION

a. SIGHTSEEING

amphitheater	anfiteatro	*ahn-fee-teh-'ah-troh*
avenue	avenida	*ah-beh-'nee-dah*
basilica	basílica	*boh-'see-lee-kah*
bell tower	campanario	*kahn-pah-'nah-ree·oh*
bridge	puente (*m*)	*'pwehn-teh*
bullring	plaza de toros	*'plah-sah deh 'toh-rohs*
castle	castillo	*kahs-'tee-yoh*
cathedral	catedral (*f*)	*kah-teh-'drahl*
church	iglesia	*ee-'gleh-see·ah*
city	ciudad (*f*)	*see·oo-'dahd*
city map	plano de la ciudad	*'plah-noh deh lah see·oh-'dahd*
corner	esquina	*ehs-'kee-nah*
downtown	centro	*'sehn-troh*
guide	guía (*m/f*)	*'gee·ah*
• guidebook	guía (*f*) del viajero	*'gee·ah dehl bee·ah-'heh-roh*
intersection	bocacalle (*f*)	*boh-kah-'kah-yeh*
kiosk	quiosco	*kee·'ohs-koh*
monument	monumento	*moh-noo-'mehn-toh*
museum	museo	*moo-'seh-oh*
• art museum	museo de arte (*m*)	*moo-'seh-oh deh 'ahr-teh*
park	parque (*m*)	*'pahr-keh*

park bench	banco	*'bahn-koh*
parking meter	parquímetro	*pahr-'kee-meh-troh*
pedestrian crosswalk	paso de peatones	*'pah-soh deh peh-ah-'toh-nehs*
public garden	jardín público	*hahr-'deen 'poo-blee-koh*
public notices	avisos públicos	*ah-'bee-sohs 'poo-blee-kohs*
public telephone	teléfono público	*teh-'leh-foh-noh 'poo-blee-koh*
public washroom	servicio público	*sehr-'bee-see-oh 'poo-blee-koh*
railway crossing	cruce (*m*) de vías	*'kroo-seh deh 'bee·ahs*
sidewalk	acera	*ah-'seh-rah*
square	plaza	*'plah-sah*
street	calle (*f*)	*'kah-yeh*
• **street sign**	letrero	*leh-'treh-roh*
take an excursion	hacer (*v**) una gira	*ah-'sehr 'oo-nah 'hee-rah*
temple	templo	*'tehm-ploh*
tower	torre (*f*)	*'toh-rreh*
traffic light	semáforo	*seh-'mah-foh-roh*
water fountain	fuente (*f*)	*'fwehn-teh*

b. GETTING OUT OF THE CITY

beach	playa	*'plah-yah*
• **get a suntan**	broncearse (*v*)	*brohn-seh-'ahr-seh*
boat	bote	*'boh-teh*
brook	arroyo	*ah-'rroh-yoh*
campground	campamento	*kahm-pah-'mehn-toh*
canoe	canoa	*kah-'noh-ah*
canteen	cantimplora	*kahn-teem-'ploh-rah*
cap	gorra	*'goh-rrah*
cruise	crucero	*kroo-'seh-roh*
fish	pescar (*v*)	*pehs-'kahr*
• **go fishing**	ir (*v**) de pesca	*eer deh 'pehs-kah*
in the country	en el campo	*ehn ehl 'kahm-poh*
in the mountains	en las montañas	*ehn lahs mohn-'tah-nyahs*
lake	lago	*'lah-goh*
mountain climbing	alpinismo	*ahl-pee-'nees-moh*
river	río	*'ree-oh*
rope	cuerda	*'kwehr-dah*
sea	mar (*m*)	*mahr*
ship	barco	*'bahr-koh*

skiing	esquí (m)	ehs-'kee
• ski resort	lugar (m) para esquiar	loo-'gahr 'pah-rah ehs-kee-'ahr
sleeping bag	saco de dormir	'sah-koh deh dohr-'meer
tent	tienda	tee-'ehn-dah
trip	viaje (m)	bee-'ah-heh
vacation	vacaciones (f)	bah-kah-see-'oh-nehs
• on vacation	de vacaciones	deh bah-kah-see-'oh-nehs

c. ASKING FOR DIRECTIONS

across	a través de	ah trah-'behs deh
ahead	adelante	ah-deh-'lahn-teh
at the end of	al final de	ahl fee-'nahl deh
at the top of	a la cumbre de	ah lah 'koom-breh deh
behind	detrás de	deh-'trahs deh
cross (over)	cruzar (v)	kroo-'sahr
• cross the street	cruzar (v) la calle	kroo-'sahr lah 'kah-yeh
down	abajo (adv)	ah-'bah-hoh
enter	entrar (v) a (en)	ehn-'trahr ah (ehn)
• entrance	entrada	ehn-'trah-dah
everywhere	en todas partes	ehn 'toh-dahs 'pahr-tehs
exit, go out	salir (v*)	sah-'leer
• exit	salida	sah-'lee-dah
far (from)	lejos (de)	'leh-hohs (deh)
follow	seguir (v*)	seh-'geer
go	ir (v*)	eer
go down	bajar (v)	bah-'hahr
go up	subir (v)	soo-'beer
here	aquí	ah-'kee
	acá	ah-'kah
in front of	delante de	ehn'lahn-teh deh
in front of (facing)	en frente de	ehn'frehn-teh deh
inside	dentro (adv)	'dehn-troh
	adentro (adv)	ah-'dehn-troh
• inside of	dentro de (prep)	'dehn-troh deh
near	cerca de (prep)	'sehr-kah deh
• nearby	cerca (adv)	'sehr-kah
outside	afuera (adv)	ah-'fweh-rah
straight ahead	derecho (adv)	deh-'reh-choh
there	allí	ah-'yee
	allá	ah-'yah
through	por (prep)	pohr
	a través de (prep)	ah trah-'behs deh
to the east	al este	ahl 'ehs-teh
to the left	a la izquierda	ah lah ees-kee-'ehr-dah

to the north	al norte	*ahl 'nohr-teh*
to the right	a la derecha	*ah lah deh-'reh-chah*
to the south	al sur	*ahl soor*
to the west	al oeste	*ahl oh-ehs-teh*
towards	hacia (*prep*)	*'ah-see·ah*
turn	dar (*v**) la vuelta	*dahr lah 'bwehl-tah*

Can you tell me where . . . ? = ¿Me puede usted decir dónde . . . ?
Where is . . . ? = ¿Dónde está . . . ?
How do you get to? = ¿Cómo se llega a . . . ?

SCHOOL AND WORK

37. SCHOOL

a. TYPES OF SCHOOLS AND GRADES

coed school	colegio mixto	*koh-'leh-gee·oh 'meeks-toh*
conservatory	conservatorio	*kohn-sehr-bah-'toh-ree·oh*
day-care center	guardería	*gwahr-deh-'ree·ah*
elementary school	escuela primaria	*ehs-'kweh-lah pree-'mah-ree·ah*
evening school	escuela nocturna	*ehs-'kweh-lah nohk-'toor-nah*
grade	clase (*f*)	*'klah-seh*
• first grade	primer grado	*pree-'mehr 'grah-doh*
high school	escuela secundaria	*ehs-'kweh-lah seh-koon-'dah-ree·ah*
junior high school	instituto de bachillerato elemental	*eens-tee-'too-toh deh bah-chee-yeh-'rah-toh eh-leh-mehn-'tahl*
kindergarten	jardín infantil	*haher-'deen een-fahn-'teel*
nursery school	escuela de párvulos	*ehs-'kweh-lah deh 'pahr-boo-lohs*
private school	escuela privada	*ehs-'kweh-lah pree-'bah-dah*
technical school	instituto laboral	*eens-tee-'too-toh lah-boh-'rahl*
university	universidad (*f*)	*oo'nee-behr-see-'dahd*
• year (*e.g., at university*)	año escolar	*'ah-nyoh ehs-koh-'lahr*
• first year	primer año	*pree-'mehr 'ah-nyoh*
• second year	segundo año	*seh-'goon-doh 'ah-nyoh*
vocational school	escuela vocacional	*ehs-'kweh-lah boh-kah-see·oh-'nahl*

b. THE CLASSROOM

atlas	atlas (*m*)	*'aht-lahs*
ballpoint pen	bolígrafo	*boh-'lee-grah-foh*
blackboard	pizarra	*pee-'sah-rrah*
blackboard eraser	borrador (*m*)	*boh-rrah-'dohr*
book	libro	*'lee-broh*
bookcase	estante (*m*)	*ehs-'tahn-teh*
chalk	tiza	*'tee-sah*

compass	compás (m)	kohm-'pahs
computer	computadora	kohm-poo-tah-'doh-rah
	ordenador	ohr-deh-nah-'dohr
date book	diario	dee-'ah-ree-oh
desk (*classroom*)	pupitre (m)	poo-'pee-treh
desk (*office*)	escritorio	ehs-kree-'toh-ree-oh
dictionary	diccionario	deek-see-oh-'nah-ree-oh
encyclopedia	enciclopedia	ehn-see-kloh-'peh-dee-ah
eraser (*pencil*)	goma	'goh-mah
	borrador (m)	boh-rrah-'dohr
eyeglasses	gafas	'gah-fahs
	anteojos	ahn-teh-'oh-hohs
film projector	proyector (m)	proh-yehk-'tohr
ink	tinta	'teen-tah
magazine	revista	reh-'bees-tah
map	mapa (m)	'mah-pah
notebook	cuaderno	kwah-'dehr-noh
overhead projector	retroproyector	reh-troh-proh-yehk-'tohr
paper	papel (m)	pah-'pehl
pen	pluma	'ploo-mah
pencil	lápiz (m)	'lah-pees
record player	tocadiscos (m)	toh-kah-'dees-kohs
ruler	regla	'reh-glah
school bag	mochila	moh-'chee-lah
slide projector	proyector de diapositivas	proh-yehk-'tohr deh dee-ah-poh-see-'tee-bahs
tack	tachuela	tah-'chweh-lah
tape recorder	grabadora	grah-bah-'doh-rah
textbook	libro de texto	'lee-broh deh 'tehks-toh
wall map	mapa mural (m)	'mah-pah moo-'rahl

c. AREAS OF A SCHOOL

campus	ciudad universitaria	see-oo-'dahd oo-nee-behr-see-'tah-ree-ah
	campus (m)	'kahm-poos
classroom	aula (f)	'ow-lah
gymnasium	gimnasio	heem-'nah-see-oh
hallway	pasillo	pah-'see-yoh
	corredor (m)	koh-rreh-'dohr
laboratory	laboratorio	lah-boh-rah-'toh-ree-oh
• chemistry lab	laboratorio de química	lah-boh-rah-'toh-ree-oh deh 'kee-mee-kah
• language lab	laboratorio de lenguas	lah-boh-rah-'toh-ree-oh deh 'lehn-gwahs

main office	oficina central	*oh-fee-'see-nah sehn-'trahl*
library	biblioteca	*bee-blee·oh-'teh-kah*
professor's office	oficina (del profesor, de la profesora)	*oh-fee-'see-nah (dehl proh-feh-'sohr, deh lah proh-feh-'soh-rah)*
school yard	patio	*'pah-tee·oh*

d. SCHOOL: PEOPLE

assistant	ayudante (*m/f*)	*ah-yoo-'dahn-teh*
class of students	clase (*f*)	*'klah-seh*
custodian	portero	*pohr-'teh-roh*
lab technician	ayudante de laboratorio	*ah-yoo-'dahn-teh deh lah-boh-rah-'toh-ree·oh*
librarian	bibliotecario(a)	*bee-blee-oh-teh-'kah-ree·oh (-ah)*
president of a university	rector (*m*)	*rehk-'tohr*
principal	director(a)	*dee-rehk-'tohr (-rah)*
schoolmate	compañero(a) de clase	*kohm-pah-'nyeh-roh (-rah) deh 'klah-seh*
secretary	secretario(a)	*seh-kre-'tah-ree·oh (-ah)*
student	alumno(a)	*ah-'loom-noh (-nah)*
	estudiante (*m/f*)	*ehs-too-dee·'ahn-teh*
teacher	profesor(a)	*proh-feh-'sohr (-rah)*
• elementary school teacher	maestro(a)	*mah-'ehs-troh (-trah)*
• high school teacher	profesor(a)	*proh-feh-'sohr (-rah)*

e. SCHOOL: SUBJECTS

accounting	contabilidad (*f*)	*kohn-tah-bee-lee-'dahd*
anatomy	anatomía	*ah-nah-toh-'mee·ah*
anthropology	antropología	*ahn-troh-poh-loh-'hee-ah*
archaeology	arqueología	*ahr-keh-oh-loh-'hee-ah*
architecture	arquitectura	*ahr-kee-tehk-'too-rah*
art	arte (*m*)	*'ahr-teh*
astronomy	astronomía	*ahs-troh-noh-'mee-ah*
biology	biología	*bee·oh-loh-'hee-ah*
botany	botánica	*boh-'tah-nee-kah*
calculus	cálculo	*'kahl-koo-loh*
chemistry	química	*'kee-mee-kah*
commerce	comercio	*koh-'mehr-see·oh*

economics	economía	*eh-koh-noh-'mee-ah*
engineering	ingeniería	*een-heh-nee-eh-'ree-ah*
fine arts	bellas artes	*'beh-yahs 'ahr-tehs*
geography	geografía	*heh-oh-grah-'fee-ah*
geometry	geometría	*heh-oh-meh-'tree-ah*
history	historia	*ees-'toh-ree-ah*
languages (foreign)	lenguas (extranjeras)	*'lehn-gwahs (ehks-trahn-'heh-rahs)*
law	derecho	*deh-'reh-choh*
	leyes (*f*)	*'leh-yehs*
literature	literatura	*lee-teh-rah-'too-rah*
mathematics	matemáticas	*mah-teh-'mah-tee-kahs*
medicine	medicina	*meh-dee-'see-nah*
music	música	*'moo-see-kah*
philosophy	filosofía	*fee-loh-soh-'fee-ah*
physics	física	*'fee-see-kah*
political science	ciencia política	*see-'ehn-see-ah poh-'lee-tee-kah*
psychology	psicología	*see-koh-loh-'hee-ah*
science	ciencia	*see-'ehn-see-ah*
sociology	sociología	*soh-see-oh-loh-'hee-ah*
statistics	estadística	*ehs-tah-'dees-tee-kah*
subject	asignatura	*ah-seeg-nah-'too-rah*
trigonometry	trigonometría	*tree-goh-noh-meh-'tree-ah*
zoology	zoología	*soh-oh-loh-'hee-ah*

f. ADDITIONAL SCHOOL VOCABULARY

> For concepts of thought, see Section 22.

answer	responder (*v*)	*rehs-pohn-'dehr*
• answer	respuesta	*reha-'pwehs-tah*
• brief	breve (*adj*)	*'breh-beh*
• long	largo (*adj*)	*'lahr-goh*
• short	corto (*adj*)	*'kohr-toh*
• right	correcto (*adj*)	*koh-'rrehk-toh*
• wrong	incorrecto (*adj*)	*een-koh-'rrehk-toh*
apply for	solicitar (*v*)	*soh-lee-see-'tahr*
assignments, homework	tarea	*tah-'reh-ah*
attend school	asistir (*v*) a la escuela	*ah-sees-'teer ah lah ehs-'kweh-lah*
be absent	estar (*v**) ausente	*ehs-'tahr ow-'sehn-teh*
be present	estar (*v**) presente	*ehs-'tahr preh-'sehn-teh*
be promoted	pasar (*v*) de año	*pah-'sahr deh ah-'nyoh*

class (*students*)	clase (*f*)	'klah-seh
• class	clase (*f*)	'klah-seh
• have a class	tener (*v**) una clase	teh-'nehr 'oo-nah 'klah-seh
• skip class	dejar (*v*) de ir a clase	deh-'hahr deh eer ah 'klah-seh
• There's no class today.	No hay clase hoy.	noh 'ah·ee 'klah-seh oy
composition	composición (*f*)	kohm-poh-see-see-'ohn
copy	copia	'koh-pee·ah
• good copy	buena copia	'bweh-nah 'koh-pee·ah
• rough draft	borrador (*m*)	boh-rrah-'dohr
course	curso	'koor-soh
• take a course	tomar (*v*) un curso	toh-'mahr oon 'koor-soh
degree (*university*)	título	'tee-too-loh
• get a degree	recibir (*v*) un título	reh-see-'beer oon 'tee-too-loh
dictation	dictado	deek-'tah-doh
diploma	diploma (*m*)	dee-'ploh-mah
• get a diploma	obtener (*v**) un diploma	ohb-teh-'nehr oon dee-'ploh-mah
draw	dibujar (*v*)	dee-boo-'hahr
• drawing	dibujo	dee-'boo-hoh
education	educación (*f*)	eh-doo-kah-see·'ohn
• get an education	recibir (*v*) una educación	reh-see-'beer 'oo-nah eh-doo-kah-see·'ohn
error	error (*m*)	eh-'rrohr
essay	ensayo	ehn-'sah-yoh
exam	examen (*m*)	ehks-'ah-mehn
• entrance exam	examen de ingreso	ehks-'ah-mehn deh een-'greh-soh
• oral exam	examen oral	ehk-'sah-mehn oh-'rahl
• pass	salir (*v**) bien	sah-'leer bee·'ehn
• fail	salir (*v**) mal	sah-'leer mahl
• take exams	tomar (*v*) exámenes	toh-'mahr ehks-'ah-meh-nehs
• written exam	examen escrito	ehks-'ah-mehn ehs-'kree-toh
exercise	ejercicio	eh-hehr-'see-see·oh
explanation	explicación (*f*)	ehks-plee-kah-see·'ohn
• explain	explicar (*v*)	ehks-plee-'kahr
field (of study)	campo (de estudio)	'kahm-poh (deh ehs-'too-dee·oh)
give back	devolver (*v**)	deh-bohl-'behr
grade	nota	'noh-tah
grammar	gramática	grah-'mah-tee-kah

learn	aprender (v)	ah-prehn-'dehr
• learn by heart	aprender (v) de memoria	ah-'prehn-dehr deh meh-'moh-ree-ah
lecture	conferencia	kohn-feh-'rehn-see-ah
• lecture	dar (v*) una conferencia	dahr 'oo-nah kohn-feh-'rehn-see-ah
listen to	escuchar (v)	ehs-koo-'chahr
mistake	error (m)	eh-'rrohr
• make a mistake	equivocarse	eh-kee-boh-'kahr-seh
notes	apuntes (m)	ah-'poon-tehs
• take notes	tomar (v) apuntes	toh-'mahr ah-'poon-tehs
problem	problema (m)	proh-'bleh-mah
• solve a problem	resolver (v*) un problema	reh-sohl-'behr 'oon proh-'bleh-mah
quarter	trimestre (m)	tree-'mehs-treh
question	pregunta	preh-'goon-tah
• ask a question	hacer (v*) una pregunta	'ah-sehr 'oo-nah preh-'goon-tah
read	leer (v)	leh-'ehr
• reading passage	lectura	lehk-'too-rah
registration	matrícula	mah-'tree-koo-lah
• registration fees	derechos de matrícula	deh-'reh-chohs deh mah-'tree-koo-lah
repeat	repetir (v*)	reh-peh-'teer
review	repasar (v)	reh-pah-'sahr
• review	repaso	reh-'pah-soh
school	escuela	ehs-'kweh-lah
semester	semestre (m)	seh-'mehs-treh
study	estudiar (v)	ehs-too-dee-'ahr
take attendance	pasar (v) lista	pah-'sahr 'lees-tah
teach	enseñar	ehn-seh-'nyahr
test	examen	ehks-'ah-mehn
thesis	tesis (f)	'teh-sees
type	escribir (v) a máquina	ehs-kree-'beer ah 'mah-kee-nah
understand	comprender (v)	kohm-prehn-'dehr
	entender (v*)	ehn-tehn-'dehr
write	escribir (v)	ehs-kree-'beer

38. WORK

a. JOBS AND PROFESSIONS

accountant	contador	kohn-tah-'dohr
actor	actor (m)	ahk-'tohr
actress	actriz (f)	ahk-'trees
announcer	locutor (m)	loh-koo-'tohr
architect	arquitecto	ahr-kee-'tehk-toh
baker	panadero	pah-nah-'deh-roh

banker	banquero	*bahn-'keh-roh*
barber	barbero	*bahr-'beh-roh*
bricklayer	albañil (*m/f*)	*ahl-bah-'nyeel*
bus driver	conductor	*kohn-dook-'tohr*
businessman	comerciante (*m/f*)	*koh-mehr-see-'ahn-teh*
butcher	carnicero	*kahr-nee-'seh-roh*
carpenter	carpintero	*kahr-peen-'teh-roh*
cashier	cajero	*kah-'heh-roh*
cook	cocinero	*koh-see-'neh-roh*
cosmetologist	cosmetólogo	*kohs-meh-'toh-loh-goh*
counselor	consejero	*kohn-seh-'heh-roh*
decorator	decorador (*m*)	*deh-koh-rah-'dohr*
dental hygienist	higienista (*m/f*) dental	*hee-jeh-'nee-stah dehn-'tahl*
dentist	dentista (*m/f*)	*dehn-'tees-tah*
dietician	dietista (*m/f*)	*dee·eh-'tee-stah*
doctor	doctor	*doh-'tohr*
	médico	*'meh-dee-koh*
drafter	dibujante (*m/f*)	*dee-boo-'hahn-teh*
driver	conductor (*m*)	*kohn-dook-'tohr*
editor	director	*dee-rehk-'tohr*
	redactor	*rreh-dahk-'tohr*
electrician	electricista (*m/f*)	*eh-'lehk-tree-'sees-tah*
engineer	ingeniero	*een-heh-nee-'eh-roh*
eye doctor	médico oculista	*'meh-dee-koh oh-koo-'lees-tah*
factory worker	obrero	*oh-'breh-roh*
farmer	campesino	*kahm-peh-'see-noh*
fashion designer	diseñador de modas	*dee-seh-nyah-'dohr deh 'moh-dahs*
fireman	bombero	*bohm-'beh-roh*
hairdresser	peluquero	*peh-loo-'keh-roh*
job	trabajo	*trah-'bah-hoh*
	puesto	*'pwehs-toh*
journalist	periodista (*m/f*)	*preh-ree·oh-'dees-tah*
lawyer	abogado	*ah-boh-'gah-doh*
machinist	maquinista (*m/f*)	*mah-kee-'nee-stah*
mechanic	mecánico	*meh-'kah-nee-koh*
miner	minero	*mee-'neh-roh*
movie director	director cinematográfico	*dee-rehk-'tohr see-neh-mah-toh-'grah-fee-koh*
musician	músico	*'moo-see-koh*
notary public	notario público	*noh-'tah-ree·oh 'poo-blee-koh*
nurse	enfermero	*ehn-fehr-'meh-roh*
occupation	profesión (*f*)	*proh-feh-see·'ohn*
painter	pintor	*peen-'tohr*
paramedic	paramédico	*pah-rah-'meh-dee-koh*

pharmacist	farmacéutico	*fahr-mah-'seh-oo-tee-koh*
pilot	piloto (*m/f*)	*pee-'loh-toh*
plumber	plomero	*ploh-'meh-roh*
police officer	policía (*m/f*)	*poh-lee-'see-ah*
profession	profesión (*f*)	*proh-feh-'see-ohn*
professor	profesor	*proh-feh-'sohr*
psychiatrist	psiquiatra (*m/f*)	*see-kee-'ah-trah*
psychologist	psicólogo	*see-'koh-loh-goh*
real estate agent	agente (*m/f*) de inmobiliaria	*ah-'hehn-teh deh een-moh-bee-lee-'ah-ree-ah*
receptionist	recepcionista (*m/f*)	*reh-sehp-see-oh-'nee-stah*
sales person	vendedor (*m*)	*behn-deh-'dohr*
scientist	científico	*see-ehn-'tee-fee-koh*
seamstress	costurera (*f*)	*kohs-too-'reh-rah*
secretary	secretario	*seh-kreh-'tah-ree-oh*
security guard	guardia (*m/f*)	*'gwahr-dee·ah*
stockbroker	bolsista (*m/f*)	*bohl-'see-stah*
supervisor	supervisor (*m*)	*soo-pehr-bee-'sohr*
surgeon	cirujano	*see-roo-'hah-noh*
tailor	sastre (*m/f*)	*'sahs-treh*
teacher	maestro	*mah-'ehs-troh*
therapist	terapeuta (*m/f*)	*teh-rah-peh-'oo-tah*
veterinarian	veterinario	*beh-teh-ree-'nah-ree-oh*
writer	escritor	*ehs-kree-'tohr*

b. INTERVIEWING FOR A JOB

> See also Section 11—Basic Personal Information.

name	nombre (*m*)	*'nohm-breh*
• first name	nombre (de pila)	*'nohm-breh (deh 'pee-lah)*
• signature	firma	*'feer-mah*
address	dirección (*f*)	*dee-rehk-see-'ohn*
• street	calle (*f*)	*'kah-yeh*
• number	número	*'noo-meh-roh*
• city	ciudad (*f*)	*see-oo-'dahd*
• postal code	código postal	*'koh-dee-goh poh-'stahl*
date of birth	fecha de nacimiento	*'feh-chah deh nah-see-mee·'ehn-toh*
place of birth	lugar (*m*) de nacimiento	*loo-'gahr deh nah-see-mee·'ehn-toh*
age	edad (*f*)	*eh-'dahd*

sex	sexo	'seh-ksoh
• **male**	hombre	'ohm-breh
• **female**	mujer	moo-'hehr
marital status	estado civil	ehs-'tah-doh see-'beel
• **married**	casado(a)	kah-'sah-doh (-dah)
• **single**	soltero (a)	sohl-'teh-roh (-rah)
• **be divorced**	estar (v*) divorciado(a)	ehs-'tahr dee-bohr-see-'ah-doh (-dah)
• **be widowed**	ser (v*) viudo(a)	sehr bee-'oo-doh (-dah)
nationality	nacionalidad (f)	nah-see-oh-nah-lee-'dahd

See also Section 30—Nationalities and Languages.

education	enseñanza	ehn-seh-'nyahn-sah
elementary school	escuela primaria	ehs-'kweh-lah pree-'mah-ree-ah
junior high school	instituto de bachillerato elemental	eens-tee-'too-toh deh bah-chee-yeh-'rah-toh eh-leh-mehn-'tahl
secondary school	escuela secundaria, colegio	ehs-'kweh-lah seh-koon-'dah-ree-ah, koh-'leh-hee-oh
university	universidad (f)	oo-nee-behr-see-'dahd
profession	profesión (f)	proh-feh-see-'ohn
resumé	curriculum vitae (m)	koo-'rree-koo-loom 'bee-teh
application	solicitud (f)	soh-lee-see-'tood

c. THE OFFICE

See also Sections 20 and 25.

adhesive tape	cinta adhesiva	'seen-tah ahd-eh-'see-bah
appointment book	agenda (f) de entrevistas	ah-'hehn-dah deh ehn-treh-'bees-tahs
briefcase	maletín (m)	mah-leh-'teen
	portafolio	pohr-tah-'foh-lee-oh
calendar	calendario	kah-lehn-'dah-ree-oh
chair	silla	'see-yah
computer	computadora	kohm-poo-tah-'doh-rah
	ordenador (m)	ohr-deh-nah-'dohr
desk	escritorio	ehs-kree-'toh-ree-oh
file	archivo	ahr-'chee-boh
• **file card**	ficha	'fee-chah

• file folder	carpeta	*kahr-'peh-tah*
• filing cabinet	archivo	*ahr-'chee-boh*
	fichero	*fee-'cheh-roh*
intercom	interfono	*een-tehr-'foh-noh*
	intercomunicador (*m*)	*een-tehr-koh-moo-nee-kah-'dohr*
pen (*ballpoint*)	bolígrafo	*boh-'lee-grah-foh*
pencil	lápiz (*m*)	*'lah-pees*
photocopier	fotocopiadora	*foh-toh-koh-pee-ah-'doh-rah*
ruler	regla	*'reh-glah*
scissors	tijeras	*tee-'heh-rahs*
staple	grapa	*'grah-pah*
stapler	engrapador (*m*)	*ehn-grah-pah-'dohr*
telephone	teléfono	*teh-'leh-foh-noh*
wastebasket	papelero	*pah-peh-'leh-roh*
word processor	procesador de texto (*m*)	*proh-seh-sah-'dohr deh 'tehks-toh*

d. ADDITIONAL WORK VOCABULARY

advertising	publicidad (*f*)	*poo-blee-see-'dahd*
boss (*in an office*)	jefe(a)	*'heh-feh (-fah)*
branch (*company*)	sucursal (*m*)	*soo-koor-'sahl*
career	carrera	*kah-'rreh-rah*
Christmas bonus	aguinaldo	*ah-gee-'nahl-doh*
classified ad	anuncios clasificados	*ah-'noon-see-ohs kla-see-fee-'kah-dohs*
commerce	comercio	*koh-'mehr-see-oh*
company	compañía	*kom-pan-'nyee-ah*
contract	contratar (*v*)	*kohn-trah-'tahr*
• **contract**	contrato	*kohn-'trah-toh*
earn	ganar (*v*)	*gah-'nahr*
employee	empleado(a)	*ehm-pleh-'ah-doh (-dah)*
employer	empresario(a)	*ehm-preh-'sah-ree-oh (-ree-ah)*
	empleador (*m*)	*ehm-pleh-ah-'dohr*
employment agency	agencia de colocaciones	*ah-'hehn-see-ah de koh-loh-kah-see-'oh-nehs*
factory	fábrica	*'fah-bree-kah*
fire	echar (*v*)	*eh-'chahr*
hire	contratar (*v*)	*kohn-trah-'tahr*
manager	gerente (*m/f*)	*heh-'rehn-teh*
market	mercado	*mehr-'kah-doh*
office	oficina	*oh-fee-'see-nah*
plant	fábrica	*'fah-bree-kah*
	planta	*'plahn-tah*

retirement, pension	jubilación (*f*)	*hoo-bee-lah-see-'ohn*
• **retire**	jubilarse (*v*)	*hoo-bee-'lahr-seh*
severance pay	indemnización por despido	*een-dehm-nee-sah-see-'ohn pohr dehs-'pee-doh*
unemployment	desempleo	*dehs-ehm-'pleh-oh*
wage, salary	sueldo	*soo-'ehl-doh*
work	trabajo	*trah-'bah-hoh*
• **work**	trabajar (*v*)	*trah-bah-'hahr*
• **work associate**	colega (*m/f*)	*koh-'leh-gah*

EMERGENCIES

39. REPORTING AN EMERGENCY

a. FIRE

alarm	alarma (*f*)	*ah-'lahr-mah*
ambulance	ambulancia	*ahm-boo-'lahn-see·ah*
building	edificio	*eh-dee-'fee-see·oh*
burn	quemar (*v*)	*keh-'mahr*
	arder (*v*)	*ahr-'dehr*
• **burn**	quemadura	*keh-mah-'doo-rah*
call the fire department	llamar a los bomberos	*yah-'mahr ah lohs bohm-'beh-rohs*
catch fire	encenderse (*v**)	*ehn-sehn-'dehr-seh*
	incendiarse (*v*)	*een-sehn-dee-'ahr-seh*
danger	peligro	*peh-'lee-groh*
destroy	destruir (*v**)	*dehs-troo-'eer*
emergency exit	salida de emergencia	*sah-'lee-dah deh eh-mehr-'gehn-see·ah*
escape, get out	escaparse (*v*)	*ehs-kah-'pahr-seh*
extinguish, put out	extinguir (*v*)	*eks-teen-'geer*
fire	fuego	*'fweh-goh*
• **be on fire**	estar (*v**) ardiendo	*ehs-'tahr ahr-dee·'ehn-doh*
• **Fire!**	¡Fuego!	*'fweh-goh*
• **fire alarm**	alarma (*f*) de incendios	*ah-'lahr-mah deh een-'sehn-dee·ohs*
• **fire escape**	escalera de incendios	*ehs-kah-'leh-rah deh een-'sehn-dee·ohs*
• **fire extinguisher**	extinguidor (*m*) de incendios	*eks-teen-gee-'dohr deh een-'sehn-dee·ohs*
• **firefighter**	bombero	*bohm-'beh-roh*
• **fire hydrant**	boca de incendio	*'boh-kah deh een-'sehn-dee·oh*
• **fireproof**	incombustible (*adj*)	*een-kohm-boos-'tee-bleh*
first aid	primeros auxilios	*pree-'meh-rohs ow-'ksee-lee·ohs*
flame	llama	*'yah-mah*
help	ayudar (*v*)	*ah-yoh-'dahr*
• **Help!**	¡Socorro!	*soh-'koh-rroh*
ladder	escalera	*ehs-kah-'leh-rah*
out	afuera (*adv*)	*ah-'fweh-rah*
• **Everybody out!**	¡Todos afuera!	*'toh-dohs ah-'fweh-rah*
paramedic	paramédico	*pah-rah-'meh-dee-koh*
protect	proteger (*v**)	*proh-teh-'hehr*

rescue	rescatar (v)	rehs-kah-'tahr
shout	gritar (v)	gree-'tahr
• shout	grito	'gree-toh
siren	sirena	see-'reh-nah
smoke	humo	'oo-moh
victim	víctima (m/f)	'beek-tee-mah

b. ROBBERY AND ASSAULT

argue	reñir (v*)	reh-'nyeer
arrest	detener (v*)	deh-teh-'nehr
	arrestar (v)	ah-rrehs-'tahr
assault	asalto	ah-'sahl-toh
Come quickly!	¡Venga inmediatamente!	'behn-gah een-meh-dee·ah-tah-'mehn-teh
crime	crimen (m)	'kree-mehn
	delito	deh-'lee-toh
• crime wave	ola de crímenes	'oh-lah deh 'kree-meh-nehs
• criminal	criminal (m/f)	kree-mee-'nahl
description	descripción	dehs-kreep-see-'ohn
fight	luchar (v)	loo-'chahr
	pelear (v)	peh-leh-'ahr
fingerprints	huellas digitales	'weh-yahs dee-hee-'tah-lehs
firearm	arma (f) de fuego	'ahr-mah deh 'fweh-goh
gun	pistola	pees-'toh-lah
handcuffs	esposas	ehs-'poh-sahs
hurry	darse (v*) prisa	'dahr-seh 'pree-sah
injure, wound	herir (v*)	eh-'reer
• injury, wound	herida	eh-'ree-dah
kill	matar (v)	mah-'tahr
• killer	asesino(a)	ah-seh-'see-noh (-nah)
knife	cuchillo	koo-'chee-yoh
• switchblade	navaja de muelle	nah-'bah-hah deh 'mweh-yeh
murder	asesinato	ah-seh-see-'nah-toh
	homicidio	oh-mee-'see-dee·oh
pickpocket	ratero(a)	rah-teh-roh (-rah)
	carterista (m/f)	kahr-teh-'rees-tah
police	policía (f)	poh-lee-'see-ah
• call the police	llamar (v) a la policía	yah-'mahr ah lah poh-lee-'see-ah
• policeman	policía (m)	poh-lee-'see-ah
• policewoman	policía (f)	poh-lee-'see-ah
rape	violar (v)	bee-oh-'lahr
• rape	violación (f)	bee-oh-lah-see-'ohn
rifle	rifle (m)	'ree-fleh

rob	robar (v)	roh-'bahr
• robber, thief	ladrón(a)	lah-'drohn ('droh-nah)
• armed robbery	robo a mano armada	'roh-boh ah 'mah-noh ahr-'mah-dah
• robbery	robo	'roh-boh
• Stop thief!	¡Ladrón!	lah-'drohn
steal	robar (v)	roh-'bahr
victim	víctima (m/f)	'beek-tee-mah
violence	violencia	bee·oh-'lehn·see·ah
weapon	arma	'ahr-mah
• shoot	disparar (v)	dees-pah-'rahr

Hurry!	¡Dese prisa!
Someone assaulted me!	¡Alguien me asaltó!
Someone stole . . .	Alquien robó . . .

c. TRAFFIC ACCIDENTS

accident	accidente (m)	ahk-see-'dehn-teh
• serious accident	accidente serio	ahk-see-'dehn-teh 'seh-ree·oh
• traffic accident	asccidente de circulación	ahk-see-'dehn-teh deh seer-koo-lah-see·'ohn
ambulance	ambulancia	ahm-boo-'lahn-see·ah
• call an ambulance	llamar una ambulancia	yah-'mahr 'oo-nah ahm-boo-'lahn-see·ah
be run over	ser (v*) atropellado(a)	sehr ah-troh-peh-'yah-doh (-dah)
bite	mordedura	mohr-deh-'doo-rah
bleed	sangrar (v)	sahn-'grahr
• blood	sangre (f)	'sahn-greh
broken bone	hueso fracturado	'weh-soh frahk-too-'rah-doh
bump into	tropezar (v*) con	troh-peh-'sahr kohn
collide, smash into	chocar (v) con	choh-'kahr kohn
• collision	choque (m)	'choh-keh
crash	choque (m)	'choh-keh
• crash into	chocar (v) con	choh-'kahr kohn
doctor	médico(a)	'meh-dee-koh (-ah)
• get a doctor	llamar a un médico	yah-'mahr ah oon 'meh-dee-koh
first aid	primeros auxilios	pree-'meh-rohs ow-'ksee-lee-ohs
• antiseptic	antiséptico	ahn-tee-'sehp-tee-koh

• **bandage**	venda	*'behn-dah*
• **gauze**	gasa	*'gah-sah*
• **iodine**	yodo	*'yoh-doh*
• **scissors**	tijeras	*tee-'heh-rahs*
• **splint**	tablilla	*tah-'blee-yah*
fracture	fractura	*frahk-'too-rah*
Help!	¡Socorro!	*soh-'koh-rroh*
hospital	hospital (*m*)	*ohs-pee-'tahl*
• **emergency room**	sala de emergencia	*'sah-lah deh eh-mehr-'gehn-see·ah*
intensive care	cuidado intensivo	*kwee-'dah-doh een-tehn-'see-boh*
police	policía (*f*)	*poh-lee-'see-ah*
• **call the police**	llamar (*v*) a la policía	*yah-'mahr ah lah poh-lee-'see-ah*
shock	choque (*m*)	*'choh-keh*
sprain	la torcedura	*lah tohr-seh-'doo-rah*
stretcher	camilla	*kah-'mee-yah*
wound, injury	herida	*eh-'ree-dah*

40. MEDICAL CARE

See also Section 12—The Body.

a. THE DOCTOR

acne	acné (*m*)	*ahk-'neh*
acupuncture	acupuntura	*ah-koo-poon-'too-rah*
AIDS	SIDA (*m*)	*'see-dah*
allergy	alergia	*ah-'lehr-gee·ah*
antibiotic	antibiótico	*ahn-tee-bee·'oh-tee-koh*
anti-coagulant	anticoagulante (*m*)	*ahn-tee-koh-ah-goo-'lahn-teh*
anti-inflammatory	antiinflamatorio	*ahn-tee-een-flah-mah-'toh-ree·oh*
appendicitis	apendicitis (*f*)	*ah'pehn-dee-'see-tees*
• **appendix**	apéndice (*m*)	*ah-'pehn-dee-seh*
appointement	cita	*'see-tah*
artery	arteria	*ahr-'teh-ree-ah*
arthritis	artritis (*f*)	*ahr-'tree-tees*
aspirin	aspirina	*ahs-pee-'ree-nah*
asthma	asma	*'ahs-mah*
backache	dolor de espalda	*doh-'lohr deh ehs-'pahl-dah*
• **have a backache**	tener (*v**) dolor de espalda	*teh-'nehr doh-'lohr deh ehs-'pahl-dah*

bandage	venda	*'behn-dah*
• **bandage**	vendar (*v*)	*behn-'dahr*
birth control	control de natalidad	*kohn-'trohl deh nah-tah-lee-'dahd*
blood	sangre (*f*)	*'sahn-greh*
• **blood pressure**	presión arterial	*preh-see-'ohn ahr-teh-ree-'ahl*
• **blood test**	análisis (*m*) de sangre	*ah-'nah-lee-sees deh 'sahn-greh*
bone	hueso	*'weh-soh*
brain	cerebro	*seh-'reh-broh*
breathe	respirar (*v*)	*rehs-pee-'rahr*
bronchitis	bronquitis (*f*)	*brohn-'kee-tees*
bruise	contusión (*f*)	*kohn-too-see-'ohn*
bunion	juanete (*m*)	*hwah-'neh-teh*
burn	quemadura	*keh-mah-'doo-rah*
calcium	calcio	*'kahl-see-oh*
chills	escalofríos (*m*)	*ehs-kah-loh-'free·ohs*
choke	atragantarse (*v*)	*ah-trah-gahn-'tahr-seh*
cold	resfriado	*rehs-free-'ah-doh*
constipation	estreñimiento	*ehs-treh-nyee-mee·'ehn-toh*
• **be constipated**	estar (*v**) estreñido	*ehs-'tahr ehs-treh-'nyee-doh*
contraceptives	anticonceptivos	*ahn-tee-kohn-sehp-'tee-bohs*
convalescence	convalecencia	*kohn-bah-leh-'sehn-see·ah*
• **convalesce**	convalecer (*v**)	*kohn-bah-leh-'sehr*
cortisone	cortisona	*kohr-tee-'soh-nah*
cough	toser (*v*)	*toh-'sehr*
• **cough**	tos (*f*)	*tohs*
• **cough drops**	pastillas para la tos	*pahs-'tee-yahs 'pah-rah lah tohs*
• **cough syrup**	jarabe para la tos	*hah-'rah-beh 'pah-rah lah tohs*
cramps	calambres (*m*)	*kah-'lahm-brehs*
crutches	muletas (*f*)	*moo-'leh-tahs*
cure	cura	*'koo-rah*
• **cure, heal**	curar (*v*)	*koo-'rahr*
	sanar (*v*)	*sah-'nahr*
cut	cortadura	*kohr-tah-'doo-rah*
• **heal**	cicatrizar (*v*)	*see-kah-tree-'sahr*
cyst	quiste (*m*)	*'kees-teh*
dandruff	caspa	*'kahs-pah*
diagnose	diagnosticar (*v*)	*dee·ahg-nohs-tee-'kahr*
diarrhea	diarrea	*dee·ah-'rreh-ah*

diet	régimen (*m*)	'*reh-hee-mehn*
	dieta (*f*)	*dee-'eh-tah*
• be on a diet	estar (*v*) a dieta	*ehs-'tahr ah dee-'eh-tah*
digest	digerir (*v**)	*dee-heh-'reer*
digestive system	sistema digestivo	*sees-teh-mah dee-hehs-'tee-boh*
• anus	ano	'*ah-noh*
• defecate	defecar (*v*)	*deh-feh-'kahr*
• esophagus	esófago	*eh-'soh-fah-goh*
• rectum	recto	'*rehk-toh*
• stomach	estómago	*ehs-'toh-mah-goh*
• have a stomach ache	tener (*v**) dolor de estómago	*teh-'nehr doh-'lohr deh ehs-'toh-mah-goh*
doctor	médico(a)	'*meh-dee-koh (-kah)*
doctor's instruments	instrumentos del médico	*eens-troo-'mehn-tohs dehl 'meh-dee-koh*
• stethoscope	estetoscopio	*ehs-teh-toh-'skoh-pee·oh*
• syringe	jeringa	*heh-'reen-gah*
• thermometer	termómetro	*tehr-'moh-meh-troh*
dose	dosis (*f*)	'*doh-sees*
eardrops	gotas para los oídos	'*goh tahs 'pah-rah lohs oh·'ee-dohs*
electrocardiograph	electrocardiógrafo	*eh-lehk-troh-kahr-dee·'oh-grah-foh*
epidemic	epidemia	*eh-pee-'deh-mee·ah*
examination	examen físico	*eh-'ksah-mehn 'fee-see-koh*
• examine	examinar (*v*)	*ehks-ah-mee-'nahr*
eye doctor	oculista (*m/f*)	*oh-koo-'lees-tah*
• contact lenses	lentes (*m*) de contacto	'*lehn-tehs deh kohn-'tahk-toh*
• eyeglasses	anteojos (*m*)	*ahn-teh-'oh-hohs*
	gafas	'*gah-fahs*
• farsighted	hipermétrope (*adj*)	*ee-pehr-'meh-troh-peh*
• nearsighted	miope (*adj*)	*mee-'oh-peh*
	corto de vista	'*kohr-toh deh 'bees-tah*
• sight	vista	'*bees-tah*
• eye drops	gotas para los ojos	'*goh-tahs 'pah-rah lohs 'oh-hohs*
feel	sentirse (*v**)	*sehn-'teer-seh*
• feel badly	sentirse (*v**) mal	*sehn-'teer-seh mahl*
• feel well	sentirse (*v**) bien	*sehn-'teer-seh bee·'ehn*
• strong	fuerte (*adj*)	'*fwehr-teh*
• weak	débil (*adj*)	'*deh-beel*
• How do you feel?	¿Cómo se siente usted?	'*koh-moh seh see·'ehn-teh oos-'tehd*

fever	fiebre (*f*)	*fee·'eh-breh*
flu	gripe (*f*)	*'gree-peh*
headache	dolor (*m*) de cabeza	*doh-'lohr deh kah-'beh-sah*
• have a headache	tener (*v**) dolor de cabeza	*teh-'nehr doh-'lohr deh kah-'beh-sah*
• migraine headache	migraña	*mee-'grah-nyah*
health	salud (*f*)	*sah-'lood*
• healthy	sano (*adj*)	*'sah-noh*
heart	corazón (*m*)	*koh-rah-'sohn*
• heart attack	ataque (*m*) cardíaco	*ah-'tah-keh kahr-'dee-ah-koh*
	infarto	*een-'fahr-toh*
hurt	doler (*v**)	*doh-'lehr*
hypertension	hipertensión	*ee-pehr-tehn-see-'ohn*
ilnesses	enfermedades (*f*)	*ehn-fehr-meh-'dah-dehs*
• blood clot	coágulo de sangre	*koh-'ah-goo-loh deh 'sahn-greh*
• cancer	cáncer (*m*)	*'kahn-sehr*
• chemotherapy	quimoterapia	*keeh-moh-the-'rah-pee-ah*
• chicken pox	varicela	*bah-ree-'seh-lah*
• depression	depresión (*f*)	*deh-preh-see-'ohn*
• diabetes	diabetes (*f*)	*dee-ah-'beh-tehs*
• epilepsy	epilepsia	*eh-pee-'lehp-see-ah*
• hepatitis	hepatitis (*f*)	*eh-pah-'tee-tees*
• laryrigitis	laringitis (*f*)	*lah-reen-'hee-tees*
• leukemia	leucemia	*leh-oo-'seh-mee-ah*
• measles	sarampión (*m*)	*sah-rahm-pee-'ohn*
• multiple sclerosis	esclerosis múltiple (*f*)	*eh-skleh-'roh-sees 'mool-tee-pleh*
• mumps	paperas	*pah-'peh-rahs*
• muscular dystrophy	distrofia muscular	*dees-'troh-fee-ah moos-koo-'lahr*
• ointment	ungüento	*oon-'gwehn-toh*
• pacemaker	marcapasos (*m*)	*mahr-kah-'pah-sohs*
• panic attack	ataque (*m*) de pánico	*ah-'tah-keh deh 'pah-nee-koh*
• protein	proteína	*proh-teh-'ee-nah*
• scar	cicatriz (*m*)	*see-kah-'trees*
• schizophrenia	esquizofrenia	*ehs-kee-soh-'freh-nee-ah*
• snore	roncar (*v*)	*rohn-'kahr*
• stroke	derrame cerebral (*m*)	*deh-'rrah-meh seh-reh-'brahl*
• transplant	trasplante (*m*)	*trahs-'plahn-teh*
• ulcer	úlcera	*'ool-seh-rah*

• **venereal disease**	enfermedad venérea	*ehn-fehr-meh-'dahd beh-'neh-reh-ah*
indigestion	indigestión (*f*)	*een-dee-hehs-tee-'ohn*
infection	infección (*f*)	*een-fehk-see-'ohn*
injection	inyección (*f*)	*een-yehk-see-'ohn*
itch	comezón (*f*)	*koh-meh-'sohn*
lose consciousness	perder (*v**) el conocimiento	*pehr-'dehr ehl koh-noh-see-mee-'ehn-toh*
lump	bulto	*'bool-toh*
lymphatic system	sistema linfático	*sees-'teh-mah leen-'fah-tee-koh*
medical records	antecedentes (*m*) médicos	*ahn-teh-seh-'dehn-tehs 'meh-dee-kohs*
medicine	medicina	*meh-dee-'see-nah*
muscle	músculo	*'moos-koo-loh*
nerves	nervios	*'nehr-bee·ohs*
• **nervous system**	sistema nervioso (*m*)	*sees-'teh-mah nehr-bee-'oh-soh*
nurse	enfermero(a)	*ehn-fehr-'meh-roh (-rah)*
operate	operar (*v*)	*oh-peh-'rahr*
operation	operación (*f*)	*oh-peh-rah-see-'ohn*
• **operating room**	sala de operaciones	*'sah-lah deh oh-peh-rah-see-'oh-nehs*
pain	dolor (*m*)	*doh-'lohr*
• **painful**	doloroso (*adj*)	*doh-loh-'roh-soh*
patient	paciente (*adj*)	*pah-see-'ehn-teh*
pill	píldora	*'peel-doh-rah*
pimple	grano	*'grah-noh*
pneumonia	pulmonía	*pool-moh-'nee·ah*
	neumonía	*neh·oo-moh-'nee·ah*
poisoning	envenenamiento	*ehn-beh-neh-nah-mee-'ehn-toh*
• **poison**	veneno (*n*)	*beh-'neh-noh*
	envenenar (*v*)	*ehn-beh-neh-'nahr*
pregnant	embarazada (*adj*)	*ehm-bah-rah-'sah-dah*
prescription	receta	*reh-'seh-tah*
pulse	pulso	*'pool-soh*
• **take someone's pulse**	tomar (*v*) el pulso	*toh-'mahr ehl 'pool-soh*
rash	salpullido	*sahl-poo-'yee-doh*
recover	recobrarse (*v*)	*reh-koh-'brahr-seh*
respiratory system	sistema respiratorio	*sees-'teh-mah rehs-pee-rah-'toh-ree·oh*
• **breathe**	respirar (*v*)	*rehs-pee-'rahr*
• **breathing**	respiración (*f*)	*rehs-pee-rah-see-'ohn*
• **bad breath**	mal aliento	*mahl ah-lee-'ehn-toh*
• **be out of breath**	estar (*v**) sin aliento	*ehs-'tahr seen ah-lee-'ehn-toh*

• lung	pulmón (*m*)	*pool-'mohn*
• nostril	ventana de la nariz	*behn-'tah-nah deh lah nah-'rees*
rheumatism	reumatismo	*reh·oo-mah-'tees-moh*
	reuma	*reh·'oo-mah*
secretary	secretario(a)	*seh-kreh-'tah-ree-oh (·ah)*
sedative	sedante (*m*)	*seh-'dahn-teh*
	calmante (*m*)	*kahl-'mahn-teh*
sick	enfermo(a)	*ehn-'fehr-moh (-ah)*
• get sick	enfermarse (*v*)	*ehn-fehr-'mahr-seh*
• sickness, disease	enfermedad (*f*)	*ehn-fehr-meh-'dahd*
sneeze	estornudar (*v*)	*ehs-tohr-noo-'dahr*
• sneeze	estornudo	*ehs-tohr-'noo-doh*
specialist	especialista (*m/f*)	*ehs-peh-see·ah-'lees-tah*
• anesthetist	anestesista	*ah-nehs-teh-'sees-tah*
• cardiologist	cardiólogo	*kahr-dee-'oh-loh-goh*
• dermatologist	dermatólogo	*dehr-mah-'toh-loh-goh*
• gynecologist	ginecólogo	*hee-neh-'koh-loh-goh*
• internist	internista	*een-tehr-'nees-tah*
• neurologist	neurólogo	*neh-oo-'roh-loh-goh*
• ophthalmologist	oftalmólogo	*ohf-tahl-'moh-loh-goh*
• pediatrician	pediatra	*peh-dee-'ah-trah*
• podiatrist	pedicuro	*peh-dee-'koo-roh*
• psychiatrist	psiquiatra	*see-kee-'ah-trah*
• urologist	urólogo	*oo-'roh-loh-goh*
suffer	sufrir (*v*)	*soo-'freer*
suffer from	padecer (*v**) de	*pah-deh-'sehr deh*
sunburn	quemadura del sol	*keh-mah-'doo-rah dehl sohl*
suppository	supositorio	*soo-poh-see-'toh-ree-oh*
surgeon	cirujano	*see-roo-'hah-noh*
• surgery	cirugía	*see-roo-'hee-ah*
swallow	tragar (*v*)	*trah-'gahr*
swell	hinchar (*v*)	*een-'chahr*
• swollen	hinchado (*adj*)	*een-'chah-doh*
tablet	pastilla	*pahs-'tee-yah*
temperature	fiebre (*f*)	*fee-'eh-breh*
• take one's temperature	tomar (*v*) la temperatura	*toh-'mahr lah tehm-peh-rah-'too-rah*
throat	garganta	*gahr-'gahn-tah*
• have a sore throat	tener (*v*) dolor de garganta	*teh-'nehr doh-'lohr deh gahr-'gahn-tah*
throw up, vomit	vomitar (*v*)	*voh-mee-'tahr*
tonsils	amígdalas	*ah-'meeg-dah-lahs*
urinary system	sistema urinario	*sees-'teh-mah oo-ree-'nah-ree-oh*

• **bladder**	vejiga	*beh-'hee-gah*
• **kidney**	riñón (*m*)	*ree-'nyohn*
• **urinate**	orinar (*v*)	*oh-ree-'nahr*
vaccinate	vacunar (*v*)	*bah-koo-'nahr*
vein	vena	*'beh-nah*
vitamin	vitamina	*bee-tah-'mee-nah*
wheelchair	silla de ruedas	*'see-yah deh roo-'eh-dahs*

b. THE DENTIST

anesthetic	anestésico	*ah-nehs-'teh-see-koh*
appointment	cita	*'see-tah*
bridge	puente (*m*)	*poo-'ehn-teh*
cavity	carie (*f*)	*'kah-ree·eh*
clean, brush	cepillarse (*v*)	*seh-pee-'yahr-seh*
crown	corona	*koh-'roh-nah*
dental floss	hilo dental	*'ee-loh dehn-'tahl*
dentist	dentista	*dehn-'tees-tah*
• **dentist's office**	oficina del dentista	*oh-fee-'see-nah dehl dehn-'tees-tah*
• **go to the dentist**	ir (*v**) al dentista	*eer ahl dehn-'tees-tah*
dentures	dientes postizos	*dee·'ehn-tehs poh-'stee-sohs*
drill	taladro	*tah-'lah-droh*
examine	examinar (*v*)	*ehk-sah-mee-'nahr*
filling	empaste (*m*)	*ehm-'pah-steh*
mouth	boca	*'boh-kah*
• **gums**	encías	*ehn-'see-ahs*
• **jaw**	mandíbula	*mahn-'dee-boo-lah*
• **lip**	labio	*'lah-bee-oh*
• **Open your mouth.**	Abra usted la boca.	*'ah-brah oos-'tehd lah 'boh-kah*
• **palate**	paladar (*m*)	*pah-lah-'dahr*
• **tongue**	lengua	*'lehn-gwah*
needle	aguja	*ah-'goo-hah*
Novocaine	Novocaína	*noh-boh-cah-'ee-nah*
office hours	horas de consulta	*'oh-rahs deh kohn-'sool-tah*
rinse	enjuagar(se) (*v*)	*ehn-hoo·ah-'gahr (-seh)*
spit	escupir (*v*)	*ehs-koo-'peer*
tooth	diente (*m*)	*dee·'ehn-teh*
• **canine tooth**	canino (*m*)	*kah-'nee-noh*
• **incisor**	diente incisivo	*dee·'ehn-teh een-see-'see-boh*
• **molar**	muela	*'mweh-lah*
• **root**	raíz (*f*)	*rah-'ees*

• **wisdom tooth**	muela del juicio	*'mweh-lah dehl hoo·'ee-see·oh*
toothache	dolor de muelas	*doh-'lohr deh 'mweh-lahs*
• **have a toothache**	tener (*v**) dolor de muelas	*teh-'nehr doh-'lohr deh 'mweh-lahs*
• **My tooth hurts.**	Me duele el diente.	*meh 'dweh-leh ehl dee-'ehn-teh*
toothbrush	cepillo de dientes	*seh-'pee-yoh deh dee-'ehn-tehs*
tooth decay	caries (*f, pl*)	*'kah-ree·ehs*
toothpaste	pasta dentífrica	*'pahs-tah dehn-'tee-free-kah*
X rays	rayos X	*'rah-yohs 'eh-kees*

41. LEGAL MATTERS

accusation	acusación (*f*)	*ah-koo-sah-see·'ohn*
• **accuse**	acusar (*v*)	*ah-koo-'sahr*
• **accused person**	acusado (*adj*)	*ah-koo-'sah-doh*
• **bring an accusation against**	formular (*v*) una acusación contra	*fohr-moo-'lahr 'oo-nah ah-koo-sah-see·'ohn 'kohn-trah*
address oneself to	hablar (*v*) a	*ah-'blahr ah*
admit	admitir (*v*)	*ahd-mee-'teer*
agree	consentir (*v**)	*kohn-sehn-'teer*
	estar (*v**) de acuerdo	*ehs-'tahr deh ah-'kwehr-doh*
bail	fianza	*fee·'ahn-sah*
controversy	controversia	*kohn-troh-'behr-see·ah*
convince	convencer (*v**)	*kohn-behn-'sehr*
coroner	médico forense	*'meh-dee-koh foh-'rehn-seh*
court	tribunal (*m*)	*tree-boo-'nahl*
• **court of appeals**	tribunal (*m*) de apelación	*tree-boo-'nahl deh ah-peh-lah-see·'ohn*
courtroom	sala del tribunal	*'sah-lah dehl tree-boo-'nahl*
debate	debatir (*v*)	*deh-bah-'teer*
• **debate**	debate (*m*)	*deh-'bah-teh*
defend oneself	defenderse (*v**)	*deh-fehn-'dehr-seh*
defense attorney	abogado(a) defensor(a)	*ah-boh-'gah-doh (ah) deh-fehn-'sohr (rah)*
disagree	no estar (*v**) de acuerdo	*noh ehs-'tahr deh ah-'kwehr-doh*
discuss	discutir (*v*)	*dees-koo-'teer*
district attorney	fiscal (*m/f*)	*fees-'kahl*

fine	multar (v)	mool-'tahr
guilt	culpa	'kool-pah
• guilty	culpable (adj)	kool-'pah-bleh
innocence	inocencia	ee-noh-'sehn-see·ah
• innocent	inocente (adj)	ee-noh-'sehn-teh
jail, prison	cárcel (f)	'kahr-sehl
• jail	encarcelar (v)	ehn-kahr-seh-'lahr
• imprison	aprisionar (v)	ah-pree-see-oh-'nahr
	encerrar (v*)	ehn-seh-'rrahr
judge	juez (m)	hoo-'ehs
• judge	juzgar (v)	hoos-'gahr
• judgment	juicio	hoo-'ee-see·oh
	sentencia	sehn-'tehn-see·ah
jury	jurado	hoo-'rah-doh
• sit on a jury	ser (v) miembro del	sehr mee-'ehm-broh
	jurado	dehl hoo-'rah-doh
justice	justicia	hoo-'stee-see·ah
kidnap	secuestrar (v)	seh-kwehs-'trahr
law	ley (f)	'leh·ee
• civil law	derecho civil	deh-'reh-choh see-'beel
• criminal law	derecho penal	deh-'reh-choh peh-'nahl
• illegal	ilegal (adj)	ee-leh-'gahl
• lawful, legal	legal (adj)	leh-'gahl
lawsuit	pleito	pleh-'ee-toh
	demanda	deh-'mahn-dah
lawyer	abogado	ah-boh-'gah-doh
	jurista (m/f)	hoo-'rees-tah
litigation	litigio	lee-'tee-hee·oh
	pleito	pleh-'ee-toh
• litigate	litigar (v)	lee-tee-'gahr
magistrate	magistrado	mah-hees-'trah-doh
notarize	legalizar (v)	leh-gah-lee-'sahr
	certificar (v)	sehr-tee-fee-'kahr
persuade	persuadir (v)	pehr-swah-'deer
plea	alegato	ah-leh-'gah-toh
plead guilty	declararse (v)	deh-klah-'rahr-seh kool-
	culpable	'pah-bleh
plead not guilty	declararse (v)	deh-klah-'rahr-seh ee-
	inocente	noh-'sehn-teh
police station	comisaría de policía	koh-mee-sah-'ree·ah
		deh poh-lee-'see·ah
public prosecutor	acusador público	ah-koo-sah-'dohr 'poo-
		blee-koh
punish	castigar (v)	kahs-tee-'gahr
right	derecho	deh-'reh-choh
sentence	sentencia	sehn-'tehn-see·ah

• **death penalty**	pena de muerte	*'peh-nah deh 'mwehr-teh*
• **life sentence**	cadena perpetua	*kah-'deh-nah pehr-'peh-twah*
• **pass sentence**	sentenciar (*v*)	*sehn-tehn-see·'ahr*
• **prison sentence**	sentencia	*sehn-'tehn-see·ah*
sue	demandar (*v*)	*deh-mahn-'dahr*
	poner (*v**) pleito a	*poh'nehr 'pleh·ee-toh ah*
summons	citación (*f*) judicial	*see-tah-see·'ohn hoo-dee-see·'ahl*
testify	atestiguar (*v*)	*ah-tehs-tee-'gwahr*
trial	proceso	*proh-'seh-soh*
verdict	veredicto	*beh-reh-'deek-toh*
	juicio	*'hwee-see·oh*
will	testamento	*tehs-tah-'mehn-toh*
witness	testigo (*m*)	*tehs-'tee-goh*

THE CONTEMPORARY WORLD

42. SCIENCE AND TECHNOLOGY

a. THE CHANGING WORLD

> For more vocabulary on basic matter, see Section 13.

antenna	antena (*f*)	*ahn-'teh-nah*
astronaut	astronauta (*m/f*)	*ahs-troh-'now-tah*
atom	átomo	*'ah-toh-moh*
• **electron**	electrón (*m*)	*eh-lehk-'trohn*
• **molecule**	molécula	*moh-'leh-koo-lah*
• **neutron**	neutrón (*m*)	*neh-oo-'trohn*
• **proton**	protón (*m*)	*proh-'tohn*
compact disc	disco compacto	*'dees-koh kohm-'pahk-toh*
fax machine	fax (*m*)	*fahks*
laser	láser (*m*)	*'lah-sehr*
• **laser beam**	rayo láser	*'rah-yoh 'lah-sehr*
microwave	microonda	*mee-kroh-'ohn-dah*
missile	proyectil (*m*)	*proh-yehk-'teel*
• **launch**	lanzar (*v*)	*lahn-'sahr*
• **launch pad**	plataforma de lanzamiento	*plah-tah-'fohr-mah deh lahn-sah-mee-'ehn-toh*
monorail	monocarril (*m*)	*moh-noh-kah-'rreel*
nuclear industry	industria nuclear	*een-'doos-tree-ah noo-kleh-'ahr*
• **fusion reactor**	reactor (*m*) de fusión	*reh-ahk-'tohr deh foo-see-'ohn*
• **nuclear energy**	energía nuclear	*eh-nehr-'hee-ah noo-kleh-'ahr*
• **nuclear fuel**	combustible (*m*) nuclear	*kohm-boos-'tee-bleh noo-kleh-'ahr*
• **nuclear reactor**	reactor (*m*) nuclear	*reh-ahk-'tohr noo-kleh-'ahr*
robot	robot (*m*)	*roh-'boht*
satellite	satélite (*m*)	*sah-'teh-lee-teh*
• **artificial satellite**	satélite (*m*) artificial	*sah-'teh-lee-teh ahr-tee-fee-see-'ahl*
scientific research	investigación (*f*) científica	*een-behs-tee-gah-see-'ohn see-ehn-'tee-fee-kah*

spacecraft	nave (*f*) espacial	*'nah-beh ehs-pah-see-'ahl*
• lunar module	módulo lunar	*'moh-doo-loh loo-'nahr*
• space shuttle	transbordador (*m*) espacial	*trahns-bohr-dah-'dohr ehs-pah-see-'ahl*
technology	tecnología	*tehk-noh-loh-'hee-ah*
telecommunications	telecomunicaciones (*f*)	*teh-leh-koh-moo-nee-kah-see-'oh-nehs*
• teleconference	teleconferencia	*teh-leh-kohn-feh-'rehn-see·ah*
theory of relativity	teoría de relatividad	*teh-oh-'ree·ah deh reh-lah-tee-bee-'dahd*
• quantum theory	teoría cuántica	*teh-oh-'ree·ah 'kwahn-tee-kah*

b. COMPUTERS

accessories	accesorios	*ahk-seh-'soh-ree-ohs*
backup copy	copia de respaldo	*'koh-pee·ah deh reh-'spahl-doh*
	copia de seguridad	*'koh-pee·ah deh seh-goo-ree-'dahd*
byte	byte (*m*)	*'bee-teh*
	octeto	*ohk-'teh-toh*
cable	cable (*m*)	*'kah-bleh*
CD burner	grabadora de CD	*grah-bah-'doh-rah deh seh-deh*
click	hacer clic	*ah-'sehr kleek*
clipboard	portapapeles (*m*)	*pohr-tah-pah-'peh-lehs*
color printer	impresora a color	*eem-preh-'soh-rah ah koh-'lohr*
compatible	compatible (*adj*)	*kohm-pah-'tee-bleh*
compress files	comprimir archivos	*kohm-pree-'meer ahr-'chee-bohs*
computer	computadora	*kohm-poo-tah-'doh-rah*
	ordenador (*m*)	*ohr-deh-nah-'dohr*
computer language	lenguaje (*m*) de computadora	*lehn-'gwah-heh deh kohm-poo-tah-'doh-rah*
computing	informática	*een-fohr-'mah-tee-kah*
cursor	cursor (*m*)	*koor-'sohr*
data	datos	*'dah-tohs*
data base	base de texto (*f*)	*'bah-seh deh 'tehks-toh*
data processing	informatica	*een-fohr-'mah-tee-kah*
decompress files	descomprimir archivos	*dehs-kohm-pree-'meer ahr-'chee-bohs*
disk	disco	*'dees-koh*
• floppy disk	disco flexible	*'dees-koh fleh-'ksee-bleh*

• **hard disk**	disco duro	*'dees-koh 'doo-roh*
file, menu	archivo	*ahr-'chee-boh*
flat panel monitor	pantalla plana	*pahn-'tah-yah 'plah-nah*
flow chart	organigrama (*m*)	*ohr-gah-nee-'grah-mah*
function	función (*f*)	*foon-see-'ohn*
graphic design	diseño gráfico	*dee-'seh-nyoh 'grah-fee-koh*
hacker	pirata (*m*) informático	*pee-'rah-tah een-fohr-'mah-tee-koh*
hardware	hardware (*m*)	*hahrd-'wehr*
icon	icono	*ee-'koh-noh*
information technology	informática	*een-fohr-'mah-tee-kah*
ink-jet printer	impresora de inyección	*eem-preh-'soh-rah deh een-yehk-see-'ohn*
input device	dispositivo de entrada	*dees-poh-see-'tee-boh deh ehn-'trah-dah*
install	instalar (*v*)	*een-stah-'lahr*
installer	instalador (*m*)	*een-stah-lah-'dohr*
interface	conector (*m*) entre unidades	*koh-nehk-'tohr 'ehn-treh oo-nee-'dah-dehs*
	interfaz (*f*)	*een-tehr-'fahs*
internal drive	disco interno	*'dee-skoh een-'tehr-noh*
joystick	mando de juegos	*'mahn-doh deh 'hweh-gohs*
keyboard	teclado	*teh-'klah-doh*
laptop, notebook	computadora portátil	*kohm-poo-tah-'doh-rah pohr-'tah-teel*
laser printer	impresora láser	*eem-preh-'soh-rah 'lah-sehr*
manual	manual (*m*)	*mah-noo-'ahl*
megabyte	megabyte (*m*)	*meh-gah-'bee-teh*
megahertz (MHz)	megahercio (MHz)	*meh-gah-'ehr-see-oh*
memory	memoria	*meh-'moh-ree·ah*
microcomputer	microcomputadora	*mee-kroh-kohm-poo-tah-'doh-rah*
modem	módem (*m*)	*'moh-dehm*
monitor	monitor (*m*)	*moh-nee-'tohr*
mouse	ratón (*m*)	*rah-'tohn*
multimedia	multimedia	*mool-tee-'meh-dee·ah*
office automation	automatización (*f*) de oficina	*ow-toh-mah-tee-sah-see-'ohn deh oh-fee-'see-nah*
operating system	sistema (*m*) operativo	*see-'steh-mah oh-peh-rah-'tee-boh*
PDA	asistente personal digital (*m*)	*ah-see-'stehn-teh pehr-soh-'nahl dee-hee-'tahl*

peripherals	equipo periférico	*eh-'kee-poh peh-ree-'feh-ree-koh*
personal computer	computadora personal	*kohm-poo-tah-'doh-rah pehr-soh-nahl*
power switch	interruptor (*m*)	*een-teh-rroop-'tohr*
print	imprimir (*v*)	*eem-pree-'meer*
print cartridge	cartucho de tinta	*kahr-'too-choh deh 'teen-tah*
printer	impresora	*eem-preh-'soh-rah*
• **laser printer**	impresora láser	*eem-preh-'soh-rah 'lah-sehr*
processor	procesador (*m*)	*proh-seh-sah-'dohr*
program	programa (*m*)	*proh-grah-mah*
• **programmer**	programador(a)	*proh-grah-mah-'dohr (-rah)*
• **programming**	programación (*f*)	*proh-grah-mah-see-'ohn*
RAM (Random Access Memory)	memoria de acceso aleatorio	*meh-'moh-ree-ah deh ahk-'seh-soh ah-leh-ah-'toh-ree-oh*
	memoria RAM	*meh-'moh-ree-ah rahm*
ROM (Read Only Memory)	memoria permanente	*meh-'moh-ree-ah pehr-mah-'nehn-teh*
save	guardar (*v*)	*gwahr-'dahr*
scanner	escáner (*m*)	*eh-'skah-nehr*
screen	pantalla	*pahn-'tah-yah*
screensaver	salvapantallas (*m*)	*sahl-bah-pahn-'tah-yahs*
software	software (*m*)	*sohft-'wehr*
	logicial (*m*)	*loh-hee-see-'ahl*
spreadsheet	hojas de cálculo	*'oh-hahs deh 'kahl-koo-loh*
terminal	terminal (*m*)	*tehr-mee-'nahl*
user-friendly	fácil de manejar	*fah-seel deh mah-neh-'hahr*
word processing	procesamiento de texto	*proh-seh-sah-mee-'ehn-toh deh 'tehks-toh*
• **word processor**	procesador de texto	*proh-seh-sah-'dohr deh 'tehks-toh*
workstation	estación (*f*) de trabajo	*eh-stah-see-'ohn deh trah-'bah-hoh*
version	versión (*f*)	*behr-see-'ohn*

c. THE INTERNET

access	acceso	*ahk-'seh-soh*
address book	libreta de direcciones	*lee-'breh-tah deh dee-rehk-see-'oh-nehs*

attached files	archivos adjuntos	*ahr-'chee-bohs ahd-'hoon-tohs*
bookmark	marcador (*m*)	*mahr-kah-'dohr*
boot	arrancar (*v*)	*ah-rrahn-'kahr*
browse	navegar (*v*)	*nah-beh-'gahr*
chat	charla	*'chahr-lah*
command	comando	*koh-'mahn-doh*
connect	conectar (*v*)	*koh-nehk-'tahr*
download	descargar (*m*)	*dehs-kahr-'gahr*
drag	arrastrar (*v*)	*ah-rrah-'strahr*
e-mail	correo electrónico	*koh-'reh-oh eh-lehk-'troh-nee-koh*
encrypted	cifrado	*see-'frah-doh*
FAQ (frequently asked questions)	FAQ (*f*)	*fahk*
fiber optic cable	cable de fibra óptica	*'kah-bleh deh 'fee-brah 'ohp-tee-kah*
firewall	firewall, muro de protección	*'fah·eer-wahl, 'moo-roh deh proh-tehk-see-'ohn*
general delivery	lista de correo	*'lee-stah deh koh-'rreh-oh*
go back	regresar (*v*)	*reh-greh-'sahr*
go forward	adelantar (*v*)	*ah-deh-lahn-'tahr*
home page	página principal	*'pah-hee-nah preen-see-'pahl*
internet	internet (*m*)	*een-tehr-'neht*
isp	proveedor (*m*) de servicio internet	*proh-beh-eh-'dohr deh sehr-'vee-see·oh een-tehr-'neht*
keyword	palabra clave	*pah-'lah-brah 'klah-beh*
link	enlace (*m*)	*ehn-'lah-seh*
message	mensaje (*m*)	*mehn-'sah-heh*
netiquette	etiqueta de la red	*eh-tee-'keh-tah deh lah rehd*
networking	conexión (*f*) de redes	*koh-nehk-see-'ohn deh 'reh-dehs*
newsgroup	grupo de noticias	*'groo-poh deh noh-'tee-see-ahs*
network	red (*f*)	*rehd*
password	contraseña (*f*)	*kohn-trah-'seh-nyah*
net	red (*f*)	*rehd*
ports	puertos	*'pwehr-tohs*
power off	apagado	*ah-pah-'gah-doh*
power on	encendido	*ehn-sehn-'dee-doh*
search engine	buscador (*m*)	*boo-skah-'dohr*
secure web site	sitio de red seguro	*'see-tee·oh deh rehd seh-'goo-roh*

server	servidor (*m*)	*sehr-bee-'dohr*
spam	spam (*m*)	*spahm*
subscribe	suscribir (*v*)	*soo-skree-'beer*
surf	navegar (*v*)	*nah-beh-'gahr*
surfers	internautas (*m/f*)	*een-tehr-'now-tahs*
technical assistance	asistencia técnica	*ah-see-'stehn-see·ah 'tehk-nee-kah*
unsubscribe from a list	borrarse (*v*) de una lista	*boh-'rrahr-seh deh 'oo-nah 'lee-stah*
upgrade	actualizar (*v*)	*ahk-too-ah-lee-'sahr*
URL	URL (dirección de una página de la red)	*oo 'eh-re 'eh-leh (dee-rehk-see-'ohn deh 'oo-nah 'pah-hee-nah deh lah rehd)*
user name	nombre (*m*) del usuario	*'nohm-breh dehl oo-soo-'ah-ree·oh*
web browser	navegador (*m*)	*nah-beh-gah-'dohr*
webcam	webcam (*f*)	*'wehb-kahm*
webpage	página de la red	*'pah-hee-nah deh lah rehd*
web provider	portal informático (*m*)	*pohr-'tahl een-fohr-'mah-tee-koh*
website	sitio en la red	*'see-tee·oh ehn lah rehd*

43. POLITICS

> For vocabulary related to expressing yourself, see Sections 16, 17, 21, and 22.

arms reduction	disminución (*f*) de las armas	*dees-mee-noo-see-'ohn deh lahs 'ahr-mahs*
• demonstration (*public*)	manifestación (*f*) (pública)	*mah-nee-fehs-tah-see-'ohn ('poo-blee-kah)*
• unilateral	unilateral (*adj*)	*oo-nee-lah-teh-'rahl*
assembly	asamblea	*ah-sahm-'bleh-ah*
association	asociación (*f*)	*ah-soh-see·ah-see-'ohn*
communism	comunismo	*koh-moo-'nees-moh*
• communist	comunista (*m/f*)	*koh-moo-'nees-tah*
conservative	conservador(a)	*kohn-sehr-bah-'dohr (-ah)*
council	consejo	*kohn-'seh-hoh*
coup d'etat	golpe (*m*) de estado	*'gohl-peh deh ehs-'tah-doh*

democracy	democracia	*deh-moh-'krah-see·ah*
• democrat	demócrata (*m/f*)	*deh-'moh-krah-tah*
• democratic	democrático (*adj*)	*deh-moh-'krah-tee-koh*
dictator	dictador	*deek-tah-'dohr*
dictatorship	dictadura	*deek-tah-'doo-rah*
economy	economía	*eh-koh-noh-'mee·ah*
elect	elegir (*v**)	*eh-leh-'heer*
• elections	elecciones (*f*)	*eh-lehk-'see·oh-nehs*
elected political representative	representante elegido	*reh-pre-sehn-'tahn-teh eh-leh-'hee-doh*
govern	gobernar (*v**)	*goh-behr-'nahr*
• government	gobierno	*goh-bee-'ehr-noh*
house of representatives	cámara de representantes	*'kah-mah-rah deh reh-preh-sehn-'tahn-tehs*
ideology	ideología	*ee-deh-oh-loh-'hee-ah*
inflation	inflación (*f*)	*een-flah-see-'ohn*
labor/trade union	sindicato	*seen-dee-'kah-toh*
legislation	legislación (*f*)	*leh-hee-slah-see-'ohn*
liberal	liberal (*adj*)	*lee-beh-'rahl*
minister	ministro	*mee-'nees-troh*
monarchy	monarquía	*moh-nahr-'kee·ah*
• king	rey (*m*)	*'reh·ee*
• queen	reina	*'reh·ee-nah*
• prince	príncipe	*'preen-see-peh*
• princess	princesa	*preen-'seh-sah*
nuclear disarmament	desarme (*m*) nuclear	*dehs-'ahr-meh noo-kleh-'ahr*
parliament	parlamento	*pahr-lah-'mehn-toh*
peace	paz (*f*)	*pahs*
policy	política	*poh-'lee-tee-kah*
political	político (*adj*)	*poh-'lee-tee-koh*
politician	político(a)	*poh-'lee-tee-koh (-ah)*
politics	política	*poh-'lee-tee-kah*
• political party	partido político	*pahr-'tee-doh poh-'lee-tee-koh*
• political power	poder político	*poh-'dehr poh-'lee-tee-koh*
president	presidente(a)	*preh-see-'dehn-teh (-tah)*
protest	protestar (*v*)	*proh-tehs-'tahr*
• protest	protesta	*proh-'tehs-tah*
reform	reformar (*v*)	*reh-fohr-'mahr*
• reform	reforma	*reh-'fohr-mah*
republic	república	*reh-'poo-blee-kah*
revolt, riot	motín (*m*)	*moh-'teen*
revolution	revolución (*f*)	*reh-boh-loo-see-'ohn*
senate	senado	*seh-'nah-doh*

socialism	socialismo	*soh-see·ah-'lees-moh*
• **socialist**	socialista (*m/f*)	*soh-see·ah-'lees-tah*
state	estado	*ehs-'tah-doh*
• **head of state**	jefe de estado	*'heh-feh deh ehs-'tah-doh*
strike	declararse en huelga	*deh-klah-rahr-seh ehn 'wehl-gah*
• **strike**	huelga	*'wehl-gah*
terrorism	terrorismo	*tehr-roh-'rees-moh*
Third World	Tercer Mundo	*tehr-'sehr 'moon-doh*
underdeveloped countries	países subdesarrollados	*pah·'ee-sehs soob-dehs-ah-rroh-'yah-dohs*
vote	votar (*v*)	*boh-'tahr*
• **vote**	voto (*m*)	*'boh-toh*
war	guerra	*'geh-rrah*
weapons of mass destruction	armas de destrucción masiva	*'ahr-mahs deh deh-strook-see-'ohn mah-'see-vah*
welfare	asistencia pública	*ah-sees-'tehn-see·ah 'poo-blee-kah*

44. CONTROVERSIAL ISSUES

a. THE ENVIRONMENT

> See also Sections 13 and 42.

acid rain	lluvia ácida	*'yoo-bee·ah 'ah-see-dah*
air pollution	contaminación (*f*) del aire	*kohn-tah-mee-nah-see-'ohn dehl 'ah-ee-reh*
biodegradable	biodegradable	*bee·oh-deh-grah-'dah-bleh*
conservation	preservación (*f*)	*preh-sehr-bah-see-'ohn*
consumption	consumo	*kohn-'soo-moh*
deforestation	deforestación (*f*)	*deh-foh-reh-stah-see-'ohn*
ecosystem	ecosistema (*m*)	*eh-koh-sees-'teh-mah*
energy	energía	*eh-nehr-'hee-ah*
• energy crisis	crisis (*f*) energética	*'kree-sees eh-nehr-'heh-tee-kah*
• energy needs	necesidades de energía	*neh-seh-see-'dah-dehs deh eh-nehr-'hee-ah*
• energy source	fuente (*f*) de energía	*'fwehn-teh deh eh-nehr-'hee-ah*
• energy waste	malgasto de energía	*mahl-'gahs-toh deh eh-nehr-'hee-ah*

environment	medio ambiente (*m*), entorno	*'meh-dee-oh ahm-bee-'ehn-teh, ehn-'tohr-noh*
food chain	cadena alimenticia	*kah-'deh-nah ah-lee-mehn-'tee-see-ah*
fossil fuel	combustible (*m*) fósil	*kohm-boos-'tee-bleh 'foh-seel*
geothermal energy	energía geotérmica	*eh-nehr-'hee-ah heh-oh-'tehr-mee-kah*
global warming	calentamiento global	*kah-lehn-tah-mee-'ehn-toh gloh-'bahl*
greenhouse effect	efecto invernadero	*eh-'fehk-toh een-behr-nah-'deh-roh*
incinerator	incinerador (*m*)	*een-see-neh-rah-'dohr*
landfill	terraplén (*m*) de desperdicios	*teh-rrah-'plehn deh dehs-pehr-'dee-see-ohs*
natural resources	recursos naturales	*reh-'koor-sohs nah-too-'rah-lehs*
nuclear energy	energía nuclear	*eh-nehr-'hee-ah noo-kleh-'ahr*
ozone	ozono	*oh-'soh-noh*
petroleum	petróleo	*peh-'troh-leh-oh*
pollution	contaminación (*f*)	*kohn-tah-mee-nah-see-'ohn*
radiation	radiación (*f*)	*rah-dee-ah-see-'ohn*
• **radioactive waste**	desechos radioactivos	*deh-'seh-chohs rah-dee-oh-ahk-'tee-bohs*
recycle	reciclar	*reh-see-'klahr*
• **recyclable**	reciclable	*reh-see-'klah-bleh*
solar cell	célula solar	*'seh-loo-lah soh-'lahr*
solar energy	energía solar	*eh-nehr-'hee-ah soh-'lahr*
thermal energy	energía térmica	*eh-nehr-'hee-ah 'tehr-mee-kah*
toxic waste	desechos fabriles tóxicos	*dehs-'eh-chohs fahb-'ree-lehs 'toh-ksee-kohs*
water pollution	contaminación (*f*) del agua	*kohn-tah-mee-nah-see-'ohn dehl 'ah-gwah*
wind energy	energía del viento	*eh-nehr-'hee-ah dehl bee-'ehn-toh*

b. SOCIETY

abortion	aborto	*ah-'bohr-toh*
• **fetus**	feto	*'feh-toh*
AIDS	SIDA (*m*)	*'see-dah*
airport security	seguridad (*f*) aérea	*seh-goo-ree-'dahd ah-'eh-reh-ah*
anthrax	ántrax (*m*)	*'ahn-trahks*

bacteria	bacteria	*bahk-'teh-ree·ah*
biological weapons	armas biológicas	*'ahr-mahs bee·oh-'loh-hee-kahs*
bioterrorism	bioterrorismo	*bee·oh-teh-rroh-'rees-moh*
censorship	censura	*sehn-'soo-rah*
chemical weapons	armas químicas	*'ahr-mahs 'kee-mee-kahs*
child abuse	abuso de niños	*ah-'boo-soh deh 'nee-nyohs*
child support	sostenimiento de los niños	*soh-steh-nee-mee-'ehn-toh deh lohs 'nee-nyohs*
civil rights	derechos civiles	*deh-'reh-chohs see-'bee-lehs*
cloning	clonación (*f*)	*kloh-nah-see-'ohn*
cybercrime	cibercrimen (*m*)	*see-behr-'kree-mehn*
date rape	violación (*f*) durante cita	*bee-oh-lah-see-'ohn doo-'rahn-teh 'see-tah*
death penalty	pena de muerte	*'peh-nah deh 'mwehr-teh*
doctor-assisted suicide	suicidio médicamente asistido	*soo·ee-'see-dee·oh 'meh-dee-kah-mehn-teh ah-see-'stee-doh*
domestic violence	violencia doméstica	*bee-oh-'lehn-see·ah doh-'meh-stee-kah*
drug abuse	abuso de drogas	*ah-'boo-soh deh 'droh-gahs*
drugs	drogas	*'droh-gahs*
• **drug addict**	drogadicto(a)	*drohg-ah-'deek-toh (-tah)*
• **drug addiction**	drogadicción	*drohg-ah-deek-see-'ohn*
• **drug pusher**	vendedor(a) traficante de drogas	*behn-deh-'dohr (-rah) trah-fee-'kahn-teh deh 'droh-gahs*
• **take drugs**	tomar (*v*) drogas	*toh-'mahr 'droh-gahs*
ecstasy	éxtasis (*m*)	*'ehk-stah-sees*
euthanasia	eutanasia	*eh·oo-tah-'nah-see·ah*
feminism	feminismo	*feh-mee-'nees-moh*
• **feminist**	feminista (*m/f*)	*feh-mee-'nees-tah*
gambling	apostar, jugar (*v*)	*ah-poh-'stahr, hoo-'gahr*
gun control	control (*m*) de armas de fuego	*kohn-'trohl deh 'ahr-mahs deh 'fweh-goh*
home schooling	enseñanza en casa	*eh-seh-'nyahn-sah ehn 'kah-sah*
homeless	personas sin hogar	*pehr-'soh-nahs seen oh-'gahr*

homosexuality	homosexualidad (*f*)	*oh-moh-seh-ksoo·ah-lee-'dahd*
• **homosexual**	homosexual (*m*)	*oh-moh-seh-ksoo·'ahl*
• **lesbian**	lesbiana	*lehs-bee-'ah-nah*
• **lesbianism**	lesbianismo	*lehs-bee·ah-'nees-moh*
inequality	desigualdad (*f*)	*dehs-ee-gwahl-'dahd*
kidnap	secuestrar (*v*)	*seh-kweh-'strahr*
leader	líder (*m*)	*'lee-dehr*
literacy	alfabetización (*f*)	*ahl-fah-beh-tee-sah-see-'ohn*
marijuana	marihuana	*mah-ree-'wah-nah*
missile defense	defensa contra misiles	*deh-'fehn-sah 'kohn-trah mee-'see-lehs*
morality	moralidad (*f*)	*moh-rah-lee-'dahd*
nuclear weapon	arma nuclear	*'ahr-mah noo-kleh-'ahr*
• **antinuclear protest**	manifestación (*f*) antinuclear	*mah-nee-fehs-tah-see-'ohn ahn-tee-noo-kleh-'ahr*
• **atomic bomb**	bomba atómica	*'bohm-bah ah-'toh-mee-kah*
• **chemical weapon**	arma química	*'ahr-mah 'kee-mee-kah*
oppress	oprimir (*v*)	*oh-pree-'meer*
pornography	pornografía	*pohr-noh-grah-'fee-ah*
power	poder (*m*)	*poh-'dehr*
prostitution	prostitución (*f*)	*prohs-tee-too-see-'ohn*
racial profiling	opinión racialmente determinada	*oh-pee-nee-'ohn rah-see-ahl-'mehn-teh deh-tehr-mee-'nah-dah*
racism	racismo	*rah-'sees-moh*
risk	riesgo	*ree-'ehs-goh*
road rage	furia caminera	*'foo-ree·ah kah-'mee-neh-rah*
sanctions	sanciones (*f, pl*)	*sahn-see-'oh-nehs*
sexual harassment	acoso sexual	*ah-'koh-soh sehk-soo-'ahl*
suicide	suicidio	*soo·ee-'see-dee-oh*
support	apoyar (*v*)	*ah-poh-'yahr*
terrorism	terrorismo	*teh-rroh-'rees-moh*
terrorist	terrorista (*m/f*)	*teh-rroh-'ree-stah*
toxic agent	agente tóxico	*ah-'hehn-teh 'tohk-see-koh*
toxin	toxina	*tohk-'see-nahs*
transmit	transmitir (*v*)	*trahns-mee-'teer*
treason	traición (*f*)	*trah·ee-see-'ohn*
unjust	injusto	*een-'hoo-stoh*
welfare reform	reforma de asistencia pública	*reh-'fohr-mah deh ah-see-'stehn-see·ah 'poo-blee-kah*

| workplace violence | violencia en el lugar de trabajo | *bee·oh-'lehn-see·ah ehn ehl loo-'gahr deh trah-'bah-hoh* |
| zero tolerance | cero tolerancia | *'seh-roh toh-leh-'rahn-see·ah* |

c. EXPRESSING YOUR OPINION

according to . . .	según . . .	*seh-'goon*
as a matter of fact	en realidad	*ehn reh-ah-lee-'dahd*
by the way	a propósito	*ah proh-'poh-see-toh*
for example	por ejemplo	*pohr eh-'hehm-ploh*
from my point of view	desde mi punto de vista	*'dehs-deh mee 'poon-toh deh 'bees-tah*
I believe that . . .	Creo que . . .	*'kreh-oh keh*
I don't know if . . .	No sé si . . .	*noh seh see*
I doubt that . . .	Dudo que . . .	*'doo-doh keh*
I think that . . .	Pienso que . . .	*pee-'ehn-soh keh*
I would like to say that . . .	Me gustaría decir que . . .	*meh goos-tah-'ree-ah deh-'seer keh*
I'm not sure that . . .	No estoy seguro(a) de que . . .	*noh ehs-'toy seh-'goo-roh (-rah) deh keh*
I'm sure that . . .	Estoy seguro(a) de que . . .	*ehs-'toy seh-'goo-roh (-rah) deh keh*
in conclusion	en conclusión (*f*)	*ehn kohn-kloo-see-'ohn*
in my opinion	en mi opinión (*f*)	*ehn mee oh-pee-nee-'ohn*
It seems that . . .	Parece que . . .	*pah-'reh-seh keh*
It's clear that . . .	Es claro que . . .	*ehs 'klah-roh keh*
that is to say	es decir	*ehs deh-'seer*
There's no doubt that . . .	No hay duda de que . . .	*noh 'ah·ee 'doo-dah deh keh*
therefore	por eso	*pohr 'eh-soh*

APPENDIX: SPANISH VERBS

IRREGULAR VERBS

The following verbs have irregular forms in the present tense. All of them have been marked throughout the text and in the end vocabulary section with an asterisk. They are listed here only in the present tense and for your convenience are presented continuously across the page instead of in the traditional way:

me acuesto	nos acostamos
te acuestas	os acostáis
se acuesta	se acuestan

acostarse: me acuesto, te acuestas, se acuesta, nos acostamos, os acostáis, se acuestan

advertir: advierto, adviertes, advierte, advertimos, advertís, advierten

agradecer: agradezco, agradeces, agradece, agradecemos, agradecéis, agradecen

almorzar: almuerzo, almuerzas, almuerza, almorzamos, almorzáis, almuerzan

apretar: aprieto, aprietas, aprieta, apretamos, apretáis, aprietan

aprobar: apruebo, apruebas, aprueba, aprobamos, aprobáis, aprueban

aullar: aúllo, aúllas, aúlla, aullamos, aulláis, aúllan

caer: caigo, caes, cae, caemos, caéis, caen

calentarse: me caliento, te calientas, se calienta, nos calentamos, os calentáis, se calientan

coger: cojo, coges, coge, cogemos, cogéis, cogen

colgar: cuelgo, cuelgas, cuelga, colgamos, colgáis, cuelgan

comenzar: comienzo, comienzas, comienza, comenzamos, comenzáis, comienzan

concluir: concluyo, concluyes, concluye, concluimos, concluís, concluyen

conducir: conduzco, conduces, conduce, conducimos, conducís, conducen

conocer: conozco, conoces, conoce, conocemos, conocéis, conocen

consentir: consiento, consientes, consiente, consentimos, consentís, consienten

construir: construyo, construyes, construye, construimos, construís, construyen

contar: cuento, cuentas, cuenta, contamos, contáis, cuentan

continuar: continúo, continúas, continúa, continuamos, continuáis, continúan

convalecer: convalezco, convaleces, convalece, convalecemos, convalecéis, convalecen

convencer: convenzo, convences, convence, convencemos, convencéis, convencen

costar: cuesto, cuestas, cuesta, costamos, costáis, cuestan

crecer: crezco, creces, crece, crecemos, crecéis, crecen

criar: crío, crías, cría, criamos, criáis, crían

dar(se):   (me) doy, (te) das, (se) da, (nos) damos, (os) dais, (se) dan
decir: digo, dices, dice, decimos, decís, dicen
defenderse: me defiendo, te defiendes, se defiende, nos defendemos, os defendéis, se defienden
demostrar: demuestro, demuestras, demuestra, demostramos, demostráis, demuestran
despertarse: me despierto, te despiertas, se despierta, nos despertamos, os despertáis, se despiertan
destruir: destruyo, destruyes, destruye, destruimos, destruís, destruyen
detener(se):   *see tener*
devolver: *see volver*
digerir: digiero, digieres, digiere, digerimos, digerís, digieren
disminuir: disminuyo, disminuyes, disminuye, disminuimos, dismunuís, disminuyen
divertirse: me divierto, te diviertes, se divierte, nos divertimos, os divertís, se divierten
doler: duelo, dueles, duele, dolemos, doléis, duelen
dormir: duermo, duermes, duerme, dormimos, dormís, duermen
elegir: elijo, eliges, elige, elegimos, elegís, eligen
empezar: empiezo, empiezas, empieza, empezamos, empezáis, empiezan
encender(se):   (me) enciendo, (te) enciendes, (se) enciende, (nos) encendemos, (os) encendéis, (se) encienden
encerrar: encierro, encierras, encierra, encerramos, encerráis, encierran
enfriarse: me enfrío, te enfrías, se enfría, nos enfriamos, os enfriáis, se enfrían
engrandecer: engrandezco, engrandeces, engrandece, engrandecemos, engrandecéis, engrandecen
entender: entiendo, entiendes, entiende, entendemos, entendéis, entienden
entristecerse: me entristezco, te entristeces, se entristece, nos entristecemos, os entristecéis, se entristecen
envejecerse: me envejezco, te envejeces, se envejece, nos envejecemos, os envejecéis, se envejecen
esquiar: esquío, esquías, esquía, esquiamos, esquiáis, esquían
estar: estoy, estás, está, estamos, estáis, están
extinguir: extingo, extingues, extingue, extinguimos, extinguís, extinguen
extraer: extraigo, extraes, extrae, extraemos, extraéis, extraen
fluir: fluyo, fluyes, fluye, fluimos, fluís, fluyen
freír: frío, fríes, fríe, freímos freís, fríen
gobernar: gobierno, gobiernas, gobierna, gobernamos, gobernáis, gobiernan
hacer (se):   (me) hago, (te) haces, (se) hace, (nos) hacemos, (os) hacéis, (se) hacen
helar: hielo, hielas, hiela, helamos, heláis, hielan
herir: hiero, hieres, hiere, herimos, herís, hieren
invertir: invierto, inviertes, invierte, invertimos, invertís, invierten
ir: voy, vas, va, vamos, vais, van
irse: me voy, te vas, se va, nos vamos, os vais, se van
jugar: juego, juegas, juega, jugamos, jugáis, juegan
llover: llueve (*invariable*)
maldecir: *see decir*

maullar: maúllo, maúlles, maúlle, maullamos, maulláis, maúllan

medir: mido, mides, mide, medimos, medís, miden

mentir: miento, mientes, miente, mentimos, mentís, mienten

merendar: meriendo, meriendas, merienda, merendamos, merendáis, meriendan

morir: muero, mueres, muere, morimos, morís, mueren

mover: muevo, mueves, mueve, movemos, movéis, mueven

nacer: nazco, naces, nace, nacemos, nacéis, nacen

negar: niego, niegas, niega, negamos negáis, niegan

nevar: nieva (*invariable*)

obtener: *see tener*

oír: oigo, oyes, oye, oímos, oís, oyen

oler: huelo, hueles, huele, olemos, oléis, huelen

padecer: padezco, padeces, padece, padecemos, padecéis, padecen

parecerse: me parezco, te pareces, se parece, nos parecemos, os parecéis, se parecen

pedir: pido, pides, pide, pedimos, pedís, piden

pensar: pienso, piensas, piensa, pensamos, pensáis, piensan

perder: pierdo, pierdes, pierde, perdemos, perdéis, pierden

poder: puedo, puedes, puede, podemos, podéis, pueden

poner(se):   (me) pongo, (te) pones, (se) pone, (nos) ponemos, (os) ponéis, (se) ponen

predecir: *see decir*

preferir: prefiero, prefieres, prefiere, preferimos, preferís, prefieren

probar: pruebo, pruebas, prueba, probamos, probáis, prueban

proponer: *see poner*

proteger: protejo, proteges, protege, protegemos, protegéis, protegen

querer: quiero, quieres, quiere, queremos, queréis, quieren

recoger: recojo, recoges, recoge, recogemos, recogéis, recogen

recomendar: recomiendo, recomiendas, recomienda, recomendamos, recomendáis, recomiendan

recordar: recuerdo, recuerdas, recuerda, recordamos, recordáis, recuerdan

regar: riego, riegas, riega, regamos, regáis, riegan

reír(se):   (me) río, (te) ríes, (se) ríe, (nos) reímos, (os) reís, (se) ríen

remendar: remiendo, remiendas, remienda, remendamos, remendáis, remiendan

reñir: riño, riñes, riñe, reñimos, reñís, riñen

repetir: repito, repites, repite, repetimos, repetís, repiten

reproducir: reproduzco, reproduces, reproduce, reproducimos, reproducís, reproducen

resolver: resuelvo, resuelves, resuelve, resolvemos, resolvéis, resuelven

rogar: ruego, ruegas, ruega, rogamos, rogáis, ruegan

rugir: rujo, ruges, ruge, rugimos, rugís, rugen

saber: sé, sabes, sabe, sabemos, sabéis, saben

salir: salgo, sales, sale, salimos, salís, salen

satisfacer: satisfago, satisfaces, satisface, satisfacemos, satisfacéis, satisfacen

seguir: sigo, sigues, sigue, seguimos, seguís, siguen

sembrar: siembro, siembras, siembra, sembramos, sembráis, siembran

sentarse: me siento, te sientas, se sienta, nos sentamos, os sentáis, se sientan
sentirse: me siento, te sientes, se siente, nos sentimos, os sentís, se sienten
ser: soy, eres, es somos, sois, son
servir: sirvo, sirves, sirve, servimos, servís, sirven
sonar: sueno, suenas, suena, sonamos, sonáis, suenan
sonreír: *see reír*
sugerir: sugiero, sugieres, sugiere, sugerimos, sugerís, sugieren
tender(se): (me) tiendo, (te) tiendes, (se) tiende, (nos) tendemos, (os) tendéis, (se) tienden
tener: tengo, tienes, tiene, tenemos, tenéis, tienen
teñir: tiño, tiñes, tiñe, teñimos, teñís, tiñen
tostar: tuesto, tuestas, tuesta, tostamos, tostáis, tuestan
traducir: traduzco, traduces, traduce, traducimos, traducís, traducen
traer: traigo, traes, trae, traemos, traéis, traen
tronar: trueno, truenas, truena, tronamos, tronáis, truenan
tropezar: tropiezo, tropiezas, tropieza, tropezamos, tropezáis, tropiezan
vaciar: vacío, vacías, vacía, vaciamos, vaciáis, vacían
venir: vengo, vienes, viene, venimos, venís, vienen
ver: veo, ves, ve, vemos, véis, ven
verter: vierto, viertes, vierte, vertimos, vertís, vierten
vestirse: me visto, te vistes, se viste, nos vestimos, os vestís, se visten
volar: vuelo, vuelas, vuela, volamos, voláis, vuelan
volver: vuelvo, vuelves, vuelve, volvemos, volvéis, vuelven

ENGLISH-SPANISH WORDFINDER

This alphabetical listing of all of the English words in *Spanish Vocabulary* will enable you to find the information you need quickly and efficiently. If all you want is the Spanish equivalent of an entry word, you will find it here. If you also want pronunciation and usage aids, or closely associated words and phrases, use the reference number(s) and letter(s) to locate the section(s) in which the entry appears. This is especially important for words that have multiple meanings.

A

a, an   un, uno, una, unos, unas   8e

abbreviation   la abreviatura   19c

able to   poder   21a

abortion   el aborto   44b

above   arriba, sobre   3d

abroad   al extranjero   19e, 30a

absent   ausente   37f

accent   el acento   8a, 19c

accept   aceptar   21b

acceptable   aceptable   21b

access   el acceso   42c

accessories   los accesorios   42b

accident   el accidente   33c, 39c

according to   según   44c

accordion   el acordeón   28c

account   la cuenta   26

accountant   el (la) contador (ra)   38a

accounting   la contabilidad   37e

accusation   la acusación   41

accuse   acusar   41

accused   el (la) acusado (a)   41

acid   el ácido   13c

acid rain   la lluvia ácida   44a

acne   acné   40a

acquaintance   el (la) conocido (a)   10b

across   a través de   3d, 36c

act   actuar (v)   28e,   el acto   28e

active   activo   8a, 11e

activity   la actividad   11e

actor   el actor   28a, 38a

actress   la actriz   28a, 38a

actually   en realidad   17b

acupuncture   la acupuntura   40a

acute   agudo   2b

adapt   adaptar   11e

adaptable   adaptable   11e

adapter   el adaptador   20b

add   sumar   1e

addict   el (la) adicto (a)   11e

addition   la suma   1e

address   la dirección, las señas   11f, 19e, 38b

address book   la libreta de direcciones   42c

adhesive tape   la cinta adhesiva   19d, 25c, 38c

adjacent   adyacente   2b

adjective   adjetivo   8a

admit   admitir   41

adolescence   la juventud   11b

Spanish nouns are denoted with the definite article **el**, **la**, **los**, or **las**. To avoid dissonance, some Spanish feminine nouns that begin with a stressed *a* take the masculine definite article **el**; these are identified by (*f*).

adolescent   el (la) joven   11b
adult   el (la) adulto (a)   11b
adventure   la aventura   20a
adverb   el adverbio   8a
advertising   la publicidad, la
  propaganda   20a, 38d
advice   el consejo   17a
advise   aconsejar   17a
affection   el afecto, el cariño
  11e, 21a
affectionate   afectuoso, cariñoso
  11e
Africa   Africa   30b
after   después (de)   4e, 8o
afternoon   la tarde   4a
again   otra vez   4e
age   la edad   11b, 38b
aggressive   agresivo   11e
agnostic   el (la) agnóstico (a)
  11d
ago   hace   4e
agree   estar* de acuerdo   21a,
  22b, 41
agriculture   la agricultura
  14a
ahead   delante, adelante   3d,
  36c
AIDS   el SIDA   40a, 44b
air   el aire   6a, 13c
air conditioning   el aire
  acondicionado   23e, 33e
air marshal   alguacil aéreo (m)
  32a
air pollution   la contaminación
  del aire   44a
airline   la línea aérea   32a
airmail   por avión   19e
airplane   el avión   32c
airport   el aeropuerto   32a
airport security   la seguridad
  aérea   44b
aisle   el pasillo   28a, 32c
alarm   la alarma   39a
alarm clock   el despertador
  4d, 25i
albatross   el albatros   15b
alcoholic drink   la bebida
  alcohólica   24k

algebra   el álgebra   (*f*)   1f
algebraic   algebraico   1f
all   todo   3c
All aboard!   ¡Todos a bordo!
  34
all day   todo el día   4a
allegory   la alegoría   17a
allergy   la alergia   40a
allude   aludir   17a
almost   casi   3c
almost never   casi nunca   4e
alphabet   el alfabeto   8a
already   ya   4e
also   también   44c
although   aunque   8o
altitude   la altitud   32c
altruism   el altruismo   11e
altruist   el (la) altruista   11e
altruistic   altruista   11e
always   siempre   4e
amateur   aficionado   27b
ambition   la ambición   11e
ambitious   ambicioso   11e
ambulance   la ambulancia
  33a, 39a, 39c
America   América   30b
American   americano(a)   (*adj,
  n*)   30d
amethyst   la amatista   25i
ammonia   el amoníaco   13c
among   entre   3d, 8g
amphitheater   el anfiteatro
  36a
amplifier   el amplificador
  20b
analogy   la analogía   17a,
  28d
anatomy   la anatomía   37e
anchovy   la anchoa   24d
and   y   8o
anesthetic   el anestésico   40b
anesthetist   el (la) anestesista
  40a
anger   el enojo   11e, 21a
angle   el ángulo   2b
angry   enojado   11e
animal   el animal   15a
ankle   el tobillo   12a

anniversary   el aniversario   11c, 29a
announce   anunciar   17a
announcer   el locutor   38a
announcement   el anuncio   17a
annually   anualmente   4c
answer   la respuesta *(n)*; responder *(v)*   9, 17a, 18b, 37f
answering machine   el contestador automático   18a
ant   la hormiga   15d
Antarctic   Antártico   13b
Antarctic Circle   el Círculo Antártico   13e
antenna   la antena   20b, 42a
anthrax   el ántrax   44b
anthropology   la antropología   37e
anti-coagulant   el anticoagulante   40a
anti-inflammatory   el antiinflamatorio   40a
antibiotic   el antibiótico   25h, 40a
antinuclear protest   la manifestación antinuclear   44b
antique   la antigüedad   25a
antiseptic   el antiséptico   39c
antithesis   la antítesis   28d
anus   el ano   40a
anxiety   el ansia *(f)*   21a
anxious   inquieto   11e, 21a
anxiousness   la inquietud   11e, 21a
apartment   el apartamento, el piso   23g
apartment house   la casa de pisos   23g
aperitif   el aperitivo   24g
apostrophe   el apóstrofe   19c
appendicitis   la apendicitis   40a
appendix   el apéndice   20a, 28d, 40a

appetizer   la tapa, el bocadillo   24g
appetizing   apetitoso   24p
applaud   aplaudir   28e
applause   el aplauso   28e
apple   la manzana   14d, 24f
apple tree   el manzano   14c
application   la solicitud   38b
apply for   solicitar   37f
appointment   la cita   40a, 40b
appointment book   la agenda de entrevistas   38c
approval   la aprobación   21b
approve   aprobar*   21b
approximately   aproximadamente   3c
apricot   el albaricoque   14d, 24f
April   abril   5b
Aquarius   Acuario   5d
Arabic   árabe *(adj, n)*   30d
Arabic numerals   la numeración arábica   1d
archaeology   la arqueología   37e
archipelago   el archipiélago   13b
architect   el (la) arquitecto (a)   38a
architecture   la arquitectura   28b, 37e
Arctic   Ártico   13b
Arctic Circle   el Círculo Ártico   13e
area   el área *(f)*   3a, 13d
area code   la zona telefónica   18b
Argentinian   argentino(a) *(adj, n)*   30d
argue   reñir*   17a, 39b
argument   la disputa   17a
Aries   Aries   5d
arithmetic   la aritmética   1f
arithmetical   aritmético   1e
arm   el brazo   12a
armchair   el sillón   23c, 35c

armed robbery   robo a mano
armada   39b
arms reduction   la disminución
de las armas   43
arrest   detener*, arrestar   39b
arrival   la llegada   32a
arrive   llegar   3e
arrogant   arrogante   11e
art   el (la) arte   28b, 37e
art museum   el museo de arte
36a
artery   la arteria   40a
arthritis   la artritis   40a
artichoke   la alcachofa   14e,
24e
article   el artículo   8a, 20a
articulate   articular   17a
artificial   artificial   13d, 25i
artificial satellite   el satélite
artificial   42a
artist   el (la) artista   28b
artistic   artístico   11e
as   como   8o
as a matter of fact   en realidad
17d, 44c
as if   como si   8o
ashtray   el cenicero   23c
Asia   Asia   30b
ask   preguntar   9, 17a
ask a question   hacer* una
pregunta   9
asparagus   el espárrago   14e,
24e
aspirin   la aspirina   25h, 40a
assault   el asalto   39b
assembly   la asamblea   43
assignments   la tarea   37f
assistant   el (la) ayudante
37d
association   la asociación   43
assure   asegurar   21a
asterisk   el asterisco   19c
asthma   el asma *(f)*   40a
astronaut   el (la) astronauta
42a
astronomy   la astronomía
13a, 37e
astute   astuto   11e

astuteness   la astucia   11e
at   en   8g
at home   en casa   23f
at midnight   a la medianoche
4a
at night   de noche   4a
at noon   al mediodía   4a
at the end of   al final de   36c
at the top   en lo alto de   36c
At what time?   ¿A qué hora?
4b
atheism   el ateísmo   11d
atheist   ateo   11d
athlete   el (la) atleta   27b
Atlantic   el Atlántico   13b
atlas   el atlas   20a, 37b
atmosphere   la atmósfera   6a,
13b
atmospheric   atmosférico
13b
atmospheric conditions   las
condiciones atmosféricas   6a
atom   el átomo   13c, 42a
atomic bomb   la bomba atómica
44b
attached files   los archivos
adjuntos   42c
attend   asistir   37f
attic   el ático   23a
attitude   la actitud   21a
attractive   atractivo   11a, 11e
audience   el público   28e
audio equipment   el equipo
auditivo   20b
August   agosto   5b
aunt   la tía   10a
Australia   Australia   30b
Australian   australiano(a) *(adj,
n)*   30d
Austria   Austria   30b
authentic   auténtico   13d
author   el (la) autor (a)   20a
autobiography   la autobiografía
28d
automobile   el automóvil
33a
avarice, greed   la avaricia
11e

avenue   la avenida   11f, 36a
average   el promedio   1f
avocado   el aguacate   24e
away   fuera   3d
axis   el eje   2b

B

baby   el (la) bebé   11b
bachelor   el (la) soltero (a)   11c
back   la espalda   12a
backache   el dolor de espalda   40a
backpack   la mochila   27a, 31
backup copy   la copia de respaldo; copia de seguridad   42b
back up   retroceder   33c
bacon   el tocino   24c
bacteria   la bacteria   44b
bad   malo   11e, 24p
bad breath   el mal aliento   40a
bad mood   mal humor   21a
bag   el saco, la bolsa   23d, 25a
baggage   el equipaje   31
bagpipes   la gaita   28c
bail   la fianza   41
baked   asado   24b, 24p
baker   el panadero   38a
bakery   la panadería   24n
balcony   el balcón   23a, 35c
bald   calvo *(adj)*   12d
ball   la pelota   27b
ballad   el romance   28d
ballet   el ballet   28c
ballpoint pen   el bolígrafo   19d, 25c, 37b
banana   la banana, el plátano   14d, 24f
bandage   la venda   25h, 39c, 40a   vendar *(v)*   40a
bangs   el flequillo   12d
bank   el banco   26
bank book   la libreta de depósitos   26

bank rate   el tipo de descuento bancario   26
banker   el banquero   38a
banknote   (see *bill*)
baptism   el bautismo   11d
barber   el barbero   12d, 38a
barber shop   la barbería   12d
bark   ladrar   15a
barn   el establo   15a
barometer   el barómetro   6c
barometric pressure   la presión barométrica   6c
baroque   barroco *(n, adj)*   28d
barrel   el barril   23d
bartender   el cantinero   24m
baseball   el béisbol   27b
basement   el sótano   23a
basil   la albahaca   14e, 24j
basilica   la basílica   36a
basin   la cuenca   13b
basket   la cesta, la canasta   23d, 27b
basketball   el básquetbol, el baloncesto   27b
basketball court   la cancha   27b
bass drum   el bombo   28c
bassoon   el bajón   28c
bat   el murciélago   15a
bat *(baseball)*   el bate   27b
bathing suit   el traje de baño   25k
bath oil   el aceite de baño   25f
bathroom   el cuarto de baño   23b, 35c
bathtub   la bañera   23a, 35c
batter *(baseball)*   el bateador   27b
battery *(car)*   el acumulador   25b, 33e
battery   la pila   25b
battery charger   el cargador de pilas   20b
bay   la bahía   13b
beach   la playa   13b, 36b
beak   el pico   15b

beans los frijoles   14e, 24e
bear el oso   15a
beard la barba   12a
beast la bestia   15a
beautician el (la) peluquero (a)   12d
beautiful hermoso   11a, 25l
beauty la belleza   11a
because porque   8o
become hacerse*   10b, 25a
become bored aburrirse *(v)*   21a
bed la cama   23c, 35c
bedbug la chinche   15d
bedroom la alcoba, el cuarto   23b
bedside table la mesilla de noche   23c, 35c
bedspread el cubrecama   23d, 35c
bee la abeja   15d
beech tree el (la) haya *(f)*   14c
beefsteak el bistec   24c
beer la cerveza   24k
beet la remolacha   14e, 24e
before antes (de)   4e, 8o
beg rogar*   17a
begin empezar*, comenzar*   4e
beginning el principio   4e
behind detrás   3d, 36c
Belgian belga   30d
belief la creencia   11d
believe creer   11d, 22b
bellboy el botones   35b
bell tower el campanario   36a
below zero bajo cero   6c
belt el cinturón   25k
Berlin Berlín   30c
beside junto a   3d
besides además de   8g
best seller el éxito de librería   20a, 25o
between entre   3d, 8g
beyond más allá   3d
Bible la Biblia   28d

bicycle la bicicleta   33a
bicycle racing el ciclismo   27b
big grande   3c, 11a, 25l
bill la cuenta   24m, 25a, 35b
bill facturar *(v)*   25a
bill, banknote el billete   26
billiard ball la bola de billar   27a
billiard table la mesa de billar   27a
billiards el billar   27a
billionth mil millonésimo   1b
bingo el bingo   27a
bingo card la tarjeta de bingo   27a
binoculars los prismáticos   27b
biodegradable biodegradable   44a
biography la biografía   28d
biological weapons las armas biológicas   44b
biology la biología   37e
bioterrorism el bioterrorismo   44b
bird el pájaro   15b
birth el nacimiento   11c
birth control el control de natalidad   40a
birthday el cumpleaños   11c, 29a
bisector la bisectriz   2b
bishop *(chess)* el alfil   27a
bite la mordedura   39c
black negro   7a
blackberry la zarzamora   14d
blackbird el mirlo   15b
blackboard la pizarra   37b
blackboard eraser el borrador   37b
bladder la vejiga   40a
blade *(of knife)* la hoja   23d, 25f
blanket la manta   23d, 35c
bleat balar   15a

bleed sangrar 39c

blender la licuadora 23d

blindness la ceguera 12c

blind person el (la) ciego(a) 12c

block *(city)* la manzana, la cuadra 33c

blond(e) rubio(a) 11a

blood la sangre 12a, 39c, 40a

blood clot el coágulo de sangre 40a

blood pressure la presión arterial 40a

blood test el análisis de sangre 40a

bloom florecer 14a

blouse la blusa 25k

blue azul 7a

blueberry el mirtilo 24f

blueprint el cianotipo 28b

blush, rouge el colorete 25f

board subir a 32a

boarding el embarque 32a

boardinghouse la casa de huéspedes 35a, la pensión *(f)* 35b

boarding pass la tarjeta de embarque 32a

boat el bote 36b

bobbypins las horquillas 25f

body el cuerpo 11a, 12a, 19a

body build desarrollar la musculatura 27a

boiled guisado *(adj)* 24b

boiling point el punto de ebullición 6c

bold audaz 11e

Bolivian boliviano(a) *(adj, n)* 30d

bond el bono 26

bone el hueso 12a, 40a

book el libro 20a, 25o, 37b

bookcase el estante 23c, 37b

bookmark el marcador 42c

bookstore la librería 25o

boot arrancar *(v)* 42c

boot la bota 25n

border la frontera 13e, 31

bore aburrir 21a

bored aburrido 21a

boredom el aburrimiento 21a

boss el (la) jefe (a) 38d

botanical botánico 14a

botany la botánica 14a, 37e

both ambos 3c

bottle la botella 23d, 24l

bottom el fondo 3d

bouquet of flowers el ramo de flores 14b

bow el arco 28c

bowl el tazón 23d, 24l

bowl jugar* a los bolos 27a

bowling alley la bolera 27a

bowling ball la bola 27a

box la caja 23d

box office la taquilla 28a

boxing el boxeo 27b

boxing gloves los guantes de boxeo 27b

boxing ring el ring 27b

boy el chico, el muchacho 11a, 11b

boyfriend novio, amigo 10b

bra el sostén 25k

bracelet la pulsera 25i

bracket el corchete 19c

brain el cerebro 12a, 40a

brake el freno 33a, 33e

brake frenar 33c

branch la rama 14a

branch *(of a company)* la sucursal 38d

brash atrevido 11e

brass el latón 13c

brass instruments los cobres 28c

Brazil el Brasil 30b

Brazilian brasileño(a) *(adj, n)* 30d

breakfast el desayuno 24a, 35b

breast el seno 12a

breath el aliento 40a

breathe respirar 12b, 40a

bricklayer el albañil 38a
bride la novia 11c
bridge el puente 33c, 36a, 40b
brief breve (*adj*) 4e, 37f
briefcase la cartera, el portafolio 25c, 38c
briefly brevemente 4e, 17b
briefs los calzoncillos 25k
bright vivo 7b
brilliant brillante 11e
bring traer* 25a
brocade el brocado 251
broccoli el brécol, el bróculi 14e, 24e
brochure el folleto 20a, 30a
broiled a la parrilla 24b
broken bone el hueso fracturado 39c
broken line la línea quebrada 2b
bronchitis la bronquitis 40a
bronze el bronce 13c
brooch el broche 25i
brook el arroyo 36b
broom la escoba 23d
broth el caldo 24g
brother el hermano 10a
brother-in-law el cuñado 10a
brown marrón 7a
browse navegar (*v*) 42c
bruise la contusión 40a
brunet(te) moreno(a) 11a
brush el cepillo 12d, 25f
brush (*art*) el pincel 28b
brush cepillarse (*v*) 12d, 40b
buckle up abrocharse (*v*) 32c
bud el brote 14a
Buddhism el budismo 11d
Buddhist el (la) budista (*n, adj*) 11d
budget el presupuesto 26
buffalo el búfalo 15a
bug el insecto 15d
build construir 23f

building el edificio 23g, 39a
bulb el bulbo 14a
bull el toro 15a
bullring la plaza de toros 36a
bumper el parachoques 33e
bump into tropezar* con 39c
bunion el juanete 40a
burn quemar 39a
burn la quemadura 39a, 40a
bus el autobús, el camión 33a, 34
bus driver el conductor 34, 38a
bus station la estación de autobuses, la camionera 34
bush el arbusto 14a
business letter carta comercial 19e
businessman el comerciante 38a
businesswoman la comerciante 38a
busy ocupado 18b
but pero, sino 8o
butcher el carnicero 38a
butcher shop la carnicería 24n
butter la mantequilla 24h
butterfly la mariposa 15d
buttocks el trasero 12a
button el botón 25g
buttonhole el ojal 25g
buy comprar 23f, 25a
byte el byte, el octeto 42b

C

cabbage la col, el repollo 14e, 24e
cabin (*plane*) la cabina 32c
cable el cable 18a, 25b, 42b
cafeteria la cafetería 24m
cake la torta 24g
calcium el calcio 40a
calculate calcular 1f
calculation el cálculo 1f
calculus el cálculo 37e

calendar el calendario 5b, 38c

calf la pantorrilla 12a

call llamar 17a

calling card (*phone*) la tarjeta telefónica 18b

calling card (*etiquette*) tarjeta de visita 16b

calm tranquilo 11e

calmness la tranquilidad 11e

camel el camello 15a

camera la cámara 25d

camp acampar 36b

campground el campamento 36b

campus la ciudad universitaria, el campus 37c

can la lata 23d

can, be able poder* 21a

Canada el Canadá 30b

Canadian el (la) canadiense (*n, adj*) 30d

canceled cancelado 32b

cancer el cáncer 40a

Cancer Cáncer 5d

canine tooth el canino 40b

canoe la canoa 36b

canteen la cantimplora 36b

canvas el lienzo 7c, 28b

cap la gorra 36b

capacity la capacidad 3c

cape el cabo 13b

capital la capital 13e

capital city la ciudad capital 13e, 30a

capital letter la letra mayúscula 19c

Capricorn Capricornio 5d

car el carro, el coche 33a

car body la carrocería 33e

car racing las carreras de coches 27b

car window la ventanilla 33e

carat el quilate 25i

carbon el carbono 13c

carburetor el carburador 33e

card la tarjeta 19e

cardinal number número cardinal 1d

cardiologist el (la) cardiólogo(a) 40a

career la carrera 11f, 38d

carnation el clavel 14b

carpenter el carpintero 38a

carpet la alfombra 23c

carriage (*typewriter*) el carro 19d

carrot la zanahoria 14e, 24e

carry llevar 31

case el estuche 23d

cash el dinero en efectivo 25a, 26

cash cobrar, cambiar 26

cash account la cuenta de caja 26

cash payment el pago al contado 26

cash register la caja registradora 25a

cashier el (la) cajero (a) 25a, 26, 38a

cassette el casete 20b, 25j

cast el reparto 28e

castle el castillo 36a

cat el gato 15a

catch (*ball*) agarrar, coger* 27b

catechism el catecismo 11d

caterpillar la oruga 15d

cathedral la catedral 36a

Catholic católico(a) (*adj, n*) 11d

Catholicism el catolicismo 11d

cauliflower la coliflor 14e, 24e

caution el cuidado 33d

cave la cueva 13b

cavity la carie 40b

CD burner la grabadora de CD 42b

ceiling el techo 23a

celery el apio 14e, 24e

cell la célula   14a
cello el violoncelo   28c
cellphone el teléfono celular, móvil   20b
Celsius Celsius   6c
censorship la censura   44b
center el centro   2a
centimeter el centímetro   3a
century el siglo   4c
chain la cadena   25i, 33a
chain guard *(bicycle)* el cárter   33a
chair la silla   23c, 38c
chalk la tiza   37b
change cambiar   4e, 25a
change gears cambiar de velocidad   33c
change the subject cambiar el tema   17a
changing room el vestuario   25k
channel el cauce   13b
channel *(TV, radio)* el canal   20b
chapter el capítulo   28d
character el carácter   11e
character *(in a book, etc.)* el personaje   28d, 28e
characteristic la característica   11e
characterize caracterizar   11e
charm el dije   25i
charter flight el vuelo fletado   30a
chat la charla   42c
chat charlar *(v)*   17a
cheap barato   24p
check *(banking)* el cheque   25a, 26
check *(luggage)* facturar, depositar   32a
check *(restaurant)* la cuenta   24m
checkbook la libreta de cheques   26
checkerboard el tablero de damas   27a

checkers las damas   27a
checking account la cuenta corriente   26
checkmate el jaque mate   27a
cheek la mejilla   12a
cheese el queso   24h
chemical el producto químico   13c
chemical weapon el arma química *(f)*   44b
chemistry la química   13c, 37e
chemistry lab el laboratorio de química   37c
chemotherapy la quimoterapia   40a
cherry la cereza   14d, 24f
cherry tree el cerezo   14c
chess el ajedrez   27a
chessboard el tablero de ajedrez   27a
chest el pecho   12a
chestnut la castaña   14d
chest of drawers la cómoda   23c, 35c
chicken el pollo   24c
chicken pox la varicela   40a
child el niño   11b
child abuse el abuso de niños   44b
child support el sostenimiento de los niños   44b
children los niños   11b
Chilean chileno(a) *(adj, n)*   30d
chills los escalofríos   40a
chimney la chimenea   23a
chin la barbilla   12a
china la porcelana   23d
China China   30b
Chinese chino(a) *(adj, n)*   30d
chlorine el cloro   13c
chlorophyll la clorofila   14a
choke atragantarse *(v)*   40a
Christian cristiano(a) *(adj, n)*   11d

Christianity el cristianismo 11d

Christmas la Navidad 5f, 29a

Christmas bonus el aguinaldo 38d

Christmas Eve la Nochebuena 5f

church la iglesia 11d, 36a

cigar el puro, el cigarro 25e

cigarette el cigarrillo 25e

cinnamon la canela 24j

circle el círculo 2a

circumference la circunferencia 2a

citrus la fruta agria 14d

city la ciudad 11f, 13e, 30a, 36a, 38b

city map el plano de la ciudad 36a

civil law el derecho civil 41

civil rights los derechos civiles 44b

clam la almeja 24d

clamp la abrazadera 25b

clarinet el clarinete 28c

class (*travel*) la clase (*f*) 30a

class (*of students*) la clase 37d, 37f

classical music la música clásica 25j, 28c

classified ads los anuncios clasificados 38d

classroom el aula (*f*) 37c

clause la cláusula 8a

clay la arcilla 13c

clean limpio (*adj*) 11a

clean limpiar (*v*) 23f, 25g

clean oneself limpiarse (*v*) 12d

clear claro (*photo*) 25d

clear (*weather*) despejado 6a

clear the table quitar (limpiar) la mesa 23f, 24o

clerk el (la) dependiente 19e

clerk's window la ventanilla 19e

click hacer (*v*) elic 42b

climate el clima 6a

clipboard el portapapeles 42b

clippers la maquinilla 12d

clock el reloj 4d

cloning la clonación 44b

close an account liquidar una cuenta 26

closed cerrado 25a

closed circuit el circuito cerrado 20b

closet el ropero 23a

closet, cupboard el armario 23b, 35c

closing la despedida 19c

closing time hora de cerrar 25a

clothes la ropa 25g

clothes basket la cesta para la ropa sucia 25g

clothes hanger la percha, el gancho 23d, 35c

clothespin la pinza 25g

clothing store la tienda de ropa 25k

cloud la nube 6a, 13b

cloudy nublado 6a

clown (see *fool*)

clubs (*cards*) los bastos 27a

clutch el embrague 33e

coach (*sports*) el (la) entrenador (ra) 27b

coach (*train*) el vagón (*m*) 34

coach class la segunda clase 34

coal el carbón 13c

coal mine la mina de carbón 13c

coal mining la extracción del carbón 13c

coast la costa 13b

coat el abrigo 25k

cockroach la cucaracha 15d

COD contra reembolso 19e

codfish el bacalao   15c, 24d
coed school el colegio mixto
  37a
coffee el café   24k
coffee pot la cafetera   23d
coffee table la mesa de
  centro   23c
coin la moneda   26, 27a
coin collecting la numismática
  27a
colander el colador   23d
cold *(illness)* el resfriado
  40a
cold *(weather)* frío *(adj)*;
  el frío   *(n)*   6a, 24p
cold cuts los fiambres   24c
cold water el agua fría   35c
collar el cuello   25g
colleague el (la) colega   10b
collect call la llamada de
  cobro revertido   18b
collide chocar con   39c
collision el choque   39c
cologne la colonia   25f
Colombian colombiano(a)
  (adj, n)   30d
colon *(punctuation sign)* dos
  puntos   19c
color el color   7c, 25d
color printer la impresora
  a color   42b
colored coloreado   7c
coloring la coloración   7c
comb el peine   12d, 25f
comb one's hair peinarse *(v)*
  12d
come venir*   3e
comedian, comedienne el (la)
  comediante   28e
comedy la comedia   20a, 28e
comet el cometa   13a
comics las tiras cómicas
  20a, 25o
comma la coma   19c
command el comando   42c
commerce el comercio   37e,
  38d
commercial el anuncio   20b

communicate comunicar
  17a
communication la
  comunicación   17a
communism el comunismo
  43
communist el (la) comunista
  43
compact car el coche pequeño
  33a
compact disc el disco compacto
  20b, 25j, 42a
company la compañía   38d
compare comparar   17a
comparison la comparación
  8a, 17a
compartment el compartimiento
  34
compass *(drawing instrument)*
  el compás   2b, 37b
compass *(navigating instrument)*
  la brújula   3d
compatible compatible   42b
competition la competencia
  27b
complain quejarse   21a, 35b
complaint la queja   21a, 35b
complementary complementario
  2b
complex complejo   1d
complex number el número
  complejo   1d
complicated complicado
  22a
composer el (la) compositor
  (ra)   25j, 28c
composition la composición
  28c, 37f
compound el compuesto
  13c
compound interest el interés
  compuesto   26
compress files comprimir *(v)*
  archivos   42b
computer la computadora, el
  ordenador   19d, 37b, 38c, 42b
computer language el lenguaje
  de computadora   42b

concave cóncavo 2b

concept el concepto 22a

concert el concierto 28c

conclude concluir* 17a

conclusion la conclusión 17a

conditional condicional 8a

condom el condón 25h

condominium el condominio 23g

conductor *(train)* el (la) revisor(a) 34

conductor *(bus)* el (la) conductor(a) 34

cone el cono 2a

confirmation la confirmación 11d

conflict el conflicto 28d

conformist el (la) conformista 11e

congratulate felicitar 17a

Congratulations. Felicitaciones. 16c, 29c

conjugation la conjugación 8a

conjunction la conjunción 8a

connect conectar (v) 42c

connection la conexión, el enlace 32a, 34

conscience la conciencia 11e, 22a

conscientious concienzudo 11e, 22a

consecutive consecutivo 2b

consent *(agree)* consentir* 41

conservation la preservación 44a

conservative conservador 11e, 43

conservatory el conservatorio 37a

consonant la consonante 8a

constipation el estreñimiento 40a

consumption el consumo 44a

contact lenses los lentes de contacto 40a

continent el continente 13e, 30a

continental continental 6a, 13e

continually continuamente 4e

continue continuar* 4e

contraceptives los anticonceptivos 40a

contract el contrato *(n);* contratar *(v)* 38d

controversy la controversia 41

convalesce convalecer* 40a

convalescence la convalecencia 40a

conversation la conversación 17a

convex convexo 2b

convince convencer* 22b, 41

cook cocinar *(v)* 24o

cook el (la) cocinero(a) 38a

cool fresco 6a

coordinate la coordenada 2b

copier la copiadora 20b

copilot el copiloto 32c

copper el cobre 13c

copy la copia 37f

copy paper el papel de fotocopiadora 25c

cordless phone el teléfono remoto 20b

corduroy la pana 251

corkscrew el sacacorchos 23d

corn el maíz 14e, 24i

corner *(of a room)* el rincón 23b

corner *(street)* la esquina 33c, 36a

coroner el médico forense 41

correspondence la correspondencia 19e

corridor el pasillo 23a

cortisone   la cortisona   25h, 40a
cosecant   la cosecante   2b
cosine   el coseno   2b
cosmetics store   la perfumería   25f
cosmetologist   el cosmetólogo   38a
cosmos   el cosmos   13a
cost   costar*   24o, 25a
cost of living   el coste de vida   26
Costa Rican   el (la) costarricense *(n, adj)*   30d
cotangent   la cotangente   2b
cotton   el algodón   13c, 25l
cough   toser *(v)*; la tos *(n)*   40a
cough drops   las pastillas para la tos   40a
cough syrup   el jarabe para la tos   40a
council   el consejo   43
counselor   el consejero   38a
counter   el mostrador   25a
country   el país   11f, 13e, 30a
countryside   el campo, la campiña   13b, 36b
courage   el valor   11e
courageous   valiente   11e
courier   el mensajero   19e
course *(meal)*   el plato   24g
course *(school)*   el curso   37f
court   el tribunal   41
court of appeals   el tribunal de apelación   41
courteous   cortés   11e
courtesy   la cortesía   11e
courtroom   la sala de un tribunal   41
cousin   el primo   10a
cover   la portada   20a
cover charge   el precio del cubierto   24m
cow   la vaca   15a
cramps   los calambres   40a
crash   el choque   39c
crash into   chocar con   39c

crayon   el creyón   7c
crazy   loco   11e
cream   la crema   24h, 25f
create   crear   11e
creative   creativo   11e
creativity   la creatividad   11e
credit   el crédito   26
credit card   la tarjeta de crédito   25a, 26
crew *(plane)*   la tripulación   32c
cricket   el grillo   15d
crime   el crimen, el delito   39b
crime wave   la ola de crímenes   39b
criminal   el (la) criminal   39b
criminal law   el derecho penal   41
critical   crítico   11e
criticism   la crítica   20a, 28d
crocodile   el cocodrilo   15c
cross   cruzar   36c
crown   la corona   40b
cruise   el crucero   36b
crutches   las muletas   40a
cry   llorar   11e, 21a
crying   el llanto   11e, 21a
Cuban   cubano(a) *(adj, n)*   30d
cubed   la cubo   1e
cube root   la raíz cúbica   1e
cucumber   el pepino   14e, 24e
cue *(billiards)*   el taco   27a
cultivate   cultivar   14a
cultivation   el cultivo   14a
cultured   culto   11e
cup   la taza   23d, 24l
cure   curar, sanar *(v)*; la cura *(n)*   40a
curiosity   la curiosidad   11e
curler   el rulo, el rizador   12d, 25f
curling iron   las tenacillas   12d
curls   los bucles   12d
curly   rizado   11a

curly-haired de pelo rizado
11a

currency el dinero en
circulación 26

current la corriente 35c

current account la cuenta
corriente 26

cursor el cursor 42b

curtain *(theater)* el telón
28e, 35c

curtain *(window)* la cortina
23c, 35c

curve la curva 33c

cushion el cojín 23c

custodian el portero 37d

customer el (la) cliente 25a,
26

customs la aduana 31

customs officer el aduanero
31

cut cortar *(v)* 12d, 24o

cut la cortadura 40a

cutlet la chuleta 24g

cybercrime el cibercrimen
44b

cyclamen el ciclamen 14b

cylinder el cilindro 2a

cymbals los címbalos 28c

cypress tree el ciprés 14c

cyst el quiste 40a

D

dad el papá 10a

dahlia la dalia 14b

daily diario 4c

daily newspaper (el) diario
(n, adj) 20a

dairy la lechería 24n

dairy products los productos
lácteos 24h

daisy la margarita 14b

dam el dique, la presa 13b

dance bailar *(v)*; el baile *(n)*
28c, 29b

dance music la música de baile
25j

dancer el (la) bailarín(a)
28c

dandruff la caspa 40a

danger el peligro 33d, 39a

dangerous peligroso 33d

dangerous crossing el cruce
peligroso 33d

Danish danés *(adj, n)* 30d

dark oscuro 6a, 7b

dark blue azul oscuro 7a

dark-haired moreno, de pelo
oscuro 11a

darkroom la cámara oscura,
el cuarto oscuro 25d

darts los dardos 27a

dashboard el tablero de
instrumentos 33e

data los datos 42b

data base la base de texto
42b

data processing la informática
42b

date la fecha 19c

date *(fruit)* el dátil 14d, 24f

date book el diario 37b

date rape la violación durante
cita 44b

daughter la hija 10a

daughter-in-law la nuera
10a

dawn el amanecer 4a

day el día 4a, 4c

day after tomorrow pasado
mañana 4a

day before yesterday anteayer
4a

day-care center la guardería
37a

deaf person el (la) sordo(a)
12c

deafness la sordera 12c

death la muerte 11c

death penalty la pena de muerte
41, 44b

debate el debate *(n)*; debatir *(v)*
17a, 41

debt la deuda 26

decade la década 4c

decagon el decágono 2a

December diciembre 5b

decimal   decimal   1f
declarative   declarativo   8a
declare   declarar   17a, 31
decompress files   descomprimir (*v*) archivos   42b
decor   la decoración   23c
decorate   decorar   23f
decrease   disminuir* (*v*); la disminución (*n*)   3c
deer   el venado, el ciervo   15a
defecate   defecar   40a
defend oneself   defenderse*   41
defense attorney   el (la) abogado(a) defensor(a)   41
definite   definido   8a
definition   la definición   20a
deforestation   la deforestación   44a
degree   el grado   2b
degree (*university*)   el título   37f
delicate   delicado   11e
democracy   la democracia   43
democrat   el (la) demócrata   43
democratic   democrático   43
demonstrate   demostrar*   22b
demonstration   la manifestación pública   43
Denmark   Dinamarca   30b
dense   denso   3b
density   la densidad   3b
dental floss   el hilo dental   25h, 40b
dental hygienist   higienista (*m/f*) dental   38a
dentist   el (la) dentista   38a, 40b
dentist's office   la oficina del dentista   40b
dentures, false teeth   los dientes postizos   40b
deny   negar   17a
deodorant   el desodorante   25f

depart   salir*, partir   3e, 34
department   el departamento   25a
department store   el almacén   25a
departure   la salida   32a
deposit   el depósito (*n*); depositar (*v*)   26
deposit slip   la hoja de depósito   26
depressed   deprimido   21a
depression   la depresión   21a, 40a
dermatologist   el dermatólogo   40a
describe   describir   17a
description   la descripción   17a, 39b
descriptive   descriptivo   8a
desert   el desierto   13b
desk (*classroom*)   el pupitre   37b
desk (*office*)   el escritorio   37b, 38c
desperate   desesperado   21a
desperation   la desesperación   21a
dessert   el postre   24g
destroy   destruir*   39a
detest   detestar, odiar   21b
detour   el desvío   33d
develop   desarrollar (*v*)   17a
develop (*photos*)   revelar (*v*)   25d
diabetes   la diabetes   40a
diagnose   diagnosticar   40a
dial   la esfera   4d, 25i
dial   marcar   18b
dial direct   marcar directo   18b
dialogue   el diálogo   28d
diameter   el diámetro   2a
diamond   el diamante   25i
diamonds (*cards*)   los diamantes   27a
diarrhea   la diarrea   40a
dice   los dados   27a
dictate   dictar   17a

dictator el dictador 43
dictatorship la dictadura 43
dictionary el diccionario 20a, 25o, 37b
die morirse* 11c
diesel el diesel 33c
diet el régimen, la dieta; estar* a dieta 40a
dietician dietista (*m/f*) 38a
difference la diferencia 1f
difficult difícil 22a
dig cavar 14a
digest digerir* 40a
digestive system el sistema digestivo 40a
digit el dígito 1d
digital camera la cámara digital 25d
digital image stabilization la estabilización de imagen 20b
digital video camera la videocámara digital 20b
digress divagar 17a
diligence la diligencia 11e
diligent diligente 11e
dimension la dimensión 3b
dining room el comedor 23b
dinner la cena 24a
diploma el diploma 11f, 37f
diplomatic diplomático 11e
direct directo 8a
direct dialing marcación directa 18b
direction la dirección 3d
dirty sucio 11a, 12d, 25g
disagree no estar* de acuerdo 21a, 41
disagreement el desacuerdo 21a
disappoint decepcionar 21a
disappointed decepcionado 21a
disarmament el desarme 43
discothèque la discoteca 29b
discount el descuento 25a, 26

discourse el discurso 8a
discourteous descortés 11e
discuss discutir 17a, 41
discussion la discusión 17a
disgust el disgusto 21b
disgusted disgustado 21b
dishonest deshonesto 11e
dishonesty la deshonestidad 11e
dishwasher el lavaplatos 23d
dislike tener* aversión a 21b
disorganized desorganizado 11e
dissatisfaction el descontento 21a
dissatisfied descontento (*adj*) 21a
distance la distancia 3d, 33c
district attorney el (la) fiscal 41
divide dividir 1e
division la división 1e
divorce el divorcio 11c
divorced (*be*) estar* divorciado(a) 11c, 38b
doctor el médico 38a, 39c, 40a
doctor-assisted suicide el suicidio médicamente asistido 44b
documentary el documentario 20b
documents los documentos 31
dodecahedron el dodecaedro 2a
dog el perro 15a
dollar el dólar 26
dolphin el delfín 15c
domestic violence la violencia doméstica 44b
Dominican dominicano(a) 30d
donkey el burro 15a
door la puerta 23a, 33e
doorbell el timbre 23a
doorman el portero 35b

dose   la dosis   40a
double   doble   3c
double bass   el contrabajo   28c
double bed   la cama matrimonial   35b, 35c
double room   el cuarto doble   35b
doubt   dudar (v)   22b
doubt   la duda   22a
dove   la paloma   15b
down   abajo (adv)   36c
down below   abajo   3d
downhill   calle abajo   33c
download   descargar (v)   42c
downtown   el centro   30a, 36a
draft (*banking*)   la letra de cambio   26
drafter   dibujante (m/f)   38a
drag   arrastrar (v)   42c
drama   el drama   20a, 28e
draw (*lines*)   trazar   2b
draw (*sketch*)   dibujar   37f
drawer   el cajón   23c
drawing   el dibujo   28b, 37f
dress   el vestido   25k
dresser   la cómoda, el tocador   23c, 35c
dried fruit   las frutas secas   14d
drill   taladrar (v)   25b
drill   el taladro   25b, 40b
drink   beber (v)   12b, 24o; tomar (v)   24o
drink   la bebida   24k
drive   conducir*, manejar   3e, 33c
driver   el (la) conductor(a)   33b, 38a
driver's license   la licencia para conducir   33b
drop   la gota   6a
drug abuse   el abuso de drogas   44b
drug addict   el (la) drogadicto(a)   44b

drug addiction   la drogadicción   44b
drug pusher   el vendedor (traficante) de drogas   44b
drugs   las drogas   44b
drug store/pharmacy   la farmacia   25h
drums   los tambores   28c
dry   secar (v)   12d
dry   seco (adj)   6a
dry cleaner   la tintorería   25g
dryer   la secadora   23d
dry oneself   secarse (v)   12d
duck   el pato   15b
dull   apagado   7b
during   durante   4e
Dutch   holandés   30d
duty tax   los derechos de aduana   31
DVD player   la grabadora de DVD   20b
dynamic   dinámico   11e

E

each   cada   3c
eagle   el águila (f)   15b
ear   la oreja   12a
eardrops (*medication*)   las gotas para los oídos   40a
early   temprano   4e, 32b, 34
earn   ganar   38d
earphone   el auricular   18a
earphones with microphone   los auriculares (mpl) con micrófono   20b
earring   el arete, el pendiente   25i
Earth   la Tierra   13a
earthquake   el terremoto   13b
easel   el caballete   28b
east   el este   3d
Easter   la Pascua Florida   5f
eastern   oriental   3d
easy   fácil   22a
eat   comer   12b, 24o
eat breakfast   desayunar (v)   24a

eat dinner cenar (*v*) 24a
eat lunch almorzar (*v*) 24a
eccentric excéntrico 11e
eclipse el eclipse 13a
economics la economía 37e
economy la economía 43
economy class la clase turista 30a, 32a, 34
ecosystem el ecosistema 44a
ecstasy el éxtasis 44b
Ecuadorian ecuatoriano(a) (*adj*, *n*) 30b
edge el borde 3d
editor el (la) director(a), el (la) redactor(a) 20a, 38a
editorial el editorial 20a
education la enseñanza 11f, 37f, 38b
eel la anguila 15c, 24d
egg el huevo 24h
eggplant la berenjena 14e, 24e
egoism el egoísmo 11e
egoist el egoísta 11e
Egypt Egipto 30b
elastic elástico 13d
elbow el codo 12a
elect elegir* 43
elected political representative el representante elegido 43
election la elección 43
electric adaptor el adaptador eléctrico 35b
electric razor la afeitadora eléctrica 12d, 25f
electrical eléctrico 13c, 25b
electrical system el sistema eléctrico 33e
electrician el (la) electricista 38a
electricity la electricidad 13c, 23e
electrocardiograph el electrocardiógrafo 40a
electron el electrón 13c, 42a
elegance la elegancia 11a
elegant elegante 11a, 25l

elegantly elegantemente 11a
element el elemento 13c
elementary school la escuela primaria 37a, 38b
elementary school teacher el maestro, la maestra 37d
elephant el elefante 15a
elevator el ascensor 23g, 25a, 35b
eloquence la elocuencia 11e
eloquent elocuente 11e
e-mail el correo electrónico 42c
emerald la esmeralda 25i
emergency la emergencia 39a
emergency exit la salida de emergencia 39a
emergency lane el carril de emergencia 33d
emergency procedures los procedimientos de emergencia 32c
emergency room la sala de emergencia 39c
emphasis el énfasis 17a
emphasize enfatizar 17a
employee el empleado 26, 38d
employer el empleador 38d
employment agency la agencia de colocaciones 38d
empty vacío 3c
encourage animar, estimular 21a
encrypted cifrado 42c
encyclopedia la enciclopedia 20a, 25o, 37b
end el fin 4e
end, finish terminar 4e
end table la mesa auxiliar 23c
ending (*verb*) la terminación 8a
endorse endosar 26
endorsement el endoso 26
enemy el enemigo 10b

energetic enérgico 11e
energy la energía 11e, 13c, 44a
energy crisis la crisis energética 44a
energy needs las necesidades de energía 44a
energy source la fuente de energía 44a
energy waste el malgasto de energía 44a
engaged prometido, comprometido 11c
engagement el noviazgo 11c, 29a
engine el motor 33e
engineer el ingeniero 38a
engineering la ingeniería 37e
England Inglaterra 30b
English el inglés(esa) (*adj, n*) 30d
enjoyment (*fun*) la diversión 21a
enjoy oneself (*have fun*) divertirse* 21a
enlarge agrandar, ampliar 25d, 25m
enlargement la ampliación 25d
enough bastante 3c
enter entrar 3e, 36c
entire entero 3c
entrance la entrada 23a, 25a, 35b, 36c
envelope el sobre 19d, 19e, 25c
envious envidioso 11e
environment el medio ambiente, el entorno 13b, 44a
envy la envidia 11e
epidemic la epidemia 40a
equality la igualdad 1f
equation la ecuación 1f
equator el ecuador 13e
equilateral equilátero 2a
equinox el equinoccio 5c

eraser (*pencil*) la goma de borrar, el borrador 2b, 19d, 37b
error el error 37f
eruption la erupción 13b
escalator la escalera movediza 25a
escape escaparse (*v*) 39a
esophagus el esófago 40a
essay el ensayo 20a, 28d, 37f
etching el aguafuerte 28b
euphemism el eufemismo 28d
Europe Europa 30b
euthanasia la eutanasia 44b
even par 1d
evening la tarde 4a
evening school la escuela nocturna 37a
every cada 3c
everyone todo el mundo 3c, 8n
everything todo 3c, 8n
everywhere en todas partes 36c
exam el examen 37f
examination el examen físico 40a
examine examinar 40a, 40b
exchange cambiar, canjear (*v*) 25a, 26
exchange el cambio 26
exchange rate el tipo de cambio 26
exclamation point el signo de admiración 19c
excursion la gira 30a
excuse la excusa 17a
excuse oneself disculparse (*v*) 17a
exercise el ejercicio 37f
exhibiton la exhibición 28b
existence la existencia 22a
exit la salida 25a, 35b, 36c
exit salir* 3e, 36c
expensive caro 24p, 25a

expiration date   la fecha de vencimiento   26

explain   explicar   17a, 37f

explanation   la explicación   17a, 37f

expression   la expresión   17a

express oneself   expresarse (v)   17a

extension   la extensión   3b

extinguish   extinguir*   39a

extract   extraer*   1e

extraction   la extracción   1e

eye   el ojo   12a

eye doctor   el médico oculista   38a, 40a

eyebrow   la ceja   12a

eyedrops   las gotas para los ojos   40a

eyeglasses   las gafas, los anteojos   37b, 40a

eyelash   la pestaña   12a

eyelid   el párpado   12a

F

fable   la fábula   28d

fabric   la tela, el paño   25l

face   la cara   12a

face powder   los polvos para la cara   25f

factor   el factor   1f

factory   la fábrica   38d

factory worker   el obrero   38a

fail   no aprobar (v)   37f

fairy tale   el cuento de hadas   28d

faith   la fe   11d, 21a

faithful   fiel   11d, 11e

fake   falso   13d

fall   caer*   3e

fall (season)   el otoño   5c

fall asleep   dormirse*   12b

fall in love   enamorarse   11c

false   falso   25i

false teeth   (see *dentures*)

family   la familia   10a

fan   el ventilador   33e

fan belt   la correa de ventilador   33e

FAQ (frequently asked questions)   FAQ (*f*)   42c

far   lejos   3d, 36c

farm   la granja, la hacienda   15a

farmer   el campesino, el labrador   15a, 38a

farmland   tierras de labrantío   13b

farsighted   hipermétrope (*adj*)   40a

fascinate   fascinar   11e

fascinating   fascinante   11e

fascination   la fascinación   11e

fashion   la moda   25k

fashion designer   el diseñador de modas   38a

fast   rápido   3e

fasten   asegurar   32c

fat   gordo   11a

father   el padre   10a

father-in-law   el suegro   10a

faucet   el grifo   23a, 35c

fax machine   el fax   18a, 18b, 42a

fear   el miedo   11e

feather   la pluma   15b

February   febrero   5b

feel   sentirse*   12c (see *sense*), 21a, 40a

feel badly   sentirse* mal   12b, 40a

feel like   tener* ganas de   21a

feel well   sentirse* bien   12b, 40a

feeling   el sentimiento   21a

felt   el fieltro   25l

felt pen   el rotulador   7c, 19d

female   la hembra   11a

feminine   femenino   8a, 11a

feminism   el feminismo   44b

fence   la cerca   15a

fencing (*sport*)   la esgrima   27b

fencing bout   el encuentro de esgrima   27b

fender   el parachoques   33e

fennel   el hinojo   14e

fetus   el feto   44b

fever   la fiebre   40a

fiancé   el novio   10b, 11c

fiancée   la novia   10b, 11c

fiber   la fibra   13c

fiber optic cable   el cable de fibra óptica   42c

fiction   la ficción   20a, 28d

field   el campo   13b, 27b

field (of study)   el campo (de estudio)   37f

field hockey   el hockey sobre hierba   27b

fig   el higo   14d, 24f

fig tree   la higuera   14c

fight   luchar, pelear (*v*); la pelea (*n*)   39b

figure   la figura   2a

figure of speech   la figura retórica   17a

file (*office*)   el archivo   38c, 42b

file (*tool*)   la lima   25b

file card   la ficha   38c

filet   el filete   24g

filing cabinet   el archivo, el fichero   38c

fill   llenar   3c

filling (*dental*)   el empaste   40b

film   la película   25d

film projector   el proyector   37b

filter   el filtro   33e

fine   multar, dar* una multa   41

fine, ticket   la multa   33c

fine arts   las bellas artes   37e

finger   el dedo   12a

fingernail   la uña   12a

fingerprints   las huellas digitales   39b

finish, end   terminar   4e

Finland   Finlandia   30b

fire (*dismiss from job*)   echar   38d

fire   el fuego   13c, 39a

fire alarm   la alarma de incendios   39a

fire escape   la escalera de incendios   39a

fire extinguisher   el extinguidor de incendios   39a

fire hydrant   la boca de incendio   39a

firearm   el arma de fuego (*f*)   39b

firefighter   el bombero   39a

firefly   la luciérnaga   15d

fireman   el bombero   38a

fireplace   la chimenea   23a

fireproof   incombustible   39a

firewall   el firewall, muro de protección   42c

first aid   los primeros auxilios   39a, 39c

first class   la primera clase   30a, 32a, 34

first name   nombre (de pila)   11f, 38b

fir tree   el abeto   14c

fish   el pescado, el pez   15c, 24d

fish   pescar (*v*)   15c, 36b

fish store   la pescadería   24n

fishbone   la espina   15c

fisherman   el pescador   15c

fishhook   el anzuelo   15c

fishing   la pesca   15c

fishing rod   la caña de pescar   15c

fix   reparar   25i, 33c

fixed price   el precio fijo   24m, 25a

flame   la llama   39a

flannel   la franela   251

flash (*photo/camera*)   el flash   25d

flashlight   la linterna   25b

flat panel monitor   la pantalla plana   42b

flatter   adular (*v*)   21a

flattery   la adulación   21a
flavor   el sabor   12c
flea   la pulga   15d
flight   el vuelo   32a
flight attendant   el (la) aeromozo(a), la azafata   32c
floor   el suelo   23a
floor (*level*)   el piso   23a, 35b
floppy disk   el disco flexible   42b
flour   la harina   24i
flour sifter   el cernidor de harina   23d
flow   fluir*   13b
flow chart   el organigrama   42b
flower   florecer (*v*)   14a
flower   la flor   14b
flowerbed   el arriate, el macizo   14b
flu   la gripe   40a
fluorescent   fluorescente   25b
flute   la flauta   25c
fly   la mosca   15d
fly   volar*   15b, 32c
focus   enfocar (*v*)   25d
fog   la neblina   6a
foggy   brumoso   6a
foliage   el follaje   14a
folklore   el folklore   28d
folk music   la música folklórica   28c
follow   seguir*   3e, 36c
food   la comida   24a
food chain   la cadena alimenticia   44a
food coloring   colorante alimentario   7c
fool, clown   el (la) tonto(a), el (la) bufón(ona)   11e
foolish   tonto   11e
foot   el pie   12a
football   el fútbol americano   27b
footnote   la nota   20a
for   para, por   8g

for example   por ejemplo   44c
for sale   de venta   25a
forehead   la frente   12a
foreign currency   la moneda extranjera   31
foreign exchange   las divisas   26
foreigner   el (la) extranjero(a)   31
forest   la selva, el bosque   13b
forget   olvidar(se)   22b
fork   el tenedor   23d, 24l
form   el formulario   31
fossil   el fósil   13c
fossil fuel   el combustible de fósil   13c, 44a
fox   el zorro   15a
fraction   la fracción   1f
fracture   la fractura   39c
France   Francia   30b
free   gratis   25a
free (*phone*)   libre   18b
freeze   helarse*, congelarse   6a
freezer   el congelador   23d
French   francés(esa) (*adj, n*)   30d
French fries   las papas fritas   24g
frequent   frecuente   4e
frequently   con frecuencia   4e
fresco painting   el fresco   28b
Friday   el viernes   5a
fried   frito (*adj*)   24p
friend   el (la) amigo(a)   10b
friendly   amistoso   11e
friendship   la amistad   10b
frog   la rana   15c
from   de   3d, 8g
front page   la primera plana   20a
frosted (*hair*)   escarchado (*adj*)   12d
frozen   helado   6a

fruit   la fruta   14d, 24f
fruit store   la frutería   24n
fruit tree   el frutero   14c
fry   freír (v)   24b
frying pan   la sartén   23d
fuel   el combustible   13c
full   lleno   3c
fun   la alegría, la diversión   21a
function   la función   42b
funnel   el embudo   23d
funny   cómico   11e
fur coat   el abrigo de piel   25k
furnace   el calorífero   23e
furniture   los muebles   23c
fuse   el fusible   25b
fusion reactor   el reactor de fusión   42a

G

galaxy   la galaxia   13a
gambling   apostar, jugar (v)   44a
game   el juego, el partido   27a, 27b
garage   el garaje   23a, 35b
garden   el jardín   14e, 23a
garlic   el ajo   14e, 24j
gas   el gas   13c, 23e
gas pedal   el acelerador   33e
gas station   la gasolinera   33c
gas tank   el tanque   33e
gasoline   la gasolina   13c, 33c
gate   la puerta   32a
gather   recoger*   14a
gauze   la gasa   39a
gearshift   el cambio de velocidad   33e
Gemini   Géminis   5d
gender   el género   8a
general delivery   la lista de correo   42c
generator   el generador   33e
generosity   la generosidad   11e
generous   generoso   11e

genre   el género   28d
gentle (*mild*)   suave   11e
gentle (*tame*)   manso   11e
gentleman   el caballero   11a
geography   la geografía   13e, 37e
geometry   la geometría   2b, 37e
geotermal energy   la energía geotérmica   44a
geranium   el geranio   14b
German   alemán(-ana) (*adj, n*)   30d
Germany   Alemania   30b
gerund   el gerundio   8a
get dressed   vestirse*   25m
get up   levantarse (v)   3e, 12b
gift   el regalo   11c, 25a
giraffe   la jirafa   15a
girl   la chica, la muchacha   11a, 11b
girlfriend   la novia, la amiga   10b
gladiolus   el gladiolo   14b
glass (*drinking*)   el vaso   23d, 241
global warming   el calentamiento global   44a
globe   el globo   13e
glossy finish   el acabado brillante   25d
glove   el guante   25k, 27b
glove compartment   la guantera   33e
glue   el pegamento   19d, 25c
go   ir*   3e, 36c
go away   irse (v)   3e
go back   regresar (v)   42c
go down   bajar   3e, 36c
go forward   adelantar (v)   33c, 42c
go out   salir*   3e, 29b
go to bed   acostarse*   12b
go up   subir   3e, 36c
goal (*soccer*)   el gol   27b
goalie (*soccer*)   el (la) portero(a)   27b

goat la cabra, el cabrito 15a, 24c

God Dios 11d

gold el oro 13c, 25i

gold dorado (*adj*) 7a

golden anniversary aniversario de oro 11c

goldfish la carpa dorada 15c

golf el golf 27b

good bueno 11e, 24p

goose el ganso, el ánsar 15b

gossip chismear, el chisme 17a

govern gobernar* 43

government el gobierno 43

GPS (global position satellite) el sistema de posicionamiento global 20b

graceful gracioso 11e

grade (*school class*) la clase 37a

grade (*school mark*) la nota 37f

graduate graduarse 11f

grain el grano 14a, 24i

gram el gramo 3a

grammar la gramática 8a, 37f

grandchild el nieto 10a

grandfather el abuelo 10a

grandfather clock el reloj de caja 4d

grandmother la abuela 10a

grand piano el piano de cola 28c

grapefruit la toronja, el pomelo 14d, 24f

grapes las uvas 14d, 24f

graphic design el diseño gráfico 42b

grass la hierba, el césped 13b, 14e

grasshopper el saltamontes, el chapulín 15d

grater el rallador 23d

gravity la gravedad 13a

gray gris 7a

great-aunt la tía abuela 10a

great-grandchild el bisnieto 10a

great-grandfather el bisabuelo 10a

great-grandmother la bisabuela 10a

great-uncle el tío abuelo 10a

Greece Grecia 30b

greed, avarice la avaricia 11e

greedy avaro, avaricioso 11e

Greek griego(a) (*adj, n*) 30d

green verde 7a

green pepper el pimiento verde 14e

greenhouse el invernadero 14a

greenhouse effect el efecto invernadero 44a

Greenland Groenlandia 30b

greeting et saludo 16a

grocery store la tienda de comestibles 24n

groom el novio 11c

ground floor la planta baja 23a, 23g

grow crecer* 3c, 11b

grow up hacerse* mayor 11b

growth el crecimiento 3c

Guatemalan guatemalteco(a) (*adj, n*) 30d

guesthouse la casa de huéspedes 35a

guide el (la) guía 36a

guidebook la guía del viajero 25o, 36a

guilt la culpa 41

guilty culpable 41

guitar la guitarra 28c

guitarist el (la) guitarrista 28c

gulf el golfo 13b

gums las encías 40b

gun la pistola 39b

gun control el control de armas de fuego 44b

gymnasium el gimnasio
27a, 37c
gynecologist el (la)
ginecólogo(a) 40a

H

habit el hábito 11e
hacker el pirata informático
42b
hail el granizo 6a
hair el pelo 12a, 12b
hair dryer el secador 12d
hair spray la laca 12d, 25f
haircut el corte de pelo
12d
hairdresser el peluquero, la
peluquera 12d, 38a
hake la merluza 15c, 24d
half la mitad (*n*); medio (*adj*)
3c
hall el vestíbulo 23b
hallway el pasillo, el corredor
23a, 37c
ham el jamón 24c
hammer el martillo (*n*);
martillar (*v*) 25b
hand la mano 12a, 25i
hand (*of watch*) la manecilla
4d, 25i
handcuffs las esposas 39b
handheld organizer el
organizador de mano 25c
handicapped minusválido,
incapacitado 11a
handkerchief el pañuelo
25k
handle (*car door*) la manija
33e
handle (*knife*) el mango
23d
handlebar el manillar 33a
handshake el apretón de manos
16a
handsome guapo 11a
hang up colgar* 18b
hanging folder la carpeta
colgante 25c
happen pasar, ocurrir 4e

happiness la felicidad 11e,
21a
happy alegre, contento 11e,
21a
Happy Birthday! ¡Feliz
cumpleaños! 11c, 29c
hard duro 13d
hardware (*computer*) el
elemento físico, el hardware
42b
hardware store la ferretería
25b
hard-working trabajador
11e
hare la liebre 15a
harmony la armonía 28c
harp el arpa 28c
harpsichord el clavicordio
28c
hat el sombrero 25k
hate el odio (*n*); odiar (*v*)
11e, 21b
hateful odioso 11e
hatred el odio 21b
have to tener* que 21a
hazard flash las luces de
emergencia 33e
he él 8h
head la cabeza 12a
head of state el (la) jefe de
estado 43
headache el dolor de cabeza
40a
heading el membrete 19c
headlight el faro delantero
33e
headline el titular 20a
headphones los auriculares
20b, 32c
heal (*a cut*) cicatrizar 40a
health la salud 11a, 40a
healthy saludable, sano 11a,
40a
hear oír* 12c
hearing el oído 12c
heart el corazón 12a, 40a
heart attack el ataque cardíaco
el infarto 40a

hearts (*cards*) los corazones 27a
heat el calor 13c
heater la calefacción 33e
heating la calefacción (*n*) 23e
heavy (*liquid*) espeso 3b
heavy (*weight*) pesado 3b, 11a, 13d, 31
hectare la hectárea 3a
hectogram el hectogramo 3a
hedge el seto vivo 14a
height la estatura 11a
helicopter el helicóptero 32c
helmet el casco 27b
help ayudar (*v*) 39a
Help! ¡Socorro! 39a, 39c
hemisphere el hemisferio 13e
hen la gallina 15b
hepatitis la hepatitis (*f*) 40a
heptagon el heptágono 2a
her su, sus 8f
herb la hierba, la yerba 24j
here aquí, acá 3d, 36c
heredity la herencia 11c
hero el héroe 28e
heroine la heroina 28e
herring el arenque 24d
herself se 8k
hesitate vacilar 17a
hesitation la vacilación 17a
hexagon el hexágono 2a
hiccup hipar (*v*) 40a
hiccup el hipo 40a
high (*temperature*) alto 6c
high school el colegio, la escuela secundaria 37a, 38b
high school teacher el profesor, la profesora 37d
highway la carretera 33c
hill la colina 13b
him lo, le 8i
himself se 8k

Hindu el (la) hindú (*adj, n*) 11d
hip la cadera 12a
hippopotamus el hipopótamo 15a
hire contratar (*v*) 38d
his su, sus 8e
history la historia 37e
hit (*ball*) pegarle a (*v*) 27b
hobby el pasatiempo 27a
hockey el hockey 27b
hole el agujero 25g
holepuncher la perforadora 25c
holiday (*official*) el día de fiesta 5a, 29a
Holland Holanda 30b
home base la base meta 27b
homeless person la persona sin hogar 20b
home page la página principal 42c
home run el jonrón 27b
home schooling la enseñanza en casa 44b
homework la tarea 37f
homosexual homosexual 44b
homosexuality la homosexualidad 44b
Honduran hondureño(a) (*adj, n*) 30d
honest honesto, recto 11e
honesty la honradez 11e
honey la miel 24j
honeymoon la luna de miel 11c
hood el capó 33e
hook el anzuelo 15c
hope la esperanza (*n*); esperar (*v*) 21a
horizontal horizontal 3d
horn la corneta 28c
horn (*car*) la bocina 33e
horoscope el horóscopo 5d
horse el caballo 15a
horse racing las carreras de caballo 27b

horsepower el caballo de fuerza 33e
horseradish el rábano picante 24j
horticulture la horticultura 14a
hospital el hospital 39c
hot caliente 24p
hot water el agua caliente 35c
hotel el hotel 35a
hour la hora 4c
hourly por hora, cada hora 4c
house la casa 23a
house of representatives la cámara de representantes 43
How? ¿Cómo? 9
How much? ¿Cuánto? 3c, 9
howl aullar* 15a
hug el abrazo 19b
human humano 11d, 15a
human being el ser humano 11d
humanitarian humanitario 11e
humanity la humanidad 11d
humble humilde 11e
humid húmedo 6a
humidity la humedad 6a
humility la humildad 11e
humor el humor 11e
hunger el hambre (*f*) 12b
hunt cazar 15a
hunter el cazador 15a
hunting la caza (*n*) 15a
hurricane el huracán 6a, 13b
hurry darse* prisa 39b
hurt doler* 40a, 40b
husband el marido 10a, 11c
hydrogen el hidrógeno 13c
hyena la hiena 15a
hygiene la higiene 12d
hygienic higiénico 12d
hyperbole la hipérbole 28d
hypertension la hipertensión 40a

hyphen el guión 19c
hypothesis la hipótesis 22a

I

I yo 8h
ice el hielo 6a, 13b
ice cream el helado 24h
ice cream parlor la heladería 24n
ice cubes los cubitos de hielo 35b
ice hockey el hockey sobre hielo 27b
icon el ícono 42b
icosahedron el icosaedro 2a
idea la idea 22a
idealism el idealismo 11e
idealist el (la) idealista 11e
identification la identificación 11f
identification card la tarjeta de identificación 31, 35b
identify identificar 17a
ideology la ideología 43
idiom el modismo 28d
if si 8o
ignition el encendido 33e
ignorance la ignorancia 11e
ignorant ignorante 11e, 22a
illegal ilegal 41
illness la enfermedad 40a
illustration la ilustración 20a
imaginary imaginario 1d
imagination la imaginación 11e, 22a
imaginative imaginativo 11e
imagine imaginar 22b
impatient impaciente 11e
imperative imperativo 8a
imperfect imperfecto 8a
import importar 31
impossible imposible 21c
imprison aprisionar, encerrar* 41
imprudent imprudente 11e
impudence la insolencia 11e
impudent insolente 11e

impulse el impulso 11e
impulsive impulsivo 11e
in en 3d, 8g
in front of delante de, en frente
  de 3d, 36c
incinerator el incinerador
  44a
incisor el diente incisivo
  40b
income los ingresos 26
increase aumentar 3c
indecision la indecisión 11e
indecisive indecisivo 11e
indefinite indefinido 8a
independent independiente
  11e
index el índice 20a
index finger el dedo índice
  12a
Indian indio(a) *(adj, n)*
  13b
indicate señalar 17a
indication la indicación 17a
indicative indicativo 8a
indifference la indiferencia
  11e, 21a
indifferent indiferente 11e,
  21a
indigestion la indigestión
  40a
indirect indirecto 8a
industrial industrial 13c
industry la industria 13c
inequality la desigualdad
  44b
inexpensive barato 25a
infection la infección 40a
infinitive el infinitivo 8a
inflation la inflación 43
inform avisar 17a
information la información
  18b
information technology la
  informática 42b
infrared light la luz infrarroja
  13a
ingenious ingenioso 11e
inherit heredar 11c

injection la inyección 25h,
  40a
injure herir* 39b
injury la herida 39b
ink-jet printer la impresora de
  inyección 42b
ink la tinta 19d, 37b
inn la posada, hostería 35a
innocence la inocencia 11e,
  41
innocent inocente 11e, 41
input device el dispositivo de
  entrada 42b
insect el insecto 15d
inside *(of)* dentro (de) 3d,
  36c
insolent insolente 11e
install instalar *(v)* 42b
installer el instalador 42b
instant instante *(adj, n)*
  4c
instrument el instrumento
  27a, 28c
insulation wire el alambre
  aislante 25b
insulin la insulina 25h
insurance el seguro 26, 30a
insurance card la tarjeta de
  seguro 33b
insurance policy la póliza de
  seguros 26
insurance premium la prima de
  seguros 26
insured asegurado 19e
integer entero 1d
intelligence la inteligencia
  11e
intelligent inteligente 11e
intensive care el cuidado
  intensivo 39c
intercom el interfono, el
  intercomunicador 18a, 38c
interest el interés 26
interest rate la tasa de interés
  26
interesting interesante 22a
interface el conector *(m)* entre
  unidades, la interfaz *(f)* 42b

intermission   el entreacto
    28e
internal drive   el disco interno
    42b
internet   el internet   42c
internist   el internista   40a
interrogative . interrogativo
    8a
interrupt   interrumpir   17a
interruption   la interrupción
    17a
intersection   la bocacalle, el
    cruce   33c, 33d, 36a
interview   la entrevista   20a,
    20b, 21o
intransitive   intransitivo   8a
introduce (someone)   presentar
    16b
invertebrate   invertebrado
    (adj, n)   15a
invest   invertir*   26
investment   la inversión   26
invite   invitar   17a
invitation   la invitación   17a,
    29b
iodine   el yodo   13c, 39c
irascible   colérico   11e
Ireland   Irlanda   30b
Irish   irlandés(-desa)   (adj, n)
    30d
iron (metal)   el hierro   13c
iron (appliance)   planchar   (v);
    la plancha   (n)   23d, 25g
ironic   irónico   11e
ironing board   la tabla de
    planchar   25g
irony   la ironía   11e, 28d
irrational number   el número
    irracional   1d
irregular   irregular   8a
irritable   irritable   11e
Islamic   islámico   11d
island   la isla   13d
isosceles   isósceles   2a
ISP   el proveedor de servicio
    internet   42c
Israel   Israel   30b
Israeli   israelí   30d

it   lo, la   8i
Italian   italiano(a)   (adj, n)
    30d
italics   la bastardilla   19c
Italy   Italia   30b
itch   la comezón   40a
its   su, sus   8e

J

jack (car)   el gato   33e
jacket   la chaqueta   25k
jail   la cárcel   41
jail   encarcelar   (v)   41
jam   la mermelada   24j
January   enero   5b
Japan   el Japón   30b
Japanese   japonés   (adj, n)
    30d
jaw   la mandíbula   12a, 40b
jazz   el jazz   25j, 28c
jealous   celoso   11e
jealousy   los celos   11e
jest   bromear   17a
jewel   la joya   25i
jewelry store   la joyería   25i
Jewish   judío(a)   (adj, n)
    11d
job   el trabajo, el puesto   11f,
    38a
jog   correr a trote corto   27a
joke   el chiste   17a
journalist   el (la) periodista
    20a, 38a
journey   el viaje   30a
joy   la alegría   21a
joystick   el mando de juegos
    42b
Judaism   el judaísmo   11d
judge   el juez   (n); juzgar   (v)
    41
judgment   el juicio   22a, 41
juice   el jugo, el zumo   24k
July   julio   5b
June   junio   5b
jungle   la selva, la jungla   13b
junior high school   el instituto
    de bachillerato elemental   37a,
    38b

Jupiter Júpiter 13a
jury el jurado 41
just justo 4e
justice la justicia 22a, 41

K

keep quiet callarse (v) 17a
Keep to the right. Conserve su derecha. 33d
ketchup la salsa de tomate 24j
kettle el hervidor, la cafetera 23d
key la llave 23d, 35b
keyboard el teclado 19d, 42b
keyboard instruments los instrumentos de teclado 28c
keyword la palabra clave 42c
kick *(ball)* patear 27b
kidnap secuestrar (v) 41, 44b
kidney el riñón 40a
kill matar 39b
killer el asesino 39b
kilogram el kilogramo 3a
kilometer el kilómetro 3a
kindergarten el jardín infantil 37a
king el rey 27a, 43
kiss besar 11c, 21b
kiss el beso 11c
kitchen la cocina 23b
knee la rodilla 12a
knife el cuchillo 23d, 241, 39b
knight *(chess)* el caballo 27a
know saber*, conocer* 16b, 22b
knowledge el conocimiento 22a
knowledgeable informado 22a
uckle el nudillo 12a

L

lab technician el (la) ayudante de laboratorio 37d
label el rótulo, la etiqueta 25a, 25c
laboratory el laboratorio 13c, 37c
labor union el sindicato 43
lace el encaje 251
lack faltar 25a
ladder la escalera 39a
ladle el cucharón 23d
lady la señora 11a
laity el laicado 11d
lake el lago 13b, 36b
lamb el cordero 15a, 24c
lamp la lámpara 23c, 35c
land la tierra, el terreno 13b
land aterrizar (v) 32c
landfill el terraplén de desperdicios 44a
landing el aterrizaje 32c
landing gear el tren de aterrizaje 32c
landlord el propietario, el patrón 23g
landscape el paisaje 13b
lane *(traffic)* el carril 33c
language lab el laboratorio de lenguas 37c
languages (foreign) las lenguas (extranjeras) 37e
laptop, notebook la computadora portátil 42b
large grande 3c, 11a
laryngitis la laringitis 40a
laser el láser 42a
laser beam el rayo láser 42a
laser printer la impresora láser 42b
last durar 4e
late tarde 4e, 32b, 34
Latin America Latinoamérica 30b
latitude la latitud 13e
laugh reírse* 11e, 21a
laughter la risa 11e, 21a
launch lanzar 42a

launch pad la plataforma de lanzamiento   42a
laundry la lavandería   25g
lava la lava   13b
law el derecho, las leyes   37e, 41
lawful legal   41
lawsuit el pleito, la demanda   41
lawyer el abogado   38a, 41
laxative el laxante   25h
lay person el laico   11d
layer el estrato   13b
laziness la pereza   11e
lazy perezoso   11e
lead el plomo   13c
leaded gas la gasolina con plomo   33c
leader el líder   44b
leaf la hoja   14a
leaf through *(pages)* hojear   20a
leap year el año bisiesto   5b
learn aprender   22b, 37f
leather de cuero, de piel *(adj)*   13c
leather el cuero   25l
leave salir*, partir   3e, 34
lecture la conferencia *(n)*; dar* *(v)* una conferencia   17a, 37f
left izquierdo   3d
leg la pierna   12a
legal legal   41
legend la layenda   28d
legislation la legislación   43
lemon el limón   14d, 24f
lemon tree el limonero   14c
length la longitud   3a
lengthen alargar   25m
lens (camera) el lente   25d
lentil la lenteja   14e
Leo Leo   5d
leopard el leopardo   15a
lesbian la lesbiana   44b
lesbianism el lesbianismo   44b
less menos   3c
letter la carta   19d

letter *(of the alphabet)* la letra   8a, 19c
letter carrier el cartero   19e
letterhead el papel con membrete   19d
lettuce la lechuga   14e, 24e
leukemia la leucemia   40a
level llano   3d
liberal liberal   11e, 43
Libra Libra   5d
librarian el (la) bibliotecario(a)   37d
library la biblioteca   37c
license plate la placa   33e
lid la tapa   23d
lie mentir* *(v)*; la mentira *(n)*   17a
lie down acostarse*, tumbarse   3e
life la vida   11c
life jacket el chaleco salvavidas   32c
life sentence la cadena perpetua   41
lift levantar   3e
liftoff el despegue   32c
light la luz   6a, 13a
light *(color)* claro *(adj)*   7b
light *(weight)* ligero *(adj)*   3b, 13d
light blue azul claro   7a
light bulb la bombilla   25b
lighter el mechero, el encendedor   25e
lightning relampaguear *(v)*   6a, 6b
lightning el relámpago   6a
lights las luces   35c
like gustarle a uno *(v)*   21b
lily la azucena   14b
lima bean el frijol de media luna   14e
lime la lima   24f
line la línea   2b
line *(queue)* la cola   26
line up hacer* cola   26
lining el forro   25g
link el enlace   42c

lion el león 15a

lip el labio 12a, 40b

lipstick el lápiz de labios 25f

liqueur el licor 24k

liquid el líquido 13c

Lisbon Lisboa 30c

listen to escuchar 12c, 17a, 37f

liter el litro 3a

literacy la alfabetización (*f*) 44b

literal literal 17a

literature la literatura 28d, 37e

lithium battery la batería de litio, pila de litio 20b

litigate litigar 41

litigation el litigio, el pleito 41

little pequeño 3c, 11a

little finger el dedo meñique 12a

live vivir 11c, 23f

lively vivo 7b, 11e

liver el hígado 24c

living room la sala 23b

loan el préstamo 26

lobby el vestíbulo 28a, 35b

lobster la langosta 24d

locate localizar 13e

location la localización 13e

logarithm logaritmo 1f

London Londres 30c

long largo 3b, 37f

long-distance call la llamada de larga distancia 18b

longitude la longitud 13e

long-term a largo plazo 4e

look after cuidar 14a, 40a

look at mirar 12c, 20b

look for buscar 25a

look forward to esperar con placer anticipado 4e

loose suelto 25l

lose perder* 27b

lose consciousness perder* el conocimiento 40a

lose weight perder peso 11a

loss la pérdida 26, 27b

lost and found la oficina de objetos perdidos 32a

lotion la loción 25f

louse el piojo 15d

lovable amable 11e

love querer*, amar (*v*); el amor (*n*) 11c, 11e, 21b

love affair el amorío 10b

lover el (la) amante 10b

loving cariñoso 11e

low bajo 6c

luggage el equipaje 31, 35b

luggage inspection la inspección del equipaje 32a

luggage rack el portaequipajes 35b

lump el bulto 40a

lunar lunar 13a

lunar eclipse el eclipse lunar 13a

lunar module el módulo lunar 42a

lunch el almuerzo 24a

lung el pulmón 12a, 40a

Lutheran luterano(a) (*adj, n*) 11d

Luxembourg Luxemburgo 30b

luxury hotel el hotel de primera categoría 35a

lymphatic system el sistema linfático 40a

M

machinist maquinista (*m/f*) 38a

mad enojado, enfadado 11e

madness la locura 11e

magazine la revista 20a, 25o, 37b

magistrate el magistrado 41

maid la criada 35b

mail el correo 19e

mail delivery la distribución de correo 19e
mailbox el buzón 19e, 23a
mailman el cartero 19e
main principal 8a
main character el (la) protagonista 28d
main office la oficina central 37c
make a call hacer* una llamada 18b
make a mistake equivocarse (v) 37f
make a stop hacer* una escala 32c
make the bed hacer* la cama 23f
makeup el maquillaje 12d, 25f
male el macho 11a, 38b
malicious malévolo 11e
malign hablar mal de (v) 17a
malleable maleable 13d
mammal el mamífero 15a
man el hombre 11a
manager el (la) gerente 26, 35b, 38d
mandolin la mandolina 28c
manicure la manicura 12d
manual el manual 42b
many muchos 8n
map el mapa 13e, 37b
maple tree el arce 14c
March marzo 5b
margarine la margarina 24h
margin el margen 19c, 19d
marijuana la marihuana 44b
marker el marcador 19d, 25c
market el mercado 24n, 38d
marital status el estado civil 11c, 38b
marriage el matrimonio 11c
marriage ceremony la boda 11c

marry (someone) casar 11c
Mars Marte 13a
marsh el pantano 13b
martial arts las artes marciales 27b
mascara el rimel 12d, 25f
masculine masculino 8a, 11a
masking tape la cinta adhesiva 25b
mass la masa 3d
Mass la misa 11d
massage el masaje 12d
masterpiece la obra maestra 28b
matches las (los) cerillas(-os), los fósforos 25e
mathematics las matemáticas 37e
matrimony el matrimonio 11c
matte finish el acabado mate 25d
matter la materia 13c
matter importar 21a
maximum máximo 3b, 6c, 31
May el mayo 5b
mayonnaise la mayonesa 24j
me me 8i, 8j
meadow el prado 13b
meal la comida 24a
mean querer* decir, significar (v) 17a
meaning el significado 17a
meanness la maldad 11e
measles el sarampión 40a
measure medir* 3b
measuring cups juego de tazas de medir 23d
measuring spoons juego de cucharitas de medir 23d
measuring tape cinta métrica 3b
mechanic el mecánico 33c, 38a
mechanical mecánico 25b, 33c

medical records los antecedentes médicos 40a

medicine la medicina 25h, 37e, 40a

mediocre mediocre 21b

Mediterranean Mediterráneo 6a

medium mediano 11a

meet conocer* 16b

megabyte el megabyte 42b

megahertz (MHz) el megahercio (MHz) 42b

megapixel el megapíxel 25d

melon el melón 14d, 24f

melting point punto de fusión 6c

membrane la membrana 14a

memory card la tarjeta de memoria 25d

memory card reader el lector de tarjeta de memoria 25d

memory la memoria 22a, 42b

mend remendar* 25g

mention mencionar 17a

menu el menú, la lista de platos 24g

meow maullar* 15a

mercury mercurio 6c, 13c

Mercury Mercurio 13a

merge el empalme 33d

meridian meridiano 13e

Merry Christmas. Feliz Navidad. 16c, 29c

message el mensaje 18b, 35b, 42c

metal el metal 13c

metamorphosis la metamorfosis 15d

metaphor la metáfora 17a, 28d

meteor el meteoro 13a

meter el metro 3a

methane el metano 13c

Methodist el (la) metodista (adj, n) 11d

Mexico México 30b

Mexico City la Ciudad de México 30c

microcomputer la microcomputadora 42b

microphone el micrófono 20b

microscope el microscopio 13c

microwave la microonda 42a

microwave oven el horno de microondas 23d

middle finger el dedo medio 12a

midnight la medianoche 4a

mild *(weather)* templado 6a, 6b

mild *(flavor)* suave 24p

mileage el kilometraje 33e

milk la leche 24h

millimeter el milímetro 3a

millionth millonésimo 1b

mind la mente 22a

miner el minero 38a

mineral el mineral 13c

mineral water el agua mineral *(f)* 24k

minimum mínimo 3b, 6c

minister el ministro 11d, 43

mint la menta 14e, 24j

minus menos 1e, 6c

minute el minuto 4c

mirror el espejo 23c, 35c

mischievous travieso 11e

miss *(the train)* perder* 34

Miss Señorita (Srta.) 11f, 16b

missile el proyectil 42a

missile defense la defensa contra misiles 44b

mistake el error 37f

mixer la batidora 23d

mobile phone el teléfono móvil 20b

model el modelo 13c

modem el módem   42b
molar la muela   40b
mole el topo   15a
molecular molecular   13c
molecule la molécula   13c, 42a
mom la mamá   10a
moment el momento   4c
monarchy la monarquía   43
Monday el lunes   5a
money el dinero   26
money order el giro postal   19e, 26
monitor el monitor   42b
monk el monje   11d
monkey el mono   15a
monologue el monólogo   28d
monorail el monocarril   42a
month el mes   4c
monthly mensualmente   4c, 5b
monument el monumento   36a
mood (*grammar*) el modo   8a
mood el humor   11e, 21a
moon la luna   5c, 6a, 13a
moonbeam el rayo de luna   13a
morality la moralidad   44b
more más   3c
morning la mañana   4a
mortgage la hipoteca   26
mosque la mezquita   11d
mosquito el mosquito   15d
motel el motel   35a
moth la polilla   15d
mother la madre   10a
mother-in-law la suegra   10a
motion la moción   3e
motor el motor   33e
motorcycle la motocicleta   33a
mountain la montaña   13b
mountain climbing el alpinismo   27a, 36b

mountain lion, cougar el puma   15a
mountainous montañoso   13b
mountain range la cordillera   13b
mouse el ratón   15a, 42b
mouth la boca   12a, 40b
move mover*   3e
move (*residence*) mudarse   (*v*) 23f
movement el movimiento   3e
movie le película   28a
movie camera la cámara cinematográfica   25d
movie director el director cinematográfico   38a
movie star la estrella de cine   28a
mp3 player el reproductor de mp3   20b
Mr. Señor (Sr.)   11f, 16b
Mrs. Señora (Sra.)   11f, 16b
much mucho   3c
muffler el silenciador   33e
mugginess el bochorno   6a
muggy bochornoso   6a, 6b
mule el mulo   15a
multimedia la multimedia   42b
multiple sclerosis la esclerosis múltiple   40a
multiple múltiple   1f
multiplication la multiplicación   1e
multiplication table la tabla de multiplicación   1e
multiply multiplicar   1e
mumble mascullar   17a
mumps las paperas   40a
murder el asesinato, el homicidio   39b
murmur murmurar   17a
muscle el músculo   12a, 40a
muscular dystrophy la distrofia muscular   40a

museum   el museo   36a
mushroom   la seta, el hongo, el champiñón   14e, 24e
music   la música   25j, 28c, 37e
musician   el (la) músico(a)   28c, 38a
Muslim   el musulmán   11d
mussels   los mejillones   24d
mustache   el bigote   12a
mustard   la mostaza   24j
mute person   el (la) mudo(a)   12c
my   mi, mis   8e
myself   me   8k
mystery   el misterio   20a, 25o
myth   el mito   11d, 28d
mythology   la mitología   28d

N

nag   regañar   17a
nail   el clavo (n); clavar (v)   25b
nail clippers   el cortauñas   25f
nail polish   el esmalte para las uñas   12d, 25f
naïve   ingenuo   11e
name   el nombre   11f, 38b
napkin   la servilleta   23d, 241
narrow   estrecho   3b
nation   la nación   13e, 30a
national   nacional   13e
nationality   la nacionalidad   11f, 38b
natural   natural   1d, 13b
natural gas   el gas natural   13c
natural resources   los recursos naturales   13c, 44a
nature   la naturaleza   13b
navigable   navegable   13b
navy blue   azul marino   7a
near   cerca   3d, 36c
nearsighted   miope   (adj)   40a
neat   limpio   11e
neck   el cuello   12a

necklace   el collar   25i
need   necesitar (v); la necesidad (n)   21a
needle   la aguja   40b
negative   negativo   1d
neigh   rebuznar   15a
neon light   el alumbrado de neón   25b
nephew   el sobrino   10a
Neptune   Neptuno   13a
nerves   los nervios   40a
nervous system   el sistema nervioso   40a
net   la red   27b, 42c
netiquette   la etiqueta de la red   42c
network   la cadena   20b
network (internet)   la red   42c
networking   la conexión de redes   42c
neurologist   el neurólogo   40a
neutron   el neutrón   13c, 42a
never   nunca   4e
New York   Nueva York   30c
news report   las noticias   20a
newscast   el noticiario   20b
newsgroup   el grupo de noticias   42c
newspaper   el periódico   20a, 25o
newsstand   el quiosco   34
next to   al lado de   3d
Nicaraguan   el (la) nicaragüense (n, adj)   30d
nice   simpático   11e
niece   la sobrina   10a
night   la noche   4a
night table   la mesita de noche   23c
nightingale   el ruiseñor   15b
no   no   16c
no one   nadie   3c, 8n
no smoking   no fumar   32a, 34
no smoking section   la sección de no fumar   32a, 34

noise el ruido 12c
noisy ruidoso 12c
nonconformist el (la) disidente 11e
non-fiction la literatura no novelesca 20a
non-stop flight el vuelo sin escala 32b
noodles los fideos 24i
noon el mediodía 4a
north el norte 3d
North America Norteamérica 30b
North Pole el Polo Norte 13e
Norway Noruega 30b
Norwegian noruego(a) (*adj, n*) 30d
nose la nariz 12a
nostril la ventana de la nariz 12a, 40a
notarize legalizar, certificar 41
notary public el notario público 41
note la nota 19e, 20a, 28c
notebook el cuaderno 37b
notepad el bloc de papel 25c
notes los apuntes 37f
nothing nada 3c
noun el sustantivo 8a
novel (*literature*) la novela 20a, 25o, 28d
November noviembre 5b
Novocain la novocaína 40b
now ahora 4e, 17b
nowadays hoy día 4e
nowhere en ninguna parte 3d
nuclear nuclear 42a
nuclear disarmament el desarme nuclear 42a
nuclear energy la energía nuclear 13c, 42a, 44a
nuclear industry la industria nuclear 42a

nuclear reactor el reactor nuclear 42a
nuclear weapon el arma nuclear (*f*) 44b
nucleus el núcleo 13c, 14a
number el número 1d, 8a, 38b
numeral el número 1d
numerical numérico 1d
nun la monja 11d
nurse el (la) enfermero(a) 38a, 40a
nursery school la escuela de párvulos 37a
nut la tuerca 25b
nylon el nailon, el nilón 25l

O

oak tree el roble 14c
oat la avena 24i
obesity la obesidad 11a
obituaries la necrología 20a
obituary el obituario 20a
object el objeto 8a
oboe el oboe 28c
obstinate obstinado 11e
obtuse obtuso 2b
occasionally de vez en cuando 4e
occupation la profesión 38a
occur occurrir, suceder 4e
ocean océano 13b
octagon el octógono 2a
octahedron el octaedro 2a
October octubre 5b
octopus el pulpo 15c
odd impar (*adj, n*) 1d
of de 8g
offend ofender 17a
office la oficina 38d
office automation la automatización de oficina 42b
office hours las horas de consulta 40b
often con frecuencia 4e
oil el aceite 13c, 24j, 33e
oil painting el óleo 28b

ointment   el ungüento   25h, 40a

old   viejo   11b

old age   la vejez   11c

older *(in age)*   mayor   11b

olive   la aceituna   14d, 24e

olive tree   el olivo   14c

omelette   la tortilla   24h

on   encima de   3d, 8g

on time   a tiempo   32b, 34

once   una vez   4e

one way *(road sign)*   la dirección única   33d

onion   la cebolla   14e, 24e

only   solo, único *(adj)*   4e

only   sólo, solamente *(adv)*   4e

onomatopoeia   la onomatopeya   28d

opal   el ópalo   25j

opaque   opaco   7b, 13d

open   abierto *(pp)*, abrir *(v)*   25a

open *(a play)*   estrenar   28e

open an account   abrir una cuenta   26

opening hour   hora de abrir   25a

opening night   el estreno   28e

opera   la ópera   28c

operate   operar   40a

operating room   la sala de operaciones   40a

operating system   el sistema operativo   42b

operation   la operación   40a

operator   el operador   18b

ophthalmologist   el oftalmólogo   40a

opinion   la opinión   22a

opposite   opuesto   2b

oppress   oprimir *(v)*   44b

optimism   el optimismo   11e

optimist   el (la) optimista   11e

optimistic   optimista   11e

oral   oral   17a

orally   oralmente   17a

orange *(color)*   anaranjado   7a

orange *(fruit)*   la naranja   14d, 24f

orange tree   el naranjo   14c

orbit   estar* en órbita, órbita   13a

orchestra   la orquesta   28c

orchestra conductor   el director de orquesta   28c

orchid   la orquídea   14b

order   mandar *(v)*; el mandato *(n)*   17a, 24o

order   pedir*   24o

ordinal   ordinal   1d

organ   el órgano   28c

organic   orgánico   13c

organism   el organismo   14a

organizer   el organizador   20b

oriental   oriental   11d

original   original   11e

original invoice   la factura original   31

ostrich   el avestruz   15b

others   otros   8n

our   nuestro, nuestra, nuestros, nuestras   8e

ourselves   nos   8k

out   afuera *(adv)*   39a

outgoing   extravertido   11e

outlet *(electrical, telephone)*   la toma   18a, 25b

outside   fuera   3d, 36c

outskirts   las afueras   30a

outspoken   franco   17a

oven   el horno   23d

overhead projector   el retroproyector   37b

owl   el búho   15b

ox   el buey   15a

oxygen   el oxígeno   13c, 32c

oyster   la ostra   24d

ozone   el ozono   44a

P

pacemaker   el marcapasos   40a

Pacific   el Pacífico   13b
package   el paquete   19e, 25a
pad   el bloc   19d
pagan   pagano *(adj, n)*   11d
page   la página   19d, 20a
pager   el localizador
  alfanumérico   20b
pail   el cubo   23d
pain   el dolor   40a
painful   doloroso   40a
paint   la pintura   7c, 23f, 28b
paintbrush   la brocha   25b
painter   el pintor, la pintora
  7c, 28b
painting   la pintura, el cuadro
  23c, 28b
pair   el par   3c, 25n
pajamas   las pijamas   25k
palate   el paladar   40b
palette   la paleta   28b
palm tree   la palma   14c
pamphlet   el folleto   20a
pan   la cacerola   23d
Panamanian   panameño(a)
  (adj, n)   30d
panic attack   el ataque de pánico
  40a
panties   las bragas   25k
pantry   la despensa   23a
pants   los pantalones   25k
paper   el papel   19d, 25c, 37b
paper clip   el sujetapapeles
  19d
paper feeder   la bandeja de
  alimentación   42b
paperback book   el libro en
  rústica   25o
parable   la parábola   28d
paradox   la paradoja   28d
paragraph   el párrafo   19c
Paraguayan   paraguayo(a)
  (adj, n)   30d
parakeet   el perico   15b
parallel   paralelo   2b
parallelogram   paralelogramo
  2a
paramedic   el paramédico
  38a, 39a

parenthesis   el paréntesis
  19c
parents   los padres   10a
Paris   París   30c
park   aparcar, estacionar *(v)*
  33c
park   el parque   36a
parkbench   el banco   36a
parking   el estacionamiento
  33c
parking meter   el parquímetro
  36a
parliament   el parlamento
  43
parrot   el loro   15b
parsley   el perejil   14e, 24j
part   la parte   3c
participle   el participio   8a
particle   la partícula   13c
party   la fiesta   29b
party *(political)*   el partido
  43
pass   pasar, adelantar *(v)*
  33c
pass *(ball)*   pasar *(v)*
  27b
pass *(football)*   el pase
  27b
pass by   pasar   3e
passenger   el pasajero   32c,
  33b
passive   pasivo   8a
passport   el pasaporte   31,
  35b
password   la contraseña   42c
past   pasado   4e, 8a
pastel *(art)*   el pastel   28b
pastry   el pastel   24i
pastry shop   la pastelería
  24n
patience   la paciencia   11e,
  21a
patient   paciente   11e, 40a
paw   la pata   15a
pawn *(chess)*   el peón   27a
pay   pagar   25a, 26, 35b
pay telephone   el teléfono
  público   18a

payment el pago 26

PDA el asistente personal digital 42b

pea el guisante 14e, 24e

peace la paz 43

peach el melocotón, el durazno 14d, 24f

peach tree el melocotonero, el duraznero 14c

peak el pico 13b

peanut el cacahuete 24f

pear la pera 14d

pear tree el peral 14c

pearl la perla 25i

pedal el pedal 33a

pedestrian el peatón 33b

pedestrian crossing el paso de peatones 33c, 33d, 36a

pediatrician el pediatra 40a

peel pelar (v) 24o

pelican el pelícano 15b

pen la pluma 2b, 7c, 19d, 25c, 37b, 38c

pen name el seudónimo 28d

penalty (soccer) el tiro penal 27b

pencil el lápiz 2b, 19d, 37b, 38c

pencil sharpener el sacapuntas 25c

penicillin la penicilina 25h

peninsula la península 13b

penis el pene 12a

pension la jubilación 38d

pentagon el pentágono 2a

people la gente 11d

pepper la pimienta 24j

pepper shaker el pimentero 24 l

perceive percibir 12c

percent el porcentaje 1f

perception la percepción 12c

percussion instruments los instrumentos de percusión 28c

perfect perfecto 8a

perfection la perfección 11e

perfectionist el (la) perfeccionista 11e

perform representar 28e

performance la representación 28e

perfume el perfume 12d, 25f

period (punctuation sign) el punto 19c

peripherals el equipo periférico 42b

permanent press inarrugable (adj) 251

permanent wave la permanente 12d

person la persona 8a, 11d

personal personal 8a

personal computer la computadora personal 42b

personality la personalidad 11e

personification la personificación 28d

personify personificar 28d

perspire sudar 6b

persuade persuadir 22b, 41

Peruvian peruano(a) (adj, n) 30d

pessimism el pesimismo 11e

pessimist el (la) pesimista 11e

pessimistic pesimista 11e

pet el animal doméstico 15a

petal el pétalo 14b

petroleum el petróleo 13c, 44a

petunia la petunia 14b

pharmacist el (la) farmacéutico(a) 25h, 38a

philosophy la filosofía 37e

phone llamar por teléfono 18b

phonetics la fonética 8a

photocopier la fotocopiadora 38c

photo(graph) la foto(grafía) 20a, 25d

photosynthesis   la fotosíntesis
14a

phrase   la frase   19c

physical   físico   13c

physics   la física   13c, 37e

pianist   el (la) pianista   28c

piano   el piano   28c

pick   la piqueta   25b

pickpocket   el ratero, el carterista
39b

picky   difícil   11e

pie   el pastel   24g

piece   el pedazo   3c

piece of furniture   el mueble
23c

pig   el cerdo   15a

pigeon   el pichón   15b

pill   la píldora   25h, 40a

pillow   la almohada   23d, 35c

pillowcase   la funda   23d

pilot   el (la) piloto   32c, 38a

pimple   el grano   40a

pincers   las tenazas   25b

pineapple   la piña   14d, 24f

pine tree   el pino   14c

pink   rosado   7a

pipe *(smoking)*   la pipa   25e

Pisces   Piscis   5d

place   el lugar   3d, 19c, 38b

place of birth   el lugar de
nacimiento   11f

plagiarism   el plagio   28d

plaid   a cuadros   251

plain   el llano   13b

plane figures   las figuras planas
2a

planet   el planeta   13a

plant   la planta   14a

plant *(factory)*   la fábrica
38d

plastic   el plástico   13c

plate   el plato   23d, 241

platform   la plataforma   34

platinum   el platino   13c

play *(a record)*   tocar   20a,
28c

play *(a sport)*   jugar*   27a

play *(sports)*   la jugada   *(n)*
27b

play *(theater)*   el drama   *(n)*
20a

player *(music)*   el (la) músico(a)
28c

player *(sports)*   el jugador, la
jugadora   27b

playing cards   las cartas, los
naipes   27a

playoffs   el partido de desempate
27b

playwright   el dramaturgo
28e

plea   el alegato   41

plead guilty   declararse culpable
41

plead not guilty   declararse
inocente   41

pleasant   agradable   11e,
21b

please *(courtesy)*   por favor
16c

pliers   los alicates   25b

plot   la trama, el argumento
20a, 28d, 28e

plug *(telephone)*   la clavija
18a

plug *(electric)*   el enchufe
25b

plum   la ciruela   14d, 24f

plumage   el plumaje   15b

plumber   el plomero   38a

plumbing   la fontanería   25b

plural   plural   8a

plus   más   1e, 6b

Pluto   Plutón   13a

pneumonia   la pulmonía, la
neumonía   40a

pocket   el bolsillo   25g, 27a

podiatrist   el pedicuro   40a

poem   el poema   20a

poet   el (la) poeta(tisa)   28d

poetry   la poesía   20a, 25o

point   el punto   2b

point *(score)*   el punto, el tanto
27b

point of view   el punto de vista
28d
poison   el veneno   (*n*);
envenenar   (*v*)   40a
poisoning   el envenenamiento
40a
Poland   Polonia   30b
pole   el polo   13e
police   la policía   33b, 39b,
39c, 42b
police station   la comisaría
41
policeman   el policía   33b,
39b, 42b
policewoman   la policía   33b
policy   la política   43
policy (insurance)   la póliza
26
Polish   polaco(a)   (*adj, n*)
30d
political   político   43
political party   el partido
político   43
political science   la ciencia
política   37e
politician   el político   43
politics   la política   43
polka dots   a lunares   (*mpl*)
251
pollen   el polen   14a
pollution   la contaminación
13c, 44a
polyester   el poliéster   251
polyhedron   el poliedro   2a
pond   el estanque   13b, 37b
pool   la alberca, la piscina
35b
poor   pobre   11e
poplar tree   el álamo   14c
poppy   la amapola   14a
porch   el portal, la terraza
cubierta   23a
pork   el cerdo   24c
pork chop   la chuleta de cerdo
24c
pornography   la pornografía
44b
port   el puerto   42c

portable CD player   el
reproductor portátil de CD
20b
portable phone   el teléfono
remoto   18a
porter   el maletero   32a, 34,
35b
portion   la porción   3c
portrait   el retrato   28b
Portugal   Portugal   30b
Portuguese   portugués (esa)
(*adj, n*)   30d
position   la posición   3d
positive   positivo   1d
possessive   posesivo   8e, 8f,
11e
postage   el franqueo   19e
postal code   el código postal
19e, 38b
postal rate   la tarifa postal
19e
postcard   la tarjeta postal
19e
postdate   posfechar   (*v*); la
posfecha   (*n*)   26
pot   la olla   23d
potato   la papa, la patata
14e, 24e
pound sign   el signo de libra
18b
pour   echar, verter*   24o
powder   el polvo   25h
power   la potencia   1e
power   el poder   44b
power off   apagado   42c
power on   encendido   42c
power switch   el interruptor
42b
practice   practicar   27b
praise   alabar   17a
pray   orar, rezar   11d, 17a
prayer   la oración   11d,
17a
preach   predicar (*v*)   17a
precious   precioso   25i
predicate   el predicado   8a
preface   el prefacio   28d
prefer   preferir*   21b

pregnancy   el embarazo   11c
pregnant   embarazada   11c,
 40a
prelude   el preludio   28c
preposition   la preposición
 8g
Presbyterian   el presbiteriano
 (*n, adj*)   11d
prescription   la receta   25h,
 40a
present   el presente   4e, 8a
present   presente (*adj*)   4e
president   el presidente   43
president (*of a university*)   el
 rector   37d
presumptuous   presuntuoso
 11e
pretentious   pretencioso   11e
preterite   el preténto   8a
previous   anterior   4e
price   el precio   24m, 25a,
 35b
price tag   la etiqueta   25a
priest   el cura, el sacerdote
 11d
primate   el primate   15a
prime (*number*)   primo   1d
prince   el príncipe   43
princess   la princesa   43
principal (*school*)   el director, la
 directora   37d
print   escribir con letras de
 molde (*v*)   11f
print   la impresión, imprimir (*v*)
 20a
print   la prueba positiva   25d
print cartridge   el cartucho de
 tinta   42b
printed matter   los impresos
 19e
printer   la impresora   42b
printing   la imprenta   20a,
 42b
prison   la cárcel   41
private school   la escuela
 privada   39a
problem   el problema   1f,
 22a, 37f

processor   el procesador   42b
product   el producto   1f
profession   la profesión   11f,
 38a, 38b
professional   profesional   11f,
 27b
professor   el (la) profesor(a)
 37d, 38a
profit   la ganancia   26
program   el programa   20b,
 28e, 42b
programmer   el programador
 42b
programming   la programación
 42b
projector   el proyector   20b
prologue   el prólogo   28d
promise   prometer (*v*); la
 promesa (*n*)   17a
pronoun   el pronombre   8a
pronounce   pronunciar   17a
pronunciation   la pronunciación
 8a, 17a
propose   proponer*   17a
prostitution   la prostitución
 44b
protect   proteger*   39a
protein   la proteína   40a
protest   la protesta (*n*);
 protestar (*v*)   43
Protestant   el (la) protestante
 (*n, adj*)   11d
Protestantism   el protestantismo
 11d
proton   el protón   13c, 42a
protractor (*drawing instrument*)
 el transportador   2b
proud   orgulloso   11e
proverb   el proverbio   28d
provided that   con tal que
 8o
province   la provincia   13e
prudent   prudente   11e
prune   la ciruela pasa   14d,
 24f
P.S.   PD   19c
psychiatrist   el (la) psiquiatra
 38a, 40a

psychologist   el (la) psicólogo(a) 38a

psychology   la psicología 37e

pubis   el pubis   12a

public garden   el jardín público 36a

public notices   los avisos públicos   36a

public parking   el estacionamiento público   33c

public prosecutor   el acusador público   41

public washroom   el servicio público   36a

publish   publicar   20a

publisher   el (la) editor(a) 20a

puck   el disco   27b

pudding   el budín   24g

Puerto Rican   puertorriqueño(a) (*adj, n*)   30d

pull   tirar   3e

pulse   el pulso   40a

pumpkin   la calabaza   14e

pun   el retruécano   28d

punch   el punzón   25b

punctuation   la puntuación 19c

punish   castigar   41

purchase   la compra (*n*); comprar (*v*)   25a

pure   puro   7b, 13d

purple   morado   7a

purse   la bolsa   25n

push   empujar   3e

put   poner*   3e

put on   ponerse*   25m

pyramid   la pirámide   2a

Q

quadratic equation   la ecuación de segundo grado   1f

quadruplets   los cuatrillizos 10a

quantity   la cantidad   3c

quantum theory   la teoría cuántica   42a

quart   el cuarto   3a

quarter, trimester   el trimestre 37f

queen   la reina   27a, 43

question   la pregunta   37f

question mark   el signo de interrogación   19c

quickly   rápidamente   3e

quotation mark   las comillas 19c

quotient   el cociente   1f

R

rabbi   el rabino, el rabí   11d

rabbit   el conejo   15a

race *(sports)*   la carrera   27b

race   la raza   11d

racetrack   el hipódromo   27b

racial profiling   la opinión racialment determinada   44b

racism   el racismo   44b

radiation   la radiación   44a

radio   el radio   20b, 23d, 35c

radioactive   radioactivo   44a

radioactive waste   los desechos radioactivos   44a

radish   el rábano   14e

radius   el radio   2a

railroad   el ferrocarril   34

railroad station   la estación del ferrocarril   34

railway crossing   el cruce de vías   36a

rain   llover*   6a

rain   la lluvia   6a

rainbow   el arco iris   6a

raincoat   el impermeable 25k

rainy   lluvioso   6a

raise someone   criar   11c

RAM (Random Access Memory) la memoria de acceso aleatorio 42b; la memoria (RAM) 42b

ramp   la rampa   33c

rape   violar (*v*); la violación (*n*)   39b

rare   raro   4e, 24b

rarely raramente, raras veces 4e

rash el salpullido 40a

raspberry la frambuesa 14d, 24f

rat la rata 15a

ratio la proporción 1e

rational racional 1d

razor la afeitadora; la najava de afeitar 12d, 25f

razor blade la hoja de afeitar 25a

read leer 20a, 37f

reader el (la) lector(a) 20a

reading lamp la lámpara para leer 35c

reading passage la lectura 37f

real real 1d

real estate los bienes raíces 26

real estate agent el agente de inmobiliaria 38a

rearview mirror el espejo retrovisor 33e

reason la razón 22a

reason razonar (v) 22b

rebellious rebelde 11e

receipt el recibo 26, 31, 35b

receive recibir 19e

receiver el receptor 18a, 20b

recent reciente 4e

recently recientemente 4e

reception la recepción 11c

reception desk la recepción 35b

receptionist recepcionista (m/f) 38a

rechargeable batteries las pilas recargables 25d

recipe la receta 23d

reciprocal recíproco 1d

recommend recomendar* 17a

record *(audio)* el disco 25j

record *(audio)* grabar 20b

record player el tocadiscos 20b, 37b

recover recobrarse (v) 40a

rectangle el rectángulo 2a

rectum el recto 40a

recyclable reciclable 44a

recycle reciclar (v) 44a

red rojo 7a

red-haired pelirrojo 11a

red snapper el huachinango 15c

referee el árbitro 27b

reference book el libro de consulta 20a, 25o

refined refinado 11e

reflect reflexionar, meditar 22b

reflexive reflexivo 8a, 8k

reform la reforma (n); reformar (v) 43

refrigerator la nevera, el frigorífico 23d

refund reembolsar (v) 25a

refund el reembolso 25a

region la región 13e

registered letter la carta certificada 19e

registration la matrícula 37f

registration fees los derechos de matrícula 37f

regular regular 4e, 8a

rehearsal el ensayo 28e

rehearse ensayar 28e

relate relatar 17a

relative relativo 8a, 8m

relatives los parientes 10a

relax relajarse (v) 12b

relief el alivio 21a

relieve aliviar 21a

religion la religión 11d

religious religioso 11d

remain quedarse (v) 29b

remember recordar* 22b

remote control el control remoto 20b

rent alquilar (v); el alquiler (n) 23g

rented car el coche alquilado 33a

repair reparar (*v*) 33e
repeat repetir* 17a, 37f
repetition la repetición 17a
reply responder, contestar 19e
report relatar (*v*) 17a
report el informe 17a
reporter el reportero 20a
representative el (la) representante 43
reproach reprochar 17a
reproduce reproducir* 14a
reproduction la reproducción 14a
reptile el reptil 15c
republic la república 43
request pedir* (*v*); la petición (*n*) 17a
rescue rescatar, el rescate 39a
reservation la reservación, la reserva 24m, 32a, 35b
reserved reservado 11e, 24m
residence la residencia 11f
resistant resistente 13d
respiratory system el sistema respiratorio 40a
rest descansar 12b
restaurant el restaurante 24m
restless incansable 11e
restore restaurar 23f
résumé el curriculum vitae 38b
retail la venta al por menor 26
retire jubilarse (*v*) 38d
retirement la jubilación 38d
return volver*, regresar 3e
return (*an object*) devolver* 3e, 25a
return address la dirección del remitente 19e
return ticket el boleto de regreso 30a
review repasar (*v*); el repaso (*n*) 37f

review (*book*) la reseña 20a
revolt el motín 43
revolution la revolución 43
rhetoric la retórica 17a, 28d
rhetorical retórico 17a
rheumatism el reumatismo, la reuma 40a
rhinoceros el rinoceronte 15a
rhombus el rombo 2a
rhubarb el ruibarbo 14e
rhyme la rima 28d
rhythm el ritmo 28c
ribbon (*typewriter*) la cinta de máquina de escribir 19d
rice el arroz 24i
rich rico 11e
rifle el rifle 39b
right correcto, recto (*adj*) 2b, 37f
right el derecho (*n*) 3d, 41
ring sonar (*v*) 18b
ring el anillo, la sortija 25i
ring finger el dedo anular 12a
rinse enjuagar(se) (*v*) 40b
rinse el enjuague 12d, 40b
riot el motín 43
ripe maduro 14a
risk el riesgo 44b
rite el rito 11d
river el río 13b, 36b
road el camino 33c
road map el mapa de carreteras 33b
road rage la furia caminera 44b
roar rugir* 15a
rob robar 39b
robber el ladrón 39b
robbery el robo 39b
robot el robot 42a
robust robusto 13d
rock la roca, la peña 13b
rock music la música rock 25j, 28c
role el papel 28e

rollerskating   el patinaje sobre ruedas   27a
ROM (Read Only Memory)   la memoria permanente   42b
Roman numeral   el número romano   1d
romantic   romántico   11e
Rome   Roma   30c
roof   el tejado   23a
rook (*chess*)   la torre   27a
room   el cuarto, la habitación   23b, 35b
rooster   el gallo   15b
root   la raíz   1e, 14a, 40b
rope   la cuerda   27a, 36b
rose   la rosa   14b
rosemary   el romero   14e, 24j
rotten   podrido   14a
rough   áspero   11e, 13d
rough draft   el borrador   37f
round-trip ticket   el boleto de ida y vuelta   30a
row   la fila   28a
rubber bands   las gomitas   25c
ruby   el rubí   25i
rude   mal educado   11e
rug   la alfombra   23c
ruler   la regla   2b, 19d, 37b, 38c
rumor   el rumor   17a
run   correr   3e, 12b, 27b
run over   atropellar   39c
runway   la pista   32c
rush hour   la hora punta   33c
Russia   Rusia   30b
Russian   ruso(a) (*adj, n*)   30d

S

sad   triste   11e, 21a
sadness   la tristeza   11e, 21a
safe   la caja fuerte   26
safe deposit box   la caja de seguridad   26
Sagittarius   Sagitario   5d
salad   la ensalada   24g
salamander   la salamandra   15c

salary   el salario, el sueldo   26, 38d
sale   la venta   25a
salesperson   el vendedor   38a
salmon   el salmón   15c, 24d
salt   la sal   13c, 24j
salt shaker   el salero   24l
salty   salado   24p
salutation   la salutación, el saludo   19c
Salvadoran   salvadoreño(a) (*adj, n*)   30d
sanctions   las sanciones   44b
sand   la arena   13b
sandwich   la torta, el bocadillo   24g
sanitary napkins   las toallitas higiénicas   25h
sapphire   el zafiro   25i
sarcasm   el sarcasmo   11e
sarcastic   sarcástico   11e
sardine   la sardina   15c, 24d
satellite   el satélite   13a, 42a
satire   la sátira   28d
satisfaction   la satisfacción   21a
satisfied   satisfecho   21a
satisfy   satisfacer*   21a
Saturday   el sábado   5a
Saturn   Saturno   13a
saucer   el platillo   23d, 24l
sausage   la salchicha   24c
save   ahorrar, guardar (*v*)   26, 42b
savings   los ahorros   26
savings account   la cuenta de ahorros   26
savings bank   la caja de ahorros   26
saw   la sierra   25b
saxophone   el saxofón   28c
say   decir*   17a
scalene   escaleno   2a
scanner   el escáner   42b
scar   la cicatriz   40a
scarf   la bufanda   25k
scene   la escena   28e, 38c
scenery   el decorado   28e

schedule el horario 4e, 34
schizophrenia la esquizofrenia 40a
school la escuela 37f
school bag la mochila 37b
schoolmate el (la) compañero(a) de clase 37d
school yard el patio 37c
school year el año escolar 5b, 37a
science la ciencia 37e
science fiction la ciencia ficción 20a, 25o
scientific research la investigación científica 42a
scientist el científico 38a
scissors las tijeras 12d, 19d, 38c, 39c
scorch chamuscar 25g
score marcar 27b
Scorpio Escorpión 5d
scorpion el alacrán 15d
Scotland Escocia 30b
screen la pantalla 25d, 28a, 42b
screensaver el salvapantallas 42b
screw el tornillo (n); atornillar (v) 25b
screwdriver el destornillador 25b
scuba diving el submarinismo 27b
sculpt esculpir 28b
sculptor el escultor 28b
sculptress la escultora 28b
sculpture la escultura 28b
sea el mar 6a, 13b, 36b
seafood el pescado, el marisco 24d
seagull la gaviota 15b
sea lion, seal la foca 15a
seamstress la costurera 38a
search registrar 41
earch engine el buscador (m) 42c
·son la estación 5c
· el asiento 28a, 32c, 34

seat (bicycle) el sillín 33a
seat belt el cinturón de seguridad 32c
secant la secante 2b
second el segundo 4c, 8a
secretary el (la) secretario(a) 37d, 38a, 40a
secure web site el sitio de red seguro 42c
securities (stocks and bonds) los valores 26
security check inspección de seguridad 32a
security guard guardia (m/f) 38a
sedative el sedante, el calmante 40a
seduction la seducción 11e
seductive seductivo 11e
see ver* 12c, 30a
seed la semilla (n); sembrar* (v) 14a
segment el segmento 2b
selfish egoísta 11e
self-service el autoservicio 33c
self-sufficient independiente 11e
sell vender 23f, 25a
semester el semestre 37f
semicolon el punto y coma 19c
senate el senado 43
send mandar 3e, 19e
sender el remitente 19e
sense, feel sentirse* 12c
sense el sentido 12c
sensitive sensible 11e
sentence (grammar) la frase, la oración 8a, 19c
sentence la sentencia 41
sentimental sentimental 11e
separate separado 11c
separation (marital) la separación matrimonial 11c
September septiembre 5b
series la serie 20b
serious serio 11e

sermon el sermón   11d
serve servir*   24o
server el servidor   42c
services los servicios   24m, 35b
set *(hair)* el peinado   12d
set el conjunto   1f
set the table poner* la mesa 23f, 24o
several varios   3c
severance pay la indemnización por despido   38d
sew coser   25g
sewing machine la máquina de coser   23d
sex el sexo   11a, 38b
sexual harassment el acoso sexual   44b
sexy atractivo   11a
shade, shadow la sombra   6a
shake hands dar *(v)* la mano a 16a
shame la vergüenza   21a
shampoo el champú   12d, 25f, 35c
share compartir *(v)*   17a
shark el tiburón   15c
shave afeitarse *(v)*   12d
shaving cream la crema de afeitar   25f
she ella   8h
sheep el carnero, la oveja 15a
sheet *(bed)* la sábana   23d, 35c
sheet *(of paper)* la hoja   25c
shelf el estante   23a
ship el barco   36b
shirt la camisa   25k
shock el choque   39c
shoe el zapato   25n
shoe polish el betún, la crema para zapato   25n
shoe store la zapatería   25n
shoelaces los cordones   25n
shoot disparar   39b
shop la tienda *(n)*; ir* de compras *(v)*   25a

short *(length)* corto   3b, 12d
short *(stature)* bajo   11a
short story el cuento   20a, 28d
shorten acortar   25m
shorts *(underwear)* los calzoncillos   25k
shorts los pantalones cortos 25k
shoulder el hombro   12a
shout gritar *(v)*; el grito *(n)* 17a, 39a
shovel la pala   25b
show la función   20b, 28c
shower la ducha   23a, 35c
shrewd sagaz, listo   11e
shrimp la (las) gamba(s), el (los) camarón(-rones)   24d
shuffle cards barajar   27a
shut up callarse   17a
shy tímido   11e
sick enfermo   11a, 40a
sickness la enfermedad   11a, 40a
side el lado   2b
sideburn la patilla   13b
sidewalk la acera   36a
sight la vista   12c, 40a
sign firmar   11f, 19c, 26
signal la señal   33c
signature la firma   11f, 19c, 26, 38b
silence el silencio   17a
silent silencioso   17a
silk la seda   13c, 25l
sill (see *window ledge*)
silver la plata   13c, 25i
silver plateado *(adj)*   7a
silver anniversary el aniversario de plata   11c
silverware el cubierto   24 1
simile el símil   28d
simple sencillo   11e, 22a
simultaneous simultáneo   4e
since desde   4e, desde que, puesto que   8o
sincere sincero   11e
sincerity la sinceridad   11e

sine (*mathematics*)   el seno 2b

sing   cantar   28c

singer   el (la) cantante   25j, 28c

single   el (la) soltero(a)   38b

single bed   la cama sencilla 35b

single room   el cuarto sencillo 35b

singular   singular   8a

sink   el lavabo   23a, 35c

siren   la sirena   39a

sister   la hermana   10a

sister-in-law   la cuñada   10a

sit down   sentarse*   3e, 32c

size   tamaño   3b

size (*of clothes*)   la talla   25k

size (*of shoe*)   el número   25n

skate   patinar   27a

skating   el patinaje   27a

ski   esquiar*   27b

ski   el esquí   27b

ski resort   el lugar para esquiar 36b

skillet   la sartén   23d

skin   la piel   12a

skirt   la falda   25k

sky   el cielo   6a, 13b

sleep   dormir*   12b

sleeping bag   el saco de dormir 36b

sleeve   la manga   25g

slender   esbelto   11a

slice   rebanar, tajar   24o

slide (*photo*)   la diapositiva 25d

slide projector   el proyector de diapositivas   20b, 37b

sliding door   la puerta corrediza 35c

slim   delgado   11a

slip   la combinación   25k

slipper   la zapatilla   25n

slippery   resbaladizo   33d

sloppy   desorganizado   11e

slot (*for tokens*)   la ranura 18a

slow   lento   3e, 4e

slow down   ir (*v*) más despacio 33c

slowly   despacio, lentamente 3e, 4e

small   pequeño   3c, 11a, 25l

small letter (*lowercase*)   la minúscula   19c

smart   listo, inteligente   11e

smell   oler*   12c

smell (*sense of*)   el olfato 12c

smile   sonreír* (*v*); la sonrisa (*n*)   11e, 21a

smoke   el humo   13c, 39a

smoking section   la sección de fumar   32a, 34

smooth   liso   13d

snack   comer(se) (*v*) un bocadillo   24a

snack   el bocadillo   24a

snake   la serpiente   15c

snack bar   el bar, la cafetería 24m

sneeze   estornudar (*v*); el estornudo (*n*)   40a

snobbish   presuntuoso   11e

snore   roncar (*v*)   40a

snow   nevar* (*v*); la nieve (*n*) 6a, 6b

soap   el jabón   12d, 25f

soap bar   la pastilla de jabón 35c

soap opera   la telenovela 20b

soap powder   el jabón en polvo 25g

soccer   el fútbol   27b

soccer ball   el balón de fútbol 27b

soccer player   el (la) futbolista 27b

socialism   el socialismo   43

socialist   el (la) socialista 43

sociology   la sociología   37e

sock   el calcetín   25n

sodium   el sodio   13c

sodium bicarbonate   el bicarbonato de sodio   25h

sofa   el sofá   23c

soft   blando   13d

soft drink   el refresco   24k

software   el software, el logicial   42b

solar   solar   13a

solar cell   la célula solar   44a

solar eclipse   el eclipse solar   13a

solar energy   la energía solar   44a

solar system   el sistema solar   13a

sole fish   el lenguado   15c, 24d

solid   sólido   2a

soliloquy   el soliloquio   28d

solstice   el solsticio   5c

soluble   soluble   13d

solution   la solución   1f

solve   resolver*   1f, 37f

some   algunos   3c, 8n

someone   alguien   8n

something   algo   8n

somewhere   en alguna parte   3d

son   el hijo   10a

song   la canción   25j, 28c

son-in-law   el yerno   10a

sonnet   el soneto   28d

soon   pronto   4e

sorrow   el dolor, la pena   21a

soul   el alma   (*f*)   11d

sound   el sonido   12c

soundtrack   la banda sonora   28a

soup   la sopa   24g

sour   agrio   24p

south   el sur   3d

South America   Sudamérica   30b

South Pole   el Polo Sur   13e

souvenir   el recuerdo   25a

space   el espacio   2b, 13a

space bar (*typewriter*)   el espaciador   19d

space shuttle   el transbordador espacial   42a

spacecraft   la nave espacial   42a

spades (*cards*)   las espadas, los picos   27a

Spain   España   30b

spam   el spam   42c

Spanish   español(a)   (*adj, n*)   30d

spark plug   la bujía   33e

sparrow   el gorrión   15b

spatula   la espátula   23d

speak   hablar   17a

speaker   el altavoz   20b

special delivery   el correo urgente   19e

specialist   el (la) especialista   40a

species   la especie   14a

speech   el discurso   17a

speed   la velocidad   3a, 33c

speed limit   el límite de velocidad   33d

speedometer   el velocímetro   33e

speed up   acelerar   33c

spelling   la ortografía   19c

spend   gastar   25a

spend (*time*)   pasar   4e

sphere   la esfera   2a

spice   la especia   24j

spicy   picante   24p

spider   la araña   15d

spinach   la espinaca   14e, 24e

spirit   el espíritu   11d

spiritual   espiritual   11d

spit   escupir   40b

splint   la tablilla   39c

spoke   el radio   33a

spoon   la cuchara   23d, 24l

sporadic   esporádico   4e

sport   el deporte   27b

sports car   el coche deportivo   33a

sports event   el encuentro deportivo   27b

sports fan el aficionado deportivo 27b
spot, stain la mancha 25g
sprain la torcedura 39c
spreadsheet las hojas de cálculo 42b
spring la primavera 5c
spring (*of watch*) el muelle 25i
square (*geom.*) el cuadrado 2a
square (*place*) la plaza 11f, 36a
square centimeter el centímetro cuadrado 3a
square kilometer el kilómetro cuadrado 3a
square meter el metro cuadrado 3a
square millimeter el milímetro cuadrado 3a
squared al cuadrado 1e
squid el (los) calamar(es) 24d
stable estable 13d
stadium el estadio 27b
stage el escenario 28e
stain (see *spot*)
stainless steel el acero inoxidable 13c
stairs la escalera 23a, 35b
stamp el timbre, la estampilla, el sello 19e, 27a
stamp collecting la filatelia 27a
staple la grapa 19d, 25c, 38c
staple remover el sacagrapas 25c
stapler el grapador 19d, 25c, 38c
star (*celest. body*) la estrella 6a, 13a
star (*punct.*) el asterisco 18
starch el almidón 25g
starched almidonado 25g
start (*the car*) arrancar 33c
starter (*car*) el arranque 33e
state el estado 11f, 13e, 43
state declarar (*v*) 17a

statement la declaración 17a
station la estación 20b
stationery store la papelería 25c
statistics la estadística 1f, 37e
stay quedarse (*v*) 29b
steal robar 39b
steel el acero 13c
steering wheel el volante 33e
stem el tallo 14a
stepbrother el hermanastro 10a
stepdaughter la hijastra 10a
stepfather el padrastro 10a
stepmother la madrastra 10a
stepsister la hermanastra 10a
stepson el hijastro 10a
stereo system el equipo estéreo 20b
stethoscope el estetoscopio 40a
still todavía, aún 4e
stinginess la mezquindad 11e
stingy tacaño, mezquino 11e
stitch coser 25g
stock market la bolsa de valores 26
stock, share la acción 26
stockbroker bolsista (*m/f*) 38a
Stockholm Estocolmo 30c
stockings las medias 25n
stomach el estómago 12a, 40a
stone la piedra 13b
stool el banquillo 23c
Stop (*sign*) Alto 33d
stop parar, detener* 3e
stop (*e.g., bus*) la parada 34
store la tienda 25a
store clerk el (la) dependiente, (*also*) la dependienta 25a

storm   la tormenta, la tempestad
6a
story   el cuento   17a
stove   la estufa   23d
straight   plano   2b
straight ahead   derecho   36c
strait   el estrecho   13b
strawberry   la fresa   14d, 24f
street   la calle   11e, 36a, 38b
streetcar   el tranvía   33a
strength   la fuerza   11a
stretcher   la camilla   39c
strike   la huelga   43
strike   declararse (v) en huelga
43
string   el cordel   19d, 25c
string bean   la judía verde
14e, 24e
string instruments   los
instrumentos de cuerda   28c
striped   rayado   25l
stroke   el derrame cerebral
40a
strong   fuerte   11a, 11e, 13d,
40a
structure   la estructura   13c
stubborn   terco   11e
student   el (la) estudiante
37d
study   estudiar   22b, 37f
stupid   estúpido   11e
style   el estilo   28d
subject (school)   la asignatura
37e
subject (grammar)   el sujeto
8a
subjunctive   subjuntivo   8a
subordinate   subordinado   8a
subscribe   suscribir (v)
42c
substance   la substancia   13c
subtract   restar   1e
subtraction   la resta   1e
suburbs   las afueras   30a
subway   el metro, el subterráneo
34
subway station   la estación del
metro   34

sue   demandar, poner* pleito a
41
suede   la gamuza   25l
suffer   sufrir   40a
suffer from   padecer de   40a
suffice   bastar   3c
sufficient   suficiente   3c
sugar   el azúcar   24j
suggest   sugerir*   17a
suicide   el suicidio   44b
suit   el traje   25k
suitcase   la maleta   31
sulphur   el azufre   13c
summarize   resumir   17a
summary   el resumen   17a
summer   el verano   5c
summons   la citación judicial
41
sum up   sumar   1f
sun   el sol   5c, 6a, 13a
sunburn   la quemadura del sol
40a
Sunday   el domingo   5a
sunlight   la luz del sol   13a
sunrise   la salida del sol   4a
sunset   la puesta del sol   4a
supermarket   el supermercado
24n
superstitious   supersticioso
11e
supervisor   el supervisor   38a
supplementary   suplementario
2b
suppository   el supositorio
25h, 40a
support   apoyar (v)   44b
surf   navegar (v)   42c
surfers   internautas (m/f)
42c
surgeon   el cirujano   38a, 40a
surgery   la cirugía   40a
surname   el apellido   11f,
38b
surprise   la sorpresa (n);
sorprender (v)   21a
swallow   tragar   15b, 40a
swan   el cisne   15b
swear (in court)   jurar   41

swear *(profanity)* maldecir* 17a
sweater el suéter 25k
sweatshirt la sudadera 25k
Sweden Suecia 30b
Swedish sueco(a) *(adj, n)* 30d
sweet dulce 11e, 24p
sweet potato la batata 24e
swell hinchar 40a
swim nadar 27b
swimming la natación 27b
Swiss suizo(a) *(adj, n)* 30d
switch el interruptor 23a, 35c
switchblade la navaja de muelle 39b
Switzerland Suiza 30b
swollen hinchado 40a
swordfish el pez espada 15c
symbol el símbolo 1f, 17a, 28d
sympathetic compasivo 21a
sympathy *(over a death)* la condolencia, el pésame 21a
symphony la sinfonía 28c
synagogue la sinagoga 11d
synthesizer el sintetizador 28c
synthetic sintético 13d
syringe la jeringa 40a
syrup el jarabe 25h

T
tab el tabulador 19d
table la mesa 23c, 24l, 35c
tablecloth el mantel 23d, 24l
tablet *(medicine)* la pastilla 25h, 40a
tack la tachuela 37b, 38c
tag la etiqueta 25a
tail la cola 15a
tailor el sastre 25k, 38a
take *(the train, etc)* tomar 34
take attendance pasar lista 37f

take off quitarse *(v)* 25m
take off *(plane)* despegar 32c
take-off el despegue 32c
take place tener lugar 4e
talcum powder el talco 25f
tall alto 3b, 11a
tampons los tampones 25h
tangent la tangente 2a, 2b
tangerine la mandarina 14d, 24f
tape la cinta 25j
tape recorder la grabadora 20b, 37b
tapestry la tapicería 28b
tariff la tarifa 31
taste probar* 12c
tasty sabroso 24p
Taurus Tauro 5d
tax el impuesto 26
tax exemption la exención del impuesto 26
taxi el taxi 33a
taxi driver el (la) taxista 33a
tea el té 25k
teach enseñar 37f
teacher el (la) profesor(a) 37d, 38a
team el equipo 27b
teapot la tetera 23d
teaspoon la cucharita 23d, 24l
teaspoonful la cucharadita 23d
technical assistance la asistencia técnica 42c
technical school el instituto laboral 37a
technology la tecnología 42a
teenager el (la) joven 11b
telecommunication la telecomunicación 18a, 42a
teleconference la teleconferencia 42a
telephone el teléfono 18a, 23e, 37c, 38c

ticket agent el vendedor de boletos 32a, 34

ticket counter la taquilla, la boletería 34

tide la marea 13b

tie empatar (v) 27b

tie *(the score)* el empate 27b

tie *(clothing)* la corbata 25k

tiger el tigre 15a

tight ceñido 25l

tighten apretar* 25m

time el tiempo 4a

timetable el horario 4e

timpani los timbales 28c

tin el estaño 13c

tint el tinte (n); teñir* (v) 7c

tip la propina 24m

tire el neumático 33a, 33e

tissue *(paper handkerchief)* el pañuelo de papel 25h

title el título 11f, 16b, 20a

title of ownership el título 33b

to a 3d, 8g

to her le 8j

to him le 8j

to me me 8j

to them les 8j

to us nos 8j

to you te, le, os, les 8j

toad el sapo 15c

toast *(in drinking)* brindar (v); el brindis (n) 17a

toast tostar* 24o

toaster el tostador 23d

tobacco el tabaco 25e

tobacco shop la tabaquería 25e

today hoy 4a

toe el dedo del pie 12a

toilet el inodoro, el retrete, el excusado 23a, 32c, 35c

toilet paper el papel higiénico 35c

token la ficha 18a

Tokyo Tokio 30c

tolerance la tolerancia 21a

tolerate tolerar 21a

toll el peaje 33c, 33d

toll booth la barrera de peaje 33c

toll-free sin cargo, gratis 18b

tomato el tomate 14e, 24e

tomorrow mañana 4a

tongue la lengua 12a, 40b

tonight esta noche 4a

tonsils las amígdalas 40a

too much demasiado 3c

tools las herramientas 25b, 33c

tooth el diente 12a, 40b

toothache el dolor de muelas 40b

toothbrush el cepillo de dientes 12d, 25h, 40b

toothpaste la pasta dentífrica 12d, 25h, 40b

toothpick el palillo 23d, 24l

top la cumbre 3d

topaz el topacio 25i

tornado el tornado 6a

to the left a la izquierda 33c

to the right a la derecha 33c

touch tocar 12c

touch *(sense of)* el sentido del tacto 12c

touch up el retoque 12d

tour la gira 30a

tour guide el (la) guía de turismo 30a

touring bus el autobús de turismo 30a

tourist el (la) turista 30a

tow truck la grúa de remolque 33a

toward hacia 3d, 36c

towel la toalla 12d, 35c

tower la torre 36a

town el pueblo 11f

toxic agent el agente tóxico 44b

toxin la toxina 44b

track *(sports)* la pista 27b

track *(train)* la vía 34

track and field   el atletismo en pista   27b
traditional   tradicional   11e
traffic   el tráfico, la circulación   33c, 39c
traffic accident   el accidente de circulación   39c
traffic jam   el atasco   33e
traffic light   el semáforo   33c, 36a
traffic policeman   el guardia de tráfico   33b
traffic policewoman   la guardia de tráfico   33b
tragedy   la tragedia   20a, 28e
trailer   el remolque   33a
train   el tren   34
train station   la estación de trenes   34
transformer   el transformador   25b
transitive   transitivo   8a
translate   traducir*   17a
translation   la traducción   17a
transmission   la transmisión   20b, 33e
transmit   transmitir (v)   44b
transparent   transparente   7b, 13c, 13d
transplant   trasplantar, el trasplante   14a, 40a
trapezoid   el trapecio   2a
travel   viajar   30a
travel agency   el (la) agente de viajes   30a
traveler's check   el cheque de viajero   26, 35b
tray   la bandeja   23d, 24l, 32c
treason   la traición (f)   44b
tree   el árbol   14c
trial   el proceso   4l
triangle   el triángulo   2a
trigonometry   la trigonometría   2b
trim   recortar   12d
trimester   (see quarter)
trip   el viaje   30a, 36b

triple   triple   3c
triplets   los trillizos   10a
trombone   el trombón   28c
tropic   el trópico   13e
Tropic of Cancer   el trópico de Cáncer   13e
Tropic of Capricorn   el trópico de Capricornio   13e
tropical   tropical   6a, 13e
troublemaker   el perturbador   11e
trout   la trucha   15c, 24d
truck   el camión   33a
truck driver   el camionero   33a
true   verdadero   25i
trumpet   la trompeta   28c
trunk (tree)   el tronco   14a
trunk (car)   el baúl, la valija   33e
trust   la confianza (n); tener* (v) confianza   21a
try on   probar*   25m
T-shirt   la camiseta   25k
tuba   la tuba   28c
Tuesday   el martes   5a
tulip   el tulipán   14b
tuna   el atún   15c, 24d
tuner (audio)   el sintonizador   20b
tunnel   el túnel   33c
turbulence   la turbulencia   32c
turkey   el pavo   15b, 24c
turn   volver*, girar   3e; dar* la vuelta   33c, 36c
turn (pages)   hojear   20a
turnip   el nabo   14e
turn off   apagar   20b, 35c
turn on   poner*   20b, 35c
turn signal   el indicador de dirección   33e
turtle   la tortuga   15c
tweezers   las pinzas   25b
twice   dos veces   4e
twin   el (la) gemelo(a)   10a
typewriter   la máquina de escribir   19d, 38c

typist el (la) mecanógrafo(a) 38a

typography la tipografía 20a

U

ugly feo 11a, 25l
ugliness la fealdad 11a
ulcer la úlcera 40a
ultraviolet light la luz ultravioleta 13a
unbelievable increíble 22a
unbuckle desabrocharse 32c
uncle el tío 10a
under debajo (de) 3d
underdeveloped countries los países subdesarrollados 43
underlining el subrayado (n) 19c
underpass el paso subterráneo 33d
understand comprender, entender* 22b, 37f
underwear la ropa interior 25k
undress desnudarse (v) 25m
unemployment el desempleo 38d, 43
unfortunately desafortunadamente 22a
United States los Estados Unidos 30b
universe el universo 13a
university la universidad 37a, 38b
unjust injusto 44b
unleaded gas la gasolina sin plomo 33c
unless a menos que 8o
unmarried soltero 11c
unpleasant desagradable 21b
unscrew destornillar 25b
unsubscribe from a list borrarse (v) de una lista 42c
until hasta que 4e, 8o

up arriba 3d
upgrade actualizar (v) 42c
uphill calle arriba 33c
upholstery el tapizado 23c
Uranus Urano 13a
urinary system el sistema urinario 40a
urinate orinar 12b, 40a
URL la URL (dirección de una página de la red) 42c
urologist el urólogo 40a
Uruguayan uruguayo(a) (*adj*, *n*) 30d
us nos 8i, 8j
user friendly fácil de manejar 42b
user name el nombre del usuario 42c
usher el acomodador 28e
usually normalmente 4e
utensils los utensilios 23d
utter pronunciar 17a

V

vacation las vacaciones 29a, 36b
vaccinate vacunar 40a
vacuum cleaner la aspiradora 23d
vain vanidoso 11e
valley el valle 13b
van el furgón 33a
vapor el vapor 13c
variable variable 1f, 26
vase el florero 23d
VCR la videocasetera 20b; la videograbadora 20b
veal la ternera 24c
vector el vector 2b
vegetable la legumbre, el vegetal 14e, 24e
vegetation la vegetación 13b
vehicle el vehículo 33a
vein la vena 40a
velvet el terciopelo 25l
venereal disease la enfermedad venérea 40a

venetian blinds   las persianas
23c
Venezuelan   venezolano(a)
(*adj, n*) 30d
Venus   Venus 13a
verb   el verbo 8a
verdict   el veredicto, el juicio
41
versatile   versátil 11e
verse   el verso 28d
version   la versión 42b
vertebrate   vertebrado 15a
vertex   el vértice 2b
vertical   vertical 3d
veterinarian   el veterinario
38a
vibrant   vibrante 7b
victim   el (la) víctima 39a,
39b
video game   el juego eléctronico
20b
videocamera   la videocámara
25d
videocassette   el videocasete
20b
videotape   la cinta (magnética)
de video 20b
view   la vista 35b
vinegar   el vinagre 24j
viola   la viola 28c
violence   la violencia 39b
violet   violeta 14b
violin   el violín 28c
violinist   el (la) violinista
28c
Virgo   Virgo 5d
virile   viril 11a
visa   el visado, la visa 31
visit   visitar 29b
vitamin   la vitamina 25h,
40a
vocabulary   el vocabulario
17a
vocational school   la escuela
vocacional 37a
volcano   el volcán 13b
volleyball   el voleibol 27b
volume   el volumen 3a

vomit   vomitar 40a
vote   el voto (*n*); votar (*v*)
43
vowel   la vocal 8a
vulture   el buitre 15b

W

wage   el sueldo 38d
waist   la cintura 12a
wait for   esperar 4e, 19e,
34
waiter   el camarero, el mesero
24m
waitress   la camarera 24m
waiting room   la sala de espera
32a
wake up   despertarse* 12b
wake-up call   despertar(se)* con
una llamada 35b
walk   andar, caminar 3e,
12b
walk   la caminata 3e
wall *(exterior)*   el muro 23a
wall *(inside)*   la pared 23a
wallpaper   el empapelado
23c
walnut   la nuez 14d
walnut tree   el nogal 14c
want to   querer* 21a
war   la guerra 43
warm up   calentarse* 6b
warn   advertir* 17a
warning   el aviso, la advertencia
17a
wash   lavar (*v*) 23f, 25g
wash oneself   lavarse (*v*)
12d
washable   lavable 25g
washing machine   la lavadora
23d
washroom *(public)*   los servicios
23b, 36a
wasp   la avispa 15d
wastebasket   el papelero
38c
watch   el reloj 4d, 25i
watchband   la correa de reloj
4d

water el agua 13c, 14a, 23e, 25k

water fountain la fuente 36a

water glass el vaso para agua 24l

water pollution la contaminación del agua 44a

watercolor la acuarela 28b

watermelon la sandía 14d, 24f

wave la ola 13b, 39b

we nosotros 8h

weak débil 11a, 11e, 13d, 40a

weakness la debilidad 11a

weapon el arma (f) 39b

weapons of mass destruction armas de destrucción masiva 43

wear llevar 25g, 25m

weather el tiempo 6a

weather forecast el pronóstico del tiempo 6c

web browser el navegador (m) 42c

webcam la webcam (f) 42c

webpage la página de la red 42c

web provider el portal informático 42c

website el sitio en la red 42c

wedding la boda 11c, 29a

Wednesday el miércoles 5a

week la semana 4c

weekend el fin de semana 5a

weekly semanal, por semana 4c

weigh pesar 3b, 11a, 24o

weight el peso 3a, 11a, 31

welfare la asistencia pública 43

welfare reform la reforma de asistencia pública 44b

well-mannered cortés, bien 11e

west el oeste 3d

western occidental 3d, 11d

whale la ballena 15c

What? ¿Cómo? 9

what qué (adj, pron) 9

wheat el trigo 14a, 24i

wheel la rueda 32c, 33e

wheelchair la silla de ruedas 40a

When? ¿Cuándo? 9

when cuando (conj) 4e

Where? ¿Dónde? 9

where donde 3d

whether si 8o

Which (one)? ¿Cuál? 9

while mientras 4e, 8o

whiskey el whiski 24k

whisper cuchichear, susurrar 17a

white blanco 7a

Who? ¿Quién? 9

who que, quien 8m

wholesale la venta al por mayor 26

whose cuyo 8l

Why? ¿Por qué? 9

wide ancho 3b

widow viuda 11c, 38b

widower viudo 11c, 38b

width la anchura 3b

wife la esposa 10a, 11c

will (document) el testamento 41

willing dispuesto 11e

win ganar (v); la victoria (n) 27b

wind el viento 6a

wind dar* cuerda a (v) 4d, 25i

window la ventana 23a, 32c

windshield el parabrisas 33

windshield wiper el limpiaparabrisas 33e

wine el vino 24k

wine cellar la bodega 23b

wine list la lista de vinos 24m

wing el ala (f) 15b, 32c

winter   el invierno   5c
wire   el alambre   25b
wireless   inalámbrico   20b
wireless phone   el teléfono móvil   20b
wisdom   la sabiduría   11e, 22a
wise   sabio   11e
with   con   8g
withdraw   retirar   26
withdrawal   el retiro   26
within   dentro de   4e
without   sin   8g, 8o
witness   el testigo   41
wolf   el lobo   15a
woman   la mujer   11a
woods   el bosque   13b
wool   la lana   13c, 25l
word   la palabra, el vocablo   17a, 19c
word processor   el procesador de texto   19d, 38c, 42b
work   el trabajo   (n); trabajar   (v)   11f, 38d
work *(literature, art)*   la obra   28d
workplace violence   la violencia en el lugar de trabajo   44b
workstation   la estación   (f) de trabajo   42b
world   el mundo   13a, 30a
worm   el gusano   15d
wound   herir*   (v); la herida   (n)   39b, 39c
wrench   la llave inglesa   25b
wrestling   la lucha libre   27b
wrist   la muñeca   12a
wristwatch   el reloj (de pulsera)   4d
write   escribir   19e, 20a, 37f
writer   el (la) escritor(a)   28d, 38a
wrong   incorrecto   37f

X, Y, Z
X rays   rayos X   40b
yard   el patio   23a
yawn   bostezar   (v); el bostezo   (n)   17a
year   el año   4c, 37a
yearly   anual, anualmente   4c
yell   gritar   (v)   17a
yellow   amarillo   7a
yellow pages   las páginas amarillas   18a
yes   sí   16c
yesterday   ayer   4a
yet   todavía   4e
yield   ceder el paso   33d
yogurt   el yogur   24h
you   tú, usted, nosotros, ustedes   8h; te, lo, la, os, los, las   8i
young   joven   11b
young lady   la señorita, la joven   11a
young man   el joven   11a
your   tu, tus, su, sus, vuestro, vuestra, vuestros, vuestras   8e
yourself   te, se   8k
yourselves   os   8k
youthful   juvenil   11b
youth hostel   el albergue juvenil   35a
zebra   la cebra   15a
zero   cero   1a, 6c
zero tolerance   la cero tolerancia   44b
zipper   la cremallera   25g
Zodiac   el Zodíaco   5d
zone   la zona   13e
zoo   el parque zoológico   15a
zoological   zoológico   15a
zoology   la zoología   15a, 37e
zoom   el zoom   25d
zucchini   el calabacín   14e, 24e

NOTES

NOTES

NOTES

3 Foreign Language Series From Barron's!

The **VERB SERIES** offers more than 300 of the most frequently used verbs.
The **GRAMMAR SERIES** provides complete coverage of the elements of grammar. The **VOCABULARY SERIES** offers more than 3500 words and phrases with their foreign language translations. Each book: paperback.

**FRENCH
GRAMMAR**
ISBN: 0-7641-1351-8
$5.95, Can. $8.50

**GERMAN
GRAMMAR**
ISBN: 0-8120-4296-4
$6.95, Can. $8.95

**ITALIAN
GRAMMAR**
ISBN: 0-7641-2060-3
$6.95, Can. $9.95

**JAPANESE
GRAMMAR**
ISBN: 0-7641-2061-1
$6.95, Can. $9.95

**RUSSIAN
GRAMMAR**
ISBN: 0-8120-4902-0
$6.95, Can. $8.95

**SPANISH
GRAMMAR**
ISBN: 0-7641-1615-0
$5.95, Can. $8.50

**FRENCH
VERBS**
ISBN: 0-7641-1356-9
$5.95, Can. $8.50

**GERMAN
VERBS**
ISBN: 0-8120-4310-3
$7.95 Can. $11.50

**ITALIAN
VERBS**
ISBN: 0-7641-2063-8
$5.95, Can. $8.50

**SPANISH
VERBS**
ISBN: 0-7641-1357-7
$5.95, Can. $8.50

**FRENCH
VOCABULARY**
ISBN: 0-7641-1999-0
$6.95, Can. $9.95

**GERMAN
VOCABULARY**
ISBN: 0-8120-4497-5
$6.95, Can. $8.95

**ITALIAN
VOCABULARY**
ISBN: 0-7641-2190-1
$6.95, Can. $9.95

**JAPANESE
VOCABULARY**
ISBN: 0-8120-4743-5
$6.95, Can. $8.95

**RUSSIAN
VOCABULARY**
ISBN: 0-8120-1554-1
$6.95, Can. $8.95

**SPANISH
VOCABULARY**
ISBN: 0-7641-1985-3
$6.95, Can. $9.95

Barron's Educational Series, Inc.
250 Wireless Blvd., Hauppauge, NY 11788 • Call toll-free: 1-800-645-3476
In Canada: Georgetown Book Warehouse
34 Armstrong Ave., Georgetown, Ontario L7G 4R9 • Call toll-free: 1-800-247-7160
www.barronseduc.com

Can. $ = Canadian dollars

Books may be purchased at your bookstore or by mail from Barron's. Enclose check or money order for total amount plus sales tax where applicable and 18% for postage and handling (minimum charge $5.95 U.S. and Canada). Prices subject to change without notice. New York State and California residents, please add sales tax to total after postage and handling. (#26) R 5/04

NOTES

NOTES

AT A GLANCE Series

Barron's new series gives travelers instant access to the most common idiomatic expressions used during a trip—the kind one needs to know instantly, like "Where can I find a taxi?" and "How much does this cost?"

Organized by situation (arrival, customs, hotel, health, etc.) and containing additional information about pronunciation, grammar, shopping plus special facts about the country, these convenient, pocket-size reference books will be the tourist's most helpful guides.

Special features include a bilingual dictionary section with over 2000 key words, maps of each country and major cities, and helpful phonetic spellings throughout.

Each book paperback, 256 pp., 3 ³/₄" x 6"

ARABIC AT A GLANCE, Wise (0-7641-1248-1) $8.95, Can. $12.50
CHINESE AT A GLANCE, Seligman & Chen (0-7641-1250-3) $8.95, Can. $12.50
FRENCH AT A GLANCE, 4th, Stein & Wald (0-7641-2512-5) $6.95, Can. $9.95
GERMAN AT A GLANCE, 4th, Strutz (0-7641-2516-8) $6.95, Can. $9.95
ITALIAN AT A GLANCE, 4th, Costantino (0-7641-2513-3) $6.95, Can. $9.95
JAPANESE AT A GLANCE, 3rd, Akiyama (0-7641-0320-2) $8.95, Can. $11.95
KOREAN AT A GLANCE, Holt (0-8120-3998-X) $8.95, Can. $11.95
RUSSIAN AT A GLANCE, Beyer (0-7641-1251-1) $8.95, Can. $12.50
SPANISH AT A GLANCE, 4th, Wald (0-7641-2514-1) $6.95, Can. $9.95

Barron's Educational Series, Inc.
250 Wireless Blvd., Hauppauge, NY 11788
Call toll-free: 1-800-645-3476
In Canada: Georgetown Book Warehouse, 34 Armstrong Ave.
Georgetown, Ont. L7G 4R9, Call toll-free: 1-800-247-7160
Visit our website at: www.barronseduc.com

NOTES

LEARN A NEW LANGUAGE
THE FAST, FUN WAY!

These lively full-color activity books help you pick up the language you need in just minutes a day. Emphasis is on everyday situations—from meeting people and handling simple business transactions to shopping and dining out—and more. All words and phrases are accompanied by pronunciation.

There are hundreds of amusing color illustrations plus puzzles, maps, quizzes and vocabulary cards for practice. *Special bonus for business and vacation travelers:* pull-out bilingual dictionary complete with Food and Drink Guide.

"LEARN A LANGUAGE THE FAST AND FUN WAY" AVAILABLE IN:

	US	Canada
CHINESE (0-8120-9689-4)	$18.95	$26.50
LEARN ENGLISH THE FAST AND FUN WAY (For Russian Speakers) (0-7641-1327-5)	$18.95	$26.50
FRENCH, 3rd Ed. (0-7641-2559-1)	$18.95	$27.50
GERMAN, 3rd Ed. (0-7641-2540-0)	$18.95	$27.50
ITALIAN, 3rd Ed. (0-7641-2530-3)	$18.95	$27.50
JAPANESE, 2nd Ed. (0-7641-0623-6)	$18.95	$26.50
RUSSIAN (0-8120-4846-6)	$18.95	$26.50
SPANISH, 3d Ed. (0-7641-2550-8)	$18.95	$27.50
APRENDA INGLÉS FÁCIL Y RÁPIDO (For Spanish Speakers) (0-7641-0622-8)	$19.95	$28.95

Books may be purchased at your bookstore, or by mail from Barron's. Enclose check or money order for the total amount plus sales tax where applicable and 18% for postage and handling (minimum charge $5.95). NY State and California residents add sales tax. Prices are subject to change without notice.

Barron's Educational Series, Inc.
250 Wireless Blvd., Hauppauge, NY 11788
In Canada: Georgetown Book Warehouse
34 Armstrong Ave., Georgetown, Ont. L7G 4R9
Visit our website at: www.barronseduc.com

(#27) R 5/04

NOTES